365 ENTRIES FROM SEVEN FIELDS OF KNOWLEDGE

THE INTELLECTUAL DEVOTIONAL

MODERN CULTURE

Revive Your Mind,

Complete Your Education,

and

Converse Confidently

with the Culturati

• • ● • •

DAVID S. KIDDER & NOAH D. OPPENHEIM

New York Times Best-Selling Authors of *The Intellectual Devotional*

RODALE

© 2008 by TID Volumes, LLC

Rodale books may be purchased for business or promotional use or for special sales.
For information, please write to:
Special Markets Department, Rodale Inc., 733 Third Avenue, New York, NY 10017

Printed in the United States of America

Rodale Inc. makes every effort to use acid-free ∞, recycled paper ♻.

Book design by Anthony Serge, principal designer;
initial interior creative by Nelson Kunkel, The Ingredient
For image credits, see page 377.
The lines from "anyone lived in a pretty how town": Copyright 1940, © 1968, 1991
by the Trustees for the E. E. Cummings Trust, from COMPLETE POEMS: 1904-1962
by E. E. Cummings, edited by George J. Firmage. Used by permission of
Liveright Publishing Corporation.

Library of Congress Cataloging-in-Publication Data

Kidder, David S.
    The intellectual devotional modern culture : revive your mind, complete your
education, and converse confidently with the culturati / David S. Kidder and
Noah D. Oppenheim.
        p.   cm.
    ISBN-13 978–1–59486–745–3 hardcover
    ISBN-10 1-59486-745-3 hardcover
        1. Civilization, Modern—Miscellanea.   2. Intellectual life—Miscellanea.
3. Learning and scholarship—Miscellanea.   4. Devotional calendars.
I. Oppenheim, Noah D.   II. Title.
CB358.K45 2008
909.8—dc22   2008013834

Distributed to the trade by Macmillan

2   4   6   8   10   9   7   5   3   1   hardcover

We inspire and enable people to improve their lives and the world around them

For more of our products visit **rodalestore.com** or call 800-848-4735

To Leigh, my beloved sister and Pop Culture Maestro—N.O.

To Amy, for your inspirational faith and courage—D.K.

Contributing Editor
Alan Wirzbicki

Contributing Writers
Daniel K. Fleschner
Kristin Meyer

Introduction

For generations, readers have kept devotionals at their bedsides—collections of 365 short daily readings selected to foster spiritual growth. *The Intellectual Devotional* is also a collection of daily readings, and this volume focuses on the rich tapestry of modern culture. Like our previous devotionals, these readings offer regular stimulation for the mind, a refreshing escape, and an education in critical realms of knowledge. Each entry is an in-depth treatment of the subject, yet it is easily digestible in a short sitting.

There are few more powerful sources of influence than the popular culture—those people, works of art, ideas, and phenomena that capture the collective imagination. With the advent of mass media in the twentieth century, that influence has only grown—the television shows we grew up with, the films that touched us, the music that formed the soundtrack of our lives. The study of our modern culture is essential to understanding common frames of reference. These readings offer a nostalgic and entertaining immersion in the most enduring cultural touchstones of the past 100 years.

The 365 readings are divided into the following fields of knowledge:

PERSONALITIES

Larger-than-life characters from the front pages and the tabloids

LITERATURE

Authors and works that transformed hearts and minds

MUSIC

From timeless works of genius to the Top 40

FILM

The directors, actors, and blockbusters that leapt off the silver screen and into our consciousness

IDEAS AND TRENDS

Ideologies, movements, and innovations that changed our world

SPORTS

Athletes and events that transcended the playing field

POP

The fizzy fun that had water coolers buzzing for the past 100 years

Sigmund Freud

Sigmund Freud (1856–1939) was a leading intellectual and psychologist who shaped the study of the human mind in the twentieth century. Through his controversial concept of psychoanalysis, use of hypnosis, and analysis of dreams, he sought to bring light to people's inner lives and motivations, and in doing so, he had a dramatic impact on not only psychology but also philosophy, sociology, and art.

Freud's work has seemingly prompted just as many people to call him a charlatan as call him a genius. After graduating from the University of Vienna with a medical degree in neurology, he went to Paris to study under Jean-Martin Charcot (1825–1893), who specialized in the study of hysteria. What Freud saw in treating patients led him to conclude that mental disorders stemmed from psychological or emotional trauma, not physical problems or natural development.

While in Paris, Freud began using hypnosis on his patients during psychoanalysis, which led to the development of his central theory: that man is endowed with an unconscious, made up of repressed memories, that has strong emotional and sexual drives. These drives, some of which are born in infancy, battle one another for control and ultimately guide human behavior.

In 1899 he published *The Interpretation of Dreams,* his most widely known work. He theorized that dreams were full of complex symbolism and were an effort by the subconscious to provide clues to human desires.

In *The Ego and the Id* (1923), Freud introduced his theory of the three competing areas of the mind: the id, which is home to the most primitive drives; the ego, which is the conscious self that interacts with reality; and the superego, which recognizes and observes the restrictions imposed by societal norms.

His focus on and belief in the power of the unconscious mind led Freud to think that all jokes, slips of the tongue, and dreams had meaning or showed insight into the human mind.

ADDITIONAL FACTS

1. *Freud experimented with cocaine and studied its euphoric effects on himself and others.*

2. *Before devoting himself to psychology, Freud conducted zoological research and is credited with discovering testicles in eels—a small detail that had escaped earlier studies.*

3. *Freud came from an Austrian Jewish family, and four of his sisters died in Nazi concentration camps during World War II.*

4. *Freud's impact on pop culture is clearly visible in works ranging from the television show* The Sopranos *to the films of Woody Allen (1935–) to the surrealist art of Salvador Dalí (1904–1989).*

•••••

Crime and Punishment

In many respects, Fyodor Dostoyevsky's *Crime and Punishment* was the first true twentieth-century novel—even though it was published in 1866. This story of murder, guilt, alienation, and redemption set the stage for many modernist and existentialist works of the century that followed, and it continues to make its mark on both literature and film today.

Set in St. Petersburg, Russia, the novel focuses on Raskolnikov, a young student who believes himself capable of greatness but feels frustrated by poverty and lack of opportunity. He decides that, because of his extraordinary potential, it would be justifiable for him to kill a miserly old pawnbroker and use her amassed fortune to achieve great things. When he acts on his plan, though, he panics, botches the robbery, and inadvertently kills a second woman without managing to steal the money. Tormented by this failure, Raskolnikov sinks into malaise and questions his real motives for the crime—and all the while is hounded by an investigator who may or may not have any proof of his guilt.

Crime and Punishment is renowned as one of the first—and still one of the greatest—examples of the psychological novel, in light of its intricate explorations of Raskolnikov's motivations and mental state. At the same time, it is a remarkable work of suspense: Tension builds as we wonder whether Raskolnikov will get caught or whether he might even confess of his own accord. In fact, much like a crime pot-boiler, *Crime and Punishment* was published serially over the course of a year. The novel brought Dostoyevsky (1821–1881) a desperately needed financial windfall that enabled him to catch up on his gambling debts, and his contemporaries, including the novelist Leo Tolstoy (1828–1910), immediately hailed it as a landmark. In the years since, Sigmund Freud (1856–1939), Friedrich Nietzsche (1844–1900), Jean-Paul Sartre (1905–1980), and Albert Camus (1913–1960), among others, have cited it as a direct influence.

ADDITIONAL FACTS

1. Crime and Punishment *inspired two of Woody Allen's (1935–) most highly regarded films,* Crimes and Misdemeanors *(1989) and* Match Point *(2005).*

2. *In his late twenties, Dostoyevsky was sentenced to death by firing squad for participating in meetings of a clandestine left-wing political group. Czar Nicholas I (1796–1855) commuted the sentence at the last minute, and the author was sent to a Siberian labor camp for four years instead—an experience that indisputably inspired parts of* Crime and Punishment.

3. *Dostoyevsky struggled for years with a compulsive gambling habit. Luckily, he was able to mine this compulsion for its literary value, producing the novel* The Gambler *in 1866.*

••●••

Pyotr Ilyich Tchaikovsky

Russian composer Pyotr Ilyich Tchaikovsky (1840–1893) wrote several of the most popular ballets in music history, including *Swan Lake* (1877), *The Sleeping Beauty* (1890), and his Christmas classic, *The Nutcracker* (1892). In addition to his dance works, Tchaikovsky composed dozens of orchestral works, including seven symphonies.

Tchaikovsky was born in the small Russian town of Votkinsk and began studying piano at the age of five. At first, his parents did not encourage his musical pursuits, believing that a "passionate" hobby would be dangerous for an already frail and sickly child. Eventually, however, Tchaikovsky moved to the Russian capital of St. Petersburg, where he completed his musical education. Czar Alexander III (1845–1894) was an admirer of his work. Another patron, Nadezhda von Meck (1831–1894), granted him a yearly stipend that allowed him to continue his musical endeavors.

In addition to his ballets, Tchaikovsky is best known today for his bombastic *1812 Overture* (1880), which commemorated the Russian victory over the French emperor Napoléon Bonaparte (1769–1821) and includes cannon fire and church bells as part of the instrumentation. Tchaikovsky also wrote eleven operas. The most famous are *Eugene Onegin* (1879) and *The Queen of Spades* (1890), both based on dramatic poems by the nineteenth-century Russian poet Aleksandr Pushkin (1799–1837).

Tchaikovsky became popular around the world during his career and toured the United States in 1891, introducing Americans to his now-classic compositions. Two of his works—the *1812 Overture* and *The Nutcracker*—have become sentimental favorites in American culture and are often performed on the Fourth of July and at Christmastime, respectively.

ADDITIONAL FACTS

1. *Tchaikovsky's last work was his Symphony no. 6, entitled* Pathétique *(1893). The composer died nine days after premiering the work, which was played as a requiem at his memorial.*

2. *Though there was once speculation that Tchaikovsky committed suicide after being exposed in a homosexual affair, most scholars today believe that he died of cholera.*

3. *Though Tchaikovsky's opera* Eugene Onegin *is considered a masterpiece, the Russian author Vladimir Nabokov (1899–1977) dismissed it as "silly" and "slapdash," saying that everything in it "insults Pushkin's masterpiece."*

••●••

The Lumière Brothers

The French duo of Louis and Auguste Lumière did not invent cinema, but they are considered the founding fathers of modern film for creating the primitive motion-picture projector they patented in 1895. The brothers were inspired by the work of American inventor Thomas Edison (1847–1931), who in 1893 had unveiled a machine called the Kinetoscope, which allowed viewers to watch short films by peering into a wooden box that held the device's components.

The Lumières, whose family business manufactured photographic equipment and supplies, improved on the Kinetoscope with the Cinématographe, a lightweight, hand-cranked apparatus that was both a camera and a projector. And unlike the Kinetoscope, which allowed only one viewer to watch the moving pictures, the Cinématographe could project movies onto a screen, allowing members of an audience to watch a movie together.

The Lumières patented the Cinématographe in February 1895, and many historians consider December 28, 1895, to be the birthday of cinema. On that day, the Lumière brothers projected films for the first time for a paying audience at the Grand Café on the Boulevard des Capucines in Paris. The program included ten films—among them *Workers Leaving the Lumière Factory* (1895)—and lasted about twenty minutes.

In 1896, the brothers took the Cinématographe and their films on a world tour, including stops in London and New York City. According to legend, some spectators were so spooked by *Arrival of a Train at La Ciotat* (1895)—which was a single shot of a train as it approached a station from the background—that they ran away in terror.

By 1900, the brothers had created 2,000 films. But believing that "cinema is an invention without any future," the brothers did not sell their camera to other film-makers and went on to focus their efforts on still photography.

ADDITIONAL FACTS

1. *Louis Lumière (1864–1948) was a trained physicist.*

2. *Auguste Lumière (1862–1954) ran the family business, which manufactured photographic equipment and supplies.*

3. *The Lumières hired a pianist to provide live musical accompaniment to their short movies at the first screening in Paris.*

••●●••

Communism

"A specter is haunting Europe—the specter of communism." With those words, Karl Marx (1818–1883) and Friedrich Engels (1820–1895) opened their 1848 *Communist Manifesto,* a political broadside that launched one of the most powerful political movements of the nineteenth and twentieth centuries.

At the time that Marx and Engels published their pamphlet, communism was a fringe movement associated with a few failed revolts and some obscure and difficult works of German philosophy. A century later, however, it dominated half the globe.

The communists believed that the Industrial Revolution of the early nineteenth century had created deep economic inequalities, as factory owners and investors reaped enormous profits while workers toiled in poverty. Capitalism, the communists believed, created great wealth, but the middle class—the bourgeoisie—wanted to maintain their position of power in society instead of sharing it with workers—the proletariat.

The solution, Marx and Engels proposed, was for the working class to take control of the means of production themselves, establishing what they termed a "dictatorship of the proletariat." Since the bourgeoisie would never surrender their power voluntarily, Marx and Engels believed, violent revolution was necessary.

The communists were hostile not only to capitalism but also to imperialism and religion—which Marx described as "the opium of the people." Indeed, in the eyes of its opponents, communism posed a direct threat to the Western way of life.

Amid the poverty and social strife of nineteenth-century Europe, however, communism found many adherents and spread steadily in the years after Marx and Engels's manifesto. With the Russian Revolution of 1917, communists gained the ability to put their ideas into practice.

The growing clash between capitalism and communism defined the world politics of much of the twentieth century, particularly the four decades of the Cold War. Although a few nations, such as China, remain nominally communist, the ideology lost much of its allure after the horrors of life in the "worker's paradise" of the Soviet Union were exposed to the world.

ADDITIONAL FACTS

1. *Marx is best known for books such as* The Communist Manifesto *and the three-volume* Capital, *but he also worked for many years as a journalist, publishing in British and American newspapers, including the* New York Daily Tribune.

2. *Though communism achieved its first great victory in Russia, Marx and Engels regarded that country as backward and underdeveloped and hoped the communist future would be ushered in by the United States.*

3. *Marx was annoyed when communist philosophy was later labeled Marxism; he once reportedly proclaimed, "I am not a Marxist."*

• • ● • •

James Naismith

Of the three great American sports—baseball, basketball, and football—only one has a true inventor. On December 21, 1891, James Naismith, a Canadian-born physical education teacher, nailed peach baskets to two opposite walls of a gymnasium in Springfield, Massachusetts, handed his students a soccer ball, and announced thirteen rules for his new game—and "basket ball" was born.

Naismith (1861–1939), the son of Scottish immigrants, grew up in Ontario and was orphaned by age nine. (His parents died of typhoid fever.) After dropping out of high school at fifteen to work as a lumberjack, he eventually returned to school, earning degrees from McGill University and Presbyterian College, where he studied to become a minister.

In 1890, he enrolled at the Young Men's Christian Association (YMCA) International Training School in Springfield. While there, he and his fellow students were given the task of devising an indoor activity for the men at the YMCA to play during the winter, between football and baseball seasons.

At the time, calisthenics and gymnastics were essentially the only indoor athletic activities, but they were deemed too boring by many of the men. The only stipulations for the new game were to "make it fair for all players and free of rough play."

Naismith's invention proved popular, and his thirteen rules were soon published in a sports magazine to an enthusiastic response. In the following years, Naismith remained prominently involved with the game as it grew, particularly in the evolution of its rules into their current form. In 1898, he took a job at the University of Kansas, where he coached for ten years and remained as an athletic administrator and campus chaplain until shortly before his death at age seventy-eight.

ADDITIONAL FACTS

1. *Naismith's original rules did not permit dribbling—players could advance the ball only by passing.*

2. *Naismith became an American citizen in 1925.*

3. *In his senior year at McGill, an incident on the rugby field changed his life—another player uttered an expletive and, upon seeing Naismith (an aspiring minister), he said, "I beg your pardon, James. I forgot you were there." At this point, Naismith realized that he might be able to help young men improve their lives through spiritual and physical development.*

4. *Naismith is the only coach in University of Kansas history with a losing record. He notched fifty-five wins and sixty losses between 1898 and 1907.*

•••••

Coney Island

Located at the southern edge of Brooklyn, the amusement parks at Coney Island first opened in the 1890s and reigned for decades as the biggest and most popular in the United States. At its peak, Coney Island drew millions of visitors annually and was famous for carousels, Ferris wheels, roller coasters, fortune-tellers, horse racing, freak shows, and, of course, hot dogs.

The first rides to open at Coney Island were rickety, often unsafe contraptions. In 1911, for instance, two women died after the roller coaster they were riding, the Giant Racer, jumped from its tracks eighty feet in the air.

Still, the parks were enormously popular and attracted an estimated 32 million visitors in 1904. Several vintage rides from the parks' golden age, including the Cyclone, a wooden roller coaster built in 1927, remain in operation.

In an era before movies and television, amusement parks were one of the first forms of mass entertainment. Most large American cities built amusement parks in the 1910s and 1920s, although none rivaled the hurly-burly of Coney Island, which comprised several sprawling, privately owned amusement resorts, including Luna Park and Steeplechase Park.

Over time, however, the resort acquired a seedy reputation thanks to prostitution, drug dealing, and other less family-friendly activities found on the boardwalk. The Great Depression also dealt a severe blow to the park. Luna Park closed in 1946. Most of Coney Island's remaining rides had been dismantled by the 1980s.

However, the Cyclone remains in operation during the summer, and the annual Coney Island hot dog eating contest—a vestige of the resort's glory days—has become an international event.

ADDITIONAL FACTS

1. *American Joey Chestnut (1983–) won the Coney Island hot dog eating competition in 2007 by eating sixty-six hot dogs in twelve minutes, defeating six-time champion Takeru Kobayashi (1978–) of Japan.*

2. *The name Coney Island comes from the original seventeenth-century Dutch settlers of New York, who named the area Konijn Eiland—"Rabbit Island" in Dutch.*

3. *The resort is currently the home of the Brooklyn Cyclones baseball team, a minor-league affiliate of the New York Mets.*

•• • ••

Albert Einstein

If anyone personified the word *genius* in the twentieth century, it was Albert Einstein (1879–1955). No other person had as significant an impact on modern science and technology as the German-born physicist, whose ideas changed the way scientists look at the universe and laid the foundation for many of the century's technological advances.

Einstein's rise to fame began in 1905, while he was working as a technical assistant at the Swiss patent office. That year he submitted four papers he had written in his spare time to the scientific journal *Annalen der Physik*. All would change the world.

In one paper, Einstein updated the quantum theory of radiation, declaring that light travels both as a wave and as particles. In a second paper, he explained the previously unexplained phenomenon of Brownian motion, which involves the bouncing of molecules. In the most famous of the papers, he outlined his special theory of relativity and unveiled what has become the most famous equation in science: $E = mc^2$.

After the publication of the papers, he was granted a professorship at a Swiss university. Then, in 1916, he disclosed his greatest achievement, the general theory of relativity, which redefined the nature of gravity and argued that space and time can be curved. In 1921, his work earned him the Nobel Prize in Physics.

Einstein's theories baffle the public as much today as they did in his time, but the impact is clear. He broke down old notions that the universe was a logical, mechanical place and also allowed for new thinking in science, politics, and art. One need not understand quantum physics or the meaning of $E = mc^2$ to know that his work led to modern marvels such as semiconductors, lasers, and television.

His achievements turned him into a global celebrity noted for his absentmindedness, love of children, and pacifism.

Ironically, though, he played a key role in the development of the atomic bomb. In 1939, while teaching at Princeton University, he warned President Franklin D. Roosevelt (1882–1945) that the Germans were developing a nuclear weapon. That warning started a chain reaction that ultimately led the United States to embark upon its own atomic program, which in turn resulted in the destruction of the Japanese cities of Hiroshima and Nagasaki in 1945.

ADDITIONAL FACTS

1. *In 2000,* Time *magazine named Einstein its Person of the Century.*

2. *Einstein was an ardent Zionist and after World War II was offered the presidency of Israel, a position he declined.*

3. *Einstein was "no Einstein" as a child. He did not learn to speak until age three, and he was an indifferent student for much of his academic career. After he finally earned his university degree in 1900, he was unable to find a job in his trained profession—as a teacher of physics and mathematics.*

· · ● ● · ·

Anna Karenina

Leo Tolstoy's *Anna Karenina* (1877), though written more than a century ago, continues to surprise readers with its immediacy and freshness. Along with Tolstoy's (1828–1910) other magnum opus, *War and Peace,* it is regarded as one of the finest novels ever written in any language.

The title character is a beautiful, intelligent, and charismatic St. Petersburg high-society woman who, on the surface, lives a perfect life. She has a devoted government official for a husband, dotes on her charming and intelligent young son, and enjoys the frequent company of close friends and family. Though Anna's married life is agreeable, everything is upended when a dashing military officer named Vronsky arrives, sparking a longing in Anna that she has never felt for her bland, passionless husband. Anna and Vronsky begin an affair that quickly becomes public, costing Anna both her family and her reputation. As her relationship with Vronsky deteriorates, Anna is left teetering on the brink of social ruin yet cringing at the idea of returning to her defunct marriage.

Anna Karenina is seen as one of the great tragic characters in literature, and certainly one of the most fully realized. She virtually leaps off the page, a fascinating woman who is condemnable for her indiscretions yet admirable for her dignity, elegance, and unwillingness to live her life dishonestly. Various generations of readers have seen her as a feminist icon, a romantic heroine, and a tragic victim.

Although it focuses on Anna, the novel also deals with Russian society as a whole: its government, its peasants, its transition to modernity, and its relationship with the West. Many of these themes are explored through the novel's lesser-known co-protagonist, a wealthy yet earthy landowner named Levin, who is generally seen as a stand-in for Tolstoy himself.

ADDITIONAL FACTS

1. Anna Karenina *is considered one of the greatest works of realism, a movement that swept Western literature during the mid- to late 1800s.*

2. *The selection of* Anna Karenina *by Oprah Winfrey (1954–) for her televised book club brought the novel back to US bestseller lists in May 2004.*

3. *Since its publication,* Anna Karenina *has inspired more than twenty different major adaptations, including numerous films, TV miniseries, radio plays, stage plays, ballets, an opera, and even a Broadway musical.*

••●••

Scott Joplin

Scott Joplin (c. 1867–1917) was the best-known composer of ragtime music, a unique and unusual American musical style that flourished around the turn of the twentieth century and is considered to have been a significant influence on the development of jazz music.

Born in Texas, Joplin showed musical aptitude from an early age and studied music theory, harmony, and composition at George R. Smith College in Sedalia, Missouri. Throughout his career, Joplin applied his extensive knowledge of European classical music to his ragtime compositions, producing works that were far more complex than the rags written by his competitors.

Joplin's first major hit was "Maple Leaf Rag," which he sold in 1899. In the following years, he composed a number of hits, including one of his most famous pieces, "The Entertainer" (1902). He realized his most ambitious goals by producing two ragtime operas: *A Guest of Honor* (1903, now lost) and *Treemonisha* (1911).

Ragtime music was originally performed in African-American communities as dance music long before it was introduced to a mainstream audience. Joplin was not the first artist to write and perform music in the genre, but he is generally regarded as the finest. (His publisher claimed that Joplin elevated ragtime from a popular form "and lined it up with Beethoven and Bach.") Ragtime is a modification of the march form that depends heavily on syncopation, or the accenting of unexpected beats. Because of its unique rhythm, this style of playing was known as *ragged time,* later condensed to *ragtime.*

Soon after Joplin's death, ragtime declined significantly in popularity as jazz came to prominence. The genre did enjoy a brief revival in the 1970s, however, and Joplin's most popular compositions are still among the most recognizable American classics.

ADDITIONAL FACTS

1. *A version of Joplin's rag "The Entertainer" used in the film* The Sting *(1973) reached number three on the Billboard charts in 1974.*

2. *In 1971, pianist Joshua Rifkin (1944–) was nominated for a Best Classical Performance Grammy for his collection of Joplin piano rags.*

3. *In 2006, a collector claimed to have discovered a copy of Joplin's "Pleasant Moments," a 1916 piano roll composition that had been considered lost.*

•••••

D. W. Griffith and *The Birth of a Nation* (1915)

D. W. Griffith's place in cinematic history was largely established before 1915, but his legacy will always be defined by his controversial film of that year, *The Birth of a Nation*. Considered a masterpiece by many, *The Birth of a Nation* was the first American epic, using technical advances that Griffith had been perfecting throughout his career. But the film's content is unabashedly racist and has sparked enormous debate since its first screening almost a century ago.

Griffith (1875–1948) grew up in Kentucky, the son of a Confederate colonel. In 1908, he shifted from actor to director, making one-reel films, which were usually twelve to fifteen minutes in length. He was astoundingly prolific: In 1909 alone, Griffith directed more than 140 films.

Among the innovations he is credited with perfecting during this era are:

- Crosscutting, or the editing together of different narratives in different locations to build suspense
- Judicious use of wide, medium, and close-up shots to help tell a story and create emotional resonance
- Rehearsing with actors to put an emphasis on performance and facial expressions

Although Griffith did not invent any of these techniques, he is considered the first director to bring these and many other innovations together to create a cinematic language, or "film grammar." His contributions helped turn the primitive movies of the early twentieth century into an art form.

The content of the movie has somewhat obscured many of those contributions. Based on the novel *The Clansman* (which was also the film's original title), the film focuses on the Civil War aftermath, glorifying the Ku Klux Klan. Upon the film's release, riots broke out in several cities, and many theaters refused to show it. The National Association for the Advancement of Colored People (NAACP) called for the film to be banned, to no avail. Indeed, *The Birth of a Nation* was the most profitable film of all time and would remain so for more than twenty years.

As a response to the cries of racism, Griffith directed *Intolerance* (1916), another colossal epic that dealt with intolerant attitudes throughout human history. It was a commercial failure, and from then on, Griffith frequently struggled with debt. He made his last film in 1931.

ADDITIONAL FACTS

1. *When* The Birth of a Nation *was finally passed by* Snow White and the Seven Dwarfs *(1937) as the biggest box office smash of all time, it had made $18 million—and initially cost $110,000 to make.*

2. *Key black characters in* The Birth of a Nation *were portrayed by white actors in blackface.*

3. The Birth of a Nation *is considered responsible for increasing membership in the Ku Klux Klan for the decade following its release.*

•• ● ••

Luddites

Luddism—a hatred of technology—takes its name from a group of disgruntled nineteenth-century English textile workers who rebelled against new factory methods that threatened their livelihood. Although the original Luddite Revolt was swiftly quashed, fear and distrust of new scientific advances continues to play a role in politics and has colored contemporary debates about a variety of topics ranging from computers to genetically modified foods.

The original Luddites took their name from Ned Ludd, who may or may not have been a real person. According to legend, Ludd broke into a house sometime in the late 1770s and destroyed a pair of stocking frames, recently invented knitting machines that were blamed for putting textile workers out of work. Whether or not this event actually occurred, the phrase "Ludd must have been here" became a common refrain in English factories whenever a piece of newfangled machinery was found damaged.

By 1812, a group of textile workers who had crowned Ned "King Ludd" began destroying stocking frames and weaving frames all over England. The first organized Luddite Revolts occurred in 1811; it took 2,500 troops to quell the violence. Soon thereafter, "machine breaking" was made a capital crime. (After one 1813 trial in York, seventeen men were hanged for breaking this law.)

Although the original Luddite Revolt faded away, the term *Luddite* entered the political lexicon as a way of describing opponents of the relentless onslaught of technology.

ADDITIONAL FACTS

1. *Harvard-educated terrorist Ted Kaczynski (1942–), a.k.a. the Unabomber, targeted scientists in his bombing campaign and is sometimes referred to as a modern-day Luddite.*

2. *A famous supporter of the Luddites was the English poet Lord Byron (1788–1824). His posthumously published "Song for the Luddites" included the lines ". . . we / Will die fighting, or live free, / And down with all kings but King Ludd!"*

3. *Luddites carried sledgehammers they called "Enoch's hammers" in honor of a Yorkshire blacksmith named Enoch Thompson who made some of the weapons.*

Cy Young

The name Cy Young has become synonymous with pitching excellence in baseball. Born on a farm in Ohio as Denton True Young (1867–1955), the great right-hander pitched in the big leagues for twenty-two years and owned several career records that will almost certainly never be broken: most wins (511), losses (316), innings pitched (7,356), games started (815), and complete games (749).

Young's career spanned 1890 to 1911, when the game of baseball was still in its formative stages. In that era, pitchers logged a tremendous number of innings and rarely came out of games for a reliever. In 1892, at age twenty-five, Young threw an astounding 453 innings. (In today's game, the league's leader usually pitches only about 250 innings in a season.)

Young played for five teams, winning at least 30 games five times and 20 games fifteen times. In 1901, the inaugural season of the upstart American League (AL), which was formed as a rival to the National League, Young had the best season of his career with the newly created Boston Americans. He led the new league in wins (33), earned run average (1.62), and strikeouts (158).

Two years later, he pitched the Americans—soon to be renamed the Red Sox—into the first-ever World Series, winning two games in Boston's victory over the Pittsburgh Pirates. In 1904, he added to his legend, throwing the first perfect game in AL history over the Philadelphia Athletics.

Young retired after the 1911 season and was inducted into the Baseball Hall of Fame in 1937. Every year, the top pitcher in both the National League and the American League receives the Cy Young Award, based on balloting by the Baseball Writers of America.

ADDITIONAL FACTS

1. *Young's nickname was short for Cyclone—it's said that while in the minor leagues, Young warmed up by throwing pitches against a wooden fence, and a bystander noted that it looked as if the fence had been hit by a cyclone.*

2. *Only one pitcher—Walter Johnson—has finished his career within 100 victories of Young's mark. Johnson, who pitched for the Washington Senators from 1907 to 1927, had 417 wins.*

3. *The Boston Americans went by several different names in the early twentieth century, including the Somersets and the Pilgrims, before finally settling on the Red Sox in 1907.*

4. *Young is the only major-league pitcher to record no-hitters in both the nineteenth and twentieth centuries (in 1897 against the Cincinnati Reds and his 1904 perfect game).*

5. *Young played for the Cleveland Spiders (1890–1898), St. Louis Perfectos/Cardinals (1899–1900), Boston Americans/Somersets/Pilgrims/Red Sox (1901–1908), Cleveland Naps/Indians (1909–1911), and Boston Braves (1911).*

• •••••

Mahjong

The Chinese board game mahjong was carried to the West by British nationals as early as 1907 and caught on in the United States—reaching frenzied popularity—in the 1920s. At the height of the craze, mahjong was a $1.5 million industry in China, with cow bones being exported from the United States to Shanghai and then rushed back to the States as completed game pieces just to keep up with the burgeoning demand. By 1923, it was estimated that between 10 million and 15 million Americans were playing the game regularly.

Mahjong is played with four players; many Americans in the 1920s made the game a social occasion by hosting mahjong nights and dressing up in Chinese-style robes. A set consists of 144 decorated bone tiles: 36 tiles in the bamboo suit, 36 in the circle suit, 36 in the character suit, 16 wind tiles, 12 dragon tiles, and 8 bonus tiles. The purpose of the game is to assemble a winning combination of different suits.

Mahjong remains a popular game in the United States, primarily among middle-aged and elderly women, as represented in such films as *Driving Miss Daisy* (1989) and *Cocoon* (1985). Mahjong has sometimes been seen as a Jewish women's game; its prevalence in Jewish communities may be attributed to the sharing of the game between Chinese and Jewish immigrant communities living in close proximity in tenement buildings in the 1920s.

ADDITIONAL FACTS

1. *A recent study conducted by doctors in Hong Kong concluded that mahjong competitions are so intense they can induce seizures—even in spectators—a condition the researchers called "mahjong epilepsy."*

2. *There have been several hit songs written about the game, such as "Since Ma Is Playing Mah Jong" (1923) by Eddie Cantor (1892–1964).*

3. *Mahjong is said to have saved the Milton Bradley Company from bankruptcy by keeping its factories working twenty-four hours a day to meet the demand for sets.*

•••••

Pablo Picasso

The day after artist Pablo Picasso (1881–1973) died, the *New York Times* declared, "Pablo Picasso remains without doubt the most original, the most protean and the most forceful personality in the visual arts in the first three-quarters of this century."

With the perspective of three more decades, that assessment remains true. The Spanish-born artist is best known for his paintings, but he also produced drawings, lithographs, etchings, sculptures, ceramics, mosaics, and murals.

Unlike most of the other artistic giants of the past century, Picasso did not confine himself to a particular movement or genre. Rather, he was constantly innovating and exploring, developing a style unto himself. One of his most profound achievements was the blurring (or, in some cases, destruction) of the distinction between beauty and ugliness.

He is considered to have been the cofounder of the cubist style with Georges Braque (1882–1963) around 1907. Cubism broke from Renaissance tradition by representing objects from multiple views, conveying more information than could be seen through traditional perspective.

Picasso's first major work that was considered a turning point toward cubism was *Les Demoiselles d'Avignon* (1907), which deconstructed the traditional ideas of beauty, anatomy, and perspective.

His further work took on elements of other styles, including surrealism, which at least partially inspired his greatest masterpiece, *Guernica* (1937). An oil painting on canvas that measured approximately $11\frac{1}{4}$ feet high and $25\frac{1}{2}$ feet wide, *Guernica* shows the suffering of a series of abstract figures. The painting was Picasso's reaction to the bombing of a Spanish town by Nazi airmen during the Spanish civil war.

Picasso remained vital and productive well into his eighties. He reportedly created more than 6,000 paintings, most of which he kept in his personal collection until his death. In 1969 alone, at age eighty-eight, he produced 165 paintings and 45 drawings.

He died at age ninety-one.

ADDITIONAL FACTS

1. *Picasso is also known for the parade of wives, mistresses, and muses that moved through his life during the course of his career. He had two wives and fathered four children with three different women.*

2. *Though he deeply identified himself as Spanish (and created his most enduring painting as a reaction to the Spanish civil war), he lived almost exclusively in France beginning in 1904. He even remained in France through the Nazi occupation during World War II.*

3. *As a child, Picasso attended bullfights in Spain with his father, and bullfighting would become an important and recurring theme in his work.*

• • • •

William Butler Yeats

The poet William Butler Yeats (1865–1939) holds an enormous place in the Irish cultural consciousness—even larger, arguably, than his compatriots James Joyce (1882–1941) and Oscar Wilde (1854–1900). As a central figure in the Celtic Revival movement of the late 1800s, Yeats became not only an Irish literary figure, but also a political and nationalist figure as well. In his works, he advocated a return to Ireland's earliest roots—its myths and folktales—as an escape from the Catholic–Protestant conflict that continues to complicate Irish politics today.

A Dubliner by birth, Yeats grew up in an artistic household—both his father and his brother were painters. Although Yeats himself dabbled in painting, he settled on poetry and by his thirties had already amassed a large oeuvre of poems. Influenced by the poetry of William Blake (1757–1827) and the burgeoning Irish literary revival, he developed a worldview that blended mysticism with native Irish sources of cultural inspiration.

Yeats's subject matter varies widely, from pastoral nature, as in "The Lake Isle of Innisfree" (1892), to time and transience, as in "When You Are Old" (1892), to unrequited love, as in "No Second Troy" (1910). He also wrote about Irish politics, notably in "Easter 1916," about the Easter Rising of 1916, in which Irish nationalists took up arms in the name of Irish independence but were executed by the British government. Though Yeats generally relied on very traditional verse forms, he brought a modern sensibility to them, especially as his career progressed.

Yeats's poetry only grew richer as he grew older, and he composed many of his best works during his sixties and seventies. The apocalyptic "The Second Coming" (1921), probably his best-known poem, uses dizzying doomsday imagery to elucidate Yeats's unique, cyclical view of history. And "Sailing to Byzantium" (1928), another late masterpiece, intertwines Yeats's fascination with aging and art into one sublime poem.

ADDITIONAL FACTS

1. *Yeats spent much of his life madly in love with an Irish nationalist and actress named Maud Gonne (1865–1953). Though she rejected his advances, he continued to pine for her even after marrying another woman.*

2. *Yeats won the Nobel Prize in Literature in 1923 but continued to produce prolifically—and arguably wrote his best work—after receiving the award.*

3. *Yeats is buried in Drumcliff, County Sligo, Ireland, under a tombstone inscribed with an epitaph from his own pen: "Cast a cold Eye / On Life, on Death. / Horseman, pass by!"*

·•●•·

Arnold Schoenberg

Unlike some artists, whose best-known accomplishments came in their youth, the Austrian composer Arnold Schoenberg (1874–1951) produced his most famous works later in his career. In dozens of orchestral works, Schoenberg helped popularize atonality, a revolutionary style of classical music that rejected traditional harmonies in favor of discordant arrangements and would prove highly influential for twentieth-century musicians.

Born in Vienna, Schoenberg taught himself music as a teenager and produced his first compositions in the 1890s. Most of his early works relied on conventional styles, but in the years preceding World War I, Schoenberg began to create a radically new musical genre. His goal, he famously decreed, was to transcend "every restriction of a bygone aesthetic."

Schoenberg's most famous innovation was his use of atonality. In traditional classical music, a *dissonant* chord or note is one that sounds unresolved, hanging in the air, and requires a *consonant* sound to balance it out. Schoenberg ignored the distinction between consonant and dissonant sounds. He declared this an "emancipation of dissonance"—still perhaps the best definition of atonality. The use of atonality often gave his works an unsettled, haunting sound.

Schoenberg, who was Jewish, moved to Germany in the 1920s to teach music but was forced to flee after the Nazis took power in 1933. He moved to the United States, where he taught at the University of California and continued to compose until his death.

ADDITIONAL FACTS

1. *Schoenberg was highly superstitious and was especially fearful of the number thirteen, a psychological condition known as triskaidekaphobia.*

2. *In addition to composing music, Schoenberg painted for many years. He considered himself a German Expressionist, similar to Paul Klee (1879–1940) and Wassily Kandinsky (1866–1944).*

3. *In response to his rejection by the traditional music world, in 1918 Schoenberg founded the Society for the Private Performance of Music, a concert space that did no advance publicity and forbade audience members to write reviews of performances.*

•••••

Charlie Chaplin

Legendary actor Charlie Chaplin's famous character, the Little Tramp, is the most enduring symbol of Hollywood's silent-film era. In the 1910s and 1920s, the Tramp was said to be the most recognizable image on the planet, a humorous figure embraced by viewers in every moviegoing country around the world.

Chaplin (1889–1977) was born in London and was a child actor on the English stage. After his second tour of the United States, he remained in America and embarked on a career in silent films in 1913. Within two years, he was an international star.

He debuted the Tramp in his second film appearance, *Kid Auto Races at Venice* (1914). The character featured a mustache, a bowler hat, baggy pants, oversize shoes, a walking cane, and a bowlegged stride. Chaplin's mastery of physical comedy and emotive body language made him a global star who was not restricted by the limitations of spoken language.

In 1914, he began directing his own films, and he would later control nearly every aspect of his works—as actor, director, producer, writer, musical composer, and editor. He directed two of his most beloved films in the 1920s—*The Kid* (1921) and *The Gold Rush* (1925).

In the following decade, Chaplin was less prolific, completing just two films, but both were masterpieces. *City Lights* (1931), which is often considered his finest film, was released three years after the advent of talking pictures, but Chaplin stuck to his belief that silent films were a purer form of expression than talkies. (*City Lights* is not technically a silent film; it includes music and sound effects.) The film combines slapstick comedy, pathos, and social satire, culminating in an emotional conclusion.

Modern Times (1936) is another Chaplin classic, focusing on man's struggles with machines in the Industrial Age—and on the era's unemployment, poverty, and hunger.

The Great Dictator (1940), a satire on the rise of German dictator Adolf Hitler (1889–1945), is the last appearance of the Tramp, and the first in which he speaks. As he aged, Chaplin worked less, directing just five films after 1940. In 1952, following a trip to Europe, he was denied reentry into the United States on the basis that he was an "undesirable alien." For many years, US authorities suspected him of communist leanings, and he was involved in several high-profile affairs with young women.

He lived out his remaining years in Switzerland before dying at age eighty-eight.

ADDITIONAL FACTS

1. *Chaplin was knighted by Queen Elizabeth II (1926–) in 1975.*

2. *His fourth and final wife, Oona, was eighteen at the time of their marriage; Chaplin was fifty-four. Oona was the daughter of American playwright Eugene O'Neill (1888–1953), and father and daughter did not speak after Oona's wedding to Chaplin.*

3. *In 1972, Chaplin returned to the United States after two decades in exile to receive an honorary Academy Award.*

•• • ••

Zionism

In 1894, Theodor Herzl (1860–1904), a young Hungarian Jew working as a journalist in Paris, witnessed a horrifying spectacle. A French artillery officer who was Jewish, Captain Alfred Dreyfus (1859–1935), had been wrongfully convicted of treason, and mobs in Paris had assembled, chanting, "Death to the Jews."

At that moment, Herzl had an epiphany that led him to create the modern Zionist movement: The Jewish people needed a homeland of their own, and they needed it fast.

The so-called Dreyfus affair underscored the depth of vitriolic anti-Semitism that Jews faced in nineteenth-century Europe. Dreyfus was eventually cleared of the trumped-up charges against him and pardoned by the French president, but only after spending four years at an isolated prison in South America.

Although the notion of a Jewish state was hardly new—Jews had prayed for a return to Jerusalem since its destruction by the Romans in 70 AD—Herzl began the first organized campaign to bring together under one banner Jews that were scattered around the world.

Working with Nathan Birnbaum (1864–1937), Herzl swiftly organized the First Zionist Congress in 1897 in Basel, Switzerland. During the three-day summit, the delegates devised the World Zionist Organization (WZO) as well as the Basel Program, in which they agreed to "establish a home for the Jewish people in Palestine under public law."

The World Zionist Congress met every four years thereafter, until the outbreak of World War II caused leaders to step up the pace. Meanwhile, the WZO immediately began pursuing the goals enunciated in the Basel Program by encouraging small-scale immigration to Palestine, the province of the Ottoman Empire that contained Jerusalem.

Although anti-Semitism was a major factor in shaping and expediting the Zionist movement, Jews also sought to return to their homeland in order to govern themselves as an independent nation. Thanks to the efforts of Herzl and Birnbaum, among others, the creation of the modern world's first Jewish state on May 14, 1948—the date Israel declared its independence—finally gave them that chance.

ADDITIONAL FACTS

1. *Birnbaum coined the term* Zionism *in an 1890 issue of his journal,* Selbstemanzipation *(Self-Emancipation).*

2. *In his 1896 book* Der Judenstaat, *Herzl proposed two possible homelands for the Jewish people: their "ever-memorable historic home" in Palestine, or Argentina, "one of the most fertile countries in the world."*

3. *Herzl coined the phrase "If you will, it is no fairy tale"—which became a motto for the Zionist movement.*

•• ◉ ••

Jim Thorpe

For much of the twentieth century, Jim Thorpe (1888–1953) was considered the greatest American athlete ever. During his stellar career, Thorpe was the ultimate athletic renaissance man: He earned letters in eleven different sports in college, played professional baseball and football, and was an Olympic champion in track and field.

Thorpe was born in a one-room cabin near Prague, Oklahoma, to a Native American family. He first garnered attention for his athletic prowess in 1907, when he stunned the track team at the Carlisle Industrial Indian School in Pennsylvania by clearing five feet nine inches in the high jump—even though he was not on the team and was wearing heavy work clothes.

An all-American halfback for the Carlisle football team in 1911 and 1912, Thorpe became an international sensation at the 1912 Olympics in Stockholm, Sweden. He won gold medals in two of the most grueling events at the games: the pentathlon and the decathlon, in which he broke the world record.

After his Olympic successes, Thorpe was feted with a ticker-tape parade down Broadway in New York City, but the celebration would not last. In 1913, the International Olympic Committee stripped him of his medals and records, ruling that he had forfeited his amateur status by playing two seasons of minor-league baseball in 1909 and 1910.

Thorpe then played six seasons of major-league baseball (1913–1915 and 1917–1919), mostly with the New York Giants, and spent parts of twelve seasons playing professional football (1915–1928) for six different teams. In 1920, he helped found the American Professional Football Association, which later evolved into the National Football League.

Beset by alcoholism, Thorpe worked mostly at odd jobs in his later years, until he died of a heart attack at a trailer home in California at age sixty-four. After years of lobbying, Thorpe's Olympic medals and marks were reinstated in 1982.

ADDITIONAL FACTS

1. *In an Associated Press (AP) poll in 1950, Thorpe was named the top male athlete and top football player of the first half of the twentieth century. In 1999, the AP named him the number three athlete of the century.*

2. *Thorpe's medals should not have been stripped, because Olympic rules at the time stipulated that a challenge to an athlete's qualification as a competitor had to be submitted within thirty days of the distribution of prizes. The American Amateur Union did not object until six months after the 1912 Olympics.*

3. *A town in Pennsylvania, formerly known as Mauch Chunk, bought Thorpe's remains and the rights to his name in 1953. The town is now called Jim Thorpe.*

4. *At the 1912 Olympic pentathlon medal ceremony, Sweden's King Gustav V (1858–1950) told Thorpe, "Sir, you are the greatest athlete in the world." Thorpe reportedly responded, "Thanks, King."*

• • ● • •

Little Rascals

Created by American film director Hal Roach (1892–1992), the children's show *Our Gang* debuted in 1922 and ran in theaters and on television for decades thereafter. Each episode followed the adventures of a group of neighborhood children, including such memorable characters as Spanky, Alfalfa, and Buckwheat. The show was eventually renamed *Little Rascals* and moved to television starting in 1955.

According to Roach, he got the idea for *Our Gang* in 1922 after auditioning a young girl for another film project. The young actress wore makeup and did her best to act like a small adult, but Roach was bored by the audition. Yet he found himself captivated by something he saw outside his office later that day: a playground argument between a group of kids.

He decided to direct a series in which child actors would act like real children and released the first *Our Gang* short in 1922. As a "short" film played in theaters before a feature film, *Our Gang* was a hit. Roach continued the series until 1938, with a few changes along the way: Sound was introduced in 1929, and the first (and only) *Our Gang* feature—*General Spanky*—was released in 1936. Roach left the project in 1938, but the MGM studio continued to produce new *Little Rascals* episodes until 1944.

One of Roach's biggest innovations was to cast both whites and blacks. Today, many of the stereotypes used in depicting black characters in particular are seen as racist, but merely by having regular black characters, Roach was pathbreaking for his time.

ADDITIONAL FACTS

1. *Frank Capra (1897–1991), the famous director of* It's a Wonderful Life *(1946) and* Mr. Smith Goes to Washington *(1939), was an early screenwriter for* Our Gang.

2. *Comedian Eddie Murphy (1961–) famously parodied the* Little Rascals *character Buckwheat for* Saturday Night Live.

3. *Roach also directed the classic films of the comedy duo Stan Laurel (1890–1965) and Oliver Hardy (1892–1957).*

Mohandas Gandhi

Political activist Mohandas Gandhi (1869–1948) is regarded as the father of independent India and became a global symbol of freedom and morality for his strategies of nonviolence and passive resistance that helped India throw off the chains of British colonial rule after World War II. His simple loincloth, cheap spectacles, and bamboo staff helped make him an international icon who inspired generations of human-rights activists around the world.

 After honing his philosophy while fighting discrimination as a lawyer in South Africa, Gandhi in 1915 returned to India, which had been ruled by the British since the eighteenth century. He immediately began working toward Indian self-rule and quickly transformed the drive toward independence from an upper-class struggle to a mass movement, uniting all classes, religions, and ethnic factions against British governance.

From 1918 to 1922, he led a series of nonviolent strikes, urging Indians to boycott British institutions. This civil disobedience led to mass arrests (about 30,000 of his followers) but also had the unintended consequence of instigating bloody riots. Gandhi himself was jailed for twenty-two months.

In 1930, Gandhi undertook his most significant act of civil disobedience. Protesting a law that prohibited Indians from making their own salt, he led seventy-eight followers on a 200-mile march to the sea, known as the Great Salt March, to make salt until the law was repealed. The march mobilized Indians across the country, and soon tens of thousands of nonviolent resisters—including Gandhi—were in jail.

With Great Britain weakened by World War II in 1942, Gandhi endorsed the Quit India campaign, which demanded that Britain give India its immediate independence. The movement led to huge demonstrations and violence in which almost 1,000 Indians were killed. Gandhi was soon arrested again, but by 1945, the British government had begun negotiating to grant India its freedom.

The year 1947 was one of both great triumph and crushing defeat for Gandhi. Britain gave India its independence but also carved out a separate Muslim country, Pakistan. Gandhi had always preached ethnic and religious tolerance, and he opposed partition. Amid the religious strife in the region following the partition, Gandhi was assassinated the next year, at age seventy-eight, by a Hindu fanatic.

ADDITIONAL FACTS

1. *Some of the human-rights leaders Gandhi inspired with his teachings of nonviolence and passive resistance were Martin Luther King Jr. (1929–1968) in the United States, Nelson Mandela (1918–) in South Africa, and Lech Walesa (1943–) in Poland.*

2. *Gandhi was known in India as Mahatma, or "Great Soul," and also as Bapu, or "Father."*

3. *Gandhi was not without his eccentricities: He did not speak on Mondays, adhered to strict dietary restrictions, used ashes to bathe instead of soap, and renounced sex at age thirty-six.*

••◆••

E. M. Forster

British novelist and critic E. M. Forster (1879–1970) occupied a somewhat unusual place in twentieth-century literature: His meticulously crafted works straddle the boundary between the Victorian and modern eras, appearing traditional and old-fashioned on the surface but expressing remarkably modern ideas within their pages. In particular, Forster's novels explore the concept of connection among individuals, as well as the various barriers—social, cultural, or otherwise—that prevent such connection from occurring.

From his earliest years, Forster displayed a gift for insightful observation. He found a creative outlet for that gift at Cambridge, and upon graduation he traveled widely throughout the Mediterranean, writing full-time. *A Room with a View* (1908), his first notable novel, tells a deceptively simple, romantic story about an Englishwoman visiting Italy. His next work, *Howards End* (1910), about three families and an English country house, likewise has the veneer of a traditional novel of manners. But its message about the value of human connection—and the foolishness of the English class system that inhibits such connection—jumps off the page in remarkably fresh and urgent terms, even today.

Forster's later fiction grew darker and more complex, culminating in *A Passage to India* (1924), his greatest and last fictional work. Set during the sunset of British colonial rule in India, this final novel ends on a pessimistic—or at best ambiguous—note about the possibility of true friendship and understanding across cultural lines. After its publication, the forty-five–year–old Forster ceased to write novels, focusing instead on literary criticism.

Although his vision became somewhat less optimistic by the end of his career, Forster is remembered as a remarkably liberal, humanist voice for his time. His works express a confidence in the power of human understanding in spite of the odds against it and a nearly mystical view of the connectedness of humankind.

ADDITIONAL FACTS

1. *Though it was rarely discussed during his lifetime, Forster was openly gay. He even wrote a gay-themed novel,* Maurice, *which was not published until 1971, the year after his death.*

2. *British novelist Zadie Smith's (1975–) bestseller* On Beauty *(2005) is a loose retelling of* Howards End *set in the suburbs of present-day Boston.*

3. *During his early career, Forster was loosely involved with the Bloomsbury group, the informal but influential literary salon that novelist Virginia Woolf ran from her sister's London home.*

•••••

The Rite of Spring

The Russian composer Igor Stravinsky (1882–1971) first conceived of *The Rite of Spring* while working on another of his ballets, *The Firebird,* in 1910. While composing the earlier piece, Stravinsky briefly imagined a pagan ritual that involved a young girl who was forced to dance herself to death as a sacrifice to the god of spring.

The resulting ballet, which Stravinsky completed two years later and is considered a milestone in the evolution of modern music, is often referred to by its French title, *Le sacre du printemps.* The landmark work is divided into two sections: "The Adoration of the Earth" and "The Sacrifice."

It's hard today to imagine a riot breaking out at a ballet, but when *The Rite of Spring* premiered at the Théâtre des Champs-Élysées in Paris on May 29, 1913, the French police could barely control the crowd. Stravinsky's work, which was choreographed by the great Russian dancer Vlasav Nijinsky (1890–1950), was a radical departure from classical strictures in almost every way. The ballet begins with a bassoon being played at a higher pitch than most had thought possible for the instrument and soon descends into what the audience heard as a cacophony of random notes. Nijinsky's choreography didn't help placate the critics, either. Rather than making graceful and demure movements on the balls of their feet, the dancers swayed their hips in an erotic manner that shocked the Parisian audience. In almost every way, *The Rite of Spring* was a brash and dramatic announcement that modernism had arrived in Western music.

The ballet is considered one of the most significant orchestral compositions of the twentieth century. It received wide popular exposure when cartoonist Walt Disney (1901–1966) included parts of *The Rite of Spring* on the sound track of his 1940 animated classic *Fantasia,* alongside works by Ludwig van Beethoven (1770–1827) and Johann Sebastian Bach (1685–1750).

ADDITIONAL FACTS

1. *Reactions to the premiere of* The Rite of Spring *differed even among the top French composers in attendance. Maurice Ravel (1875–1937) reportedly shouted, "Genius! Genius!" from the audience, while Camille Saint-Saëns (1835–1921) stormed out in the opening minutes.*

2. *While Stravinsky admired Nijinsky's dancing, he found it frustrating to work with the choreographer, who (according to Stravinsky, at least) knew "nothing" about music.*

3. *Over the course of his career, Stravinsky would collaborate with other great artists, including the British poet and playwright W. H. Auden (1907–1973), who wrote the aria for Stravinsky's 1951 opera* The Rake's Progress, *and the French writer Jean Cocteau (1889–1963).*

4. *Stravinsky's impact extended beyond classical music: The rock musician Frank Zappa (1940–1993) considered him a major influence.*

•• • ••

Douglas Fairbanks and Mary Pickford

In the 1920s, Douglas Fairbanks Sr. and Mary Pickford were two of the world's most popular silent-film stars. Pickford was beloved for her portrayals of ingenues and sentimental heroines; Fairbanks, after beginning his career in light comedies, became the preeminent swashbuckler of the silent era.

Today, their films are not nearly as well known as what their personas came to represent: They were the first example of "Hollywood royalty." After a three-year courtship, they married in 1920, a union of America's Sweetheart and the handsome, athletic box office star.

Though ten years younger than her counterpart, Canadian-born Pickford (1892–1979) made her film debut first, in 1909. She appeared in more than seventy-five films by trendsetting director D. W. Griffith (1875–1948) between 1909 and 1912. During this period, she set a fashion trend with her blonde corkscrew curls.

As her popularity grew, "the Girl with the Golden Hair" aggressively fought for higher wages, successfully jumping from one studio to the next in search of more money. Examples of her ingenue roles include *The Poor Little Rich Girl* (1917) and *Pollyanna* (1920).

Fairbanks (1883–1939) made his film debut in 1915, initially appearing as naïve, middle-class heroes. In 1920, he began the transition to playing more manly roles in costume epics including *The Mark of Zorro* (1920), *The Three Musketeers* (1921), *Robin Hood* (1922), and *The Thief of Baghdad* (1924).

A year before their wedding, Fairbanks and Pickford cofounded—with Charlie Chaplin (1889–1977) and Griffith—the distribution company United Artists, which gave them a degree of independence previously unknown to actors and directors. Pickford remained a partner in the company until 1956.

Pickford was one of several silent-era stars who were unsuccessful in transitioning to talking pictures. Though she won an Academy Award for Best Actress for *Coquette* (1929), her first all-talking film, she made just four more pictures before her retirement in 1933.

Fairbanks and Pickford separated in 1933 and divorced in 1936. Within three years, Fairbanks was dead of a heart attack at age fifty-six. Pickford, who received an honorary Academy Award in 1976, lived to be eighty-seven.

ADDITIONAL FACTS

1. *Together, Fairbanks and Pickford costarred in just one film*—The Taming of the Shrew *(1929)— which was also Fairbanks's first talking film.*

2. *Fairbanks was born Douglas Ulman; Pickford was born Gladys Smith.*

3. *Fairbanks and Pickford were the first two stars to officially leave their handprints in cement in the courtyard of Grauman's Chinese Theater in Hollywood, in 1927.*

··●●··

Anarchism

Amid the twentieth century's great clashes between communism, fascism, and democracy, one small, militant political movement opted for a different course: none of the above.

Anarchism—the opposition to all forms of government—was founded by European political theorists including Pierre-Joseph Proudhon (1809–1865) and Mikhail Bakunin (1814–1876). The movement enjoyed its greatest popularity in the late nineteenth and early twentieth centuries in both Europe and the United States.

To its adherents, anarchism promised an end to government oppression as well as the depredations of capitalism. Anarchists believed that private property should be abolished and control of factories turned over to workers. Although anarchism had many similarities with communism, philosophers such as Proudhon did not envision any role for the state whatsoever.

In practice, anarchists launched a global wave of violence, with a special emphasis on assassinations of authority figures that they hoped would eventually bring down governments across the world. In Russia, Czar Alexander II (1818–1881) was killed by an anarchist bomb. The king of Italy, Umberto I (1844–1900), was shot dead. Leon Czolgosz (1873–1901), the assassin of President William McKinley (1843–1901), was an anarchist. Anarchists were also blamed for an attack on Wall Street that killed thirty-eight bystanders in 1920, although the crime was never solved.

Anarchists, by their very nature, lacked a cohesive national leadership structure, although the most well-known American anarchist was Emma Goldman (1869–1940). But their secretiveness only made them appear more fearsome; fears of anarchism helped trigger the Red Scare after World War I, in which Goldman and many suspected anarchists and communists were deported from the United States.

Anarchism still has followers, although its violence ended in the United States after the 1920s.

ADDITIONAL FACTS

1. *Goldman was implicated in a plot to kill industrialist Henry Clay Frick (1849–1919), a steel baron who had crushed a strike in 1892.*

2. The Secret Agent, *a classic 1907 novel by Joseph Conrad (1857–1924), tells the story of an anarchist plot to blow up Greenwich Observatory in England.*

3. *Rebels in Paris seized control of the French capital for two months in 1871, setting up a quasi-anarchist government called the Paris Commune. Most of the commune's leadership was executed after French troops reasserted control.*

• • ● • •

Ty Cobb

On the baseball diamond, Ty Cobb (1886–1961) was one of the fiercest and most successful competitors the game has ever seen. Off the field, he was just as ferocious.

Known for his aggressive style of play, Cobb is regarded by many as the greatest all-around player of all time. He still owns the record for highest career batting average (.367), and his twelve batting titles have never been matched. Cobb also set many stolen-base records, which at the time were thought to be unbreakable. In 1936, he received more votes for the inaugural Hall of Fame class than Babe Ruth (1895–1948).

But unlike the Babe, who was beloved by fans and fellow players, Cobb was almost universally despised. On the field, he played with a barely controlled rage, his spikes flying in the direction of anyone who crossed his path. Off the field, he was equally feared—he once went into the stands to attack a heckling fan.

Cobb said that he never recovered from an incident that occurred when he was eighteen. His father, believing that Cobb's mother was having an affair, came home unexpectedly and climbed to the balcony outside their bedroom. Thinking an intruder was outside, Cobb's mother shot his father and killed him. She was later acquitted of manslaughter charges.

In his twenty-four seasons, Cobb racked up 4,191 hits, 2,245 runs, and 892 stolen bases, records that would not be topped for decades. In 1909, he won the triple crown for the Detroit Tigers, leading the league in batting average (.377), home runs (9), and runs batted in (107). In 1911, he won the first-ever American League Most Valuable Player award, leading the league in several categories, including batting (.420), runs (147), and runs batted in (127).

He died a rich man, having made millions in the stock market and through his investments in the Coca-Cola Company. But only four members of the baseball community attended his funeral.

ADDITIONAL FACTS

1. *Born in Narrows, Georgia, Cobb was nicknamed the Georgia Peach.*

2. *He played for the Detroit Tigers (1905–1926) and Philadelphia A's (1927–1928). He also was the Tigers' player-manager from 1921 to 1926.*

3. *Among Cobb's remarkable feats: He batted at least .320 for twenty-three consecutive years.*

4. *Cobb played in three World Series with the Detroit Tigers (1907, 1908, and 1909) but did not win any. Indeed, the great batsman hit just .262 in his World Series career.*

•••••

Flagpole Sitting

In 1924, a professional daredevil named Alvin "Shipwreck" Kelly (1893–1952) sat for thirteen hours and thirteen minutes on top of a flagpole in Hollywood, California. Kelly's feat set a world record—mostly because he was the first person to try—and sparked an unlikely craze.

After news of Kelly's feat spread throughout the country, many others began to make attempts at the world record, which soon ranged from twelve to twenty-one days. Crowds, attracted by the novelty, gathered to watch the latest contender for the title of King of the Pole, and newspapers eagerly printed results.

In 1928, for instance, Kelly arrived in Louisville, Kentucky, where the headline of the *Courier-Journal and Times* blared: "Daredevil Kelly, Content on Pole, in 100 Hour Attempt."

Flagpole sitting took its inspiration from Simeon Stylites (c. 390–459), an early Christian saint in Syria who reputedly sat for thirty-seven years on top of a small elevated platform to escape the pressures of daily existence and died atop his perch. He inspired a wave of other pole sitters in the ancient world, who were known as stylites.

In 1930, after several competitors had broken his modern record, Kelly decided to reclaim the title for himself by sitting on a pole in Atlantic City, New Jersey, for forty-nine days. Unfortunately for Kelly, by then Americans had better things to worry about: The stock market had crashed in 1929, and pole sitting soon lost its popularity.

ADDITIONAL FACTS

1. *The current record for pole sitting is held by Daniel Baraniuk (1975–) of Poland, who spent 196 days on top of a pole in 2002.*

2. *The current rules of the World Pole-Sitting Championship allow contestants to take short breaks every two hours.*

3. *The Spanish filmmaker Luis Buñuel (1900–1983) based his 1965 film* Simón del desierto *on Simeon Stylites.*

•••••

Howard Hughes

Howard Hughes (1905–1976) was one of the most enigmatic and mysterious personalities of the twentieth century. He was a manufacturing magnate, an innovative film producer and director, a record-setting aviator, an ambitious airplane builder, and a giant in the Las Vegas hotel and casino industry. But he was also a terrible businessman and eccentric whose film, aviation, hotel, and casino companies lost tens of millions of dollars.

Hughes is perhaps best known for his secrecy and his fear of germs, particularly late in his life, when he lived in isolation in a series of hotel rooms. As biographers Donald L. Barlett (1936–) and James B. Steele (1943–) wrote, during the last years of his life, Hughes was a "hopeless psychotic."

In his earlier years, however, Hughes cut as public and dashing a figure as there was in American culture.

His father had developed the first successful rotary bit to drill oil wells through rock, an invention that would bring the Hughes Tool Company enormous sums of money. Hughes inherited the business in 1924, and its profits would give him the freedom to explore two of his life's passions—movies and flying.

In Hollywood, Hughes produced several successful films and had romances with some of the town's biggest female stars, including Katharine Hepburn (1907–2003) and Ava Gardner (1922–1990).

But most of his business ventures ended in disaster. His most spectacular failure was the construction of the H-4 Hercules seaplane, derisively dubbed the Spruce Goose. The US government contracted Hughes to build three of these mammoth, eight-engine seaplanes (with a wingspan of 320 feet) for $18 million, for use during World War II. Even after adding millions of dollars of his own money, Hughes was able to produce only one plane, which flew just once, in 1947, for one mile.

Hughes spent his last years shuttling between a variety of hotels and countries. Toward the end, he was seen by only five men, who served as secretaries, advisors, nurses, and his messengers to the outside world. He died of kidney failure at age seventy.

ADDITIONAL FACTS

1. *Some of Hughes's successful films include Hell's Angels (1930), Scarface (1932), and the controversial film The Outlaw (1943). At the time, Hell's Angels (which Hughes directed as well as produced) was the most expensive film ever made, with a budget of $4 million. It grossed $8 million and turned actress Jean Harlow (1911–1937) into a star.*

2. *Hughes had a series of spectacular plane crashes, including one in 1946 in which he suffered a fractured skull, a crushed chest and left lung, and nine broken ribs.*

3. *Late in his life, Hughes secretly shuttled between hotels not only to keep his appearance and mental illness from the public, but also to avoid establishing residency in any state, thereby avoiding having to pay state income tax.*

D. H. Lawrence

The English novelist D. H. Lawrence (1885–1930) attracted nearly constant controversy during his literary career. Even for decades after his death, discussions of his works focused almost exclusively on their candid sexuality. Despite the hostility that Lawrence's novels elicited in his day, though, they are anything but pornographic. They provide profound insight, ahead of their time, into the tensions that occur when individuals' unconscious, primitive desires run headlong into society's rules and constraints.

Lawrence was born to oddly matched parents—a nearly illiterate coal miner and an educated schoolmistress—in the Nottinghamshire region of England. With encouragement from a childhood friend, Lawrence began to write articles and short fiction. By his late twenties, he had finished his first novel, attracted the attention of prominent editors, married, and begun traveling through Europe and writing full-time.

The largely autobiographical *Sons and Lovers* (1913) explores the oedipal romantic and sexual dramas of a family much like Lawrence's own. His editor toned down some of Lawrence's particularly forthright passages about sex, so the novel managed to escape censorship and win acclaim as a landmark work. But Lawrence's next and more daring novel, *The Rainbow* (1915), was banned in many jurisdictions for obscenity—the first of many such controversies that would arise over Lawrence's writing.

After another well-received novel, *Women in Love* (1920), Lawrence traveled extensively, writing short stories, travelogues, poems, and letters. During his travels, he grew more deeply fascinated with humankind's primal aspects—instinct, ritual, dreams, power, and will—and their inevitable clash with societal forces. His last and most infamous major work, *Lady Chatterley's Lover* (1928), reflects this fascination. The novel, about a woman whose passionless marriage drives her to embark on a sexual affair outside of her social class, was decried so vehemently as pornographic that it was not officially published in the United States until 1959, nearly thirty years after Lawrence's death.

ADDITIONAL FACTS

1. *During World War I, Lawrence's pacifist stance raised the suspicion of the British government, which attempted to suppress some of his writings from the period.*

2. *Lawrence was heavily influenced by the theories of Sigmund Freud, particularly his studies of the unconscious mind and repressed sexual desires.*

3. *Lawrence was sickly throughout most of his childhood and adult life, struggling with recurrent pneumonia and later tuberculosis, which took his life in 1930.*

•••••

Irving Berlin

The great American songwriter Irving Berlin (1888–1989) was born Israel Isidore Baline to a Jewish family in the Russian town of Mogilev. When he was five, the Balines fled to the United States to escape violent pogroms against the area's Jewish population. Berlin's father died shortly after the family settled in New York City, and the young boy had to find work to support his family. One of his first jobs was as a singing waiter; he would stay in music for the rest of his life.

Berlin's first songs earned him only modest success. His big break came in 1911, when he published "Alexander's Ragtime Band." A tremendous success when it was first released, reaching the top spot on sheet-music charts, the song launched Berlin's career and established overnight his reputation as the greatest star among the composers and lyricists of Tin Pan Alley. (Berlin was one of the few Tin Pan Alley artists who wrote both words and music.) Berlin soon progressed from hit songs to hit musicals, creating Broadway classics such as *Annie Get Your Gun* (1946) and *Stop! Look! Listen!* (1915).

As new media were invented, Berlin always stayed at the forefront. He was among the first songwriters to work with "talkies"; in *The Jazz Singer* (1927), the first full-length motion picture with sound, Al Jolson (1886–1950) sings "Blue Skies," a 1926 Berlin hit.

Berlin's biggest hit came with the 1942 film *Holiday Inn,* in which Bing Crosby (1903–1977) first performed the song "White Christmas." As Berlin told an interviewer in 1920, "The song writer must look upon his work as a business, that is, to make a success of it, he must work and work, and then WORK." The work paid off: Berlin's first song, "Marie from Sunny Italy," made only thirty-seven cents. "White Christmas" is the best-selling song of all time.

ADDITIONAL FACTS

1. *Hours after the terrorist attacks of September 11, 2001, many members of Congress assembled at the steps of the United States Capitol and sang Berlin's patriotic classic "God Bless America" (1938).*

2. *Berlin wasn't the only Jewish songwriter to create a Christmas classic. Other holiday standards penned by Jewish artists include "Rudolph the Red-Nosed Reindeer" (1939), by Johnny Marks (1909–1985), and "Silver Bells" (1951), by Jay Livingston (1915–2001) and Ray Evans (1915–2007).*

3. *In 1944, Berlin had lunch with Winston Churchill (1874–1965), who mistook him for the political philosopher Isaiah Berlin (1909–1997). When the British prime minister asked Berlin what his most important recent work had been, the confused songwriter responded, "I don't know. It should be 'A White Christmas,' I guess."*

The Jazz Singer (1927)

"Wait a minute, wait a minute. You ain't heard nothing yet."
—Al Jolson, as Jack Robin

With those words, actor Al Jolson (1886–1950) brought synchronous speech to a Hollywood feature film, ushering in the beginning of the sound era and signaling the imminent demise of the silent cinema.

Synchronous sound had previously been used in short films, and nonsynchronous words had appeared on film sound tracks. But never before had the words of an actor in a fictional feature film been synchronized with his image on film.

Directed by Alan Crosland (1894–1936), the film debuted in Los Angeles on October 6, 1927, and caused an immediate sensation. It was the biggest box office hit to that point for Warner Bros., which had developed the groundbreaking Vitaphone sound system.

The film's success triggered a revolution in film production, forcing the Hollywood studios to change how they made pictures. From then on, they had to construct quiet studio stages with microphones hanging overhead; create soundproof boxes in which to put the camera, camera operator, cinematographer, and director; and install speakers and amplification in their theaters.

Within two years, most of Hollywood's productions were sound films.

The Jazz Singer itself is not an all-talking picture. It includes two scenes of dialogue and ten songs, six of which Jolson performs. He sings his principal songs in blackface, which has made the movie somewhat controversial.

The story focuses on a cantor's son who wants to enter show business, turning his back on the synagogue to sing jazz songs. (Jolson himself was the son of a cantor, a Jewish religious figure who directs the musical sections of services. And like the title character, who changes his name from Jakie Rabinowitz to Jack Robin, the Lithuanian-born Jolson changed his from Asa Yoelson.)

The film deals with themes of generational conflict, cultural assimilation, and religious tolerance. It was based on Samson Raphaelson's 1921 short story "The Day of Atonement," which Raphaelson had also adapted into a 1925 Broadway play.

ADDITIONAL FACTS

1. *Jolson was the third choice to play the title role. George Jessel, who had played Jakie Rabinowitz on Broadway, and Eddie Cantor both turned down the film.*

2. *The first "all-talking" feature-length film was* Lights of New York *(1928).*

3. The Jazz Singer *was twice remade in Hollywood—in 1952 and 1980.*

4. *In 1929, Warner Bros. production head Darryl F. Zanuck accepted an honorary Academy Award given to the studio "for producing* The Jazz Singer, *the pioneer outstanding talking picture, which has revolutionized the industry."*

•••••

Henry Ford and the Model T

In the early twentieth century, industrialist Henry Ford (1863–1947) helped popularize the automobile with new manufacturing techniques that made it possible to produce inexpensive cars that middle-class Americans could afford. His two major innovations, the automated assembly line and the $5 daily wage, revolutionized both the auto industry and all of American manufacturing and ensured that the automobile would quickly become the primary mode of transportation in the United States.

Ford introduced the Model T on October 1, 1908. Though not the first car on the market, it was far and away the most reliable and the cheapest. And it only got cheaper: The initial price tag was $850, and it soon fell to $260.

Ford was able to keep prices low by implementing an extremely efficient, automated assembly line in his factories. Beginning with the simplest components of a Model T, the parts moved down the line to specialized laborers who would each perform a single, discrete task. Using this process, an entire Model T could be constructed in ninety-three minutes.

But the $260 price tag was still steep by the standards of the day. (In 1908, the per capita annual income in the United States was only $326.) To help create a demand for his cars, Ford upped his workers' wages to $5 a day, realizing that his employees were also potential customers.

Over the next two decades, Ford sold more than 15 million Model T's. The model was discontinued in 1927, but other automakers and manufacturers soon copied the industrial practices Ford had pioneered. Today, his Ford Motor Company remains one of the world's largest carmakers.

ADDITIONAL FACTS

1. *Though Ford denied being an anti-Semite, a newspaper he owned—the* Dearborn Independent—*published the viciously anti-Semitic book* The Protocols of the Elders of Zion. *In 1938, Ford himself was awarded the Grand Cross of the German Eagle, the highest honor Nazi Germany awarded to foreigners.*

2. *Members of the Ford family still run the Ford Motor Company to this day. The current executive chairman is William Clay Ford Jr. (1957–), Henry Ford's great-grandson.*

3. *Henry Ford was a race-car driver before becoming an automobile manufacturer, and he was inducted into the Motorsports Hall of Fame of America in 1996.*

··•··

Babe Ruth

On May 6, 1915, George Herman "Babe" Ruth hit his first major-league home run. At the time, few realized that it was a revolutionary act that would change the face of American sports.

When Ruth (1895–1948) hit that first home run, he was an outstanding left-handed pitcher for the Boston Red Sox. But he would soon become an international folk hero and arguably the most influential player in the history of baseball as a left-handed slugger for the New York Yankees.

In the dead ball era before Ruth, home runs occurred infrequently. Instead, teams focused on scoring runs with singles, bunts, and stolen bases. So in 1919, when Ruth hit twenty-nine home runs for the Red Sox, breaking the major-league record of twenty-seven set by Ned Williamson (1857–1894) in 1884, he became a sensation and single-handedly brought baseball into the modern age.

After that season, however, cash-strapped Red Sox owner Harry Frazee famously sold his star player to the New York Yankees for $125,000. The deal would have far-reaching consequences for both teams. Ruth turned the Yankees, who had never won a World Series before the trade, into a legendary powerhouse. The Red Sox, on the other hand, would not win another title for eighty-six years.

In 1920, his first season with the Yankees, Ruth hit fifty-four round-trippers. (The next-best home-run hitter that year, George Sisler, had nineteen.) The following year, he swatted fifty-nine, while also recording a .378 batting average with 171 runs batted in. In his most celebrated season, 1927, he anchored the famous Yankees "Murderer's Row" team and hit sixty home runs.

Ruth finished his career with 714 home runs, among dozens of other batting records. He also helped the Yankees win seven pennants and four World Series titles (1923, 1927, 1928, and 1932).

But Ruth was not merely a transcendent ballplayer; he was also a legendary personality, known for his outsize appetites—for hot dogs, beer, and women, not necessarily in that order—and his often-mythical exploits off the field. His car accidents, affairs, illnesses, and Hollywood roles, and just about every other part of his life, made headlines, ushering in the era when athletes would be considered national celebrities.

ADDITIONAL FACTS

1. *Ruth's nickname originated in 1914, when he signed his first professional contract at age nineteen with the minor-league Baltimore Orioles. In spring training that year, his teammates referred to him as owner Jack Dunn's "babe," and the name stuck.*

2. *In 1920, Ruth's first with New York, the Yankees doubled their attendance and became the first team to draw more than 1 million fans in a season. Three years later, Yankee Stadium—also known as "The House That Ruth Built"—opened.*

3. *Ruth played in an era of colorful sportswriting and acquired an array of nicknames, most notably the Bambino and the Sultan of Swat.*

•• ● ••

Dance Marathons

On June 10, 1928, the most famous dance marathon of the decade began at New York City's Madison Square Garden. Vying for a top prize of $5,000, 132 couples took the floor at the famous arena in the culmination of one of the most improbable fads in American history.

The dance marathon craze had been triggered by an American woman named Alma Cummings, who in 1923 reportedly danced for twenty-seven hours without stopping. Her record was soon broken by Vera Sheppard, a file clerk who danced for sixty-nine hours at a New York City ballroom. ("The only thing that annoyed me was having a man's arm around me all the time," Sheppard told newspapers.) Sheppard's record, in turn, quickly fell to a Cleveland woman.

Similar marathons sprang up in cities across the country, and promoters began to offer cash prizes to the couple with the greatest endurance. The marathon at Madison Square Garden, however, was by far the highest-profile such event.

Dance marathons took a heavy physical toll on competitors. Two days into the event at the Garden, the *New York Times* said, "The dancers resembled mechanical toys when they are about to run down and need winding." Contestants weren't judged on their dancing skills—only their stamina (although the New York marathon did allow dancers periodic fifteen-minute breaks).

The 1928 Madison Square Garden marathon ended up lasting for twenty days and was only shut down because the city's health commissioner feared for the well-being of the eight remaining couples onstage.

In 1935, the novelist Horace McCoy (1897–1955) published *They Shoot Horses, Don't They?* a murder mystery whose plot revolves around a Depression-era dance marathon. Director Sydney Pollack (1934–) adapted the book into a 1969 film starring Jane Fonda (1937–); it won one Academy Award and was nominated for eight others. Today, Pollack's film is a lasting testament to an era when impoverished but impassioned amateurs tried to make ends meet by dancing the night away.

ADDITIONAL FACTS

1. *The American Society of Teachers of Dancing organized a petition drive against dance marathons in 1923, saying they were "dangerous to health, useless as entertainment and a disgrace to the art and profession of dancing."*

2. *According to legend, the first recorded dance marathon—at Renshaw Hall in Butte, Montana—was also shut down by a health commissioner, this time after fifteen hours.*

3. *Mexico City banned dance marathons in 1933, after determining that a proposed marathon "benefited nobody."*

·•●•·

Salvador Dalí

With his large eyes, comically upturned mustache, large collection of canes, and outrageous comments, painter Salvador Dalí (1904–1989) was himself an embodiment of his most famous art: surrealism. Dalí developed the persona of an eccentric genius, known as much for his showmanship and marketability as for his innovative work.

Surrealism, with its fantastical visual imagery and exploration of the subconscious, emerged as a major movement in the European art world in the 1920s. Dalí's first major international breakthrough occurred in 1928, when three of his paintings were shown at the Carnegie International Exhibition in Pittsburgh. A year later, he had his first one-man show in Paris.

Around this time, he developed his "paranoiac-critical method," in which he induced his own psychotic hallucinations to create art. Soon, he became the leader of the surrealist movement, confirming his place with *The Persistence of Memory* (1931), the most famous painting in the genre's history. The work features some of Dalí's most characteristic images, including melting clocks (representing the bending of time), ants (decay), and the landscape of his home region of Catalonia in Spain.

Although he continued to show paintings in surrealist exhibitions for the rest of the decade, he was expelled from the movement in 1934 for his apolitical views. (Most of the other surrealists were Marxists.)

Starting around 1940, he began to focus more on scientific, historical, and religious themes. He was prolific throughout his career, as demonstrated by a 1980 retrospective exhibition in Paris that included 168 paintings, 219 drawings, 38 objects, and more than 2,000 documents.

Dalí's showmanship, abundant work, and arrogance won him many critics, most of whom he shrugged off as lesser, jealous artists. When asked in 1958 by the journalist Mike Wallace (1918–) which contemporary artists he admired, Dalí replied, "First Dalí. After Dalí, Picasso." That was the list.

Dalí died of heart failure at age eighty-four.

ADDITIONAL FACTS

1. *Dalí worked in various media, producing oil paintings, watercolors, drawings, graphics, sculptures, films, photographs, performance pieces, and jewelry.*

2. *His contributions to film are noteworthy. He collaborated with the Spanish director Luis Buñuel (1900–1983) on two seminal surrealist films, Un chien andalou (1929) and L'âge d'or (1930). Dalí also provided the vivid dreamscapes in the Alfred Hitchcock (1899–1980) film Spellbound (1945) and worked with Walt Disney (1901–1966) on the animated short Destino, which was completed and released in 2003. (Dalí worked on it in 1945 and 1946.)*

3. *Part of Dalí's persona was to make outrageous statements to cause a sensation. He once called nineteenth-century French master Paul Cézanne (1839–1906) "the clumsiest painter I have ever come across."*

••●••

Carl Sandburg

One of the most thoroughly American poets in the nation's history, Carl Sandburg (1878–1967) is best remembered for "Chicago" (1914), his celebration of the strength, productivity, and character of the Midwest's great industrial city, as well as for a lengthy biography of Abraham Lincoln he published decades later. Sandburg's accessible, exuberant poems made him immensely popular during his lifetime, and his works still retain a wide readership today.

Born to a poor Swedish immigrant couple in Galesburg, a small city in western Illinois, Sandburg left school early and worked at a succession of odd jobs throughout his teens and twenties. This period steeped him in the local culture and traditions of the Midwest, as he grew familiar with everything from local political campaigns to barbershops to farm fields. By 1913, he had put down roots in Chicago and settled into journalism, writing poems on the side.

Sandburg's first major collection, *Chicago Poems* (1916), was an instant hit, and its best-known poem, titled simply "Chicago," brought him renown. This work typifies Sandburg's approach to poetry: It relies on bold, declarative statements and simple but evocative imagery, such as his now-legendary description of Chicago: "Stormy, husky, brawling / City of the Big Shoulders." Moreover, the poem is written in unrhymed free verse, making the language more accessible and less rigid than that of more traditional poetry. Throughout, Sandburg displays great pride in Chicago, acknowledging the city's problems—crime, prostitution, poverty—but reveling in its endurance and resilience.

Sandburg is often compared to Walt Whitman (1819–1892), the great populist American poet of the nineteenth century. Indeed, Sandburg openly admired Whitman's masterwork, *Leaves of Grass* (1855), for its pioneering use of free verse and its celebration of humble, everyday, distinctively American subjects. Like Whitman, Sandburg was fascinated by America's folklore and its democratic system: Besides his poetry, he also wrote nearly a dozen books about American history and music.

ADDITIONAL FACTS

1. *Also an avid performer, Sandburg enjoyed entertaining audiences at his readings with folk songs and stories.*

2. *Sandburg, like his predecessor Walt Whitman, admired Abraham Lincoln enormously. He spent many years writing a sprawling, multivolume biography of Lincoln and won the Pulitzer Prize for History for one of the volumes in 1940.*

3. *Concerned that most of the fairy tales available to American children were European in origin, Sandburg decided to write several volumes of fairy tales himself, with distinctively American characters and settings.*

••••

Bessie Smith

When Columbia Records nicknamed Bessie Smith (c. 1894–1937) the Queen of the Blues, the music press made it clear that they disagreed. *Queen* wasn't quite regal enough: The nickname that stuck for the famous singer was "the Empress of the Blues."

Bessie Smith was the most popular blues singer of the 1920s and 1930s and had already achieved considerable success as a performer before she entered the recording studio. In 1912, Smith sang in a revue with legendary blues singer Gertrude "Ma" Rainey (1886–1939), nicknamed the Mother of the Blues, and the older star was impressed. Rainey gave the Tennessee native some pointers—particularly on how to maintain a strong stage presence—and the pupil soon outshined her teacher.

Smith had her own show in Atlantic City by 1920, and in 1923 she moved to New York City, where she was a huge hit on the vaudeville circuit. This was also the year that she signed a recording contract with Columbia and made her first albums.

Columbia signed Smith as the first artist for its new "race records" series, hoping to exploit the popularity of African-American blues music. Smith's first releases— "Gulf Coast Blues" (1923) and "Down Hearted Blues" (1923)—were big sellers. Other hits included "Baby Won't You Please Come Home" (1923) and "Nobody Knows When You're Down and Out" (1929).

Smith's prominence began to wane as the Great Depression cut into the nation's budget for entertainment and vaudeville gave ground to "talkies." Once motion pictures could be recorded with sound, the market for vaudeville performances nearly vanished. Smith was in peak form at the time, and still quite young. Some believe that she was ready to make a comeback in the late 1930s, but she didn't get the chance: The Empress of the Blues died in a car accident in Mississippi on September 26, 1937.

ADDITIONAL FACTS

1. *The folk-rock group the Band wrote a song named after Bessie Smith in 1975.*

2. *Smith's birth date has been officially listed as sometime in July 1892 and as April 15, 1894. There is no consensus on which is the correct date, but Smith always observed April 15 as her birthday.*

3. *In 1929, Smith starred in the movie* St. Louis Blues, *which contains the only known footage of her.*

••●••

Greta Garbo

Swedish-born Greta Garbo (1905–1990) was the biggest box office star of the 1930s and one of the few performers to successfully make the transition from silent films to sound pictures. Her career was relatively brief—she retired at age thirty-six—but her luminous on-screen presence and mysterious off-camera persona have bewitched film lovers for generations.

Born Greta Lovisa Gustafsson in Stockholm, Garbo appeared in films in Sweden and Germany before she caught the eye of the legendary Hollywood producer Louis B. Mayer. He signed her to a contract with MGM, and she made her first three Hollywood films in 1926: *The Torrent, The Temptress,* and *Flesh and the Devil.*

With her androgynous beauty, Garbo quickly emerged as a major silent-film star, earning the nickname "the Swedish Sphinx." Concerns about her Scandinavian accent kept MGM from casting her in a talking picture until 1930, when she starred in an adaptation of the Eugene O'Neill play *Anna Christie.* Her first speaking role was such a sensation that MGM promoted the film with a "Garbo Talks!" advertising campaign.

Portraying a weary Swedish-American prostitute, she delivered her first line: "Gimme a whiskey, ginger ale on the side. And don't be stingy, baby!" Concerns about her accent proved unwarranted, as her throaty delivery only enhanced her allure and mystique—and for much of the 1930s, in the midst of the Great Depression, she reportedly commanded upward of an astounding $500,000 per picture.

Of all her famous lines of dialogue, perhaps the one that is best remembered is from *Grand Hotel* (1932), an Academy Award winner for Best Picture. Playing a Russian ballerina, Garbo says, "I want to be alone," a line that resonated for the rest of her days, particularly after her retirement to a life of seclusion in 1941.

Her last major performance came in *Ninotchka* (1939), a classic romantic comedy that MGM promoted with the tagline "Garbo Laughs!" She earned her fourth Academy Award nomination for Best Actress for the role but lost for the fourth time. Two years later, she appeared in her final film, *Two-Faced Woman* (1941).

Garbo then retreated from the public eye for nearly fifty years, granting no interviews, as her legend continued to grow until her death at age eighty-four.

ADDITIONAL FACTS

1. *Garbo was engaged to* Flesh and the Devil *costar John Gilbert in 1926, but she left him at the altar; she never married and is believed to have been bisexual.*

2. *She starred in* The Kiss *(1929), the last picture MGM produced without dialogue.*

3. *In 1954, the* Guinness Book of World Records *named Garbo "the most beautiful woman who ever lived."*

4. *She was awarded an honorary Academy Award in 1955.*

•••••

Fundamentalism

The term *fundamentalism* was coined in the 1910s to refer to Christians who rejected modern science and insisted that the Bible represented the literal word of God. Almost a century later, fundamentalism remains a major part of American religious thought and is embraced by millions of self-identified evangelical Christians in the United States and around the world.

Major scientific breakthroughs of the late nineteenth and early twentieth century posed a serious challenge to long-held Christian beliefs. Biological research by Charles Darwin (1809–1882) showed that animals had evolved from other life forms, contradicting the biblical story of Genesis. New discoveries by scientists such as Albert Einstein (1879–1955) suggested that the universe was far vaster and more complex than it was depicted in ancient scriptures.

In response to these discoveries, some Christian scholars sought to update traditional religious beliefs at the dawn of the twentieth century. Charles W. Eliot (1834–1926), a retired president of Harvard, gave a famous speech in 1909 called "The Religion of the Future." In it, he argued that religion in times to come would not be based on authority, would include no worship of "dead ancestors, teachers, or rulers," would not be obsessed with personal salvation, and would not be "gloomy."

But Eliot's speech, and the prevailing skepticism about religious beliefs during the early part of the century, provoked a ferocious backlash from some conservative Christians. A year after Eliot's speech, members of the Princeton Theological Seminary responded by issuing a list of "fundamentals" they regarded as essential to Christianity, including the literal inerrancy of the Bible and the bodily resurrection of Jesus after his crucifixion.

Fundamentalism found a ready audience, especially among Baptists and some Methodists. Beginning in the 1920s, fundamentalism fueled attacks on the teaching of evolution in public schools, as Christian groups sought to force educators to teach creationism instead. Today, fundamentalism claims many adherents from a variety of Christian denominations.

ADDITIONAL FACTS

1. *A strong proponent of fundamentalism was former presidential candidate William Jennings Bryan (1860–1925), who was mocked by the journalist H. L. Mencken (1880–1956) after expressing his literal belief in the Bible during the Scopes "Monkey Trial."*

2. *The first use of the term* fundamentalist *to describe some Muslims occurred during the Lebanese hostage crisis of the 1980s.*

3. *According to a 2007 poll, 39 percent of Americans think it is "definitely true" that God created people in their present form.*

•••••

Lou Gehrig

In his day, Lou Gehrig (1903–1941) was known as the Iron Horse: an indestructible machine who hit a baseball like few men before or after him and played in a record 2,130 consecutive games. He was also known as the quiet, unassuming man in the shadow of his flamboyant New York Yankees teammate Babe Ruth (1895–1948).

Yet today, Gehrig's name is synonymous with the rare disease that prematurely ended his career and life, and he is best remembered for the moving farewell speech he gave to a Yankee Stadium crowd two months after his retirement.

Gehrig was born in Manhattan and attended Columbia University. The Yankees signed him in 1923, and he became a regular at first base in 1925. A day after appearing in a game as a pinch hitter, Gehrig famously replaced veteran Wally Pipp (1893–1965) at first base. He would not leave the lineup for more than thirteen years. Gehrig's streak of 2,130 consecutive games would remain intact until Cal Ripken Jr. (1960–) of the Baltimore Orioles broke it in 1995.

Gehrig soon developed into one of the best hitters in baseball history. In 1927, he hit 47 home runs and 175 runs batted in with a .373 batting average; no player besides Ruth (who hit 60 homers that year) had ever hit so many home runs in a season.

In 1931, Gehrig set an American League (AL) record that still stands with 184 RBIs. In 1934, he won the AL's triple crown (.363 batting average, 49 home runs, 165 RBIs).

In 1938, Gehrig's average fell below .300 for the first time since 1925, and he could feel his strength beginning to wane. He stayed in the starting lineup every day that season, but just eight games into the 1939 season, he held himself out of a game for the first time. The streak—and his career—ended on May 2, 1939.

A month later, Gehrig was diagnosed with amyotrophic lateral sclerosis (ALS), a neurological disorder in which the nerve cells in the central nervous system slowly degenerate. The disease is now commonly referred to as Lou Gehrig's disease.

On July 4, 1939, the Yankees held Lou Gehrig Appreciation Day, during which the reticent star haltingly told the 62,000 fans in attendance, "Today, I consider myself the luckiest man on the face of the earth." Later that year, he was inducted into the Baseball Hall of Fame. Less than two years later, he died of ALS at age thirty-seven.

ADDITIONAL FACTS

1. *Gehrig's uniform number, 4, was the first number ever to be retired in professional sports history.*

2. *Gehrig helped the Yankees win seven pennants and six World Series crowns, batting .361 in World Series games.*

3. *Gehrig still owns the major-league record for career grand slams, with 23. He finished his career with a .340 batting average, 493 home runs, and 1,995 RBIs.*

•••••

Al Jolson

Al Jolson (1886–1950) was among the most popular American entertainers of his day in vaudeville, on Broadway, and in recordings. He is also remembered for his role in the pioneering movie *The Jazz Singer* (1927) and for symbolizing an era when mainstream stage and screen performers routinely appeared in blackface.

Jolson's family immigrated to Washington, DC, from Lithuania when he was a child. Jolson was a street and stage performer by his early teens and entertained US troops during the Spanish-American War in 1898. By 1911 he was starring on Broadway and in national tours.

In contrast to the reserved, rigid presence of some contemporaries, Jolson was animated and charismatic on stage. To the delight of the crowd, he often stepped out of character to perform a solo concert in lieu of the scheduled show. Through the 1910s and 1920s, he also maintained a hugely successful recording career, becoming the first singer to sell more than 10 million records.

In *The Jazz Singer*, loosely based on his own biography, Jolson portrayed a synagogue cantor's son who rises to fame as a secular entertainer. The first feature-length film with synchronized singing and dialogue sequences, *The Jazz Singer* was a huge box office hit that Jolson followed with an even bigger hit, *The Singing Fool* (1928).

On stage and screen, Jolson was the most prominent blackface performer of his time. Although blackface was a widely accepted entertainment convention at the time, controversy surrounding the practice has clouded Jolson's popularity and image since his death.

Jolson spent the 1940s in semiretirement, starring in occasional tours and Broadway shows to moderate success. He enjoyed a career resurgence with the release of the biopic *The Jolson Story* in 1946 and the reissue of many of his older recordings.

Despite failing health, he entertained American troops during World War II and in 1950 traveled at his own expense to do the same in Korea. The following month, Jolson died of a heart attack at age sixty-four.

ADDITIONAL FACTS

1. *For some live performances, Jolson had ramps built from the stage into the audience so that he could walk among the crowd. He would occasionally strike up conversations with audience members.*

2. *Although record charts were not kept at the time,* Billboard *magazine estimated that Jolson recorded about twenty-three number one hits.*

3. *Jolson improvised much of the dialogue in* The Jazz Singer, *but the film's famous opening line, "You ain't heard nothing yet," was a mainstay of his stage act.*

• • ◆ • •

J. Edgar Hoover

J. Edgar Hoover (1895–1972) was the first director of the Federal Bureau of Investigation (FBI) and remained at the helm of the vast law enforcement agency for almost five decades. Under his direction, the FBI battled bootleggers, spies, and the Mafia, but Hoover was frequently criticized for his agents' disregard for civil liberties.

Hoover was born in Washington, DC, and joined the Justice Department after graduating from law school. As a twenty-nine-year-old bureaucrat, he took over the department's small Bureau of Investigation in 1924.

Under his direction, the bureau aggressively expanded in the 1920s, focusing its efforts on rumrunners and bank robbers. In one of its most famous exploits, Hoover's G-men chased down bank robber John Dillinger (1903–1934), killing him in a hail of bullets outside the Biograph Theater in Chicago. Hoover was quick to claim credit for the bureau's victories and came to be regarded as the face of law and order during the crime-ridden years of the Great Depression.

In 1935, the bureau was renamed the Federal Bureau of Investigation, and President Franklin D. Roosevelt (1882–1945) named Hoover director. Hoover would remain in office until his death, serving under eight US presidents.

During the Cold War, Hoover became particularly concerned with identifying Communist agents in the United States. In one of his most widely condemned decisions, he authorized his agents to infiltrate civil rights groups and plant illegal wiretaps to listen in on leaders such as Martin Luther King Jr. (1929–1968) whom he feared were Communist operatives. The program, known as COINTELPRO, was revealed in the 1970s and condemned by Congress.

Several presidents considered firing Hoover, but his popularity as a crime fighter—and his thick background files on virtually every figure in public life—made him a permanent institution in Washington.

In his personal life, Hoover was an enigma who appeared completely immersed in his job. He never married, and rumors have long persisted that he was gay.

After Hoover's death, reforms at the FBI curbed the use of wiretaps and limited future directors to terms of ten years—a measure intended to prevent another director from accumulating Hoover's unprecedented power.

ADDITIONAL FACTS

1. *The sprawling FBI headquarters in downtown Washington, DC, was named for Hoover after his death.*

2. *It was Hoover's idea to issue the first FBI Ten Most Wanted list in 1950.*

3. *During Hoover's tenure, the FBI turned down an application from a young law-school graduate from California: Richard M. Nixon (1913–1994).*

• • ● • •

Robert Frost

Robert Frost (1874–1963) was the elder statesman of twentieth-century American letters, a rare national poet who was read and respected by both literary critics and everyday citizens. Though he remains frequently quoted, Frost also enjoys the dubious distinction of being one of the most misunderstood writers in the American canon. Readers often interpret Frost's works as quaint, folksy pictures of rural life, when in fact his subtly complex poems brim with dark, ironic humor and even pessimism.

Though born in California, Frost was raised in New England, the region with which he is inextricably linked. After dropping out of Dartmouth to pursue a poetry career, he remained frustrated for years, producing volumes of work but failing to get enough of it published to make his efforts financially worthwhile.

Finally, Frost left the United States in 1912 to see whether his work might be better received in London. It was, and in 1913 his first full collection was published in Great Britain. Fellow American poet Amy Lowell (1874–1925) adored Frost's work and brought it back to the United States, promoting it relentlessly. Largely as a result of Lowell's efforts, Frost's collections became bestsellers, and he catapulted to near-instant fame.

Frost's work departed from the romantic tradition of nineteenth-century New England poetry, forsaking sublime depictions of nature in favor of darker portraits of marginal, troubled landscapes. His pastoral imagery and seemingly simple language belie the fact that his poems are complex, ambiguous works that evade tidy interpretation.

Frost's most famous poems include "Mending Wall," about the human tendency to build barriers; "The Road Not Taken," an oft-misunderstood meditation on the arbitrariness of life's choices; "Fire and Ice," a cheeky imagining of the end of the world; and "Stopping By Woods on a Snowy Evening," a beautiful but dark poem about the boundary between nature and civilization.

ADDITIONAL FACTS

1. *Frost won four Pulitzer Prizes for his work—more than any other poet in American history.*

2. *He wrote a poem, "Dedication," for the presidential inauguration of John F. Kennedy (1917–1963) in 1961. But the eighty-six-year-old's poor eyesight and the glare from the winter sun made it difficult for him to read his notes, so he decided at the last minute to recite an earlier poem, "The Gift Outright," from memory instead.*

3. *Frost preferred time-tested poetic forms and rhyme schemes over looser, contemporary styles such as free verse. He famously derided free verse by saying he would "just as soon play tennis with the net down."*

•••••

Aaron Copland

Classical music has sometimes been regarded as an elite art form, created by and for the upper crust of society, but composers often draw inspiration from popular traditions. One of the best examples of this tendency is the American composer Aaron Copland (1900–1990), who set out to create a uniquely American classical music and based his project on a uniquely American popular form: jazz.

Born in Brooklyn, Copland took piano lessons as a teenager and learned the fundamentals of classical music and composition. After completing high school, though, he left home to study composition in Paris, where he became a committed champion of avant-garde modern music and resolved to use jazz as the basis for his art.

Music historians divide Copland's career into two periods. The first was his *austere* period, in which the influence of jazz and the commitment to modernism were most apparent. Major works from this period include *Symphony for Organ and Orchestra* (1924), *Music for the Theater* (1925), and *Dance Symphony* (1925).

Later in his career, Copland's more populist tendencies became more pronounced, and he began producing the works of his *vernacular* period. These often drew their inspiration from American folk traditions, such as the tale of the infamous outlaw used as the basis for the ballet *Billy the Kid* (1938) and the story of the great American president commemorated in *Lincoln Portrait* (1942).

Although he continued to produce avant-garde works throughout his career, Copland increasingly focused his efforts on popular works. He even produced a number of film scores, including sound tracks for *Of Mice and Men* (1939) and *Our Town* (1940). One of his most famous songs, the patriotic and brassy "Fanfare for the Common Man," debuted in 1943 and remains perhaps his best-known and most frequently performed composition.

ADDITIONAL FACTS

1. *Copland was a close friend of New York Philharmonic conductor Leonard Bernstein (1918–1990), who was regarded as the greatest conductor of his work.*

2. *Because he defended the Communist Party in the mid-1930s, Copland was wrongly accused for many years of being a member of the party, particularly during the Red Scare of the 1950s.*

3. *Copland's piano teacher when he was a teenager was Rubin Goldmark (1872–1936), who also tutored fellow Brooklyn native George Gershwin (1898–1937).*

•••••

The Marx Brothers

The Marx Brothers were one of the most successful family comedy teams in movie history. Their thirteen films together, released between 1929 and 1949, contain some of the most memorable gags, bits, and dialogue ever captured on film.

The brothers' personas are recognizable to anyone acquainted with film comedy:

- Groucho (born Julius Henry, 1890–1977), the bespectacled, mustachioed verbal acrobat and hustler
- Chico (born Leonard, 1887–1961), the Italian-accented, piano-playing tramp
- Harpo (born Adolph, 1888–1964), the zany, harp-playing mute

A fourth brother, Zeppo (born Herbert, 1901–1979), who often played a straight man, appeared in only five of the films.

The Marx Brothers were all born in New York City to immigrant parents Sam and Minnie. With prodding from their ambitious mother, the brothers followed their uncle, comedian Al Shean, into show business.

Their careers began on the vaudeville stage and later moved to Broadway. In 1929, they made their major film debut in *The Cocoanuts*, a version of their hit Broadway play. Their best films—including *Animal Crackers* (1930), *Monkey Business* (1931), *Horse Feathers* (1932), and *Duck Soup* (1933)—are characterized by anarchic, slapstick comedy, musical performances, and general zaniness.

Groucho, with his greasepaint mustache, prominent eyebrows, and quick one-liners, was the linchpin of the group, the star around whom the other characters and the plot revolved. Although his character was part of the film's action, he also connected with the audience by self-consciously winking at them with every joke. As critic Roger Ebert wrote, "It is impossible to discuss Groucho's dialogue without quoting it, and pointless to quote it since Groucho's delivery is essential to the effect."

Duck Soup, a satire of war, politics, and government, is regarded as the brothers' best film. Though it was a box office flop when it was released, it managed to threaten Benito Mussolini enough that the fascist leader banned it from Italy.

Of all the Marx Brothers, Groucho was the only one to go on to an independent career of note—he hosted the successful radio and TV game show *You Bet Your Life* from 1947 to 1961.

ADDITIONAL FACTS

1. *Another brother, Milton, or Gummo (1892–1977), appeared onstage with the other four but never in any of the films; he became a talent agent for actors and writers.*

2. *Groucho first used what would become his signature characteristic, a greasepaint mustache, in 1924 for a stage production of* I'll Say She Is; *he had arrived late to the theater and did not have time to attach a proper mustache.*

3. *The brothers' last official move together,* Love Happy *(1949), featured a twenty-three-year-old starlet named Marilyn Monroe.*

•• ● ● ••

The Armory Show

The Armory Show, a seminal monthlong art exhibition held in 1913 at a military barracks in New York City, exposed Americans for the first time to cutting-edge European painters such as Marcel Duchamp (1887–1968) and has been credited with introducing modern art to American culture.

More than 300 artists participated in the show, including European painters Wassily Kandinsky (1866–1944) and Pablo Picasso (1881–1973), as well as American artists such as Mary Cassatt (1845–1926) and George Bellows (1882–1925). Painters and sculptors representing cubism, futurism, postimpressionism, and other avant-garde European styles were included in the show, marking the first time most had been shown to an American audience.

The exhibition opened in New York City's Sixty-Ninth Regiment armory building on February 17, 1913. Over the next month, thousands of Americans, including former president Theodore Roosevelt (1858–1919), toured the show.

Reactions ranged from hostile to ecstatic. Many critics singled out for ridicule Duchamp's *Nude Descending a Staircase*, a cubist work that depicted a figure in motion by superimposing successive images on top of one another. Fans praised Duchamp for inventing a new way to represent motion in painting, but critics— including Roosevelt—hated it.

To fans, the exhibit was a watershed event, and it immediately had a profound impact on American art. American social realism—lifelike paintings that depicted street and factory scenes—almost immediately gave way to a more abstract style inspired by the paintings at the Armory Show.

After closing in New York, the show moved to Chicago, where it continued to amaze, inspire, and befuddle in equal proportions.

ADDITIONAL FACTS

1. Nude Descending a Staircase *is now permanently housed at the Philadelphia Museum of Art.*

2. *Although Duchamp was a successful artist, he largely abandoned painting in the 1920s to become a full-time chess player.*

3. *New York City has staged a new Armory Show annually since 1999.*

• • ● • •

Babe Didrikson

Many regard Mildred "Babe" Didrikson (1911–1956) as the greatest female athlete of the twentieth century. A brash and cocky Texan, she was primarily known for her achievements in track-and-field events and golf. Her impact is still felt today as one of the founders of the Ladies Professional Golf Association (LPGA) in 1949.

Born to a Norwegian immigrant family, Didrikson first gained notice for her skills on the baseball and softball diamonds, and she was an all-American basketball player when she was in high school.

She emerged as one of the world's track-and-field stars at the 1932 Amateur Athletic Union (AAU) Championships, where she won five events and tied for first in a sixth—breaking three world records in the process. She single-handedly won the AAU team competition for her employer, the Employers Casualty Insurance Company of Dallas; in second place was the twenty-two-member team from the University of Illinois.

Though Didrikson qualified for five events in that year's Olympics in Los Angeles, women were permitted to enter only three. She won gold in the first-ever Olympic women's javelin and eighty-meter hurdles events (breaking her own world records) and claimed silver in the high jump. (She actually tied for first but was relegated to silver on a controversial rule technicality.)

Didrikson then embarked on her hugely successful golfing career and became the world's top player, a position she retained for most of the next two decades. She was named the country's top female athlete five times by the Associated Press during her golfing career (1945, 1946, 1947, 1950, and 1954—along with her first award, in 1931, for track and field).

Of her ten career major tournament victories, her final win, at the 1954 US Open, came a year after her diagnosis of—and subsequent surgery for—colon cancer. She died two years later, at age forty-five, after the cancer returned.

ADDITIONAL FACTS

1. *Didrikson said she'd acquired the name "Babe" because her long home runs on the baseball diamond reminded onlookers of slugger Babe Ruth (1895–1948).*

2. *She was named the top female athlete of the twentieth century by the Associated Press, ESPN, and Sports Illustrated.*

3. *She cofounded the LPGA with Patty Berg (1918–2006) and Fred Corcoran (1905–1977).*

4. *Didrikson married professional wrestler George Zaharias (1908–1984) in 1938. She changed her name to Babe Didrikson Zaharias but is still more commonly known as Babe Didrikson.*

•••••

Mickey Mouse

Mickey Mouse was "born" on November 18, 1928, when the short cartoon *Steamboat Willie* was screened at the Colony Theater in New York City. Although the animated mouse had appeared in two films before, *Plane Crazy* and *Gallopin' Gaucho, Steamboat Willie* was the first of Walt Disney's films to sync with sound. An instant hit, the film propelled Mickey to pop culture stardom.

Disney lore claims that Mickey Mouse was invented on a train when Disney (1901–1966), depressed by the loss of his copyright on an earlier creation, Oswald the Rabbit, dreamed up a new character named Mortimer Mouse. Disney's wife, Lillian (1900–1997), didn't like the name Mortimer and suggested the gentler moniker Mickey.

Always a playful and rambunctious character, the original Mickey was a bit more mischievous than today's family-friendly rodent. The studio later edited out a full thirty seconds of *Steamboat Willie* because of the original Mickey's violent behavior. Mickey went on to star in many more films after *Steamboat Willie,* including the 1940 musical *Fantasia.*

Mickey's film career took a backseat for many years while he transitioned into the corporate logo of the Walt Disney Corporation. However, he made a comeback in 1955 with the launch of the *Mickey Mouse Club* TV program and the opening of the Disneyland amusement park. Mickey appeared on watches, lunch boxes, T-shirts, and everything associated with Disney's theme parks.

Synonymous with all-American family entertainment, to some critics Mickey has also come to symbolize American cultural and commercial imperialism. Regardless, he is one of the most recognizable symbols worldwide.

ADDITIONAL FACTS

1. *On Mickey's fiftieth birthday, he became the first cartoon character to have his name immortalized on a star on the Hollywood Walk of Fame.*

2. *Walt Disney himself was the original voice of the mouse and continued to voice Mickey until the demands of running a studio became too great.*

3. *In 2007, a Hamas-run TV channel broadcast a children's show featuring a Mickey look-alike named Farfour. After great controversy over the alleged anti-Israeli and anti-American preaching of Farfour the mouse, the Palestinian terrorist group replaced the character with a bumblebee.*

•••••

Winston Churchill

The unwavering leadership of Winston Churchill (1874–1965) brought Great Britain through its darkest hours during World War II and made him one of the giant figures of the twentieth century. Churchill was a romantic and a British nationalist, but most of all, he was a steadfast defender of the moral superiority of democracy.

Although he was born into a prominent British family, Churchill's success as a military or political leader was not always assured. He entered Parliament in 1900 at age twenty-six and rose to First Lord of the Admiralty in 1911. But during World War I, Churchill was blamed for the disastrous British defeat at the Battle of Gallipoli in 1915 and forced to resign.

He put his career back together and served as chancellor of the exchequer (1924–1929), a position akin to that of finance minister, but his decision to return Britain to the gold standard proved to be a disaster. He spent most of the 1930s in the political wilderness, without an influential role in government. He concentrated on writing and also became an outspoken critic of German rearmament and the rise of Adolf Hitler (1889–1945) and the Nazi regime.

He bitterly opposed the appeasement policies of prime minister Neville Chamberlain (1869–1940), and when Chamberlain resigned in 1940, Churchill succeeded him. He was immediately tested—in June 1940, with Germany's defeat of France, it appeared as though Britain would be successfully invaded for the first time since 1066.

But Germany did not invade, and Churchill convinced his beleaguered people to continue fighting against the tyranny and barbarism of Fascism. Britain scored a series of military victories over both Italy and Germany, stemming the tide before the United States and the Soviet Union joined the Allies to defeat the Axis powers.

After the Allies' victory, Churchill was celebrated as one of the great leaders of modern times, and he remains a legendary figure in Western history. After serving an undistinguished second stint as prime minister (1951–1955), he spent the final years of his life in declining health. He died at age ninety.

ADDITIONAL FACTS

1. *Churchill is generally credited with keeping the Big Three—Churchill, Franklin D. Roosevelt (1882–1945), and Joseph Stalin (1879–1953)—together during World War II. He conceived the idea for the famed summit meetings at Tehran, Yalta, and Potsdam.*

2. *Churchill famously popularized the term* Iron Curtain *in a 1946 speech to refer to the symbolic boundary between Western and Eastern Europe—and, more generally, between democracy and the Communist bloc.*

3. *In addition to his success as a statesman, Churchill was also a celebrated writer and the author of the six-volume series* The Second World War. *He won the Nobel Prize in Literature in 1953.*

4. *In a 2002 poll conducted by the BBC, Churchill was voted the greatest Briton of all time. He was also celebrated in the United States: In 1963, President John F. Kennedy (1917–1963) conferred honorary US citizenship on Churchill (whose mother was an American).*

• • • •

Modernism

The modernist movement in literature thrived from roughly 1900 to 1940 in both Europe and the United States. Its major figures, including James Joyce (1882–1941), Virginia Woolf (1882–1941), Gertrude Stein (1874–1946), William Faulkner (1897–1962), and T. S. Eliot (1888–1965), experimented with radical new techniques in an attempt to depict reality and arrive at truth in unexpected ways.

Modernism was a reaction against realism, the approach that many Western authors had pursued during the second half of the nineteenth century. The realists had tried to portray people and society in a way that was as detailed and true to life as possible. In the early twentieth century, though, a number of new theories and scientific discoveries called the validity of the realists' approach into question. Thinkers such as Albert Einstein (1879–1955) and Sigmund Freud (1856–1939) revealed that some of the seemingly most familiar things in the world—space, time, language, and even the human mind—were inherently unknowable and enigmatic.

In light of these new ideas, modernist authors and artists of the period began to wonder whether concrete reality and objective truth existed at all. They rejected the realists' obsession with accurate depiction of the world as a futile enterprise. Instead, they tried to formulate new ways of exploring truth and reality.

As a result, modernist literature is rife with experimentation—experimentation with language, structure, narration, chronology, and other formerly unassailable underpinnings of literature. To explore the inner thoughts of characters more fully, Joyce, Woolf, and others pioneered stream-of-consciousness narration. To try to arrive at objective truth, they used multiple narrators within individual works, so that the various narrators' subjective viewpoints could be compared and contrasted and the areas of convergence and divergence made apparent. And to highlight the connectedness of past, present, and future events, they abandoned chronological plots in favor of scattered narratives that bounce back and forth in time.

ADDITIONAL FACTS

1. *The peak of literary modernism came in the 1920s, which is often referred to as the high modernist period.*

2. *Modernist poets loosened the strict rules of verse and meter that had governed poetry in the 1800s by experimenting with free verse, a less rigid but still complex form.*

3. *Modernism was not confined to literature, but found expression in music and the visual arts as well. Pablo Picasso (1881–1973) and other cubist painters, for example, were part of the modernist movement.*

•••••

The Carter Family

The Carter Family, a gospel and bluegrass band consisting of several members of a rural Appalachian family, were one of the first hit country acts and helped establish country as a distinctive American musical genre. Known as the First Family of Country Music, the Carters recorded many classics, including "Poor Orphan Child" (1927), "Wildwood Flower" (1928), and the traditional "Will the Circle Be Unbroken."

Hailing from Poor Valley, Virginia, the Carters grew up immersed in gospel singing at church and "hillbilly music" at home. Their music combined the two influences, applying the intricate arrangements and vocal harmonies of gospel to the driving tempos of traditional Appalachian music. The original core of the family singing group—A. P. Carter (1891–1960); his wife, Sara (1898–1979); and his sister-in-law Maybelle (1909–1978)—eventually made it to radio in 1927, performing their personal tales of sorrow and reflection.

In the climate of the Great Depression, their songs struck a chord—especially with rural folk, who were hit hardest by the economic conditions.

Due to divorce, remarriage, and children, the Carter Family roster changed over time. The original incarnation grew to incorporate Maybelle's three daughters, Anita (1933–1999), June (1929–2003), and Helen (1927–1998). June Carter went on to marry outlaw country star Johnny Cash (1932–2003) in 1968, a marriage that many saw as a fusion of traditional country music with rock and roll. June carried on the Carter Family torch by introducing her daughter, Carlene Carter, to the stage in the 1970s.

The resurgence of traditional music and the new folk movement in the 1960s built directly upon the Carter Family's foundation. Countless artists have reinterpreted Carter Family classics, and many music critics trace a direct lineage from the Carter Family to Woody Guthrie (1912–1967) to Bob Dylan (1941–).

ADDITIONAL FACTS

1. *Maybelle Carter developed a signature flat-picking style of guitar playing that came to be known as the Carter scratch. This style is now pervasive in bluegrass music.*

2. *"Wildwood Flower" was named one of the 100 most important American musical works of the twentieth century by National Public Radio.*

3. *Reese Witherspoon (1976–) won an Academy Award for Best Actress for her portrayal of June Carter in the 2005 movie* Walk the Line.

·•●•·

Frank Capra

Born on the island of Sicily, Frank Capra (1897–1991) immigrated with his family to the United States in 1903 and went on to become the foremost director of patriotic American films of his era. Just about every American who has ever watched television at Christmastime has seen Capra's most beloved film, *It's a Wonderful Life* (1946).

After he'd churned out twenty-two features, Capra's career took off when he made his first blockbuster hit, *It Happened One Night* (1934). Starring Clark Gable (1901–1960) and Claudette Colbert (1903–1996) as unlikely lovers, *It Happened One Night* was a landmark romantic screwball comedy, a huge financial success—helping Columbia Pictures ascend to major studio status—and a critical sensation. At the Academy Awards, the film swept five major categories (Best Actor, Actress, Director, Screenwriting, and Picture), an achievement that would not be duplicated until *One Flew Over the Cuckoo's Nest* (1975).

After *It Happened One Night,* Capra focused his efforts on tales of small-town heroes fighting cynicism and corruption. *Mr. Deeds Goes to Town* (1936), *Lost Horizon* (1937), and *You Can't Take It With You* (1938; Academy Award for Best Picture) were all successful efforts, leading up to an enduring American classic, *Mr. Smith Goes to Washington* (1939). In Jefferson Smith (played by Jimmy Stewart), Capra conjured his classic common-man hero, a naïve young senator who fights political corruption in Washington.

The US government tapped Capra to oversee *Why We Fight,* a series of seven documentaries designed to educate American servicemen about the stakes of World War II. Considered masterpieces of propaganda, the films came out between 1942 and 1945 and were released for theatrical distribution both in the United States and overseas.

That *It's a Wonderful Life* would be Capra's most beloved film would have been something of a surprise when it came out to lukewarm box office receipts in 1946. But thanks to its inspirational message of hope and faith in humanity at Christmastime, it has become a staple of the holiday season. *It's a Wonderful Life* was one of Capra's last major films; he directed his final movie, *Pocketful of Miracles,* in 1961 and died of a heart attack in 1991, at age ninety-four.

ADDITIONAL FACTS

1. *Capra received Academy Award nominations for Best Director six times, winning three (for* It Happened One Night, Mr. Deeds Goes to Town, *and* You Can't Take It With You*).*

2. *Capra served as host of the Academy Awards twice—in 1936 and 1939.*

3. *He received the American Film Institute's Life Achievement Award in 1982.*

•••••

Prohibition

When the states ratified the Eighteenth Amendment to the United States Constitution in 1919, banning the "manufacture, sale, or transportation of intoxicating liquors," the amendment's backers hoped the new law would help end the poverty, domestic violence, and social malaise associated with alcohol. But Prohibition failed to stop drinking, and indeed may have exacerbated many of the social problems the measure was meant to solve. Increasingly unpopular with the public, Prohibition was repealed fourteen years later to widespread rejoicing.

Reformers in the so-called temperance movement had pushed for an alcohol ban since the nineteenth century. Many abolitionist and early feminist leaders, such as Susan B. Anthony (1820–1906), also supported Prohibition, arguing that an alcohol ban would protect women from drunken husbands and ease conditions in urban slums.

Instead, Prohibition fueled a surge of crime in the 1920s and 1930s as illegal smuggling rackets sprang up to provide Americans with booze. Gangsters like Chicago's Al Capone (1899–1947) created elaborate criminal networks to import alcohol from Canada and distribute it to illegal bars known as speakeasies, which opened in virtually every American city. Vicious gang wars such as the 1929 Valentine's Day Massacre, in which Capone's henchmen gunned down seven rivals, shocked Americans.

In addition, many Americans began distilling their own "moonshine" whiskey in illegal stills. Moonshine was dangerous to make and notoriously potent. Some consumers also switched to drugs like opium, cocaine, and marijuana.

The law was widely ignored—even President Warren G. Harding (1865–1923) reportedly served liquor during poker parties at the White House—and calls for its repeal grew in the late 1920s. Congress repealed the Eighteenth Amendment in 1933, although it permitted individual states and counties to maintain prohibition, an option exercised by a handful of jurisdictions.

ADDITIONAL FACTS

1. *By most estimates, the potency of Prohibition-era beverages was more than 150 percent greater than that of alcoholic beverages produced before and after that time period.*

2. *The Eighteenth Amendment is the only constitutional amendment that abridged the rights of Americans. It was also the only amendment to be repealed—by the Twenty-First Amendment, in 1933.*

3. *Jay Gatsby, the title character of F. Scott Fitzgerald's seminal novel* The Great Gatsby, *supposedly earned his fortune through the illegal sale of alcohol.*

•••••

Jesse Owens

For German dictator Adolf Hitler, the 1936 Olympic Games in Berlin presented an opportunity to prove his theory of Aryan racial supremacy to the world. So it was to his distinct embarrassment that Jesse Owens (1913–1980), an African-American son of a sharecropper and grandson of slaves, became the star of the competition, capturing four track-and-field gold medals. By humiliating Hitler, Owens became an international hero in the period of international tension before World War II.

Owens's first performance to capture national attention came when he was a sophomore at Ohio State University, at the 1935 Big Ten Championships. In a span of about forty-five minutes, he entered four races and won all of them, breaking three world records and tying a fourth.

A year later, at the Olympics, Owens graduated from national star to international political symbol. His victories came in the 100-meter and 200-meter dashes, the long jump, and the 4x100-meter relay.

Owens was not initially on the relay team, but he and fellow African-American sprinter Ralph Metcalfe (1910–1978) were added to the roster, replacing two Jewish athletes, Marty Glickman (1917–2001) and Sam Stoller (1915–1983). As the story goes, Nazi officials asked the US delegation to remove the Jewish athletes from the team to spare the regime any further embarrassment. Hitler refused to shake hands with any of the black athletes.

After the Olympics, Owens left school to become a professional athlete. Because there were no endorsement opportunities for a black Olympic hero, however, money was often hard to come by, and Owens was forced to race all manner of opponents—from people to dogs to horses—to support his family. By the 1950s, he established himself as a successful lecturer and owned his own public relations firm. He died of lung cancer at age sixty-six.

ADDITIONAL FACTS

1. *He was born James Cleveland Owens in Alabama and moved to Cleveland, Ohio, at age nine. On his first day of school there, his teacher asked his name—"J. C.," he replied. The teacher thought he had said Jesse, and the name stuck for the rest of his life.*

2. *Owens was the first American to win four gold medals at a single Olympic Games.*

3. *In 1976, President Gerald Ford (1913–2006) bestowed upon Owens the Presidential Medal of Freedom, the nation's highest civilian honor.*

4. *Owens fouled on his first two attempts to qualify for the long-jump finals at the 1936 Games. Before Owens's third and final try, Germany's Luz Long (1913–1943), a tall, blond symbol of Hitler's so-called Aryan race, suggested that Owens jump from a few inches behind the takeoff board to ensure qualification. Owens took the German's advice and easily qualified. He went on to win the gold medal, Luz won silver, and the two embraced after the event. Luz later died in World War II, but Owens stayed in contact with the German's family.*

•• • ••

Betty Boop

Although short-lived as a cartoon character, the coy, curvaceous Betty Boop proved that animation could be more than children's entertainment. An animated version of a risqué vaudeville singer, she appeared in a series of adult-oriented cartoons produced by Paramount Pictures between 1930 and 1939.

Boop's inspiration was the 1920s singer and flapper Helen Kane (1910–1966). Kane was known for many of the things that her cartoon counterpart would make world famous: the short haircut, the high-pitched singing style, and the kick-line dancing. (She even coined the famous catchphrase "boop-oop-a-doop!")

Using Kane as his model, film producer Max Fleischer (1883–1972) created a new character for his Talkartoon series of short animated films, which were distributed by Paramount. Betty Boop was only loosely based on Kane in the beginning: In Boop's first appearance in 1930, she was a French poodle. Beginning with the January 2, 1932, film *Any Rags* she was depicted in her now-famous human role. A year earlier, a voice actress named Mae Questel (1908–1998) began performing Betty Boop's voice, a role she would keep until the last Boop cartoon—*Yip Yip Yippy*—was drawn in 1939.

Along with Fleischer Studios, the major producer of animated films in the 1930s was Walt Disney Studios. The two studios had many differences, especially Disney's preference for kid-friendly fare instead of the adult-themed shows Fleischer offered. His Betty Boop often wore skimpy outfits, and her singing and dancing were openly suggestive.

The studio was soon forced to tame Boop, however, when the Motion Pictures Producers and Distributors Association adopted a set of industry-wide decency standards known as the Hays Code in 1934. Among the rules stipulated were dress codes for women—even animated women. After the code was established, Betty Boop had to don a longer dress and a higher neckline.

ADDITIONAL FACTS

1. *In the 1934 short* Betty Boop's Rise to Fame, *the cartoon character's breast is briefly visible as she changes outfits.*

2. *The current film rating system was adopted in 1968 as an alternative to the Hays Code.*

3. *In 1934, Kane unsuccessfully sued Fleischer Studios and Paramount Pictures, claiming that she was owed compensation for Betty Boop's popularity.*

•••••

Charles de Gaulle

When France faced its greatest struggles in the twentieth century, it repeatedly turned to one man to restore law, order, and independence: General Charles de Gaulle (1890–1970). To his critics, de Gaulle was an arrogant autocrat, a man of outsize ambition for himself and his country. But those ambitions helped France recover from humiliating defeat during World War II and stemmed the tide of near civil war in the late 1950s.

As a senior army officer in 1940, he refused to accept France's capitulation to Germany and fled to London, where he set up a French government in exile, the Free French. He exhorted French soldiers and citizens to join the resistance and to continue the struggle against the Nazis.

With the liberation of Paris in 1944, de Gaulle returned home to a hero's welcome and soon was named president of the newly created provisional government. But to de Gaulle, the new constitution that ultimately led to the foundation of the Fourth Republic did not give the president enough authority, and he resigned in 1946.

De Gaulle remained an important figure in French politics in the following decade, but he was not a principal actor again until 1958. That year, a revolt in the North African French colony of Algeria exploded, and political instability within France brought down the government.

Anxious French leaders turned once again to de Gaulle, giving him complete authority for six months to bring France under control. He did so, quelling the violence in Algeria (and eventually paving the way for Algerian independence in 1962) and setting France on a stronger, more independent course.

He oversaw the writing of a new constitution (conferring more presidential authority), sanctioned the development of nuclear weapons, and pulled France out of the military wing of the North Atlantic Treaty Organization (NATO).

De Gaulle navigated through 1968, a year of student protests, demonstrations, and worker strikes, but not without losing some of his authority. A year later, he turned a vote on a reform bill into a referendum on his leadership, and when the proposal was defeated, he resigned. He died nineteen months later.

ADDITIONAL FACTS

1. *After serving in the French army during World War I, de Gaulle wrote a series of books and articles critical of the French military system. His ideas were scoffed at in France, and by 1940, using tactics similar to those he had suggested, the Nazis had conquered France.*

2. *De Gaulle named his first child after Marshal Philippe Pétain (1856–1951), who was his military mentor. Pétain later collaborated with the Nazis following the establishment of the Vichy government and became de Gaulle's archenemy.*

3. Time *magazine named de Gaulle its Man of the Year for rescuing France from chaos in 1958.*

•••••

James Joyce

In just a few landmark works, Irish novelist James Joyce (1882–1941) changed the face of Western literature more than almost any other author of the modern era. His novels and short stories were groundbreaking for their time and introduced a host of new literary techniques that continue to influence writers working today.

After spending his youth in Dublin, Joyce traveled throughout Europe, wrote, and briefly returned to Ireland hoping to get published. His first major work, *Dubliners*, appeared in 1914 and is still regarded as one of the finest short-story collections of the twentieth century. Its final story, "The Dead," exemplifies one of the literary techniques most often associated with Joyce: the epiphany, a specific moment in which a character makes a sudden, life-changing realization about himself or the world.

Joyce followed *Dubliners* with *A Portrait of the Artist as a Young Man* (1916), a largely autobiographical novel about his Catholic upbringing, his education, and his emergence as an artist. Though *Portrait* brought Joyce great acclaim, his indisputable masterpiece was his next novel, *Ulysses* (1922). This mammoth work—a retelling of Homer's *Odyssey* set in a single day in modern Dublin—is often called the greatest novel written in English. In it, Joyce experimented radically with language, style, and voice, particularly in his use of stream-of-consciousness narration—his attempt to render characters' inner thoughts verbatim, without any organization or interpretation. Joyce's experimentation reached even greater heights in his final novel, *Finnegans Wake* (1939), a work so difficult it tends to be read only by scholars.

Though Joyce's works have defied easy adaptation into plays or films, they have endured in the Western cultural imagination. They are valued not only for their literary innovation but also for their explorations of Catholicism, sexuality, art, and the often fraught politics of Joyce's native Ireland.

ADDITIONAL FACTS

1. *Throughout his life, Joyce was plagued by glaucoma, cataracts, and other eye problems that, for brief spells, left him blind.*

2. *Each year, Joyce aficionados worldwide celebrate Bloomsday on June 16, in honor of the day in 1904 on which the events of* Ulysses *take place.*

3. *Joyce is considered one of the central figures in literary modernism, along with Marcel Proust (1871–1922), Virginia Woolf (1882–1941), and William Faulkner (1897–1962).*

•••••

Fats Waller

Pianist Thomas Wright "Fats" Waller (1904–1943) was one of the most popular and influential American artists of the early twentieth century and a pioneer of early jazz. Known for his flamboyant, comedic style, Waller contributed a number of standard works to the American songbook, including "Ain't Misbehavin'" (1929) and "Honeysuckle Rose" (1934). While he was a classically trained pianist with a solid grounding in the works of Johann Sebastian Bach (1685–1750), Waller is most famous for perfecting a difficult, improvisational jazz style known as *stride*.

Along with Waller, the masters of stride piano were Willie "the Lion" Smith (1897–1973) and James P. Johnson (1894–1955), from whom Waller took piano lessons while growing up in New York City. When playing stride, the pianist contributes both the rhythm and the melody of a piece. The rhythm, which usually requires separate instruments such as an upright bass or a drum kit, is provided entirely by the pianist's left hand. Stride is notoriously difficult because the pianist's left hand can't simply maintain a beat: The pianist has to alternate between establishing the rhythm of the piece using the left side of the piano and contributing harmonies with chords from the middle of the keyboard. (The left hand's movement up and down the keyboard gives stride its name.) All the while, the pianist has to play elaborate (and fast) melodies with the right hand.

Mastering stride takes incredible talent and years of practice, but Waller had a significant natural advantage. The pianist George Shearing (1919–) once compared shaking hands with Waller to "grabbing a bunch of bananas." It wasn't much of an exaggeration: Waller had enormous hands that could span twelve white keys on a piano. He was a leading performer and a hit recording artist in the 1920s and 1930s, just as jazz was becoming nationally popular, but he died of pneumonia in 1943. He is often cited as a major influence on later jazz musicians and was awarded a posthumous Grammy for lifetime achievement in 1993.

ADDITIONAL FACTS

1. *Waller got his start when he was a teenager in New York City performing at rent parties—house parties with live music that residents would charge their guests to attend to help pay the rent.*

2. *Before selling sound recordings of his performances, Waller wrote player-piano rolls for Okeh.*

3. *In 1926, at the height of his popularity, Waller was dragged into a Chicago club by a man holding a gun to his back. He thought he was being kidnapped, but he was actually being forced to perform at a birthday party for the famous gangster Al "Scarface" Capone (1899–1947).*

•••••

James Cagney

Jimmy Cagney (1899–1986) was the quintessential star of a burgeoning genre that emerged in the 1930s: the gangster film. As his obituary in the *New York Times* said, he was a "cocky and pugnacious film star" and a legendary showman. Will Rogers said of him, "Every time I see him work, it looks to me like a bunch of firecrackers going off all at once."

Cagney was trained on Broadway and in vaudeville as a song-and-dance man. He was neither a great dancer nor a formidable singer, but his high-energy performances on stage translated well onto the screen.

A year after his film debut in *Sinners' Holiday* (1930), Cagney starred in *The Public Enemy* (1931), which made him an instant star. One of the first gangster movies, the film was noteworthy for its realistic portrayal of violence and misogyny. In one of the movie's best-known scenes, Cagney's character, Tom Powers, famously squashes half a grapefruit into the face of costar Mae Clarke.

For the remainder of the 1930s, Cagney continued to burnish his reputation as Hollywood's leading gangster, and he received an Academy Award nomination for Best Actor for his performance in *Angels with Dirty Faces* (1938), which costarred Humphrey Bogart. A year later, he teamed up with Bogart again in *The Roaring Twenties* (1939), Cagney's last gangster film for a decade.

Cagney returned to his song-and-dance roots to play renowned singer, songwriter, and dancer George M. Cohan in *Yankee Doodle Dandy* (1942). A patriotic musical, the film proved to be the biggest box office hit of the year and earned Cagney an Oscar for Best Actor.

He returned to the gangster genre for Raoul Walsh's Freudian *White Heat* (1949), playing a psychopathic mobster who utters the famous line "Made it, Ma! Top of the world!" In 1955, Cagney appeared in two noteworthy films: *Love Me or Leave Me,* which earned him his third and final Academy Award nomination, and *Mister Roberts,* alongside Henry Fonda and Jack Lemmon.

Cagney went into retirement in 1961. But on his doctors' orders to be more active, he returned to the screen two decades later to take a small role in Milos Forman's *Ragtime* (1981). It would be Cagney's final film. He died at age eighty-six of a heart attack; an old friend from Hollywood, President Ronald Reagan, delivered the eulogy at his funeral.

ADDITIONAL FACTS

1. *In addition to directing the top-grossing film of 1942,* Yankee Doodle Dandy, *Michael Curtiz also directed 1942's most beloved film,* Casablanca.

2. *Although most famous for his B-movie roles, Cagney also appeared in an adaptation of William Shakespeare's* A Midsummer Night's Dream *(1935) that won two Academy Awards.*

3. *In 1984, Cagney was awarded the Presidential Medal of Freedom, the government's highest civilian award.*

••●••

Flappers

During the 1920s, a group of young women began wearing their hair in a then-exotic style called a bob, smoking cigarettes, listening to jazz music, and otherwise defying the conventional expectations for proper young women. Nicknamed flappers—the word is thought to originate from a British slang term for *prostitute*—they symbolized a growing defiance of traditional gender norms in the United States and Europe in the years after World War I.

Famous flappers included the actress Joan Crawford (1905–1977) and Zelda Fitzgerald (1900–1948), the wife of novelist F. Scott Fitzgerald (1896–1940).

In addition to their boyish hairstyles and clothing, the flapper generation often took a more liberal attitude toward sex. Some flappers dated numerous men—a habit considered scandalous by the standards of the day.

Flappers emerged against the backdrop of the Nineteenth Amendment to the Constitution, which had extended full voting rights to women and prompted many Americans to rethink traditional gender roles.

Perhaps the best-known portrayals of flappers appeared in Fitzgerald's novels and short stories. *The Great Gatsby* (1925), his masterpiece, includes a prominent flapper character, the independent, steely, hard-drinking golf pro Jordan Baker. His story "Bernice Bobs Her Hair" features a young girl who is trained to be a society woman by her older cousin Marjorie, who teaches Bernice how to conduct herself in true flapper style.

When the Roaring Twenties came to an abrupt halt with the stock market crash of 1929, the flappers and their expensive, hedonistic lifestyle fell out of fashion.

ADDITIONAL FACTS

1. *The flapper era coincided with an explosion in the popularity of makeup, especially lipstick, which had been relatively uncommon in the United States before World War I.*

2. *Fitzgerald published a collection of short stories in 1920 called* Flappers and Philosophers.

3. *"Bernice Bobs Her Hair" was based on a letter that Fitzgerald wrote to his younger sister with instructions on how to be more attractive to men.*

•• • ••

Joe Louis

Considered by many to be the greatest heavyweight boxer who ever lived, Joe Louis (1914–1981) was heavyweight champion for nearly twelve years, successfully defending the crown a record twenty-five times. But he is remembered most for his 1938 defeat of Germany's Max Schmeling (1905–2005), whom Adolf Hitler had promoted as a symbol of Nazi superiority. The victory of an African-American man over a German made Louis one of the biggest black American folk heroes of the twentieth century.

Louis was born in Alabama, the grandson of slaves. After turning professional in 1934, he terrorized the heavyweight division, winning his first twenty-seven fights (twenty-three by knockout). Many considered him invincible and on track for the title when he was upset by Schmeling in their first bout at Yankee Stadium on June 19, 1936.

Louis rebounded and soon claimed the title, knocking out champion James J. Braddock (1905–1974) on June 22, 1937.

But Louis was not satisfied—he would not consider himself the true champion until he beat Schmeling. He got his chance on June 22, 1938, again at Yankee Stadium. This time, he knocked Schmeling out just 124 seconds into the bout. His victory left an indelible mark on American culture and made him a hero to blacks and whites alike.

Louis reigned as champion until his retirement in 1949, but financial problems brought him back to the ring in 1950—he lost his return bout to champion Ezzard Charles (1921–1975). Louis fought nine more times before retiring for good after a loss to Rocky Marciano (1923–1969) in 1951. During his illustrious professional career, Louis—known as the Brown Bomber—compiled a 68-3 record with fifty-four knockouts.

For the rest of his life, Louis battled cocaine addiction and paranoia and eventually took a job as a casino greeter in Las Vegas. Near the end of his life, he became friends with Schmeling, who had survived World War II. Louis died of a heart attack at age sixty-six.

ADDITIONAL FACTS

1. *During Louis's reign as heavyweight champion, his opponents were often called the Bum of the Month, because they had no chance against his superior skills.*

2. *From 1942 to 1945, Louis served in the US Army and fought 96 exhibition matches to raise money and morale for the troops.*

3. *His given name was Joseph Louis Barrow, but he fought as Joe Louis so his disapproving mother would not find out he had started boxing.*

•••••

Looney Tunes

In 1929, Walt Disney Studios launched a series of short animated cartoons to accompany its popular Mickey Mouse offerings. The series, called *Silly Symphonies,* was a critical darling, winning the first six Academy Awards offered for Best Animated Short. It inspired a rival studio, Warner Bros., to create two of its own music-based cartoon series: *Merrie Melodies* and *Looney Tunes.*

Mel Blanc

Because Warner owned the publishing rights to many popular songs, it had access to a vast library of music. However, unlike *Merrie Melodies, Looney Tunes* soon developed a regular cast of characters as famous as any animated cartoon characters Disney ever produced. They include Bugs Bunny, Daffy Duck, Porky Pig, Sylvester, Tweety, and Foghorn Leghorn. Remarkably, all of these characters and many others were voiced by the same actor, Mel Blanc (1908–1989).

Looney Tunes ran in theaters, before or after feature films, until 1969. Some of the episodes are rarely seen today because they made use of racial stereotypes, particularly regarding the Japanese during World War II. However, most of the *Looney Tunes* library has been widely distributed. Beginning in 1960, Warner Bros. also began syndicating the show for television broadcast. Because the episodes drawn before 1948 were in black and white, all the episodes that were distributed to the network for *The Bugs Bunny/Road Runner Hour* or *The Bugs Bunny & Tweety Show* were made after Warner adopted color for the series in July 1948.

ADDITIONAL FACTS

1. *In addition to acting as the voice of numerous* Looney Tunes *characters, Blanc also voiced Barney Rubble on* The Flintstones.

2. *Characters from* Looney Tunes *have often appeared in full-length feature films, including the 2003 half-animated/half–live-action film* Looney Tunes: Back in Action.

3. *Disney's Donald Duck made his debut in the* Silly Symphonies *episode "The Wise Little Hen" in 1934.*

•••••

Anne Frank

Perhaps no voice to emerge from the Holocaust has resonated more throughout the world than Anne Frank's. She was a Jewish girl forced into hiding with her family and four friends during the Nazi occupation of the Netherlands during World War II. All eight people lived in the secret annex of a building owned by her father's company. They went into hiding in July 1942 and remained until they were betrayed and arrested in August 1944.

For those two years in hiding, Anne (1929–1945) kept a diary that was first published posthumously in 1947 and now appears in sixty-seven languages. The American version is called *Anne Frank: The Diary of a Young Girl*.

About a year before her death in the concentration camp Bergen-Belsen, she wrote, "I want to be useful or give pleasure to people around me who yet don't really know me. I want to go on living even after my death!"

The Frank family had already fled Germany for the Netherlands in 1933. In Amsterdam, they lived safely until 1940, when the Nazis invaded and soon implemented anti-Jewish laws.

Fearing deportation, the Frank family—father Otto (1889–1980), mother Edith (1900–1945), and daughters Margot (1926–1945) and Anne—went into hiding. They received food, clothing, and supplies from four of Otto's employees, who continued to work on the lower floors of the building.

After the group in the annex was discovered, they were all sent to concentration camps in Germany. Edith, Margot, and Anne all died in camps.

Of the Frank family, only Otto survived. Miraculously, two of his former employees recovered Anne's diary and gave it to Otto when he returned to Amsterdam.

He decided to publish the diary, which first appeared in Dutch in 1947. As Roger Rosenblatt wrote in *Time* in 1999, "The passions the book ignites suggest that everyone owns Anne Frank, that she has risen above the Holocaust, Judaism, girlhood and even goodness and become a totemic figure of the modern world—the moral individual mind beset by the machinery of destruction, insisting on the right to live and question and hope for the future of human beings."

ADDITIONAL FACTS

1. *Frances Goodrich (1890–1984) and Albert Hackett (1900–1995) turned the book into a hugely successful stage play that was first produced on Broadway in 1955 and won the Pulitzer Prize for Drama. It was also made into a Hollywood film in 1959.*

2. *In May 1960, the Anne Frank House opened, preserving the annex as a museum at 263 Prinsengracht in Amsterdam.*

3. *Anne and Margot both died of typhus in March 1945 at Bergen-Belsen, three weeks before the camp was liberated by the British.*

•••••

T. S. Eliot

Anglo-American writer and critic T. S. Eliot (1888–1965) was renowned for his complex poems as well as several notable plays and essays. The surreal, often disturbing images in his landmark works, such as *The Waste Land,* came to epitomize modernist poetry and encapsulated the grief and confusion that haunted Europe after World War I.

Born in St. Louis, Eliot attended Harvard and, after a year of study in Paris, decided to move to Great Britain permanently in 1914, just at the outbreak of World War I. It's difficult to overstate the impression that the war made on Eliot and his work. The war left unfathomable destruction in Europe: Nearly 10 million people died in the conflict, which had no discernible cause. The war's pointlessness left Eliot and his contemporaries wondering about the direction, and even the viability, of Western civilization itself.

Eliot's first major work, "The Love Song of J. Alfred Prufrock" (1915), remains one of the most widely read poems of its era. This first-person monologue by a man plagued by self-doubt and paralysis—he famously asks, "Do I dare to eat a peach?"—paints an ambiguous, stream-of-consciousness portrait that continues to fascinate and confound readers.

The Waste Land (1922), Eliot's magnum opus, is a lengthy, convoluted, and densely allusive poem about the postwar spiritual state of both the West and Eliot himself. It draws on a host of ancient and medieval influences to create a disorienting depiction of the sense of barrenness that prevailed in Europe after the war. Eliot repeated the pessimistic sentiments of *The Waste Land* in "The Hollow Men" (1925), which ends in perhaps his most memorable lines: "This is the way the world ends / Not with a bang but a whimper."

ADDITIONAL FACTS

1. *In his later years, Eliot became a renowned playwright, penning* Murder in the Cathedral *(1935), about the twelfth-century archbishop of Canterbury Thomas à Becket, and* The Cocktail Party *(1950), about a couple facing marital difficulties.*

2. *Not all of Eliot's work was heavy. Andrew Lloyd Webber (1948–) adapted Eliot's volume of children's poetry,* Old Possum's Book of Practical Cats *(1939), into the long-running stage musical* Cats.

3. *In the film* Apocalypse Now *(1979), the character played by Marlon Brando (1924–2004) reads aloud from "The Hollow Men" and has two of Eliot's favorite books—*The Golden Bough, *by Sir James Frazer (1854–1941), and* From Ritual to Romance, *by Jesse L. Weston (1850–1928)—sitting on his nightstand.*

4. *Eliot completed his written doctoral dissertation at Harvard in 1916 but failed to appear for its oral defense, so he never received the degree.*

•••••

Billie Holiday

Billie Holiday (originally Eleanora Fagan, 1915–1959) was born in Philadelphia to a single teenage mother and soon moved to a poor neighborhood in Baltimore, Maryland, where she endured an extremely traumatic childhood. Holiday was raped at the age of eleven, was sent to a Catholic reform school later that year, and worked as a prostitute in a Harlem brothel while she was still only a teenager. According to her autobiography, *Lady Sings the Blues,* Holiday was eventually arrested for prostitution and needed to find other work.

One day, the legend goes, Holiday went to a Harlem speakeasy looking for work as a dancer. She was told there were no openings—but that the club did need a singer. Desperate for work, she tried out for the position—and her audition reduced the audience to tears. She got the job, and eventually became a singer in various New York City clubs. In 1933, she was discovered by CBS producer and talent scout John Hammond (1910–1987), who signed her to a recording contract.

Holiday began her recording career with some of the greatest big bands of the era, including the groups led by Benny Goodman (1909–1986), Count Basie (1904–1984), and Artie Shaw (1910–2004). Holiday's recordings are remarkable for her sad, searing vocal performances, in which she displays a haunting vocal style that is entirely her own. One of her greatest songs, a condemnation of lynching called "Strange Fruit," came early in her career. It was an extremely daring song at the time, appearing years before the civil rights movement gained momentum.

Unfortunately, Holiday would not live long enough to see that movement bear sweeter fruit. After battling heroin addiction and alcoholism for most of her life, Holiday died of cirrhosis in 1959.

ADDITIONAL FACTS

1. *In the movie version of* Lady Sings the Blues, *Holiday is played by Diana Ross (1944–), lead singer of the Supremes.*

2. *By joining the band led by Artie Shaw (1910–2004) in the 1930s, Holiday became one of the first black women to perform in an all-white orchestra.*

3. *In 1988, the Irish rock band U2 released a song in tribute to Holiday called "Angel of Harlem."*

Fred Astaire and Ginger Rogers

The dancing duo of Fred Astaire and Ginger Rogers defined Depression-era Hollywood charm and sophistication, churning out nine musicals between 1933 and 1939 and becoming known the world over simply as Fred and Ginger. As film historian David Thomson writes, they were an unlikely pairing of "the man about town and the girl next door."

Astaire (1899–1987) was a dance sensation with his sister, Adele, before coming to Hollywood in the early 1930s. He made his film debut in 1933 and was teamed with Rogers later that year in *Flying Down to Rio*. His slicked-back hair and perfectly pressed clothes created an image of elegance that appealed to a generation of Depression-weary moviegoers.

Rogers (1911–1995) was trained in vaudeville and on Broadway before her film debut in 1929. She appeared in twenty-five films before teaming with Astaire, but her career peaked during her collaboration with him. Together they mesmerized audiences with their combination of technical virtuosity, sophistication, and pure joy.

Part of their success stemmed from Astaire's insistence that their dance numbers be shot with as few edits as possible and with their entire bodies in the frame—the better for viewers to appreciate their performances. Astaire teamed with choreographer Hermes Pan on many of their routines, which were so stunning that they overcame the usually thin plots of their movies.

The pair's best films are considered to be *Top Hat* (1935), which was the RKO studio's biggest moneymaker of the 1930s (bringing in $3 million), and *Swing Time* (1936).

After their split in 1939, Astaire worked with several other partners, but without the same magic. Rogers performed in light comedies and some dramas, winning an Academy Award for Best Actress for her role in *Kitty Foyle* (1940).

Though not without their respective successes—for Astaire, *On the Beach* (1959) and *The Towering Inferno* (1974), and for Rogers, *Monkey Business* (1952) and *Kitty Foyle*—neither star was as bright without the other.

ADDITIONAL FACTS

1. *Astaire was born Frederic Austerlitz Jr.; Rogers was born Virginia Katherine McMath.*

2. *Astaire's other screen dancing partners included Rita Hayworth, Eleanor Powell, Paulette Goddard, Joan Leslie, and Lucille Bremer.*

3. *Rogers presented Astaire with an honorary Academy Award in 1950.*

•• • ••

Imperialism

At its apex in 1921, the British Empire comprised more than a quarter of the world's population, in outposts from Hong Kong to Bermuda. Other major European powers—France, Spain, Portugal, the Netherlands—each controlled vast portions of Africa and Asia, and even the United States, a latecomer to the imperial system, owned the Philippines and Puerto Rico.

Imperialism was both a political system and an ideology: To its proponents, the chance to spread "civilization" across the globe justified the subjugation of foreign countries in brutal conflicts that the poet Rudyard Kipling (1865–1936) called "savage wars of peace."

Spain and Portugal started their empires in the fifteenth century, but the pace of imperial expansion greatly accelerated in the 1800s, when faster transportation and relative peace on the continent allowed European countries to look outward. Even relatively small powers built massive empires; in 1885, Belgium claimed the Congo, a country roughly eighty times its size. European empires grew even more by absorbing the remains of the Ottoman Empire after its collapse following World War I.

For European countries, empires served primarily an economic purpose. The governing nations plundered colonies such as the Belgian Congo and British South Africa for gold, iron, copper, ivory, rubber, and other raw goods—a one-sided economic relationship that fueled the growth of Europe and the United States but often had devastating effects on the colonies.

For both better and worse, imperialism also had the effect of spreading Western legal, educational, and economic systems across the world. For instance, many ex-territories, such as India, continue to use educational systems modeled on Great Britain's.

However, the imperial system proved short-lived. World War II drained the coffers of the major European powers; afterward, the cost of defending their sprawling empires, coupled with growing resistance, spelled the demise of European imperialism. India became independent in 1947; Belgium was forced to free the Congo in 1960.

ADDITIONAL FACTS

1. *A few scattered remnants of the European empires remain; for instance, the United Kingdom still owns the Turks and Caicos Islands, and France retains control over French Guiana.*

2. *The 1902 Joseph Conrad novel* Heart of Darkness *exposed the savage methods used by Belgian King Leopold II (1835–1909) to control the Congo and helped spur some reforms in the colony.*

3. *The deal dividing the Ottoman Empire between Britain and France, known as the Sykes-Picot Agreement, was reached in secret in 1916.*

• • • • •

Joe DiMaggio

On the baseball field, Joe DiMaggio (1914–1999), nicknamed Joltin' Joe and the Yankee Clipper, was one of the most graceful and elegant players ever to play the game. Off the field, he was intensely private, even considered aloof by many. His retreat from the spotlight made him an almost mythical figure in American pop culture, immortalized in songs, movies, and novels.

Many consider DiMaggio one of the best players in baseball history, because he could hit for average (.325 career batting average) and power (361 career home runs), rarely struck out (just 369 times in his career), and was an almost flawless center fielder and an expert base runner. He was the American League's Most Valuable Player three times (1939, 1941, 1947), and his fifty-six-game hitting streak, compiled in 1941, still stands as one of the iconic records in American sports history.

He also won. The Yankees claimed World Series crowns in each of DiMaggio's first four seasons and added five more titles before the end of his career in 1951. He was elected to the Hall of Fame in 1955, and in 1969, a panel of sportswriters named him Baseball's Greatest Living Player.

After his playing career ended, DiMaggio reluctantly remained in the spotlight when he entered into the "Marriage of the Century" with Marilyn Monroe (1926–1962) in 1954. It was a union of America's foremost sports hero and Hollywood's sexiest star, and the nation loved it. The marriage, however, lasted only nine months, though DiMaggio and Monroe continued to be linked romantically until her death in 1962.

In his later years, when DiMaggio appeared in public, he was always impeccably dressed, keeping up his image of class and sophistication. He even managed to retain his reputation after becoming a spokesman for Mr. Coffee and the Bowery Savings Bank of New York. He died at age eighty-four.

ADDITIONAL FACTS

1. *Two of DiMaggio's brothers, Vince (1912–1986) and Dom (1917–), also played in the major leagues.*

2. *Like many players of his generation, DiMaggio lost three years to military service (1943–1945). Having completed his stint in the US Army, he returned to the Yankees in 1946.*

3. *After Monroe's death, DiMaggio made the arrangements for her funeral and sent six red roses to her crypt three times a week for twenty years.*

•••••

The Three Stooges

The Three Stooges, whose hilarious slapstick antics entertained audiences for four decades, debuted on film in 1930 as a trio of bumbling firemen in the film *Soup to Nuts*. They continued to appear in minor roles until 1934, when Columbia signed the three comedians to produce their own series of twenty-minute shorts.

The original Stooges—Larry (Louis Fienberg, 1902–1975), Moe (Moses Horwitz, 1897–1975), and Curly (Jerome Horwitz, 1903–1952)—had all started their acting careers on the vaudeville stage. Moe and Curly were brothers who had grown up in a Jewish immigrant neighborhood in Brooklyn.

Each Three Stooges short revolved around a crude plot, dumb jokes, and ample violent humor often pitting Moe, the group's sour-faced leader, against the impish Curly. Subtlety and sophistication were not strong points for the gang, although they did produce one of Hollywood's first satires of Nazi Germany, *You Nazty Spy*, in 1940.

The trio performed together until 1947, when Curly suffered a massive stroke. Another Horwitz brother, Shemp (Samuel Horwitz, 1895–1955), replaced him. After Shemp's death eight years later, Joe Besser (1907–1988) stepped into the role. Then, when Besser bowed out in 1958, Curly Joe (Joseph Wardell, 1909–1993) took over as the third Stooge until Larry's stroke in 1970 forced the group to disband.

In addition to their film shorts, the Stooges appeared in many feature films, including *Snow White and the Three Stooges* (1961), *The Three Stooges Meet Hercules* (1962), and *The Three Stooges in Orbit* (1962). They also made a cameo appearance in the 1963 comedy classic *It's a Mad, Mad, Mad, Mad World*.

ADDITIONAL FACTS

1. *Moe's wife, Helen, was a cousin of famed magician Harry Houdini (1874–1926).*

2. *Members of the Stooges made several unsuccessful attempts at solo careers; for instance, Moe appeared in the 1973 film* Doctor Death, Seeker of Souls.

3. *Before joining the Stooges, Larry had been a boxer in the lightweight division.*

4. *Before joining the Stooges, Shemp played a cab driver in the movie* Mississippi Gambler *(1942). Ironically, Shemp died of a heart attack in the back of a taxi.*

·•●•·

Robert Oppenheimer

Known as the father of the atomic bomb, J. Robert Oppenheimer (1904–1967) led the Manhattan Project, which eventually developed and successfully tested the first nuclear weapon in 1945. He was the leading American theoretical physicist of the era but also came to represent the moral and ethical dilemmas faced by scientists involved in nuclear physics.

Oppenheimer studied at Harvard and Cambridge and earned his PhD in Germany before becoming a professor at the California Institute of Technology and the University of California, Berkeley. In response to the report that Germany had split the atom, President Franklin D. Roosevelt (1882–1945) established the Manhattan Project in 1941. He put Oppenheimer in charge a year later.

Oppenheimer set up a new research station and assembled a brilliant scientific team in the desert at Los Alamos, New Mexico. They were successful: On July 16, 1945, Oppenheimer and others witnessed the first explosion of an atomic bomb (known as the Trinity test), which unleashed the equivalent of 18,000 tons of TNT. Said Oppenheimer at the time, "We knew the world would not be the same."

Within a month, US planes dropped two atomic bombs on the Japanese cities of Hiroshima and Nagasaki, killing more than 140,000 people. In a matter of weeks, Japan surrendered to the Allies and World War II was over.

After the war, Oppenheimer chaired the advisory committee of the US Atomic Energy Commission from 1947 until 1952 and used his position to oppose the development of a hydrogen bomb and a nuclear arms race with the Soviet Union.

In 1953, he was accused of having Communist sympathies, and following a hearing in 1954, he was stripped of his security clearance.

He retreated to Princeton University, where he was the director of the Institute of Advanced Study. In 1963, President John F. Kennedy (1917–1963) offered a public pardon of sorts, giving Oppenheimer the Fermi Award for "his outstanding contributions to theoretical physics and his scientific and administrative leadership."

Oppenheimer died of throat cancer in 1967.

ADDITIONAL FACTS

1. *In 1947, Oppenheimer admitted his ambivalence about the scientific community's role in the deaths of so many people in Hiroshima and Nagasaki: "In some sort of crude sense which no vulgarity, no humor, no overstatements can quite extinguish, the physicists have known sin; and this is a knowledge which they cannot lose."*

2. *He spoke eight languages, and as a young man, he learned enough Dutch in six weeks to give a technical lecture while visiting the Netherlands.*

3. *Oppenheimer came from a wealthy Manhattan family. His father was a textile importer and his mother was an artist. The family art collection included three Van Goghs.*

•••••

Gertrude Stein

The American intellectual Gertrude Stein (1874–1946) was a unique literary figure whose highbrow life and avant-garde writings made her a cultural phenomenon. Her experimental works, though at times tedious, are undeniably interesting and did much to push the boundaries of the English language.

After growing up in Oakland, California, Stein studied at Radcliffe, then moved to Paris in 1903. There, she immersed herself in the literature and art scene and met a fellow American, Alice B. Toklas (1877–1967), who would become her lifelong partner. In time, Stein gained a reputation as a formidable literary-society hostess: Between the world wars, she essentially ran an intellectual salon from her Paris home, holding court among Ernest Hemingway (1899–1961), Pablo Picasso (1881–1973), Henri Matisse (1869–1954), and others.

An early champion of cubist art, Stein tried to apply its principles to her writing. Just as cubist painters depicted the same object from multiple angles at once, Stein repeated individual words obsessively, attempting to uncover different shades of meaning each time. For example, one segment of her early work *Three Lives* (1909), called "The Good Anna," repeats the word *good* hundreds of times in an attempt to circle around the seemingly simple word's many subtleties. Stein also wrote largely in the present tense—using gerunds in phrases such as "she is reading"—to capture the immediate moment.

Stein had a notoriously large ego and openly labeled herself a genius—calling herself "the creative literary mind of the century"—while heaping derision upon other writers whose efforts she found lacking. Even her work *The Autobiography of Alice B. Toklas* (1933), ostensibly about her partner, is in fact about Stein herself. Throughout her career, she remained eccentric, immensely quotable, and ceaselessly self-promoting. All the while, the devoted Toklas acted as her assistant and manager, handling day-to-day tasks so that Stein could focus solely on her writing.

ADDITIONAL FACTS

1. *Perhaps the most memorable image of Stein is not a photo but Picasso's masklike 1906 portrait of her, which now hangs at the Metropolitan Museum of Art in New York City.*

2. *Stein's numerous quotable lines include "Rose is a rose is a rose is a rose" and her oft-repeated expression of distaste for Oakland, "There is no there there."*

3. *Stein once declared to Hemingway that he and his literary contemporaries were "all a lost generation." The term* Lost Generation *has been used to refer to that group of writers since.*

•••••

Porgy and Bess

The brothers George (1898–1937) and Ira (1896–1983) Gershwin composed more than a dozen successful Broadway shows and wrote enduring American standards such as "Fascinating Rhythm" (1924) and "Someone to Watch Over Me" (1926). Perhaps their single most famous work, however, was the controversial 1935 opera *Porgy and Bess*, which is widely regarded as a landmark of American theater for its unforgettable songs, including "Summertime," as well as its daring use of an all-black cast.

Porgy and Bess is based on a 1925 novel titled *Porgy*, by DuBose Heyward (1885–1940). The story takes place in a black neighborhood called Catfish Row in Charleston, South Carolina, and follows a beggar, Porgy; the object of his affection, Bess; her domineering boyfriend, Crown; and a local cocaine dealer named Sportin' Life.

George Gershwin, who wrote the music, called *Porgy and Bess* a "folk opera," and his score is an exuberant mix of influences from American folk, blues, and jazz music. However, the lyrics, penned by his brother Ira, often use African-American dialect to tell the story, which attracted criticism from blacks who felt that the opera reinforced negative stereotypes. (Both Heyward and the Gershwin brothers were white.)

Indeed, the opera was controversial from virtually its first performance. The Gershwins were determined to stage the original production with a full African-American cast, a difficult feat in the 1930s. The production did not receive immediate acclaim from white audiences and was derided as racist by many blacks. However, the individual songs in the opera, such as "Summertime," "I Got Plenty o' Nuttin'," and "It Ain't Necessarily So," became classics. Eventually some African-Americans began to accept the opera despite its use of racial stereotypes, and today *Porgy and Bess* is considered one of the greatest American operas of the twentieth century.

ADDITIONAL FACTS

1. *George Gershwin was a pioneer as a composer, pianist, and conductor, having composed* Rhapsody in Blue *(1924) and* An American in Paris *(1928) in addition to his work writing musicals and standards.*

2. *George Gershwin died of a brain tumor at the young age of thirty-eight.*

3. *The Library of Congress named its prize for popular songs after George and Ira Gershwin.*

• • • • •

Clark Gable

On-screen, Clark Gable (1901–1960) was known for his virile, tough-guy persona. Off-screen, he was a hard-drinking playboy, renowned for his affairs with some of Hollywood's leading ladies. That combination, along with his appearances in some of the era's greatest films, made him the most popular film heartthrob of the 1930s and 1940s and earned him the nickname the King of Hollywood.

Gable's career began taking off in 1931, when he appeared in twelve movies. A year later, he starred opposite Jean Harlow in *Red Dust,* which continued his trajectory toward superstardom.

In 1934, he won the Academy Award for Best Actor for his leading role in Frank Capra's *It Happened One Night.* The film was a seminal romantic comedy in which Gable proved his ability to play a character with a tough exterior but a loving, sentimental side as well.

He earned another Academy Award nomination for his portrayal of Fletcher Christian, the leader of a band of mutineers, in *Mutiny on the Bounty* (1935). Although Gable's status as the King was now in place, his greatest role was still on the horizon.

In what is widely considered the quintessential American epic, Gable crafted his most enduring role as the dashing Rhett Butler in *Gone with the Wind* (1939). The film broke box office records, won a then-record ten Academy Awards, and ensured that Gable would be a leading man for the rest of his life. The picture also gave Gable the chance to utter what the American Film Institute deemed in 2005 the most memorable line in cinema history: "Frankly, my dear, I don't give a damn."

In 1942, Gable's movie-star wife, Carole Lombard, was killed in a plane crash, and shortly thereafter, he enlisted in the US Army Air Forces, flying combat missions in World War II. None of his films after the war measured up to his previous success.

His final film, *The Misfits* (1961), directed by John Huston and written by Arthur Miller, was also the last film for costar Marilyn Monroe. Gable, who never saw the completed film, died of a heart attack at age fifty-nine.

ADDITIONAL FACTS

1. *Although* Gone with the Wind *won ten Academy Awards, Gable lost in his bid for a second Best Actor Oscar to Robert Donat (*Goodbye, Mr. Chips*).*

2. *In one scene in* It Happened One Night, *Gable removes his shirt to show his bare chest—which reportedly caused men across the country to ditch their undershirts in favor of Gable's look.*

3. *Gable starred in three movies that won the Academy Award for Best Picture—*It Happened One Night, Mutiny on the Bounty, *and* Gone with the Wind.

••◆••

Fascism

In a speech on October 28, 1925, Benito Mussolini, Italian dictator and leader of the Fascisti, summed up his ideology with one neat phrase: "*Tutto nello Stato, niente al di fuori dello Stato, nulla contro lo Stato*"—"Everything in the State, nothing outside the State, nothing against the State."

Fascism, a totalitarian system of government that emphasizes the state's complete power over every aspect of society, emerged in a handful of European countries during the period of economic upheaval and social malaise that followed World War I. Fascist leaders such as Mussolini (1883–1945) and the German dictator Adolf Hitler (1889–1945) attracted popular support by promising to impose order, restore national pride, and rule with an iron fist.

In addition to Mussolini and Hitler, Spain's Francisco Franco (1892–1975) and the Portuguese leader António de Oliveira Salazar (1889–1970) are often considered part of the fascist movement.

In Italy, the first fascist state, Mussolini and his supporters, dubbed the Blackshirts, took power in 1922 and quickly outlawed strikes, instituted newspaper censorship, and abolished elections.

In many countries, fascism attracted support amid fears of the growing power of communism. Indeed, Mussolini, Hitler, and Franco all depended on the fear of communism to hasten their ascent to power. The Nazis famously set fire to Berlin's Reichstag building in 1933, a crime they then blamed on communists in order to stoke fears of a communist takeover and build their own support.

Once in power, fascists sought to obliterate the private sector and form what they called a "corporate state" of all-encompassing government authority. Hitler's version of fascism emphasized the creation of a racially homogeneous Germany, an ideology that eventually led to the Holocaust.

The defeat of the Axis in World War II ended the fascist movement in Italy and Germany. However, fascism was not dismantled in Spain until after Franco's death in 1975.

ADDITIONAL FACTS

1. *Mussolini coined the term* fascismo *from the Italian word* fascio *and the Latin* fasces. *In ancient Rome, a fasces—a bundle of rods with a projecting ax blade—was an emblem of authority, symbolizing strength through unity.*

2. *On April 28, 1945, in a northern Italian village, Mussolini was found disguised as a German soldier. He was executed along with the secretary of the Fascist Party, four cabinet ministers, and his mistress.*

3. *Spain's fascist movement was known as the Falange. The word was derived from the name of an ancient Roman military formation, the phalanx.*

•••••

Ted Williams

Ted Williams (1918–2002) excelled at virtually everything he did. He is considered one of the best fighter pilots ever, having proved his skills in combat. He was a champion fly fisherman. And he was, according to baseball observers, the greatest hitter who ever lived.

Despite missing three complete seasons and most of two others because of his military service in two wars, World War II and Korea, Williams posted a career .344 batting average (unmatched by any player since), hit 521 home runs, was named to seventeen all-star games, won six American League (AL) batting titles, claimed the triple crown twice (1942, 1947), was twice the AL's Most Valuable Player (1946, 1949), and was the last player to hit .400 in a season, when he batted .406 in 1941.

Williams, a left fielder, combined extraordinary eyesight with obsessive study. He even wrote *The Science of Hitting,* which many consider the definitive book on the subject.

He made his debut with the Red Sox in 1939 and played for the team until 1960, when, in his final at bat at Fenway Park, he smashed home run number 521 at age forty-two. He was inducted into the Baseball Hall of Fame on the first ballot in 1966. Three years later, a media panel voted him the best hitter of baseball's first century.

Despite his hitting prowess, Williams was an indifferent fielder, and he played in only one World Series. (The Red Sox lost to the St. Louis Cardinals in 1946.) Temperamental and often angry, he also had a love-hate relationship with Boston fans and a hate-hate relationship with the town's sportswriters.

After his retirement, he spent most of his later years fishing, signing autographs, and talking about hitting. He died at age eighty-three, after a series of strokes and heart complications.

ADDITIONAL FACTS

1. *Williams flew thirty-nine combat missions in Korea and was frequently the wingman of future astronaut and US senator John Glenn (1921–).*

2. *Entering the final day of the 1941 season, Williams had a batting average of .39955, which rounded up to .400. Red Sox manager Joe Cronin gave him the chance to sit out that day's doubleheader to retain the .400 mark. Williams refused to sit out and racked up six hits in eight at bats to raise his average to .405702 (.406).*

3. *Upon Williams's death in 2002, his remains were cryogenically frozen, with his head severed from his body, and the two pieces placed in separate containers filled with liquid nitrogen. He and his son, John Henry, and daughter Claudia all agreed to the biostasis procedure in the hope of being together again at some future date.*

• • • • •

Monopoly

So emblematic of American capitalism that it was once banned in Russia and China (and is still outlawed in Cuba and North Korea), Monopoly is a game of luck, chance, and strategy with one object—to bankrupt your opponents. Since its introduction in 1935, millions of copies of the game have been produced in countless varieties.

The game was patented by an unemployed salesman in Pennsylvania named Charles Darrow (1889–1967). Darrow based the game's famous squares on streets in the resort town of Atlantic City, New Jersey. Boardwalk, the most valuable space on the board, refers to the city's famous seaside promenade.

In the middle of the Great Depression, the game was a surprise hit for toy manufacturer Parker Brothers and became the best-selling game of the year.

For years, Parker Brothers marketed the game using Darrow's life story as a rags-to-riches myth. However, the story was debunked in the early 1970s when an economics professor proved that Monopoly was, in fact, a variation of a widely distributed American game, The Landlord's Game, patented in 1904.

Inventor or not, Darrow got the monopoly on Monopoly and became the first millionaire board game designer. His game has sold more than 250 million copies in thirty-seven languages since 1935 and introduced expressions such as "'get out of jail free' card" and "do not pass 'Go,' do not collect $200" to the English lexicon. True to its folk roots, Monopoly continues to evolve today in dozens of variations based on cities (Las Vegas Monopoly), sports teams (Denver Broncos Monopoly), movies (*Lord of the Rings* Monopoly), and miscellaneous interests (Cat Lover's Monopoly).

ADDITIONAL FACTS

1. *Players can print Monopoly money from the Hasbro Toys Web site.*

2. *Players land on Illinois Avenue, "Go," and the B&O Railroad more than any other space.*

3. *The race car is the most popular playing piece.*

4. *During World War II, correspondence and money were smuggled to American POWs in Germany using Monopoly sets.*

5. *Parker Brothers initially rejected Darrow's game, citing "52 fundamental playing flaws," but changed their minds after he sold 5,000 homemade sets to a Philadelphia department store.*

•• • ••

Clement Attlee

The man who succeeded Winston Churchill (1874–1965) as prime minister of the United Kingdom could not have been more different from the blustery and heroic man who led Britain through World War II. Clement Attlee (1883–1967) was an unassuming middle-class lawyer known for his quiet nature, a self-proclaimed "ordinary chap."

But as prime minister from 1945 to 1951, Attlee fundamentally altered the British economy, initiating a welfare state to help the struggling country recover from the hardships of World War II. Changes made under his leadership included the foundation of the National Health Service; the nationalization of several industries, including coal mining and steel production; and the creation of a national insurance program.

All told, Attlee's government transferred about one-fifth of the British economy from private hands to public ownership, reflecting a fundamental shift in the economic role of the state in much of postwar Europe. This form of "pragmatic socialism" remained in place in Britain and throughout much of Europe until the late 1970s, when conservative leaders such as Margaret Thatcher (1925–) began deregulating many industries to help stimulate economic growth.

Because of his unpretentious personality, Attlee was underestimated throughout his political career. He had served in the army during World War I and entered Parliament in 1922. By 1935, he had become leader of the Parliamentary Labour Party.

During World War II, he held various roles as a member of Churchill's war coalition, including deputy prime minister and secretary of state for the dominions, which put him in charge of domestic matters while Churchill focused on the war.

After the war, Labour swept into power, allowing Attlee to replace Churchill as prime minister. In addition to his creation of the welfare state, Attlee also oversaw the dismantling of major parts of the British Empire: India, Burma (now known as Myanmar), and Ceylon (now Sri Lanka) were all granted independence during his tenure.

When the Conservatives defeated Labour in 1951, Churchill returned to 10 Downing Street, replacing Attlee as prime minister. Attlee remained as the leader of the Opposition for four more years before retiring in 1955.

He died at age eighty-four.

ADDITIONAL FACTS

1. *Unlike Churchill, who opposed Indian independence, Attlee personally introduced into the House of Commons the bill that liberated India from Britain in 1947.*

2. *After his resignation from Parliament in 1955, Attlee was given an earldom and made a Knight of the Garter, the highest rank in the British honors system.*

3. *Attlee was an amateur poet and an avid cricket fan.*

••●••

E. E. Cummings

Though probably best remembered today for his aversion to capital letters, the American poet E. E. Cummings (1894–1962) contributed far more to English-language poetry than mere quirks of punctuation and capitalization. Over a forty-year career, he published a dozen volumes of largely positive, vibrant poetry that is highly experimental yet accessible to everyday readers.

A native of the Boston area, Cummings earned two degrees at Harvard, where a number of his poems appeared in campus publications. He volunteered as an ambulance driver not long after graduation and was sent to France as part of the American effort in World War I. Shortly after the war, Cummings moved back to France and spent the better part of a decade in Paris, writing and studying art. During these early years, he read numerous works by Gertrude Stein (1874–1946), whose avant-garde experimentation with language would become a hallmark of Cummings's own writing.

Cummings first earned acclaim with a novel—*The Enormous Room* (1922), a significant but often overlooked work in the canon of World War I literature. He followed with several poetry collections that featured his trademark experimentation with typography, diction, and word order. These poems test the boundaries of English syntax and punctuation: Though Cummings typically uses simple language, he juxtaposes and combines words in ways that expose interesting, unforeseen relationships among them. For example, one well-known work that typifies his style, "anyone lived in a pretty how town," begins as follows:

> anyone lived in a pretty how town
> (with up so floating many bells down)
> spring summer autumn winter
> he sang his didn't he danced his did . . .

Among Cummings's most famous works, such as "pity this busy monster, manunkind" and "my father moved through dooms of love," many adhere to this same style, which changed little over his career.

ADDITIONAL FACTS

1. *It is a common misconception that Cummings legally changed his name to all lowercase—he actually spelled "E. E. Cummings" with capitals more often than not and never made any legal changes to his name.*

2. *Like his New England predecessor Emily Dickinson (1830–1886), Cummings gave explicit titles to very few of his poems. Instead, scholars and anthologists refer to his poems by their full first lines.*

3. *During his years at Harvard, Cummings was close friends with the novelist John Dos Passos (1896–1970), who went on to write* Manhattan Transfer *(1925) and the sprawling* U.S.A. Trilogy *(1930–1936).*

•••••

Cole Porter

While Cole Porter (1891–1964) was being groomed for Yale at a posh East Coast prep school, his headmaster taught him a valuable lesson that set the tone for his musical career. The headmaster warned, "Words and music must be so inseparably wedded to each other that they are like one."

Unlike the Gershwins, who methodically plotted their way from the slums of Brooklyn to the bright lights of Broadway, Porter came from a wealthy family and didn't need the money. A semicloseted gay man, Porter married a wealthy widow and lived the high life in Paris for years before finally making his mark on Broadway. Once he emerged, he never left.

Known for his masterful lyrics and astute pop culture references, Porter often mixed high and low culture in his writing. One of his most famous songs is "You're the Top" (1934):

> You're a melody from a symphony by Strauss
> You're a Bendel bonnet,
> A Shakespeare's sonnet,
> You're Mickey Mouse.

In his social life, Porter was the consummate dinner-party guest and bon vivant. However, he was constantly looking for love and physical connection. Having experienced the ennui that stems from excess, Porter expressed it with wry humor in his lyrics for the hit 1934 musical *Anything Goes*:

> Some get a kick from cocaine.
> I'm sure that if I took even one sniff
> That would bore me terrific'ly too
> Yet I get a kick out of you.

Porter composed more than 800 songs over the course of his career, including classics of the American songbook such as "Night and Day" (1932), "I've Got You under My Skin" (1936), and the scores for *Anything Goes* (1934) and *Kiss Me Kate* (1948).

ADDITIONAL FACTS

1. *Both of Porter's legs were crushed when he was thrown from a horse in 1937. He lived much of the rest of his life in pain before finally having his right leg amputated in 1958.*

2. *While at Yale, Porter was in the singing group the Whiffenpoofs. He also penned the classic Yale football fight songs "Yale Bulldog" and "Bingo Eli Yale."*

3. *Porter's first name is the maiden name of his mother, Kate Cole.*

Bette Davis

Born Ruth Elizabeth Davis, Bette Davis (1908–1989) broke with Hollywood convention by becoming the most successful actress of her age despite lacking what most people would call classic beauty. Instead, she established herself as an unparalleled artist with her realistic performances as tough, sometimes unsympathetic women. She possessed a depth and range that no typical starlet could match.

After a stage career that took her to Broadway, Davis moved to Hollywood in 1930 and made her film debut the following year in *The Bad Sister*. She took on roles in more than twenty films before she got her break in *Of Human Bondage* (1934), opposite star Leslie Howard. Portraying coarse waitress Mildred Rogers, Davis earned the respect of critics and moviegoers alike, though she was passed over for an Academy Award nomination—an oversight that prompted a feverish, although ultimately unsuccessful, write-in campaign.

Perhaps because of her omission from Oscar night in 1935, she won an Academy Award for Best Actress a year later for her performance as an alcoholic actress in *Dangerous* (1935). She garnered a second Oscar three years later for her portrayal of a spoiled Southern belle in *Jezebel* (1938).

Davis's most enduring role was as the aging actress Margo Channing in Joseph Mankiewicz's *All About Eve* (1950). Critic Roger Ebert calls Channing her greatest role, writing, "It seems to show her defeated by the wiles of a younger actress, but in fact marks a victory: the triumph of personality and will over the superficial power of beauty. She never played a more autobiographical role."

All About Eve, which earned fourteen Academy Award nominations (a record tied by 1997's *Titanic*) and six Oscars, would give Davis the ninth of her eleven nominations, a figure that includes the unusual write-in campaign for *Of Human Bondage*.

Her final nomination came for her performance in the 1962 psychological horror film *What Ever Happened to Baby Jane?* in which she costarred with her rival and fellow screen legend Joan Crawford. Davis continued acting until her death at age eighty-one from breast cancer.

ADDITIONAL FACTS

1. *In 1941, Davis became the first female president of the Academy of Motion Picture Arts and Sciences; she left the post after two months.*

2. *In 1977, she became the first woman to receive the American Film Institute's Life Achievement Award.*

3. *During World War II, Davis helped organize a legendary nightclub in Los Angeles called the Hollywood Canteen, which provided entertainment for American service members.*

The SAT

On June 23, 1926, about 8,000 teenagers took the first Scholastic Aptitude Test (SAT), an exam designed to measure their academic abilities and help colleges select their freshman classes.

Within a few decades, the multiple-choice test—with its analogies, reading passages, and math problems—had become a rite of passage for millions of Americans as one of the central elements of the nation's college admissions process.

At the time of its invention, the SAT represented a revolutionary concept in American higher education. The tests, administered by a nonprofit group called the College Board, were meant to measure objectively a student's aptitude, diminishing the importance of family connections, wealth, and luck in the college admissions process and theoretically leveling the playing field for all applicants.

Standardized testing spread rapidly after World War II, as more colleges embraced the goals of academic meritocracy symbolized by the SAT. By 1957, more than half a million Americans every year sharpened number two pencils for the exam. The Advanced Placement Program, another popular form of standardized test, was introduced in 1955. The ACT, a competitor to the College Board, began testing in 1959.

More recently, results from standardized tests have been used to measure educators as well as students. The No Child Left Behind Act of 2001 made standardized testing a regular feature at every level of public schools.

Many critics, however, have pointed to the shortcomings of tests like the SAT, arguing that they discriminate against students from poor and minority backgrounds who have less time and money to prepare for the exam. Many critics also charge that the importance of standardized tests has forced educators to "teach to the test" rather than follow more in-depth and creative curricula.

In 2001, the president of the University of California attracted national attention by suggesting that the state stop accepting the test. However, the university and hundreds of other schools continue to rely on SAT results for admissions.

ADDITIONAL FACTS

1. *About 26 percent of the students taking the first SAT exam were applicants to Yale, one of the first colleges to accept SAT scores.*

2. *The SAT's official name was changed in 1990 to the Scholastic Assessment Test.*

3. *In 2005, a writing section was added to the traditional multiple-choice questions on the SAT.*

•••••

Jackie Robinson

For the simple act of playing in a baseball game, Jackie Robinson (1919–1972) became one of the most important civil rights figures of the twentieth century. On April 15, 1947, Robinson—the grandson of slaves and the son of a share-cropper—played first base in a major-league game, breaking baseball's color barrier.

Robinson had been a star athlete at the University of California, Los Angeles, where he was the first student to letter in four sports in one year. After serving as an officer in the US Army during World War II, he played shortstop for the Kansas City Monarchs of the segregated Negro League in 1945.

The following year, Brooklyn Dodgers general manager Branch Rickey (1881–1965) selected Robinson—a fierce man who did not take racial discrimination lightly—to be the player to integrate baseball. After a year in the minor leagues, Robinson went to Brooklyn to play for the Dodgers.

Under strict orders from Rickey, Robinson did not respond to any physical or verbal taunts for his entire rookie year. And the taunts came—from teammates, opponents, and fans. Instead, Robinson unleashed his fury on the field, becoming an aggressive terror, particularly on the base paths.

Robinson was not only a trailblazer but also a great ballplayer. In 1947, he was named Rookie of the Year. In 1949, he was the National League's Most Valuable Player, leading the league in batting average (.342) and stolen bases (37). He was a six-time all-star who led the Dodgers to six World Series appearances and one world championship, in 1955.

In December 1956, the Dodgers traded him to the New York Giants, but Robinson chose to retire rather than join Brooklyn's hated rival. For the rest of his life, he worked in the business world and continued to campaign for civil rights. He died of a heart attack at age fifty-three.

ADDITIONAL FACTS

1. *The Dodgers retired Robinson's number, 42, in 1972, and all of major-league baseball followed suit in 1997, on the fiftieth anniversary of Robinson's debut.*

2. *In his rookie season with Brooklyn, Robinson played first base. He moved to second base the next season, where he played for most of the remainder of his career.*

3. *Robinson was inducted into the Baseball Hall of Fame in 1962.*

••●••

Superman

In June 1938, in the first issue of Action Comics, cartoonists Jerry Siegel (1914–1996) and Joe Shuster (1914–1992) introduced a muscle-bound hero named Superman, inaugurating one of the most beloved characters in American pop culture and inventing the superhero comics genre.

Superman, in his earliest incarnation, was faster than a speeding bullet, more powerful than a locomotive, and could leap tall buildings in a single bound—but he couldn't fly. (He gained that superpower in 1941.) Siegel and Shuster penned an elaborate biography for the superhero, who was born on the planet Krypton, sent to Earth by his father before Krypton's destruction, and raised as Clark Kent by a Kansas farmer. When Kent goes to work as a mild-mannered reporter at the *Daily Planet,* he meets his love interest, Lois Lane, whom he often rescues in the guise of Superman while hiding his real identity. All the while, Superman battles various supervillains, including his archenemy, Lex Luthor.

Superman's instant popularity spawned the creation of more adventure-hero comics, including *Batman,* which first appeared in 1939, and *Captain America* and *Wonder Woman,* which debuted in 1941.

While he started as a comic-book character, Superman soon appeared in various other media, including a popular radio series, cartoons, and the 1978 film starring Christopher Reeve (1952–2004). In the 1990s, Superman was adapted to the small screen in the television show *Lois & Clark: The New Adventures of Superman.* A series that debuted in 2001 named *Smallville* focuses on the life of a young Clark Kent before his transformation into Superman.

ADDITIONAL FACTS

1. *The latest film adaptation of the Superman story is the 2006 film* Superman Returns.

2. *Though he had faded from pop culture prominence by the 1990s, Superman again made news in 1993 when DC Comics issued a story line in which the famed superhero died. He was revived in another issue two months later.*

3. *Siegel and Shuster had actually created an earlier version of Superman in 1933—as a supervillain.*

• • ● • •

Jackson Pollock

Painter Jackson Pollock (1912–1956) was one of the best-known members of the abstract expressionist movement in the United States in the late 1940s and early 1950s. His style, known as *drip and splash* or *action painting,* shocked and revolutionized the art world.

Instead of placing a canvas on an easel, Pollock would lay his canvas on the floor of his studio or on the ground outside, then walk around its outside edges (or even step on the canvas itself), dripping and pouring commercial paint directly from the can onto the canvas. He also sometimes added sand or broken glass to his works for additional texture. Some critics rejected his work as chaotic and meaningless, while others found it to be highly organized, psychologically interesting, and visually captivating.

Pollock became a leader of the abstract expressionists, a group of mostly New York City–based painters who created large-scale works and had an interest in Jungian psychology (particularly the collective unconscious and primitive mythology) and a belief that finding true expression through painting was a physical process.

Pollock began painting in high school in Los Angeles before moving to New York in 1930 to study at the Art Students League under American regionalist painter Thomas Hart Benton (1889–1975). In the early years of Pollock's career, he was influenced by Benton, Pablo Picasso (1881–1973), surrealists, Mexican muralists, and Native American artists.

He worked on the Works Progress Administration Federal Art Project from 1935 to 1943 and had his first solo show at Peggy Guggenheim's Art of This Century Gallery in 1943.

Pollock started to develop the drip-and-splash technique in 1947. His best-known works, including *Autumn Rhythm* (1950) and *Lavender Mist* (1950), are in this style.

In 1951, he shifted his focus from the use of colors to working in black and white. In his last year, struggling with alcoholism and depression, he did not paint at all.

While driving drunk, Pollock was killed in a one-car accident at age forty-four.

ADDITIONAL FACTS

1. *The Hollywood film* Pollock *(2000), directed by and starring Ed Harris (1950–), was nominated for two Academy Awards, winning one for Best Actress in a Supporting Role (Marcia Gay Harden, 1959–).*

2. *Pollock married fellow artist Lee Krasner (1908–1984). Their house in the Springs section of Long Island, New York, is now known as the Pollock-Krasner House and Study Center. It is open to the public and is operated by the State University of New York at Stony Brook.*

3. *In November 2006, entertainment mogul David Geffen (1943–) sold one of Pollock's most famous paintings,* No. 5 *(1948), for \$140 million. The price was the highest ever known to have been paid for a painting.*

•••••

Mrs. Dalloway

Virginia Woolf's *Mrs. Dalloway* (1925) is one of the watershed works of the modernist period in Western literature. The novel established Woolf (1882–1941) as a bold experimenter with stream-of-consciousness narration and other new literary techniques, and also as an astute observer of the state of British society after the devastation of World War I.

Virginia Woolf

As its title suggests, *Mrs. Dalloway* focuses on a single woman: Clarissa Dalloway, a society wife living in London after the war. The novel follows the minutiae of Clarissa's life over the course of a single day as she makes preparations for a party that she and her husband are hosting in the evening. She buys flowers, receives visits from old friends, and strolls through London's upper-crust neighborhoods before returning home for the party.

The novel is less about what actually happens to Clarissa during the day than about the thoughts that run through her and the other characters' minds as those events occur. Virtually every time Clarissa enters a shop or runs into an acquaintance passing by, she is reminded of people and events from earlier in her life. Woolf's narrative follows Clarissa's train of thought closely and also jumps into the minds of other people she encounters during her errands.

Though this stream-of-consciousness technique might seem free-form and chaotic, Woolf organizes it intricately, using it to illuminate depths and dimensions of her characters in ways that would not be possible otherwise. Notably, though Clarissa encounters many people throughout her day and many of the novel's plot threads intertwine, there is little true human contact in the novel, and many voids born of miscommunication exist between even the oldest and closest friends.

ADDITIONAL FACTS

1. *Woolf continued to experiment with stream of consciousness in her later novel* To the Lighthouse *(1927) and even more aggressively in* The Waves *(1931).*

2. *Woolf's critical essay* A Room of One's Own *(1929), about the challenges and lack of opportunities facing female writers, had enormous influence on feminism and the women's movement.*

3. *Michael Cunningham's (1952–) book* The Hours *(1998) portrays three women connected to* Mrs. Dalloway: *Woolf herself, writing the novel; a 1950s housewife reading it; and a modern-day woman unwittingly reliving it over the course of a single day.*

•••••

Duke Ellington

Jazz bandleader Duke Ellington (1899–1974) summed up his entire musical philosophy with a single famous lyric: "It don't mean a thing if it ain't got that swing." As complex and intricate as Ellington's compositions became, they always had "that swing."

Edward Kennedy "Duke" Ellington was born in Washington, DC, appropriately enough for an artist who found the word *jazz* too constricting and referred to his work as nothing less than "American music." His work spanned a large number of styles over the course of his career, from standards recorded with Ella Fitzgerald (1917–1996) to collaborations with some of the most innovative jazz musicians of his time, including bassist Charles Mingus (1922–1979) and saxophonist John Coltrane (1926–1967).

The work for which Ellington is most famous, however, is his tenure as leader of the house band at Harlem's Cotton Club in the 1920s and 1930s.

Ellington played piano for the band, but many critics say that his greatest instrument was his orchestra. He began by leading a small dance troupe known as the Washingtonians but soon assembled an orchestra of fourteen players, known as the Famous Orchestra. The lineup changed over time but always contained some of the greatest jazz musicians of the period, including saxophonist Johnny Hodges (1906–1970), Charles "Cootie" Williams (1910–1985), and Rex Stewart (1907–1967), all of whom would eventually lead their own orchestras.

While leading these great bands, Ellington produced many of his best-known compositions, such as "Cottontail" (1940) and "Harlem Air Shaft" (1940).

Ellington's popularity began to wane as swing lost ground to bebop, a new style of jazz that was meant for listening, not dancing. He never completely faded from view, however. His performance at the Newport Jazz Festival in 1956 brought his music to a new audience, and artists of a younger generation, from Miles Davis (1926–1991) to Dave Brubeck (1920–), all emphasized their admiration for the Duke. And Ellington never lost his youthful charm: When he was passed over for a Pulitzer Prize at the age of sixty-seven, he remarked, "Fate is being kind to me. Fate doesn't want me to be famous too young."

ADDITIONAL FACTS

1. *Though Ellington didn't win the Pulitzer Prize during his lifetime, he was honored with a special posthumous award in 1999.*

2. *Miles Davis titled his 1974 tribute to Ellington "He Loved Him Madly" because the Duke always ended his performances (and one year even his Christmas cards) with the words "love you madly."*

3. *Richard Nixon (1913–1994) invited Ellington to play at the White House in 1969 and awarded him the Presidential Medal of Freedom, the highest civilian honor in the United States.*

• • ● • •

Katharine Hepburn

Katharine Hepburn (1907–2003) was a feminist icon who played against the classic type of the Hollywood starlet, combining an independent spirit, athleticism, wit, and intelligence to become the First Lady of Cinema.

Her film career spanned more than six decades, and she was rewarded with four Academy Awards (a record number for acting) and twelve nominations. She is perhaps best known for her patrician New England accent and her quarter-century affair with fellow screen legend Spencer Tracy (who was married throughout their relationship).

Hepburn made her film debut in *A Bill of Divorcement* (1932), and within a year, she had already won an Academy Award for Best Actress for *Morning Glory* (1933).

Hepburn's first important on-screen collaborator was Cary Grant. They starred in Howard Hawks's *Bringing Up Baby* (1938), often considered the definitive screwball comedy. But like several others of Hepburn's to that point, the film was a box office flop, and a poll that year in *Photoplay* magazine called her "box office poison."

Hepburn left Hollywood in 1939 to star on Broadway in the romantic comedy *The Philadelphia Story,* which was a smash hit. She bought the rights to the story and returned to Hollywood—where the film version of the play (released in 1940) revitalized her career.

She starred alongside Tracy (1900–1967) for the first time in *Woman of the Year* (1942), often considered Hepburn's best film. The duo would go on to make eight more pictures together, and their off-screen relationship would continue until Tracy's death in 1967.

In 1951, she teamed for the first and last time with Hollywood icon Humphrey Bogart in *The African Queen*. Hepburn played an older woman who finds love, the type of role that would define the latter part of her career.

Her run of late-career Oscars began with *Guess Who's Coming to Dinner* (1967), which many consider a tribute to costar Tracy, who died shortly after the film was completed. She added a third Oscar a year later for *The Lion in Winter* (1968) and an unprecedented fourth for *On Golden Pond* (1981), costarring with Henry Fonda and his daughter, Jane.

Hepburn's final film appearance was in 1994, nine years before her death at her Connecticut estate at age ninety-six.

ADDITIONAL FACTS

1. *Hepburn was named the number one female screen legend by the American Film Institute.*

2. *Hepburn costarred with Spencer Tracy in nine films and with Cary Grant in four.*

3. *For both Hepburn and Bogart,* The African Queen *was the first color film in which they appeared.*

•• • ••

Nativism

In 1938, President Franklin D. Roosevelt (1882–1945) gave a famous speech to the Daughters of the American Revolution pleading for toleration of immigrants. "Remember always that all of us, and you and I especially, are descended from immigrants," he said.

Roosevelt delivered his address against the backdrop of a groundswell of anti-immigrant sentiment—also known as nativism—during the 1920s and 1930s.

The term *nativism* was coined in the mid-nineteenth century, during an earlier immigration scare. The so-called Know-Nothings enjoyed brief success on a nativist, anti-Catholic platform in 1854 elections before their movement disintegrated.

Nativism returned after World War I, when worries about crime and economic uncertainty combined to foment renewed hostility toward against newcomers. In 1924, Congress passed an act restricting immigration from Asia and "undesirable" sections of Europe, including predominantly Roman Catholic countries such as Italy and Poland. During the Red Scare period, hundreds of Eastern Europeans were deported because of suspected links to anarchism.

At the same time, nativist citizen groups became more powerful. The Ku Klux Klan, which had been founded in the South to terrorize African-Americans after the Civil War, began targeting Catholics and Jews as well. The 1928 Democratic presidential nominee, Al Smith (1873–1944), encountered significant hostility because of his Catholicism and was soundly defeated by Republican Herbert Hoover (1874–1964).

The anti-immigrant mood continued during Roosevelt's presidency. In a famous incident in 1939, the ship *St. Louis* and its passengers, mostly German Jews, were refused entry to the United States and sent back to Europe, where many are believed to have died in the Holocaust.

Nativism abated during World War II, and the 1924 immigration act was superseded by legislation in 1965 that allowed far more immigrants into the United States.

Still, anti-immigrant sentiment remains a potent undercurrent in American political life and has bubbled to the surface on occasion.

ADDITIONAL FACTS

1. *A small number of job advertisements in the nineteenth century bore the infamous disclaimer "No Irish need apply," attesting to the depth of anti-Catholic and anti-immigrant feeling.*

2. *Anti-Catholic views were still an issue during the 1960 election. John F. Kennedy (1917–1963) had to explicitly state, "I am not the Catholic candidate for president, I am the Democratic Party's candidate," and he remains the only Catholic ever elected to that office.*

3. *Though best known as a violent racist organization, the Ku Klux Klan has always been a strong proponent of nativism and anti-Catholicism as well.*

•••••

Rocky Marciano

Rocky Marciano (1923–1969) wasn't the biggest, most talented, or most skilled boxer who ever lived, but he may have been the toughest. Although he was undersize at five foot ten and 185 pounds, he brawled his way to a 49-0 record and the heavyweight title, retiring as the only undefeated heavyweight champion in boxing history.

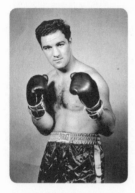

Born Rocco Francis Marchegiano outside Boston, Marciano was known as the Brockton Blockbuster and the Rock from Brockton. His childhood dream was to become a catcher in professional baseball, but an unsuccessful tryout with the Chicago Cubs in 1947 made him turn to boxing, a sport he had picked up four years earlier while serving in the US Army.

In 1948, he turned pro and began establishing himself as a rising star thanks to his powerful overhand right, which he dubbed Suzie Q. By October 1951, he was 37-0 with 32 knockouts when he faced his boxing hero, Joe Louis (1914–1981), the former champion.

Louis had reigned over the heavyweight division from 1937 to 1949, but by 1951, he was thirty-seven years old and had already retired once. After knocking out the former champ, Marciano wept in Louis's dressing room. Even though Louis was past his prime, the win gave Marciano credibility—and a title shot against Jersey Joe Walcott (1914–1994).

On September 23, 1952, Marciano trailed Walcott heading into the thirteenth round. The challenger needed a knockout, and Suzie Q provided one, leaving Walcott unconscious and giving Marciano the championship belt.

He defended his title six times, including another win over Walcott and two epic victories over Ezzard Charles (1921–1975).

Marciano retired in 1956 and was killed in a private plane crash the day before his forty-sixth birthday.

ADDITIONAL FACTS

1. *Of Marciano, Pulitzer Prize–winning sportswriter Red Smith (1905–1982) wrote, "He was the toughest, strongest, most completely dedicated fighter who ever wore gloves. Fear wasn't in his vocabulary and pain had no meaning."*

2. *The closest another heavyweight has come to approaching Marciano's 49-bout winning streak was Larry Holmes (1949–), who had notched a career tally of 48-0 before losing to Michael Spinks (1956–) in 1985.*

3. *At sixty-eight inches, Marciano had the shortest reach of any heavyweight champion.*

•• ● ••

Lassie

Perhaps the most famous dog in American pop culture, Lassie made her debut in 1938 as the canine star of a short story in the *Saturday Evening Post*. Author Eric Knight (1897–1943) built upon the story's popularity and expanded the tale into a book titled *Lassie Come Home,* which in turn inspired a 1943 film staring Elizabeth Taylor (1932–).

In the original tale, Sam Carraclough, a poor Yorkshire farmer, is forced to sell his son's collie to a Scottish duke who then moves the dog with him to Scotland. Ever faithful and loyal, Lassie stays devoted to her young owner and braves the long distance and great danger to return to the Carracloughs.

The film was an instant hit, and many more Lassie movies followed. Campbell Soup Company later agreed to sponsor a TV series, bringing Lassie to the small screen.

Lassie was the only constant character in the television show. She changed owners many times and in certain episodes seemed to travel alone. But, no matter what family she was living with, Lassie always taught her owners, and her viewing public, lessons of loyalty, friendship, and courage.

Before Lassie, a dog had never been the center of an entertainment franchise. In fact, most dogs in film and on TV were considered farm animals and kept outdoors. In 2005, Lassie was picked as one of the top 100 screen icons of all time by *Variety* magazine; she was the only nonhuman on the list.

ADDITIONAL FACTS

1. *Although the character of Lassie is a female collie, Pal, a nonpedigreed male, played the original Lassie. Most Lassies since have been one of Pal's direct descendants.*

2. *Lassie is one of three animals to have a star on the Hollywood Walk of Fame; the others are the German shepherds Rin Tin Tin and Strongheart.*

3. *Many* Lassie *episodes dealt with environmental issues such as endangered species.*

• • ● • •

Mao Zedong

In his simple gray tunic, Mao Zedong (1893–1976) symbolized the People's Republic of China, a country that he principally founded in 1949. He emerged from wars and political struggles to become the new country's leader and achieved almost godlike status during his twenty-seven years in power.

Mao was a revolutionary and a nation builder who harnessed the power of the peasantry in the name of Communism to bring China into the modern age and steer it toward its current status as a superpower. But the transition was not without costs. Mass starvation, ill-conceived policies, and paranoia marred his rule and have largely defined his legacy since his death.

Mao, who was born to a peasant family in China's Hunan Province and first exposed to the writings of Karl Marx in 1918, was a founding member of the Chinese Communist Party in 1921. During the Chinese civil war, he proved to be a skilled practitioner of guerrilla warfare and led his undermanned army to an improbable victory in 1949 over Chiang Kai-shek (1887–1975) and the Nationalists.

Following his military triumph, Mao set about remaking China in the Soviet image. His first five-year plan, begun in 1953, emphasized centralized planning, a large defense buildup, and an increase in the output from factories.

But in 1958, he put a Chinese stamp on Marxism, ordering that peasants be reorganized into communes—with the idea that the power of the peasants would compel China to dramatically increase agricultural production and catch up with the West.

But that plan, the Great Leap Forward, was a disaster, leading to the starvation deaths of at least 20 million people and a rupture in relations with the Soviet Union. The debacle also caused Mao to lose his chairmanship of the central government council (though he remained chairman of the Communist Party politburo).

His Cultural Revolution, begun in 1966 to cleanse the country of bourgeois elements (and his political opponents) and to ensure the revolution's post-Mao future, also threw China into chaos at every level of society and resulted in mass killings. Still, Mao was able to reassert his leadership of the nation and the army. In 1971, he made his final public appearance, but he continued to wield the ultimate power in China from behind closed doors until his death at age eighty-two.

ADDITIONAL FACTS

1. *Despite the peacetime deaths of tens of millions of people under his leadership, Mao remains a revered figure in China. A giant mural of his face adorns the entrance to the Forbidden City in Beijing.*

2. *In 1972, the United States ended twenty years of hostility toward China when President Richard Nixon (1913–1994) personally visited Mao in Beijing.*

3. *During his twenty-seven years as China's leader, Mao rarely appeared in public, which contributed to his mystique. Young students were taught to love Mao, and millions of little red books—Quotations from Chairman Mao Tse-tung—were distributed as Chinese state doctrine, all of which added to the so-called cult of Mao.*

• • ◆ • •

F. Scott Fitzgerald

F. Scott Fitzgerald (1896–1940) is by many accounts the greatest American novelist of the twentieth century. Marked by both technical brilliance and unmatched lyrical expression, his novels and short stories capture the sense of both promise and despair that characterized America during the Jazz Age of the 1920s.

After an upbringing in Minnesota and an education at Princeton, Fitzgerald stormed onto the American literary scene with his first novel, *This Side of Paradise*, in 1920. Though this story of a Princeton student's romantic exploits sometimes seems pretentious and juvenile, its undeniable brilliance established Fitzgerald as a major talent. The fame and proceeds from the work enabled Fitzgerald and his young wife, Zelda (1900–1948), to embark on a giddy, decadent lifestyle that made them tabloid staples.

The Great Gatsby (1925), Fitzgerald's third and shortest novel, is considered his magnum opus. The work explores both the potential and the emptiness of the American Dream through the lens of a self-made millionaire whose facade of success hides a corrupt background and a lonely personal life. Though unpopular in its time, *The Great Gatsby* now stands as perhaps the finest novel of its era and is inevitably mentioned in critics' attempts to single out one work as the Great American Novel.

Fitzgerald's turbulent marriage to the notoriously unstable Zelda influenced his later writing, particularly *Tender Is the Night* (1934), a meandering portrayal of an expatriate American psychiatrist's fraught relationship with one of his patients. Fitzgerald's marital troubles worsened his already significant drinking problem, and by the late 1930s he had descended into full-fledged alcoholism. After moving to Los Angeles in 1937 to work as a screenwriter, he died of a heart attack in 1940. His final novel, *The Love of the Last Tycoon*, about a Hollywood movie mogul, was left unfinished.

ADDITIONAL FACTS

1. *Fitzgerald's full name was Francis Scott Key Fitzgerald, derived from the name of his distant relative Francis Scott Key (1779–1843), who wrote the words to "The Star-Spangled Banner" in 1814.*

2. *After years of mental instability, Zelda Fitzgerald suffered a severe nervous breakdown in 1930 and had to be institutionalized. Never able to recover, she died in a fire at a mental hospital in 1948.*

3. *Though not known as a humor writer, Fitzgerald possessed a sharp wit. His short-story collection* The Pat Hobby Stories, *about a bumbling screenwriter in Hollywood, ranks among his least read but funniest works.*

••●••

Robert Johnson

Blues guitarist Robert Leroy Johnson was born in Hazlehurst, Mississippi, sometime in May 1911, and a death certificate found in 1968 showed that he passed away on August 16, 1938. Other than that, very little is known about his life. We do, however, have the forty-one scratchy recordings that Johnson made in Texas in 1936 and 1937. These include classics such as "Sweet Home Chicago" and many songs—including "Love in Vain Blues," "Traveling Riverside Blues," and "Cross Road Blues"—that would later become famous when they were covered by such rock artists as the Rolling Stones, Led Zeppelin, and Cream.

Because so few actual details about Johnson's life are known, an elaborate myth has grown up around him. According to legend, Johnson sold his soul to the devil at a lonely rural crossroads in return for his guitar-playing prowess. Johnson himself may have spread the legend during his lifetime, but it was most widely circulated by Son House (1902–1988), another Mississippi bluesman, who told the story to credulous fans during the blues revival of the 1960s.

Whatever the source of his talents, the King of the Delta Blues Singers was certainly one of the greatest practitioners of a truly American art form. Initially he played before small audiences at bars and on street corners before eventually earning a recording contract. His records were moderately successful in his lifetime but would have a deep influence on rock musicians such as Keith Richards (1943–) of the Rolling Stones and Robert Plant (1948–) of Led Zeppelin when they were rereleased to great acclaim in the 1960s.

ADDITIONAL FACTS

1. *Only two photographs of Robert Johnson exist; both were made public in 1974.*

2. *On the Rolling Stones' live album* Get Yer Ya-Yas Out! *(1970), a cover of Robert Johnson's "Love in Vain Blues" is credited as a "traditional" folk song, with no mention of Johnson; newer versions of the album added Johnson's name as the writer.*

3. *Johnson's records saw their first wide release in 1961, when John Hammond (1910–1987) convinced Columbia Records to issue* King of the Delta Blues Singers. *Hammond would later sign Bob Dylan (1941–), Aretha Franklin (1942–), and Bruce Springsteen (1949–), among many others.*

•••••

John Ford

Celebrated for directing some of the most acclaimed westerns ever made, John Ford (1894–1973) became known for his straightforward, classic filmmaking style, which produced such influential works as *Stagecoach* (1939), *The Grapes of Wrath* (1940), and *The Searchers* (1956).

He won an unprecedented four Academy Awards for Best Director and helped make both John Wayne and Henry Fonda major stars. He also inspired later generations of directors, including Martin Scorsese, George Lucas, Jean-Luc Godard, and Akira Kurosawa.

After two decades of making silent and sound pictures, Ford won his first Academy Award for *The Informer* (1935), set during the Irish civil war and starring Victor McLaglen (who won the Oscar for Best Actor).

Ford's *Stagecoach*, his first western with sound, helped to revitalize the genre and launched John Wayne's career. The film involved more-sophisticated themes and more-colorful characters than previous westerns as it explored the conflict between civilization and the wild frontier. *Stagecoach* was a box office smash, and Wayne and Ford would go on to work together on a dozen major films.

The year 1939 also marked the beginning of Ford's collaboration with Henry Fonda. In a two-year period, the director and star made three films, including *The Grapes of Wrath* (1940), which earned Ford his second best director Academy Award and for many years was considered one of the greatest American films ever made. Ford and Fonda also worked together on the landmark western *My Darling Clementine* (1946).

Ford helped burnish Wayne's screen image in his "cavalry series"—*Fort Apache* (1948), *She Wore a Yellow Ribbon* (1949), and *Rio Grande* (1950). Their two most enduring films, though, would be *The Quiet Man* (1952), in which Ford traded the American West for the lush Irish countryside, and *The Searchers*, his most influential film.

The Searchers featured Wayne in the role of antihero Ethan Edwards and focused on themes of obsession, racism, and moral ambiguity. It was a role that Wayne considered one of his favorites, and one that helped Hollywood come to terms with white westward expansion in the United States and its devastating impact on Native Americans.

ADDITIONAL FACTS

1. *Although Ford is principally known for westerns, none of his four Academy Awards for Best Director were for westerns.*

2. *Ford set seven major films, beginning with* Stagecoach, *in Monument Valley in Utah and Arizona.*

3. The Searchers *is considered to have been a major inspiration for Martin Scorsese's* Taxi Driver *(1976) and George Lucas's* Star Wars *(1977).*

··●··

Surrealism

Surrealism was an artistic movement of the early twentieth century that sought to translate the mysterious workings of the subconscious mind into bizarre, fantastical works of art and literature.

André Breton

Although the Spanish painter Salvador Dalí (1904–1989) was the best-known face of surrealism, the movement spanned many different genres and had a marked impact on twentieth-century art.

The surrealist movement's de facto leader was a French psychoanalyst named André Breton (1896–1966). Breton was deeply influenced by the theories of Sigmund Freud (1856–1939) and began to experiment with techniques for tapping into the subconscious mind.

The first technique he tried was automatic writing—an effort to directly record the thoughts of the subconscious. To do so, surrealist practitioners had to ignore the normal requirements of "good" writing, including narrative structure and any standard of beauty.

When Breton published the first *Surrealist Manifesto* in 1924, he defined *surrealism* as the attempt to transcribe thought "in the absence of all control exercised by the reason."

In the years that followed, the movement gained prominence. What began as a group that occasionally met in Parisian cafés became an international movement that ranged from literature to film. Major figures included the Italian Giorgio de Chirico (1888–1978), the Belgian René Magritte (1898–1967), and the Spanish painters Joan Miró (1893–1983) and Dalí. The French writer Antonin Artaud (1896–1948) used surrealist techniques to revolutionize the theater. And the Spanish director Luis Buñuel (1900–1983) brought surrealism to the cinema.

Though Buñuel was a somewhat obscure figure, he may have been the most influential. Surrealism has dwindled as an artistic and literary movement, but—from the twists in *The Twilight Zone* to the dreams in *Dumbo*—it has never faded from the screen.

ADDITIONAL FACTS

1. *The literal translation of the French* surréalisme *is "beyond realism."*

2. *In the 1930s, the surrealist movement was divided by politics: Breton and others left or were expelled from the Communist Party, while some of their colleagues remained loyal to Moscow.*

3. *Buñuel collaborated with Dalí on a well-known 1928 avant-garde short film,* Un chien andalou— *French for* An Andalusian Dog.

• • • • •

The Shot Heard Round the World

"The Giants win the pennant! The Giants win the pennant!
The Giants win the pennant!"
—Russ Hodges, October 3, 1951

On August 12, 1951, the Brooklyn Dodgers held a seemingly insurmountable lead of 13½ games over their crosstown National League rivals, the New York Giants. Just a month earlier, Dodgers manager Chuck Dressen (1898–1966) had bragged, "The Giants is dead." And after the Giants lost four consecutive games—including three to the Dodgers in mid-August—it appeared that Dressen was correct.

But on the afternoon of August 12, the Giants beat the Philadelphia Phillies. The next day, the Giants won again. And they continued to win for sixteen consecutive games. That was the start of one of the greatest comebacks in baseball history. The Giants would claim thirty-seven of their final forty-four games to catch the Dodgers and force the first three-game playoff in National League history, with the winner facing the New York Yankees in the World Series.

The teams split the first two games, leading to a winner-take-all finale at the Polo Grounds, the Giants' home field. New York was transfixed: Stockbrokers skipped work and schoolchildren cut class to watch the game or listen to the radio account by broadcaster Russ Hodges (1910–1971).

Each team had sent its star pitcher to the mound to start the game—Don Newcombe (1926–) for the Dodgers and Sal Maglie (1917–1992) for the Giants. Through seven innings, the game was tied 1–1, but at the top of the eighth, the Dodgers scored three runs to build a 4–1 lead and appeared to be on their way to the World Series.

But at the bottom of the ninth, two singles and a double made the score 4–2. And with one out and two men on, outfielder Bobby Thomson (1923–) came to the plate to face Brooklyn relief pitcher Ralph Branca (1926–).

After taking Branca's first pitch for a strike, Thompson swung at a high fastball and lined it over the left-field fence. The crowd, and the city, erupted in pandemonium. Hodges's ecstatic call of the game is one of the most famous in radio history. The next day's newspaper's called Thomson's blast the Shot Heard Round the World, and it remains arguably the most memorable walk-off home run in baseball history.

ADDITIONAL FACTS

1. *The Giants went on to lose to the Yankees in the World Series in six games.*

2. *The game is also known as the Miracle at Coogan's Bluff, the location of the Polo Grounds in Upper Manhattan. The stadium was torn down in 1964.*

3. *The phrase "the shot heard round the world" has also been used to describe more serious global events, including the opening battle of the American Revolution in 1775 and the assassination of Archduke Franz Ferdinand (1863–1914) in 1914, the event that triggered the start of World War I.*

•••••

The War of the Worlds

On October 30, 1938, 6 million listeners in the New York City area tuned in to *Mercury Theatre on the Air,* a weekly drama program on CBS Radio, and were shocked by the special bulletin read by an anxious newscaster: A fleet of Martians was invading Earth.

Orson Welles

"We know now that in the early years of the twentieth century," the broadcaster said, "this world was being watched closely by intelligences greater than man's."

The announcer, whose booming voice would soon become world famous, cut to a correspondent, supposedly stationed in New Jersey, who reported that alien ships were appearing in the skies "like a jet of blue flame."

As the hourlong program continued, the situation seemed to grow more and more desperate. Aliens had emerged from the ships, and they were headed toward Manhattan.

What many listeners missed, however, was a disclaimer at the beginning of the broadcast. Had they heard it, they would have known that they were listening not to a newscast of an actual event, but to a radio play of the science-fiction classic *The War of the Worlds,* by the British author H. G. Wells (1866–1946).

The broadcast, the brainchild of its announcer, a young actor named Orson Welles (1915–1985), was meant as an entertainment to coincide with Halloween. But many listeners, already on edge about the growing conflict between the Axis and other European powers, thought they were hearing actual news.

The stunt caused a minor panic on the East Coast and propelled Welles to fame. He went on to great acclaim as the director of *Citizen Kane* (1941), *The Magnificent Ambersons* (1942), *Othello* (1952), and *Touch of Evil* (1958).

ADDITIONAL FACTS

1. *Between 8:30 p.m. and 10:00 p.m. on the night of the broadcast, the Trenton, New Jersey, police headquarters recorded numerous calls involving "Mars attacking this country."*

2. *In the years after the broadcast, many conspiracy theories arose, including the possibility that the program was a military test of psychological warfare techniques.*

3. *Welles and Wells discussed the broadcast in an October 28, 1940, radio program. Both expressed surprise at the response.*

•• • ••

Milton Berle

Milton Berle (1908–2002) was one of the twentieth century's most popular comedians and actors, and he is best known as television's first major star. His first show, *Texaco Star Theater,* which debuted on NBC in 1948, was a runaway success and is credited with popularizing the fledgling medium.

Berle was born Milton Berlinger and worked in show business for almost his entire life. After he won a Charlie Chaplin (1889–1977) look-alike contest as a boy, his mother pushed him toward a career as a performer. He appeared in silent films shot in and around New York City, and at age ten, he joined a traveling children's vaudeville act.

He became a star of vaudeville and Broadway and also performed in Hollywood films and on the radio. But he became a superstar, known as Uncle Miltie and Mr. Television, after he transitioned to the budding medium in 1948. His zany antics (most notably dressing like a woman and blacking out his front teeth) were a sensation with television viewers. The show was similar to his nightclub and vaudeville act in that he would do some comedy, introduce guest stars, allow them to perform, and then interact with the guests.

Berle's impact was seismic: According to *Life* magazine, in 1947 there were 136,000 television sets in use, and by the end of 1948, there were 700,000. After only two months on the air, his show was so popular that it was the only program not pre-empted during coverage of the 1948 presidential election.

In 1951, he signed an unprecedented thirty-year contract with NBC (which paid him $200,000 annually), but in 1953, with his popularity waning, Texaco pulled its sponsorship of the show. Subsequent attempts failed to bring Berle back to the top of the ratings.

For the rest of his career, Berle appeared in Hollywood films and made guest appearances on a variety of television programs. He also continued to perform at nightclubs and in benefit shows.

In 1984, he was one of seven pioneers inducted into the Academy of Television Arts and Sciences Hall of Fame. He died of colon cancer at age ninety-three.

ADDITIONAL FACTS

1. *Many comedians accused Berle of stealing jokes, and gossip columnist Walter Winchell (1897–1972) famously called him the Thief of Bad Gags. Berle used this reputation as part of his comedy persona.*

2. *Berle was active with the Friars Club, a fraternal association made up mostly of entertainers. He often served as master of ceremonies for the group's famous roasts.*

3. *Two of Berle's trademarks were his ever-present cigar and the opening line from* Texaco Star Theater: *"Good evening, ladies and germs."*

•••••

William Faulkner

William Faulkner (1897–1962) was the foremost literary chronicler of the American South during a painful, difficult time in the region's history—the period between the Civil War and the civil rights era, when racial tensions simmered, the economy faltered, and the old southern aristocracy faded into irrelevance.

Faulkner himself was a product of the old South: His family dated back generations in Mississippi, counting politicians and Civil War heroes among its ranks. Though an unmotivated student, Faulkner loved reading; by his teens, he had started to try his hand at writing poems and stories. During the 1920s, while traveling and working at various odd jobs, he dreamed up the fictional setting—Yoknapatawpha County, Mississippi—that would form the landscape for most of his works.

Faulkner's first major novel, *The Sound and the Fury* (1929), is generally regarded as his masterpiece. A tale about the fall of a once-storied southern family into moral and financial ruin, the novel introduced readers to Faulkner's masterful stream-of-consciousness prose—his attempt to record characters' thoughts exactly and completely, often in jumbled fashion. In several more landmark novels—*As I Lay Dying* (1930), *Light in August* (1932), and *Absalom, Absalom!* (1936)—Faulkner continued to explore the collapse of the old South and its struggle to reconcile itself with the modern world.

Rife with lengthy sentences, unreliable narrators, and stories that unfold without any semblance of chronological order, Faulkner's novels are generally not easy reads. Nonetheless, they tell poignant, unforgettable stories and explore the ghosts of the South's past with lyricism and piercing insight. Though most of the crises that the South faced in Faulkner's day are now long gone, his works still serve as stark reminders of the lingering power of the past to shape the circumstances of the present.

ADDITIONAL FACTS

1. *In the summer of 2005, Oprah picked not one but three Faulkner novels*—The Sound and the Fury, As I Lay Dying, *and* Light in August—*as her book club's reading selection.*

2. *Faulkner was preoccupied with the past's unending effect on the present. One of his most famous lines, from his 1951 play* Requiem for a Nun, *reads, "The past is never dead. It's not even past."*

3. *In addition to his novels, Faulkner also had a somewhat incongruous career as a Hollywood screenwriter. In 1946, he adapted the famous Raymond Chandler (1888–1959) novel* The Big Sleep *(1939) into the now-classic film starring Humphrey Bogart (1899–1957) and Lauren Bacall (1924–).*

••●••

Glenn Miller

Though never a critical favorite, Glenn Miller (1904–1944) was one of the best-selling jazz artists of the swing era. To this day, many of his hits, especially his signature tune "Moonlight Serenade" (1939), are some of the most recognizable big-band arrangements of the World War II era in American music.

When the Iowa-born Miller began his musical career, he had dreams of becoming a great trombone soloist, and he did play for a number of big bands throughout the 1920s and early 1930s. His early career included stints alongside legends such as clarinetist Benny Goodman (1909–1986) and drummer Gene Krupa (1909–1973), as well as a brief period under the tutelage of Dorsey brothers Jimmy (1904–1957) and Tommy (1905–1956). He also earned a spot in the pit orchestra for George Gershwin's hit musical *Girl Crazy* (1930).

Despite his dedication, however, Miller felt that he never achieved the trombone virtuosity of some of his contemporaries, including Will Bradley (1912–1989) and Jack "Big T" Teagarden (1905–1964).

Indeed, Miller's success came not in performing but in arranging. He started his first orchestra in 1937, and it was a flop. But he tried again in 1938, and this time his band was a huge success. The second Glenn Miller Orchestra perfected the "Miller sound": a solo clarinet playing high notes over tenor saxophones, a unique arrangement that Miller used to produce hit after hit, including "In the Mood" (1939), "Tuxedo Junction" (1940), and the classic "Moonlight Serenade."

Miller led his orchestra until 1942, when he joined the Army Air Corps and was commissioned as a captain. He first led military bands in the United States but had the group transferred to London in 1943 so he could be closer to combat troops.

On December 15, 1944, Miller boarded a plane bound for Paris, where he was to perform for Allied soldiers who had just liberated the city. The plane disappeared in bad weather over the English Channel, and Miller's body was never found.

ADDITIONAL FACTS

1. *James Stewart (1908–1997) played Miller in the 1953 film* The Glenn Miller Story.

2. *Three "ghost bands" named the Glenn Miller Orchestra, officially sanctioned by the Miller estate, still perform today. One group is in the United States, one in Europe, and one in South Africa.*

3. *Miller's first instrument was a mandolin he received as a gift. He quickly traded it in for his signature trombone.*

••••

The Wizard of Oz (1939)

"Toto, I've got a feeling we're not in Kansas anymore."
—Judy Garland, as Dorothy Gale

With its unique combination of fantasy, music, comedy, suspense, and special effects, *The Wizard of Oz* is one of the most beloved films in movie history. Just about everything in the film has entered American folklore, from the Yellow Brick Road to Dorothy's dog, Toto, to classic lines of dialogue like "There's no place like home."

The film is an adaptation of the 1900 novel by L. Frank Baum (1856–1919) and features some of the most recognizable songs in American pop culture. Judy Garland (1922–1969) stars as Dorothy Gale, an orphan living on a farm in Kansas who wants to run away from home with Toto to escape the torment of her hateful neighbor. During a tornado, Dorothy is hit on the head and knocked unconscious, and in her dream state, she and Toto are transported by the twister to a land of witches, munchkins, and other strange characters: the merry old land of Oz.

Essentially, the film's plot is a lost child's quest to return home, and Dorothy's journey involves a series of often-terrifying trials. Fortunately for Dorothy, she befriends the Scarecrow (Ray Bolger), the Cowardly Lion (Bert Lahr), and the Tin Man (Jack Haley), who accompany her on her trek—and she helps them fulfill their desires as well.

Although Judy Garland went on to have a legendary career, Dorothy (whom she played at age sixteen) remained her best-known role. Several of her songs became standards, particularly "Over the Rainbow," which a poll by the American Film Institute in 2004 named the top movie song in history.

One of the noteworthy special effects occurs when Dorothy first lands in Oz—the images change from sepia-toned black and white to Technicolor. *The Wizard of Oz* and *Gone with the Wind* (1939), which was also an MGM production, dramatically helped to popularize color pictures in Hollywood.

ADDITIONAL FACTS

1. *Four directors contributed to the production, though Victor Fleming (1889–1949)—who left the film to work on* Gone with the Wind—*is officially credited with leading the film. Richard Thorpe (1886–1991), George Cukor (1889–1983), and King Vidor (1894–1982) also directed some parts.*

2. *The film was nominated for six Academy Awards and won two—for Best Song ("Over the Rainbow," by Harold Arlen and E. Y. Harburg) and Best Original Score (Herbert Stothart). Judy Garland also received an honorary Oscar for her performance.*

3. *When the film was released, it was not a commercial success, barely recouping its cost of $2.8 million.*

•••••

Plastics

In 1907, a Belgian-born chemist named Leo Baekeland (1863–1944) mixed two chemicals, phenol and formaldehyde, to create the world's first synthetic plastic. He called his sticky, amber-colored concoction Bakelite—and so the age of plastics was born.

Attempts to create a synthetic plastic dated back to the nineteenth century. A plastic is a material that can be molded into different shapes when exposed to pressure or heat; scientists like Baekeland hoped to invent a substance that could be used in place of rare natural plastics such as shellac and amber.

To create Bakelite, he mixed the two chemicals and subjected them to high heat and pressure. The resulting substance was heat-resistant, did not conduct electricity, and held its shape.

Soon, the invention was put to use to coat electrical wiring and to make toys, knife handles, radios, and even jewelry. During the plastics craze of the 1920s, the new material became widely available as a replacement for many animal-derived materials in goods such as combs and utensils.

With the success of Bakelite, other scientists rushed to develop their own plastics. Nylon, an improved form of plastic, was introduced in 1939.

The availability of plastics proved invaluable to the Allies during World War II; it was used for aircraft parts, as lids for soldiers' canteens, and even in the equipment needed to build the atomic bomb.

After the war, chemical companies began marketing a new generation of plastics to the general public. Tupperware, one of the most famous plastic products, debuted in 1946.

The 1960s saw a backlash against plastics, when the word became synonymous with materialism and the superficiality of American culture. More recently, environmentalists have objected to the heavy toll the manufacture of synthetic plastics takes on the environment.

ADDITIONAL FACTS

1. *Cellophane, another early plastic, owes its inception to a spilled bottle of wine. In 1913, Jacques Edwin Brandenberger (1872–1954), a Swiss engineer, set out to develop a flexible, protective coating for fabrics after witnessing a customer spill wine on a tablecloth in a restaurant. His discovery was too brittle for fabric but excellent for packaging.*

2. *Plastics take centuries to decompose. In 2005, plastic found in the stomach of an albatross had a serial number from a plane shot down in World War II.*

3. *One of the most popular Disneyland attractions from 1957 to 1967, the Monsanto House of the Future, was made almost entirely of plastic and showed what life would be like in the unimaginable year of 1987.*

•••••

Gordie Howe

He's called Mr. Hockey, and until Wayne Gretzky (1961–) came along in the late 1970s, Gordie Howe (1928–) was widely considered the greatest hockey player ever.

A tough, physical player, Howe distinguished himself with his deft scoring touch, his powerful fists, and his unprecedented longevity. He played a remarkable thirty-two professional seasons, from his debut at age eighteen with the Detroit Red Wings in 1946 until his retirement at age fifty-two in 1980. (He retired for two seasons before returning in 1973.)

Howe's high level of play for so many years may never be topped in the National Hockey League (NHL) or any other sport. His accolades are numerous—in the NHL, he was a six-time Most Valuable Player, led the league in scoring six times, won the Stanley Cup four times, and retired as the league's career leader in a variety of categories, including goals and points.

Gretzky has since taken Howe's scoring records, but Howe still has played in more games than any other player and compiled more points than any other right wing in hockey history.

After twenty-five seasons in Detroit, Howe retired in 1971. But two years later, he was offered the chance to play alongside his sons, Mark and Marty, for the Houston Aeros of the World Hockey Association (WHA), an upstart league that was a competitor of the NHL.

He played in Houston for four years (winning two league championships and one league MVP award) and for the New England Whalers for two years.

In 1979, the WHA and NHL merged, and Howe played his final season for the newly renamed Hartford Whalers. Though he turned fifty-two that year, he still played in all eighty games and made his twenty-third NHL all-star-game appearance—alongside nineteen-year-old Gretzky: Mr. Hockey handing the baton to the Great One.

ADDITIONAL FACTS

1. *Howe retired with 2,589 points on 1,071 goals and 1,518 assists (including WHA and playoffs). His NHL regular-season marks of 801 goals and 1,850 points were broken by Gretzky.*

2. *Howe almost died during the 1950 playoffs—he crashed headfirst into the boards during Detroit's series with Toronto, suffering a fractured skull and brain damage. He was put on the hospital's critical list but recovered after surgery to relieve pressure on his brain.*

3. *Howe played in his sixth decade in 1997, appearing in one game for the International Hockey League's Detroit Vipers.*

•••••

The Slinky

In 1943, at the height of World War II, a Pennsylvania engineer named Richard James (1914–1975) was working in his home laboratory on an obscure but crucial military issue. Because navy ships often navigated through rough seas, they needed elaborate measures to stabilize onboard instruments. James attempted to solve this problem by anchoring these instruments to a system of sensitive springs that would react to the turbulence while keeping the instruments level.

While at work one day, James accidentally dropped one of his springs and watched it smoothly step from his shelf to a stack of books to a tabletop and on down to the floor, where it coiled back into a perfect cylinder. James's thoughts immediately shifted from the war effort to the toy store. He shared the idea with his wife, Betty, and she came up with a name for the gizmo: the Slinky.

A Slinky is manufactured by coiling sixty-seven feet of steel wire, a process that James's first machines could complete in almost ten seconds. With the exception of smoothing the sharp ends, the toy hasn't changed since the first models were sold in 1945. James couldn't convince any toy sellers to purchase his idea, so he manufactured and sold Slinkys himself, beginning with a sale of 400 units to the Gimbels department store. James died in 1974, but by 1995, James Industries had sold more than a quarter-billion Slinkys.

In addition to being toys, Slinkys have often served educational purposes, especially to demonstrate the properties of waves in seismology, the study of earthquakes. NASA even uses the toy for experiments aboard the space shuttle—bringing the Slinky back full circle to its scientific origins.

ADDITIONAL FACTS

1. *Like the Slinky, Silly Putty has its origins in World War II–era scientific research, when the substance was considered as a possible substitute for rubber.*

2. *During the Vietnam War, American troops used Slinkys to construct primitive shortwave radios.*

3. *In 1960, James left his company and family and joined a Bolivian religious cult.*

• • ● • •

Dwight D. Eisenhower

Following his success as the top American general during World War II, both Democratic and Republican Party leaders tried to persuade General Dwight D. Eisenhower (1890–1969) to run for president. In 1952, the GOP prevailed.

Eisenhower's homespun manner and outstanding military credentials made him one of the most popular and respected men in the United States. After winning a tight contest for the Republican presidential nomination over Ohio senator Robert Taft (1889–1953), he trounced Democratic nominee, Adlai Stevenson (1900–1965), to become the country's thirty-fourth president.

While in the White House, Eisenhower focused on balancing the budget, bringing an end to the Korean War (1950–1953), improving relations with the Soviet Union, and working toward world peace. He generally shied away from bold political moves and as a result, achieved few major legislative accomplishments.

Eisenhower sought to relax tensions with the Soviet Union and was, at times, successful. In 1955, Soviet leaders rebuffed—but appreciated—his proposal to allow reciprocal aerial inspections between the United States and the Soviet Union.

But in 1960, the downing of an American U-2 spy plane flying over the Soviet Union led to the deterioration of relations between the two sides. Eisenhower took responsibility for the incident, but Soviet premier Nikita Khrushchev (1894–1971) boycotted that year's highly anticipated Paris peace talks.

On the domestic front, Eisenhower largely continued the policies of his Democratic predecessors, maintaining most New Deal and Fair Deal programs. He oversaw the creation of the Interstate Highway System in 1956, and a year later, he sent troops into Little Rock, Arkansas, to ensure that local authorities would comply with the federal law to desegregate schools.

Eisenhower's legacy received a significant blow when his handpicked successor, Vice President Richard M. Nixon (1913–1994), lost his 1960 bid for the presidency to Senator John F. Kennedy (1917–1963).

After leaving the White House, Eisenhower retired to his home in Gettysburg, Pennsylvania, where he wrote his memoirs and acted as an elder statesman. He died at age seventy-eight.

ADDITIONAL FACTS

1. *Following World War II, Eisenhower was president of Columbia University and also took command of the new NATO military force put together in 1950.*

2. *Eisenhower had two major health scares while in the White House. In 1955, he suffered a heart attack that kept him in the hospital for seven weeks, and in 1957 he experienced a mild stroke.*

3. *Eisenhower was the first president to be limited to two White House terms by the Twenty-Second Amendment, which was ratified in 1951.*

••••

Brave New World

Whereas many dystopian novels have depicted political systems gone awry, *Brave New World* (1932), by the British author Aldous Huxley (1894–1963), illuminated the dangers of unchecked scientific and technological progress decades before they became a reality. Prophetic even today, the novel presaged a number of still-unresolved ethical dilemmas surrounding eugenics, pharmaceuticals, psychiatry, stem cell research, and other controversial fields of biotechnology.

Taking its name from a line in Shakespeare's *The Tempest,* Huxley's novel is set in England during the twenty-sixth century. Natural childbirth is a thing of the past: Instead, the government operates an extensive system of hatcheries in which human embryos are farmed. Even before birth, humans are rigidly separated according to a caste system: Some embryos are pampered and meticulously cared for, while others are exposed to toxic chemicals and harsh temperatures so that their capabilities are stunted. The former end up at the top of society, in positions of power, while the latter reside at the bottom, as menial laborers. This conditioning continues by means of social segregation, indoctrination, and administration of antidepressants during each person's formative years, leaving free will out of the picture.

Brave New World also criticizes industrialization—particularly American-style mass production—which Huxley felt had damaged society. He intended the novel as a warning and, looking back on it decades later, expressed his belief that his predictions were being borne out. Nonetheless, the novel was not particularly well received upon publication, and only in the past few decades has it become regarded as a classic.

Although *Brave New World* is not without literary merit, its primary influence has been as a pioneering work of science fiction and dystopian literature. Later authors extended Huxley's dystopian vision with novels as varied as Ray Bradbury's *Fahrenheit 451* (1953), Stephen King's *The Running Man* (1982), and P. D. James's *The Children of Men* (1992).

ADDITIONAL FACTS

1. *Huxley came from a family that included a number of prominent biologists, and he would have studied medicine if not for an eye condition that left him nearly blind by his late teens.*

2. *During the decade following his publication of* Brave New World, *Huxley became fascinated by Hinduism, vegetarianism, and meditation. He even wrote a book about Eastern mysticism called* The Perennial Philosophy *(1944).*

3. *In his later years, Huxley experimented extensively with hallucinogenic drugs, and many of his writings on the subject inspired members of the 1960s hippie counterculture; the rock band the Doors, for instance, took their name from Huxley's drug-fueled 1954 book* The Doors of Perception.

•●●•

Woody Guthrie

Folksinger Woody Guthrie's most famous song, "This Land Is Your Land" (1940), is often played alongside Irving Berlin's "God Bless America" (1938) at Fourth of July celebrations. Guthrie's song has so many verses that many listeners don't notice its seething, angry lyrics:

> *In the shadow of the steeple I saw my people*
> *By the relief office I seen my people;*
> *As they stood there hungry, I stood there asking*
> *Is this land made for you and me?*

The song, composed in 1940, was actually written as a retort to Berlin's upbeat patriotic tune, which Guthrie found trite and sappy at a time when millions of Americans were unemployed.

An Oklahoma native, Woodrow Wilson Guthrie (1912–1967) became a dust-bowl refugee during the Great Depression. He hoboed, hitchhiked, and according to one report, actually walked to California looking for work. Affected by his wanderings, Guthrie was deeply sympathetic to plight of the American worker. Guthrie eventually settled in New York City, where he was involved with progressive politics and collaborated with musicians such as Huddie "Lead Belly" Ledbetter (1889–1949), Pete Seeger (1919–), and Burl Ives (1909–1995). During World War II, Guthrie rallied the troops with historic ballads and anti-Nazi songs, and adorned his guitar with the phrase "This Machine Kills Fascists."

Plagued by Huntington's disease for the last fifteen years of his life, Guthrie spent his final years in terrible pain in hospitals in New York and New Jersey. He lived just long enough to receive a visit at his bedside from one of his biggest fans, the young folksinger Bob Dylan (1941–).

Profoundly egalitarian and deeply patriotic, Guthrie's vast canon of music ranges from the political to the silly. He performed his own songs and evoked the voice of the common man with his direct and crackled vocals. He favored a simple style, considering ornate musical composition indulgent and bourgeois. An inspiration to new folkies such as Dylan, Joni Mitchell (1943–), Joan Baez (1941–), and eventually Bruce Springsteen (1949–), Guthrie is credited with laying the foundation for the American folk revival of the 1960s.

ADDITIONAL FACTS

1. *Woody's son, Arlo Guthrie (1947–), released his iconic antiwar protest song "Alice's Restaurant" a month after Woody passed away in 1967.*

2. *Woody's ashes were spread off the coast of Coney Island, the last place he lived in New York City.*

3. *The band Wilco collaborated with British songwriter Billy Bragg (1957–) to release much of Guthrie's previously unreleased material on the 1998 album* Mermaid Avenue *(both the title of a Guthrie tune and a street name in Brooklyn).*

•••••

Gone with the Wind (1939)

In its time—and for decades afterward—*Gone with the Wind* (1939) was considered one of the greatest American films ever made. After a two-year buildup, it caused a sensation across the country when it was released, becoming the biggest box office hit of all time. In fact, adjusted for inflation, it remains the most successful film in history ($1.3 billion in adjusted domestic box office gross).

The historical epic is a nostalgic look at the old South, focusing on the life and loves of Scarlett O'Hara (played by the British actress Vivien Leigh, 1913–1967) before, during, and after the Civil War. Her ill-fated relationship with Rhett Butler (Clark Gable) is one of the great romances in Hollywood history and provides one of the most unforgettable lines of dialogue uttered on screen. According to an American Film Institute poll, Rhett's line spurning Scarlett, "Frankly, my dear, I don't give a damn," is the most memorable in American film history.

The film won ten Academy Awards (including two special awards), a record that stood for two decades, until *Ben-Hur* (1959) claimed eleven Oscars. Among its major awards: Best Picture, Best Director (Victor Fleming), Best Actress (Leigh), Best Supporting Actress (Hattie McDaniel), and Best Screenplay (Sidney Howard, who received the first posthumous award in Oscar history).

Gone with the Wind's performance was especially noteworthy considering that many critics believe 1939 to be Hollywood's finest year. Other releases that year included *The Wizard of Oz; Mr. Smith Goes to Washington; Stagecoach; Wuthering Heights; Goodbye, Mr. Chips;* and a long list of others.

The lavish production cost more than $4 million and was lauded for the authenticity of its costumes and sets. Five directors contributed, though Victor Fleming was the only one to receive a directing credit.

From its original theatrical release through its seven subsequent rereleases (the most recent in 1998), *Gone with the Wind* has brought in $198 million in the United States and more than $400 million worldwide. It has sold more tickets than any film in history, was at one time the most-watched feature film in US television history, and remains one of Hollywood's most beloved epics.

ADDITIONAL FACTS

1. *The film is based on the novel of the same name by Margaret Mitchell (1900–1949). In 1936, producer David O. Selznick (1902–1965) bought the rights to book, paying a record sum of $50,000.*

2. *Casting the role of Scarlett proved to be difficult, with estimates of the number of actresses considered reaching 1,400. Ultimately, the only contenders to receive color screen tests were Leigh, Paulette Goddard, and two other actresses, and Leigh got the role.*

3. *Only four men were considered for the role of Rhett Butler. Gable was Selznick's first choice, but contractual conflicts made Gary Cooper (1901–1961) the early front-runner. Cooper turned down the role, and after Gable signed on, Cooper was famously quoted as saying, "Gone with the Wind is going to be the biggest flop in Hollywood history. I'm glad it'll be Clark Gable who's falling flat on his nose, not Gary Cooper."*

•• ● ••

Penicillin

Sometimes called the most important scientific innovation of the second millennium, the medicine penicillin has saved an estimated 200 million lives since its discovery in 1928. The drug has been used to cure previously debilitating diseases such as tuberculosis, leprosy, and gonorrhea, and it inspired the creation of a class of powerful medicines known as antibiotics.

Alexander Fleming

The first penicillin was created by a Scottish scientist, Alexander Fleming (1881–1955), using a type of mold called penicillium. In experiments at his hospital in London, Fleming noticed that the drug inhibited the spread of bacteria, tiny organisms that can cause a host of diseases.

At first, no one realized penicillin's importance; it was not used to treat a human until 1939. That year, Howard Walter Florey (1898–1968) and Ernst Boris Chain (1906–1979) tested the effects of penicillin on human diseases, leading the Nobel committee to award the 1945 prize for medicine jointly to Fleming, Florey, and Chain.

The effects of penicillin were perhaps most noticeable on a grand scale during World War II. In earlier conflicts such as the American Civil War and World War I, doctors were forced to treat infections with crude medicines like strychnine and arsenic—compounds that sometimes helped patients but also had toxic effects on the human body. Penicillin had no major side effects and saved the lives of thousands of Allied fighters.

The drug was not without its problems. Penicillin was extremely difficult to mass-produce, and scientists during World War II reportedly grew so desperate they asked neighbors to save kitchen mold to use in penicillin production.

After the war, scientists discovered quicker ways to manufacture penicillin and also invented new types of antibiotics. Penicillin remains the most widely used antibiotic to date and is still prescribed for certain classes of infections.

ADDITIONAL FACTS

1. *Fleming's discovery was an accident: He reportedly left a window open in his lab, which allowed an airborne fungus to contaminate a tray of bacteria cultures.*

2. *Many ancient civilizations, including the ancient Egyptians, Greeks, and Chinese, used molds and plants to treat infections. However, healers in these cultures did not know the reason for the effectiveness of these "homegrown" remedies.*

3. *The chemical formula for penicillin is $C_{16}H_{18}N_2O_4S$.*

•●●•

Red Auerbach

Known for his keen eye for talent, his pugnacity, and his victory cigars, basketball coach Arnold "Red" Auerbach (1917–2006) built the Boston Celtics into one of the greatest dynasties in the history of American professional sports.

From the time he signed on as head coach of the Celtics in 1950 until his death in 2006, Auerbach presided over sixteen National Basketball Association (NBA) championship teams: nine as head coach, six as general manager, and one as team president. From 1959 to 1966, the Celtics won eight consecutive NBA championships, a streak unmatched in American professional sports history.

Auerbach was also a trailblazer in terms of racial equality in the NBA. He was the first to draft a black player, Chuck Cooper (1926–1984) in 1950; the first to unveil a starting lineup of five black players, in the 1963–1964 season; and the first to hire a black coach, Bill Russell (1934–) in 1966.

His ability to recognize talent allowed him to pull off the series of trades and draft picks that made the Celtics so successful. He coached eleven Hall of Fame players and acquired several others as general manager, but his style was always to emphasize team play over individuality. Among the Hall of Famers he coached or acquired were Russell, Bob Cousy (1928–), Tom Heinsohn (1934–), Larry Bird (1956–), Kevin McHale (1957–), Bill Sharman (1926–), and John Havlicek (1940–).

Like his basketball acumen, Auerbach's victory cigars, which he often lit on the court before the game was over, were also legendary. His cockiness infuriated opposing players, coaches, and sometimes owners as well: Before a game in 1957, a confrontation with St. Louis Hawks owner Ben Kerner ended when Auerbach punched him in the mouth.

Auerbach died of a heart attack at age eighty-nine.

ADDITIONAL FACTS

1. *When he retired as coach before the 1966–1967 season, Auerbach had the most wins in the regular season (938) and playoffs (99) of any coach in NBA history. (Both records have since fallen.)*

2. *In 1985, the Celtics retired number 2 in Auerbach's honor. (He was deemed the second-most-important man in the franchise's history, after owner Walter Brown, for whom the Celtics retired number 1.)*

3. *The trophy given to the winner of the NBA Coach of the Year award is named for Auerbach.*

•••••

The Howdy Doody Show

Before there were Saturday morning cartoons, there was *The Howdy Doody Show.* Originally a radio program called *The Triple B Ranch,* the program made the transition to television on NBC in December 1947, becoming one of the first children's shows on the new medium.

At the time of its premiere, only 20,000 American homes even had a television. By 1960, at the end of its thirteen-year run, more than 2,000 episodes had been produced and versions existed in countries from Canada to Cuba.

Set in Doodyville, an imaginary town in Texas, the show began with its famous question, "Hey, kids, what time is it?" The peanut gallery of children in the audience would respond, "It's Howdy Doody time!" Howdy Doody, voiced by Buffalo Bob Smith (1917–1998), was a redheaded boy puppet with a freckle for every state in the Union (forty-eight at the time). Curmudgeonly mayor Phineas T. Bluster, Dilly Dally, and Flub-a-Dub were among the other Doodyville marionettes who lived side by side with live characters like Chief Thunderthud and Princess Summerfall Winterspring in the fictional town. The songs and stories were interspersed with the slapstick antics of Clarabell, a live mute clown armed with a seltzer bottle. The most famous moment of the show belonged to Clarabell, who broke his silence in the last seconds of the series to bid the kids farewell.

The show marked a number of TV firsts. *Howdy Doody* was one of the first network series to be shown in color; the first show on NBC to run five days a week; and one of the first, through split-screen technology, to connect characters in different parts of the country.

More significant still was the marketing potential the program exposed. In 1948, Howdy ran for "president of all kids" and offered free campaign buttons to viewers at home. About 60,000 children responded, and advertising space sold out. Products by sponsors such as Colgate-Palmolive-Peet were heavily marketed within the show, and after 1948, articles of Howdy Doody merchandise including records, comic books, and windup toys became bestsellers.

ADDITIONAL FACTS

1. *Three Howdy Doody puppets were used throughout the show's production: Howdy Doody for close-ups, Double Doody for long shots, and Photo Doody for still photos.*

2. *Bob Smith got the name Buffalo Bob because he was from Buffalo, New York.*

3. *The show was called* Puppet Playhouse *when it debuted, but the name was changed to* The Howdy Doody Show *within a week.*

•••••

Nikita Khrushchev

Soviet leader Nikita Khrushchev (1894–1971) is often remembered for his flamboyant and sometimes crude public behavior. But as leader of the Soviet Communist Party, he fundamentally altered the political direction of his country and improved Cold War relations with the United States.

Khrushchev, the grandson of a serf and the son of a farmer and coal miner who had little formal education, became first secretary of the Soviet Communist Party after the death of Joseph Stalin (1879–1953). In office, he promoted "peaceful coexistence" with the United States, traveled the world as a spokesman for Soviet policy, and denounced Stalin and the cult of personality.

In particular, Khrushchev's denunciation of the former dictator in his speech to the 20th Congress of the Communist Party of the Soviet Union in February 1956 was a dramatic moment in the country's history. It marked the beginning of the so-called "thaw" with the West, led to thousands of Stalin's victims being rehabilitated, and allowed criticism of Stalin to appear in print.

But Khrushchev also violently put down a Hungarian revolt in 1956, instigated the Cuban Missile Crisis in 1962, and openly quarreled with fellow Communist leader Mao Zedong (1893–1976) of China. He also failed to deliver on economic and agricultural promises to the people of the Soviet Union and embarrassed other prominent Soviet leaders with his boorish public conduct.

In 1964, conservative Soviet leaders orchestrated Khrushchev's ouster and brought the country to the right with his replacement, Leonid Brezhnev (1906–1982). But the legacy of Khrushchev's "thaw" would be felt again during the 1980s under the more liberal leadership of Mikhail Gorbachev (1931–), who ultimately oversaw the dismantling of the Soviet empire.

After his removal from office, Krushchev live in virtual isolation for the final seven years of his life. He died at age 77 of a heart attack.

ADDITIONAL FACTS

1. *The most notorious example of Khrushchev's rude public behavior occurred in 1960 at the United Nations, during a speech by Filipino delegate Lorenzo Sumulong (1905–1997). Khrushchev removed his right shoe and began banging it on the table, calling Sumulong "a jerk, a stooge, and a lackey of imperialism."*

2. *One of Khrushchev's most famous quotes was uttered to a group of Western diplomats, in reference to capitalism: "We will bury you."*

3. *Khrushchev's noted "kitchen debate" with Vice President Richard Nixon (1913–1994) in 1959 had no practical impact on the Cold War. But because of Nixon's forceful defense of capitalism in the face of the Soviet leader, the vice president's prestige increased dramatically in advance of his presidential race with John F. Kennedy (1917–1963).*

•••••

Ernest Hemingway

Over a career spanning four decades, Ernest Hemingway (1899–1961) created a body of novels and short stories whose style had enormous influence over later twentieth-century authors. Though Hemingway's spare, bare-bones prose was often parodied, it appealed to readers and earned him the Nobel Prize for Literature in 1954.

The Illinois-born Hemingway began in journalism, working as a reporter in Kansas City, Missouri. When the United States entered World War I, he served as an ambulance driver in Italy and then stayed in Europe after the war to live among a community of expatriate American writers in Paris. Comprised of Ezra Pound (1885–1972), F. Scott Fitzgerald (1896–1940), John Dos Passos (1896–1970), and others, this group—which Gertrude Stein (1874–1946) later termed the Lost Generation—created a rich outpouring of literature during the 1920s.

The Sun Also Rises (1926), Hemingway's first significant success, is set among this community of dissipated American expatriates in France and Spain. *A Farewell to Arms* (1929) and *For Whom the Bell Tolls* (1940), two tragic wartime love stories, stemmed from Hemingway's experiences during World War I and the Spanish civil war, respectively. His later masterpiece, *The Old Man and the Sea* (1952), tells a moving parable about an elderly fisherman. Over the course of these works, Hemingway developed a distinctive prose style, featuring repetitive, unadorned sentences in which the spaces between words—what is not said—are as important as what is said.

Hemingway's works attracted renown—and at times mockery—for the overt, self-conscious masculinity of their subject matter. Indeed, the majority of them feature stoic male protagonists, many engaged in endeavors such as war, bullfighting, boxing, and hunting. Hemingway's legendary globetrotting lifestyle—including everything from safaris in Africa to big-game fishing in Cuba—supported this reputation. Nonetheless, crippling depression set in during Hemingway's later years, and after a period of declining health, he took his own life in 1961.

ADDITIONAL FACTS

1. *The posthumously published* A Moveable Feast *(1964), a loosely nonfictional, beautifully written account of Hemingway's years amid the Paris café culture of the 1920s, shows a side of Hemingway's writing different from the unbridled machismo of most of his works.*

2. *Hemingway's house in Key West, Florida, now a tourist attraction, is overrun by six-toed cats who are allegedly descendants of a cat that Hemingway received as a gift in the 1930s.*

3. *The British novelist Graham Greene (1904–1991) once praised Hemingway's style by saying, "It was as though Hemingway had put words into a sieve and shaken the sieve, and from the sieve fell all the unnecessary adjectives and adverbs."*

•••••

Muddy Waters

Born in the heart of Mississippi's Delta region, the birthplace of the blues, singer and guitarist Muddy Waters (McKinley Morganfield, 1915–1983) played harmonica and guitar from a young age. But he couldn't earn enough by performing at small parties to eke out a living at it, so he also supported himself in his youth by making moonshine, illegally distilled whiskey.

Waters did not begin recording his songs until 1941, and his first records were not commercial. That year, Library of Congress archivist Alan Lomax (1915–2002) met Waters in Stovall, Mississippi, and taped some of his songs for the library's American Folk Song collection. Lomax sent Waters a copy of their session as a memento, and Waters was amazed at how good he sounded. At that moment, he decided to devote his life to playing and recording blues music.

A few years later, Waters moved to Chicago, where he became one of the founders of Chicago blues, an influential style distinctive for its heavy, wailing backbeats.

Waters received his first electric guitar soon after moving to Chicago and was one of the first musicians to make use of what became an iconic American instrument. He released most of his classic records in the 1950s, including "Mannish Boy" (1955), "I Just Want to Make Love to You" (1954), "Got My Mojo Working" (1956), and "I'm Your Hoochie Coochie Man" (1954). His music proved influential to many rock pioneers, including Eric Clapton (1945–) and the band Led Zeppelin, who borrowed heavily from the great bluesman's recordings. A pivotal figure in the history of modern music, Waters died in 1983.

ADDITIONAL FACTS

1. *Waters's 1948 song "Rollin' Stone" lent its name to both the band the Rolling Stones and the magazine* Rolling Stone.

2. *It was Waters who helped rocker Chuck Berry (1926–) secure his first deal with Chess Records. Leonard Chess (1917–1969) was hesitant at first to release Berry's "Maybellene" (1955), but Waters convinced him, and it became one of the label's biggest hits.*

3. *During his time in Chicago, Waters carried on a fierce rivalry with the bluesman Chester A. Burnett—better known as Howlin' Wolf (1910–1976)—whom many considered the only comparable performer.*

• • ● • •

James Stewart

Jimmy Stewart (1908–1997) is perhaps the most adored American screen actor of the twentieth century, particularly for his idealistic roles of the 1930s and 1940s. A tall, gangly man, Stewart earned a degree in architecture from Princeton but soon found his calling as a professional actor. After a stint onstage, he went to Hollywood, making his film debut in *The Murder Man* (1935).

Stewart became a star on the strength of two Frank Capra films: *You Can't Take It with You* (1938), which won the Academy Award for Best Picture, and *Mr. Smith Goes to Washington* (1939). The latter film is arguably Stewart's finest performance, earning him his first Academy Award nomination for Best Actor. Yet Stewart won his only best actor Oscar for his performance in the romantic comedy *The Philadelphia Story* (1940), alongside Katharine Hepburn and Cary Grant.

Stewart's film career was put on hold in March 1941 when he enlisted in the US Army Air Corps. He flew twenty combat missions during World War II, advancing from private to colonel—and eventually achieving the rank of brigadier general in the US Air Force Reserve.

Stewart's first role after the war was in Capra's *It's a Wonderful Life* (1946), a film that was a box office disappointment at the time but has become an American Christmas tradition on television. He received his third of five Academy Award nominations for *It's a Wonderful Life*—the others were for *Harvey* (1950) and *Anatomy of a Murder* (1959).

After *It's a Wonderful Life*, Stewart's screen persona took on a darker and more mature tone, particularly in thrillers directed by Alfred Hitchcock, including *Rear Window* (1954) and *Vertigo* (1958); and in westerns by Anthony Mann, including *Winchester '73* (1950) and *The Naked Spur* (1953). Stewart also costarred with John Wayne in the critically acclaimed John Ford western *The Man Who Shot Liberty Valance* (1962).

Stewart received an honorary Oscar in 1985, twelve years before his death from a heart attack and a pulmonary embolism at age eighty-nine.

ADDITIONAL FACTS

1. *Stewart costarred in two films that won the Academy Award for Best Picture*—You Can't Take It with You *and* The Greatest Show on Earth *(1952).*

2. *After winning an Oscar for* The Philadelphia Story, *Stewart sent the statue to his father, who displayed the award in the front window of his hardware store in Indiana, Pennsylvania.*

3. *Stewart starred in 5 of the top 100 American films as determined by the American Film Institute*—It's a Wonderful Life *(number 11),* Mr. Smith Goes to Washington *(29),* Rear Window *(42),* The Philadelphia Story *(51), and* Vertigo *(61). Only Robert De Niro (1943–) starred in as many films in the top 100 as Stewart.*

•••••

The America First Committee

In 1940, a student at Yale University started a peace group called the America First Committee with a single aim: to keep the United States out of the fighting in World War II.

The war had begun in 1939, when Nazi Germany invaded Poland in a lightning strike called the blitzkrieg. France and Great Britain, Poland's allies, then declared war on Germany and fascist Italy.

For many Americans, the war in Europe stirred tragic memories of World War I, in which 116,000 American soldiers had lost their lives in brutal trench warfare. A strong pacifist and isolationist movement had emerged in the 1930s, hoping to keep the United States out of the next European conflict.

Indeed, isolationism may have enjoyed higher levels of popular support in the United States in the 1930s than at any other point in the twentieth century. Beginning in 1935, Congress passed a series of Neutrality Acts designed to prevent the country from taking sides in foreign wars.

But many members of the America First Committee also had baser motives. The peace movement contained an anti-Semitic contingent, led by aviator Charles Lindbergh (1902–1974), that admired the Nazis.

Although the committee itself accounted for less than about 1 million Americans, it symbolized Americans' deep reluctance to enter World War II, a mood that hampered efforts by American president Franklin D. Roosevelt (1882–1945) to aid Great Britain and France in the early stages of the war. In 1940 and 1941, Roosevelt managed to provide some aid to Britain, but he won a declaration of war against Germany only after the surprise Japanese attack on Pearl Harbor on December 7, 1941.

The America First Committee disbanded four days after the Pearl Harbor bombing.

ADDITIONAL FACTS

1. *The committee included prominent Democrats and Republicans as well as Norman Thomas (1884–1968), the leader of the Socialist Party.*

2. *Future American president Gerald Ford (1913–2006) was a supporter of the America First Committee while a student at Yale Law School; he later changed his views and volunteered for service in World War II.*

3. *In 2004, American author Philip Roth (1933–) published* The Plot Against America, *a novel depicting a United States in which America First prevailed and Lindbergh was elected president.*

•••••

Willie Mays

Born and raised in Alabama, Willie Mays (1931–) became one of the most celebrated athletes in baseball history. With his combination of speed, power, and enthusiasm, Mays was a beloved center fielder for the New York Giants in the 1950s, and later for the San Francisco Giants after the team moved to the West Coast in 1958.

Mays, nicknamed the Say Hey Kid, was the epitome of the all-around player. He could hit for average and power, run, throw, and field. He finished his career with 3,283 hits and 660 home runs and was a two-time Most Valuable Player, a twenty-four-time all-star, and a twelve-time Gold Glove winner. He also led the Giants to the World Series crown in 1954.

He joined the Giants in 1951, following two years with the Birmingham Black Barons of the Negro League. He struggled at first, recording just one hit in his first twenty-six at bats. But after a pep talk from legendary manager Leo Durocher (1905–1991), Mays caught fire and wound up becoming the National League's Rookie of the Year.

After missing most of the 1952 season and all of 1953 due to his service in the US Army, Mays returned in 1954 and was a sensation—he batted .345 with forty-one home runs and 110 runs batted in en route to his first MVP award and a World Series championship.

He moved with the Giants to San Francisco after the 1957 season, but he was not embraced in California as he had been in New York. It was not for lack of production—in his second MVP season, 1965, he batted .317 with fifty-two home runs and 112 RBIs.

In 1972, the Giants traded Mays to the New York Mets, where he ended his career with an embarrassing performance, falling down in the outfield during the 1973 World Series. He was elected to the Baseball Hall of Fame on the first ballot in 1979.

ADDITIONAL FACTS

1. *Mays was celebrated for his magnificent defensive plays. His most famous catch came during Game 1 of the 1954 World Series. On a deep fly ball off the bat of Vic Wertz (1925–1983) of the Cleveland Indians, Mays made an over-the-shoulder catch at a dead run in center field at the Polo Grounds, about 450 feet from home plate. The catch preserved a 2–2 tie in the eighth inning; the Giants went on to win the game and sweep the series.*

2. *When he retired, Mays was third on the all-time home runs list, behind Babe Ruth (1895–1948) and Hank Aaron (1934–). Mays is now fourth, having been passed by his godson, Barry Bonds (1964–).*

3. *Mays was also renowned for his flamboyance in the outfield—he made the basket catch famous and often wore a cap too small for his head so that it would fly off when he chased fly balls.*

•••••

Lucille Ball

Lucille Désirée Ball (1911–1989) began her acting career in the movies in 1933, performing in the chorus of *Roman Scandals,* a musical. She also appeared in more highly regarded films, including *Stage Door* (1937) with Katharine Hepburn (1907–2003) and Ginger Rogers (1911–1995), and *Fancy Pants* (1950) with Bob Hope (1903–2003). As it turned out, the most important movie Ball ever starred in was the 1940 comedy *Too Many Girls;* during its filming, she met her future husband, Desi Arnaz (1917–1986).

With her film career floundering in the early 1950s, Arnaz convinced Ball to work in television, still a new medium, and the two decided to make a show together. At first, studios were reluctant to produce a show whose white female character had a husband with a Cuban accent, but CBS eventually bought the series, and the first episode of *I Love Lucy* aired on October 15, 1951, with Ball and Arnaz playing Lucy and Ricky Ricardo.

The first episode—"Lucy Thinks Ricky Is Trying to Murder Her"—didn't make much of an impact. The thirtieth episode—"Lucy Does a TV Commercial"— did. It was in that program that Ball depicted a nine-minute audition for a commercial to sell Vitameatavegamin, a combination of vitamins, meat, vegetables, and minerals meant to provide an energy boost to anyone who ate a tablespoonful after every meal. Unfortunately, the product tastes horrid, and its alcohol content is alarmingly high. By the end of the fourth take, Lucy has become extremely drunk. The episode was a classic moment in television history, and it established *I Love Lucy.*

The show had other highlights, particularly the series of episodes in which Ball, pregnant in real life, gives birth to the Ricardos' first child. The series was also a great success: It was often ranked number one in the Nielsen television ratings and never ranked below number three. Nonetheless, Ball and Arnaz decided to end the show after only six seasons, while it was still on top.

ADDITIONAL FACTS

1. *Ball first became nationally famous in 1933 as the model who played the Chesterfield Cigarette Girl in advertisements.*

2. *One of the first people to recognize Ball's potential was the great silent-film star Buster Keaton (1895–1966), who mentored her for a short time before she switched to television.*

3. *Ball's trademark red hair wasn't natural; she dyed her hair blonde until 1942, when MGM hairdressers "seeking a more distinctive look" opted for red.*

4. *Ball and Arnaz divorced in 1960.*

••●••

Fidel Castro

When Fidel Castro (1926–) and his band of revolutionaries overthrew dictator Fulgencio Batista (1901–1973) to take control of Cuba in 1959, Dwight D. Eisenhower (1890–1969) was president of the United States. Nine more presidents have sat in the White House since then, and Castro remains a towering figure in Cuban life and a revolutionary symbol around the world.

During the Cold War, Castro aligned with the Soviet Union and relished his role as the leader of a Communist country just ninety miles off American shores. For decades, the Soviet Union propped up Cuba's economy, selling it oil at deflated prices, buying the island's sugar at inflated prices, and supplying weapons and military aircraft. Since the fall of the Soviet Union in 1991, however, Cuba has endured severe economic privation.

In the history of the twentieth century, Castro figured in two of the best-known incidents of the Cold War: the Bay of Pigs invasion and the Cuban missile crisis.

The Bay of Pigs invasion in 1961 was an unsuccessful attempt by American-backed Cuban exiles to invade Cuba and overthrow the Castro regime. The debacle was a serious embarrassment to the United States and the Kennedy administration.

A year later, photographs from American reconnaissance planes revealed that the Soviets were building missile sites in Cuba to house weapons that could strike the United States. After a thirteen-day standoff, the Soviets agreed to remove the missiles—much to Castro's disgust.

Since then, Castro's supporters cite Cuba's universal-health-care system, 98 percent literacy rate, and low infant mortality rate as examples of the success of Castro's regime. Yet critics point to the abject poverty of many Cubans, the country's lack of infrastructure, and a long list of human-rights abuses.

After falling ill, Castro resigned from office in February 2008 and passed the presidency to his brother Raúl Castro (1931–). However, Fidel remains a powerful influence over Cuban politics and society.

ADDITIONAL FACTS

1. *Until he transferred power to his younger brother, Castro was the longest-serving political leader in the world. He underwent surgery for diverticulitis and has rarely been seen in public since.*

2. *The CIA has repeatedly tried to assassinate Castro. During his presidency, John F. Kennedy put his younger brother and attorney general, Robert (1925–1968), in charge of an assassination program. Attempts have included putting arsenic in Castro's milkshake, poisoning his cigars, and enlisting members of the Mafia.*

3. *Several of Castro's family members have defected to the United States and become outspoken members of the anti-Castro Cuban exile community. They include his sister, Juanita (1933–); an illegitimate daughter, Alina Fernandez Revuelta (1956–); and two nephews of his first wife: US congressmen Lincoln Diaz-Balart (1954–) and Mario Diaz-Balart (1961–).*

•••••

Bertolt Brecht

Though the German playwright Bertolt Brecht (1898–1956) produced several notable works, he is remembered less for any one play than for his overall approach to theater. Unlike earlier playwrights, who had focused on either melodrama (aiming to move and entertain audiences) or realism (striving to create the illusion of real life onstage), Brecht drew attention to the artificiality of the theater, using plays as a platform for speaking directly to audiences about his political views.

Brecht wrote his first plays in the early 1920s. While living in Berlin later in that decade, he came in contact with artists and political theorists whose anticapitalist, anti-middle-class ideas influenced him profoundly. It was during this period that he developed the foundations of his overarching theory of theater, which became known as epic theater.

Epic theater challenged the notion that a play should entertain its audience or hold a mirror up to real life. Instead, Brecht believed that a play should be a forum for the playwright to present his ideas overtly to the audience. He also felt it was important that the audience *not* experience suspension of disbelief or emotional involvement in the story. To achieve this result—which Brecht called the *Verfremdungseffekt*, or "alienation effect"—he relied on a number of unconventional techniques, including stripped-down sets, frequent interruption of the play's action, direct address of the audience, and characters who represent ideas rather than people.

A prime example of epic theater is Brecht's *Mother Courage and Her Children* (1941), about a woman who both profits from and is ruined by the Thirty Years' War. Although the story is ostensibly tragic, Brecht hinders the audience's emotional involvement by interrupting the flow with comedy, songs, announcements from the stage, and even scene titles that act as spoilers, ruining upcoming plot twists.

ADDITIONAL FACTS

1. *Some of Brecht's works border on musical theater.* The Threepenny Opera *(1928), his collaboration with the German composer Kurt Weill, includes more than twenty songs.*

2. *Brecht fled Germany in the 1930s, fearing persecution by the right-wing regime of Adolf Hitler (1889–1945). The playwright spent several years in Scandinavia before settling in the United States in 1941.*

3. *During his time in the United States, Brecht worked as a Hollywood screenwriter. In 1947, however, he was suspected of Communist ties and was blacklisted from the industry.*

•••••

Oklahoma!

The curtain rose on *Oklahoma!* on March 31, 1943. It didn't fall until 2,212 performances later, in 1948, making the production one of the longest-running musicals to date. The first collaboration of the composer Richard Rodgers (1902–1979) and the lyricist Oscar Hammerstein II (1895–1960), *Oklahoma!* forever changed the genre and marked the arrival of a new style of American musical theater: a musical play that put great storytelling at center stage.

Rodgers and Hammerstein were both well into their careers when they partnered to stage *Oklahoma!* Rodgers had worked with Lorenz Hart (1895–1943), and Hammerstein with Jerome Kern (1885–1945). Rodgers was accustomed to writing the music for his shows first and then turning the score over to a lyricist, but for the first time in his career he allowed Hammerstein to write the lyrics first.

What resulted was the first true musical play. Previously, musicals were full of show-stopping numbers that had lots of razzle-dazzle and little to do with the plot. But the songs in *Oklahoma!* furthered the action onstage and helped advance character development. For instance, the opening notes of the play are sung from offstage. Curly, a cowboy, enters singing,

> *Oh, what a beautiful mornin',*
> *Oh, what a beautiful day.*
> *I got a beautiful feelin'*
> *Ev'rything's goin' my way.*

The audience is lulled into the story with introspection rather than wowed with a kick line. Uninterested in simply entertaining a crowd, Rodgers and Hammerstein wanted to make an emotional connection. At the height of World War II, American GIs came to Broadway in droves to see *Oklahoma!* It represented something pure, simple, and distinctly American.

Rodgers and Hammerstein melded story, song, and dance into one quiet and unassuming American folktale. Unpretentious as it was, *Oklahoma!* was just the beginning of an epic run of hit musicals. *Carousel* (1945), *South Pacific* (1949), *The King and I* (1951), and *The Sound of Music* (1959) became some of the most beloved plays in the Rodgers and Hammerstein canon of musical theater classics.

ADDITIONAL FACTS

1. *Stephen Sondheim (1930–), lyricist of* West Side Story *and* Gypsy *and lyricist/composer of musicals including* Sweeney Todd *(1979) and* Into the Woods *(1987), studied under Oscar Hammerstein as a child.*

2. Oklahoma! *was awarded a special Pulitzer Prize for Letters in 1944 in recognition of its superior storytelling.*

3. *Agnes de Mille (1905–1993) choreographed* Oklahoma! *and forged new ground with the famed dream sequence that explores the inner psychology of Laurie, the female lead.*

••••

Henry Fonda

Henry Fonda (1905–1982) had a long acting career distinguished by an easy-going style and his portrayal of honest and decent characters faced with moral dilemmas. The critic Roger Ebert has described him as "an actor with the rare ability to exist on the screen without seeming to reach or try."

Trained on Broadway, Fonda made his Hollywood debut in 1935 and achieved star status with his performances in three films directed by John Ford—*Young Mr. Lincoln* (1939), *Drums Along the Mohawk* (1939), and *The Grapes of Wrath* (1940).

Most film historians consider his portrayal of Tom Joad in the adaptation of John Steinbeck's *The Grapes of Wrath* to be his finest role. He was nominated for an Academy Award for Best Actor but lost to his close friend James Stewart, who won for *The Philadelphia Story*.

After appearing in *The Ox-Bow Incident* (1943), an indictment of western lynch-mob justice, Fonda spent three years in the US Navy—he ended his service as a lieutenant in air combat intelligence.

Following World War II, he carried out another of his signature roles, as Wyatt Earp in *My Darling Clementine* (1946). But just two years later, he left Hollywood, returning to a career in the theater.

Fonda again worked in film to reprise his Tony Award–winning title role in *Mister Roberts* (1955). The picture, which costarred James Cagney and Jack Lemmon, was the last collaboration between Fonda and John Ford—they got into a fistfight on the set, Ford left the film for health reasons, and Mervyn LeRoy was brought in to complete the movie.

Fonda cemented his reputation for playing good-guy characters in Sidney Lumet's *12 Angry Men* (1957), portraying the logical and decent Juror #8. He took on his lone role as a villain in Sergio Leone's *Once upon a Time in the West* (1968) before accepting a series of less noteworthy roles in movies, on television, and onstage for more than a decade.

His last major role was in *On Golden Pond*, costarring with legendary actress Katharine Hepburn and his daughter, Jane Fonda. The surprise hit grossed almost $120 million and earned Fonda his only Academy Award for Best Actor, in 1982. He died later that year at age seventy-seven.

ADDITIONAL FACTS

1. *Henry Fonda was also the father of Hollywood star Peter Fonda and the grandfather of Bridget Fonda.*

2. *Fonda and his daughter, Jane, were the first father–daughter combination to be nominated for Academy Awards in the same year (1982, both for* On Golden Pond).

3. *Fonda is the oldest recipient of the best actor Academy Award. (He was seventy-six years old at the time.)*

·•●•·

Bretton Woods

Held in New Hampshire in 1944, the United Nations Monetary and Financial Conference at Bretton Woods laid the groundwork for the world economic system that emerged from the ruins of World War II. Delegates to the meeting created two key institutions, the World Bank and the International Monetary Fund (IMF), that have become pillars of the world economy.

The three-week meeting, which was conducted at a palatial hotel in the woods near Mount Washington, had far-reaching effects. According to economic historians, the Bretton Woods system helped ensure the world's postwar prosperity and set the stage for economic globalization in the late twentieth century.

At the time the conference opened in the summer of 1944, however, delegates had two more-immediate concerns: rebuilding Europe and ensuring that an economic disaster like the Great Depression would never occur again. Many politicians felt that nothing less than world peace was at stake, believing economic turbulence would inevitably lead to further political instability.

The delegates to Bretton Woods included the influential British economist John Maynard Keynes (1883–1946). Keynes was a supporter of active government intervention in economic affairs, a stance that was reflected in the policies adopted at Bretton Woods.

To rebuild, the delegates chartered the World Bank, an institution that lends money to national governments for infrastructure projects such as roads, dams, and bridges. Western European countries were the first to take advantage of the loans after the end of the war.

To ensure economic stability, delegates also created the IMF to regulate exchange rates between different national currencies. The fund can make emergency loans to countries experiencing economic difficulties.

Both the IMF and the World Bank still exist and are considered major parts of the world economy. A third provision of Bretton Woods, which required member countries to peg the value of their currencies to the US dollar, collapsed in the 1970s.

ADDITIONAL FACTS

1. *The meeting took place at the Mount Washington Hotel, which is still in operation as a ski resort in New Hampshire's White Mountains.*

2. *Only a few countries in the world, including Cuba and North Korea, remain outside the IMF and World Bank system.*

3. *After Bretton Woods, the value of the dollar in gold was set at $35 per ounce, a price it would maintain until 1971.*

••●••

Roger Bannister

On the morning of May 6, 1954, a twenty-five-year-old British medical student named Roger Bannister (1929–) went to work at a hospital in London, where he was training to become a neurologist. That afternoon, he left work early, took a train to Oxford, and, after changing into his running spikes, accomplished a feat once thought impossible: He ran a mile in less than four minutes.

The record for the one-mile run had steadily declined during the early twentieth century, but in 1954 it had stood at 4:01 for eight years, leading some to wonder whether runners had reached the limit of the human body's abilities. During the 1950s, however, Bannister and several other amateur runners set their sights on the four-minute barrier.

Bannister was born in Harrow-on-the-Hill, England, and attended Oxford. In an era before sophisticated sports training, endorsement contracts, and corporate sponsorship, he trained for his record-setting run between classes and stints at the hospital. Bannister was unpaid, competed as an amateur, and refused even to accept any gifts or trophies with a value greater than $20.

The fateful race was held on a windy evening before about 1,000 spectators. Bannister's training partners, Chris Brasher (1928–2003) and Chris Chataway (1931–), helped pace him during the first part of the race, ensuring that he maintained a record-setting clip.

When the race was over, the announcer read the time to a cheering crowd: 3 minutes, 59.4 seconds, a result that was soon beamed around the world.

Later that year, Bannister quit running to devote more time to his studies. He became a prominent neurologist before retiring in 2001.

ADDITIONAL FACTS

1. *The Australian John Landy (1930–) broke Bannister's record less than two months later, running a mile in 3 minutes, 57.9 seconds at a race in Finland.*

2. *Bannister was knighted in 1975 for his accomplishments as a neurologist, not for running.*

3. *The current record holder is Moroccan Hicham El Guerrouj (1974–), who ran the mile in 3:43.13 in 1999.*

••●••

Baseball Cards

The first baseball cards were distributed in packages of cigarettes or chewing tobacco in the late 1800s. Many of the biggest stars of the early twentieth century, such as Babe Ruth (1895–1948) and Honus Wagner (1874–1955), were featured on small, rectangular tobacco cards, which were given away as cheap promotional gimmicks.

Production of baseball cards temporarily ceased during World War II. After the war, however, the Topps chewing-gum company issued a series of cards in 1952 that is considered the first modern set and kicked off the baseball card craze of the 1950s and 1960s.

Each Topps baseball card featured the player's photo on the front and, in a departure from the one-sided tobacco cards, an array of batting or pitching statistics on the back. Topps also included a stick of its Day-Glo pink chewing gum in every five-cent package.

Although cards were originally intended merely as an enticement to help sell gum, they quickly became more popular than the product itself. Collecting took off in the 1950s, becoming a hobby for millions of American boys. Cards could be traded, flipped—or simply hoarded as miniature treasures.

During the 1980s, aging baby boomers seeking to recapture mementos of their lost youth fed a baseball card revival, and the prices for rare cards from the 1950s shot up. In 1991, Sotheby's, the auction house better known for its art sales, began selling baseball cards salvaged from attics, and thousands of mothers suddenly stood accused of throwing away now-valuable antiques. The Mickey Mantle card from the original 1952 Topps series has sold for $275,000 and remains one of the most treasured holy grails of baseball card collecting.

ADDITIONAL FACTS

1. *The 1909 Honus Wagner card issued by the American Tobacco Company is the most valuable baseball card in history; only about sixty exist. One sold for $2.8 million in 2007.*

2. *Topps stopped putting sticks of gum in its packs in 1991.*

3. *Trading cards have also been issued for football, soccer, basketball, hockey, and even golf.*

••●••

John F. Kennedy

Though President John F. Kennedy's time in the White House was brief, his impact was dramatic. He led the country through some of the tensest moments of the Cold War and was considered a visionary leader and brilliant speaker. Yet he became an even larger figure in American history after his shocking assassination, just over 1,000 days into his administration.

The day of his murder, November 22, 1963, remains a watershed of the twentieth century, and historians—both amateur and professional—continue to debate who killed Kennedy (1917–1963) and why.

Kennedy's 1960 election victory over Vice President Richard M. Nixon (1913–1994) was one of the closest in history. Kennedy, at age forty-three, was not only the youngest man ever elected to the White House but also the first Roman Catholic.

Without a solid mandate, however, little of Kennedy's domestic program—dubbed the New Frontier—was enacted before his death. In foreign affairs, his anti-Communist foreign policy led to several high-profile confrontations with his primary international adversary, Soviet premier Nikita Khrushchev (1894–1971).

The most dramatic such encounter occurred in 1962, when a thirteen-day standoff between the United States and the Soviet Union followed the discovery of Soviet weapons in Cuba. With nuclear war a real possibility, Khrushchev eventually blinked and pulled the missiles and troops out of Cuba.

Kennedy's brief presidency and life ended when he was shot twice while riding in a presidential motorcade in Dallas. Less than two hours later, a twenty-four-year-old named Lee Harvey Oswald (1939–1963) was arrested for killing the president. Two days after that, nightclub owner Jack Ruby (1911–1967) shot and killed Oswald.

In 1964, the Warren Commission ruled that Oswald had acted alone in killing Kennedy, a conclusion supported by voluminous evidence. But public-opinion polls have consistently shown for more than four decades that most Americans believe Kennedy was the victim of a conspiracy.

ADDITIONAL FACTS

1. *Kennedy and his wife, Jacqueline (1929–1994), formed a handsome, fashionable couple who brought glamour to the White House. With their two young children and an array of visitors to the White House, including artists, intellectuals, and entertainers, the Kennedy presidency later acquired a fairy-tale title: Camelot.*

2. *In his inspirational inaugural address, Kennedy famously urged Americans to "ask not what your country can do for you—ask what you can do for your country."*

3. *In 1961, Kennedy founded the Peace Corps and also asked Congress for $22 billion to help put an American man on the moon by the end of the 1960s. The new space program, Project Apollo, would land two men on the moon in July 1969.*

•••••

The Grapes of Wrath

When the great classic American novels are discussed, *The Grapes of Wrath* (1939) inevitably makes the list. This powerful work by California native John Steinbeck (1902–1968) awakened the American conscience to the plight of the nation's poor migrant farmers and remains a staple assignment in English classes today.

Steinbeck's novel is set during the Great Depression, which paralyzed the American economy from 1929 through the mid-1930s, bringing rampant unemployment and widespread poverty and hunger. The burden of the Depression proved especially heavy for farmers in the western United States because it came hand in hand with the dust bowl—an ecological disaster, brought on by a combination of drought and irresponsible farming practices, that laid waste to much of the region's arable land.

The Grapes of Wrath follows the Joads, a farming family from Oklahoma that flees the hardships of the dust bowl by trekking westward to California via US Route 66, along with thousands of other so-called Okies. The Joads are an archetypal salt-of-the-earth clan, anchored by strong, determined Ma Joad but ultimately led by Ma's ex-convict son, Tom. With three generations in one rickety truck, they attempt to find work and a new life in California. Although they encounter tragedy along the way, several of the family's members emerge stronger for it.

The Grapes of Wrath is part of a long tradition of American social-protest fiction, standing alongside works such as Harriet Beecher Stowe's antislavery novel *Uncle Tom's Cabin* (1852) and Upton Sinclair's *The Jungle* (1906), which exposed the grim conditions in Chicago slaughterhouses. Steinbeck's novel is not universally praised: Critics have cited his heavy-handedness, sentimentality, and tendency to paint his characters broadly but not particularly deeply. Nevertheless, Steinbeck's storytelling techniques are undeniably effective, and his novel remains a searing reminder of one of the most difficult periods in American history.

ADDITIONAL FACTS

1. The Grapes of Wrath *earned Steinbeck the personal wrath of many businessmen and landowners, who detested his openly left-leaning politics and support for organized labor.*

2. *Although* The Grapes of Wrath *arguably remains Steinbeck's most enduring work, he himself believed that his later novel* East of Eden *(1952) was his best.*

3. The Grapes of Wrath *was made into an acclaimed 1940 film starring Henry Fonda (1905–1982), Jane Darwell (1879–1967), and John Carradine (1906–1988). The novel's ending, though, was altered considerably for the film version.*

• • ● • •

Count Basie

William Allen "Count" Basie (1904–1984) was an accomplished jazz composer and pianist, but in the eyes of many historians, his greatest achievement was incubating and showcasing some of the greatest musical talent of the twentieth century in his band, the Count Basie Orchestra.

After playing piano and leading bands in Kansas City and Chicago, Basie, a native of New Jersey, settled in New York City at the end of 1936. His band was as highly regarded for its technical prowess as Duke Ellington's, and, like Ellington's, Basie's orchestra often served as a starting point for musicians and singers who went on to greater things.

One of the most famous graduates of Basie's orchestra was the tenor saxophonist Lester Young (1909–1959). When Young started out, the saxophone was regarded as more of a background instrument on the jazz scene and had not yet acquired the prominence it would later assume. Playing in Basie's band, Young helped establish the saxophone as a serious jazz instrument. Perhaps Young's most lasting influence was to establish the hipster look and attitude with which jazz would come to be associated in the bebop era, in contrast to the staid formality of the big bands.

More famous still were the singers who had their start in Basie's band. Basie had a passion for the blues and used his band to promote some of its greatest singers. Among those who benefited from Basie's support were Billie Holiday (1915–1959) and Big Joe Turner (1911–1985). Turner's case is fascinating because it demonstrates just how broad Basie's influence was. While Turner performed with the band as a blues singer, he would later become one of the early pioneers of rock and roll, recording the rock classic "Shake, Rattle and Roll" in 1954.

When big-band-music's popularity waned in the early 1950s, Basie lost some of his prominence, but he remained a cultural fixture and collaborated with artists from Frank Sinatra (1915–1998) to Mel Brooks (1926–).

ADDITIONAL FACTS

1. *Count Basie and his band have a cameo in the 1974 Mel Brooks comedy* Blazing Saddles.

2. *One of Frank Sinatra's best-selling albums was* Sinatra at the Sands, *a live album he recorded in Las Vegas with Basie's orchestra.*

3. *Many consider Basie's 1955 recording of "April in Paris" to be the greatest ever, topping versions by Louis Armstrong (1901–1971), Ella Fitzgerald (1917–1996), and Thelonious Monk (1917–1982).*

••●••

Alfred Hitchcock

The British-born director Alfred Hitchcock (1899–1980) earned the nickname the Master of Suspense on the strength of the taut psychological thrillers he made throughout his long and distinguished career. His films often featured criminals, spies, psychological drama, and victims of mistaken identity or innocent people swept up in situations beyond their control.

In his finest films, Hitchcock's masterful use of editing not only builds suspense but also includes the audience in the plot. Indeed, voyeurism is a common theme in some of his most acclaimed films, including *Vertigo* (1958), *Psycho* (1960), and, especially, *Rear Window* (1954).

Hitchcock worked in Great Britain for the first part of his career, sharpening his use of suspense in *The 39 Steps* (1935) and *The Lady Vanishes* (1938). He left for Hollywood in 1939 and met with immediate success—his first feature, *Rebecca* (1940), was a critical and box office smash, earning an Academy Award for Best Picture.

He continued his success in Hollywood with *Foreign Correspondent* (1940), *Suspicion* (1941), *Spellbound* (1945), and his midcareer masterpiece, *Notorious* (1946).

Rear Window, starring James Stewart and Grace Kelly, ushered in Hitchcock's prime era. The film focuses on an injured photographer who is immobilized in his Greenwich Village apartment, with only his neighbors' lives to entertain him. Hitchcock creates two parallel worlds—one in which Stewart's character watches his neighbors, and another in which the audience both watches Stewart and watches with him.

Vertigo, which also stars Stewart, was not a box office hit, but it has come to be appreciated as one of Hitchcock's best works. It is the clearest representation of one of the director's obsessions—the desire or need to control women. (In this case, the objectified woman is played by Kim Novak.)

North by Northwest (1959) and *The Birds* (1963) were also critical and box office successes. But the film the director is perhaps best known for is *Psycho* (1960), which spawned an entire genre of modern horror films.

Several components of *Psycho* have become iconic—from Bernard Herrmann's piercing score, to the Bates Motel, to the shower scene starring Janet Leigh.

ADDITIONAL FACTS

1. *Hitchcock was nominated for the best director Academy Award five times but never won; he eventually received the Irving G. Thalberg Memorial Award for lifetime achievement in 1968.*

2. *Hitchcock is famous for making cameos in his own films—all told, he made thirty-seven such appearances.*

3. *For much of his career, Hitchcock was not appreciated by many critics for his abilities, but the writers and directors who contributed to the French journal* Cahiers du cinéma *championed his cause as part of the auteur theory—the notion that a film's director is its author.*

•• ● ● ••

Nuclear Bomb

On August 6, 1945, the United States dropped a small uranium device code-named Little Boy over the Japanese city of Hiroshima, ending the lives of some-where between 120,000 and 140,000 Japanese citizens. Yet the significance of the nuclear bomb's development and detonation reverberated far beyond even this devastating loss of life, as the nuclear arms race played a major role in world politics for the next fifty years, and even continues today.

The nuclear bomb was developed in a top-secret program known as the Manhattan Project, which mobilized some of the top minds of the twentieth century. Many of the scientists who worked on the Manhattan Project, such as Niels Bohr (1885–1962) and Enrico Fermi (1901–1954), were displaced from the Axis countries against which the United States was fighting. Research into the use of nuclear power was first inspired by the fear that the Nazis were already developing and testing nuclear weapons of their own. (They weren't—at least, not successfully.)

The use of nuclear bombs in World War II was and continues to be extremely con-troversial. Proponents argue that the bomb ultimately *saved* the lives of countless soldiers by hastening the end of the war, since Japanese kamikaze pilots and banzai fighters had shown no sign of surrender despite the imminence of an all-but-guaranteed Allied victory.

On the other hand, critics lament the horror of killing huge numbers of enemy civil-ians, in contravention of internationally recognized rules of warfare. Other critics believe the bombings at Hiroshima and Nagasaki actually *caused* the Cold War, as they spurred the Soviet Union to develop its own nuclear arsenal.

The use of nuclear power has captivated the world imagination as epitomizing the dual propensity of humankind: to create, and to destroy. The specter of nuclear annihilation framed world affairs during the Cold War and continues to preoccupy world leaders as rogue states such as North Korea and Iran are accused of develop-ing nuclear programs.

ADDITIONAL FACTS

1. *The rock band Rush recorded a song called "Manhattan Project."*

2. *One of the chief architects of the nuclear bomb, the Italian physicist Enrico Fermi, was married to a Jewish woman; they immigrated to the United States to escape the anti-Semitic policies of Mussolini.*

3. *The classic Cold War film Dr. Strangelove (1964), directed by Stanley Kubrick (1928–1999), satirizes the fear of total world destruction through the detonation of a nuclear doomsday device.*

•••••

"The Greatest Game Ever Played"

In the Yankee Stadium twilight, on a cold Sunday in December 1958, the modern National Football League was born.

Johnny Unitas

In what has been dubbed the Greatest Game Ever Played, the Baltimore Colts beat the New York Giants 23–17 in the first NFL title game decided in overtime. The game itself was indeed exciting—the Colts rallied from a 17–14 deficit late in regulation play to send the game into overtime and eventually win.

But the game's importance went beyond Baltimore's NFL title win—it led to the birth of the modern NFL and burnished the legend of twenty-five-year-old Colts quarterback Johnny Unitas (1933–2002).

Television played a large role in raising the game to mythic status. A rare national audience tuned in to watch the heroics of Unitas and the eleven other future Pro Football Hall of Fame players, and many observers consider this the point when the NFL set a course to become the most popular American sports league by the mid-1960s.

With 1:56 remaining in regulation, Unitas and the Colts, trailing 17–14, got the ball on their own fourteen-yard line. Using passes over the middle of the field, Unitas marched the Colts deep into Giants territory, setting up a twenty-yard field goal by Steve Myhra (1934–) with seven seconds left to send the game into overtime.

The Giants began the sudden-death extra period with the ball but were forced to punt. The Colts took over at their own twenty-yard line, and Unitas completed a series of clutch passes, including a twenty-one-yard completion to wide receiver Raymond Berry (1933–) on third and fourteen.

On the thirteenth play of the drive, Colts fullback Alan Ameche (1933–1988) took a handoff from Unitas and plunged one yard for the game-winning touchdown, bringing the Greatest Game Ever Played to its conclusion.

ADDITIONAL FACTS

1. *In addition to the twelve Hall of Fame players, three future Hall of Fame coaches also stalked the sidelines—Colts head coach Weeb Ewbank (1907–1998), Giants offensive coordinator Vince Lombardi (1913–1970), and Giants defensive coordinator Tom Landry (1924–2000).*

2. *The Giants had beaten the Colts, 24–21, during the regular season that year on November 9.*

3. *Two men who played for the Giants went on to become famous broadcasters—Pat Summerall (1930–) kicked a field goal for two extra points, and Frank Gifford (1930–) fumbled twice.*

●●●●●

Leave It to Beaver

The so-called golden age of TV—the 1950s—featured many family-based sit-coms, including *I Love Lucy* and *The Adventures of Ozzie and Harriet*. But children seldom appeared on those shows, which focused instead on the adult characters.

In contrast, the sitcom *Leave It to Beaver* revolved around Theodore "Beaver" Cleaver, who was seven years old when the show premiered in 1957; his older brother, Wally; and their parents, June and Ward.

Though the show is now regarded as one of the most iconic television series of the late 1950s and early 1960s, it wasn't much of a hit during its six-season run. (CBS dropped the series after one season and ABC picked it up for an additional five.) Indeed, its best ratings came when reruns aired in the 1980s.

The show was created by Joe Connelly (1917–2003) and Bob Mosher (1915–1972). Connelly and Mosher attempted to depict what they considered realistic childish behavior rather than making the children perform like adults. In one episode, for instance, Wally gives Beaver a ridiculous haircut to try to hide the fact that Beaver lost his haircut money—an experience Mosher himself had as a child.

For the most part, episodes focused on typical "boys will be boys" escapades, from losing the pet cat to wrecking the household plumbing. Other episodes dealt with more mature (and, for the time, groundbreaking) topics such as alcoholism ("Beaver and Andy") or divorce ("Beaver's House Guest").

Toward the end of its run, the show began shifting to other topics as Wally entered his teens. This direction was cut short when the show was canceled in September 1963.

ADDITIONAL FACTS

1. *Members of the original cast reunited in 1983 for the feature-length film* Still the Beaver, *which sparked a revival of interest in the show.*

2. *The show's pilot episode—"It's a Small World"—was not aired with the original series, and it featured different actors in the roles of Ward and Wally. The pilot was lost until 1987.*

3. *Cocreator Connelly took the name Beaver from one of his shipmates on a World War II destroyer.*

••●••

Pope John XXIII

In 1962, as the world grappled with modernization, the space race, and the specter of nuclear war, Pope John XXIII (1881–1963) feared that the Catholic Church was falling behind the times. He believed it needed a new spirit to put itself in touch with this new world, and to do so, it needed to become more open and welcoming to people of all religions.

Beginning that year, John XXIII convened the Second Vatican Council (also known as Vatican II) to address the issues facing the modern Catholic Church. At the time, it was a stunning gathering of the hierarchy of the world's largest faith, and a tacit admission that the church's old, conservative attitudes were not necessarily the best ways to deal with modernity.

The results of the three-year council were largely achieved after John XXIII's death in 1963, but they included several more-liberal policies, including the decision that Mass could be performed in local languages instead of in Latin, as well as more tolerant church-state positions on religious freedom.

John XXIII was born Angelo Giuseppe Roncalli in Sotto il Monte, Italy. Before becoming pope, he was a man of the world, serving the church in Bulgaria, Turkey, Greece, and France. During the 1930s and 1940s, he used his influence in Europe to help Jews escape Nazi persecution.

He was elected pope in 1958, succeeding Pius XII (1876–1958), and was known as *il Papa Buono* ("the Good Pope") for his gentleness and warmth. His last major act before his death at age eighty-one was the publication of *Pacem in Terris* (*Peace on Earth*), an encyclical that stated that recognition of human rights was essential before world peace could be achieved.

ADDITIONAL FACTS

1. *In 2000, John XXIII was beatified, the last step before one can achieve sainthood.*

2. *He was named Man of the Year by* Time *magazine in 1962 for convening Vatican II.*

3. *His warmth is exhibited in an anecdote from a visit by Jacqueline Kennedy (1929–1994) to the Vatican. John XXIII asked an aide how to address her, and the aide said "Mrs. Kennedy" or "Madame" was appropriate. The Pope practiced both addresses, but when she arrived, John XXIII extended his arms and burst out, "Jacqueline!"*

••••

The Stranger

Albert Camus's *The Stranger* (1942) was one of the most important European works of literature and philosophy of the twentieth century and remains one of the most widely read. This brief, accessible novel both tells a gripping suspense story and expresses, clearly and concisely, the absurdist worldview that Camus (1913–1960) and many of his philosophical contemporaries shared.

Albert Camus

The "stranger" of the novel's title is Meursault, an aimless young man in the French colony of Algeria who is completely emotionally detached from the world around him. He learns at the beginning of the novel that his mother has died, but he expresses no sorrow and remembers virtually nothing about her funeral. A few weeks later, he agrees to accompany his girlfriend—to whom he is largely indifferent—to a friend's house on the ocean. On the beach, one of Meursault's companions gets into a brawl with an Arab man. Later that day, Meursault returns to the beach with his companion's gun and, in a moment of confusion, shoots and kills the Arab, seemingly for no reason.

Meursault is arrested and put on trial for the murder. The authorities are horrified by his lack of remorse and his unwillingness to profess his faith in God, even when threatened with execution. The trial becomes a farce, as the authorities take issue not so much with Meursault's killing of the Arab as with his disregard for society's notion of morality in general.

Just before his impending execution, Meursault finally displays passion, defending his view that life is absurd and meaningless and that God does not exist. For Meursault—and for Camus—this worldview is not necessarily bleak and pessimistic; in fact, it is a source of peace and calm. In the end, Meursault comes off as an almost noble figure, resigned to the "gentle indifference of the world."

ADDITIONAL FACTS

1. *Although Camus is often associated with the philosophy of existentialism, he rejected that claim and insisted that he belonged to no particular school of thought.*

2. *Camus was awarded the Nobel Prize in Literature in 1957; he died in a car accident in France just three years later.*

3. *Camus was close friends with the French philosopher and author Jean-Paul Sartre (1905–1980), whose works include* Nausea *(1938) and* No Exit *(1944).*

•••••

Louis Armstrong

The jazz critic Nat Hentoff once wrote that Louis Armstrong (1901–1971) has the same relationship to previous jazz musicians that William Shakespeare (1564–1616) has to previous poets and playwrights. There may have been jazz musicians before Satchmo, but he towered above his predecessors and had an enormous influence on everyone who followed.

Louis Daniel Armstrong was born in New Orleans, the birthplace of jazz. He first rose to prominence, however, when he moved in the early 1920s to Chicago, which by that time had become the center of jazz performance. Armstrong first played trumpet in a band led by Joe "King" Oliver (1885–1938), in which he pioneered a style that centered around improvised solos rather than composed group works.

Soon, however, Armstrong left Oliver's band to record with his two legendary groups of the mid- to late 1920s: the Hot Five and the Hot Seven. It was with these bands that Armstrong made his first classic recordings, including "Potato Head Blues" (1927) and "West End Blues" (1928).

Armstrong continued to perform and innovate for decades, most notably with the All Stars group he formed in the late 1940s. He also collaborated with a number of great musicians, including perhaps most famously Ella Fitzgerald (1917–1996). Some critics believed that these collaborations were a betrayal of Armstrong's great talents, but they were among his most commercially popular works.

Armstrong's influence on trumpet players was enormous. Miles Davis (1926–1991) said that "you can't play anything on a horn [that] Louis hasn't played." Dizzy Gillespie (1917–1993) went further, claiming that the entire history of jazz owed a debt to Armstrong: "If it hadn't been for him, there would have been none of us. I want to thank Mr. Louis Armstrong for my livelihood."

ADDITIONAL FACTS

1. *The track "Muggles" (1928) refers to a slang term for marijuana, which Armstrong used enthusiastically throughout his life.*

2. *In 1964, it was Armstrong who knocked the Beatles off the top of the Billboard pop charts with his version of "Hello, Dolly!"*

3. *In addition to an autobiography and some scattered pieces, Armstrong also published a diet book entitled* Lose Weight the Satchmo Way.

Orson Welles

No individual in the history of film has had as brilliant and as confounding a Hollywood career as Orson Welles (1915–1985). He arrived on the cinematic scene as a twenty-four-year-old wunderkind in 1939, and within two years had directed, produced, cowritten, and starred in what many critics and moviegoers believe to be the greatest film of all time, *Citizen Kane* (1941).

Welles's reputation in the theater and radio worlds was such that when he arrived in Hollywood, RKO Pictures gave him a contract that was the envy of every established filmmaker—he received complete artistic control over the film that would become *Kane*.

Welles himself played the role of media magnate Charles Foster Kane (loosely based on press baron William Randolph Hearst, among others) and directed a film that would be renowned for its technical achievements, particularly the work of the cinematographer Gregg Toland (1904–1948).

Although *Citizen Kane* was a critical success, it flopped at the box office and won just one Academy Award, for best original screenplay.

The rest of Welles's career was marked by unfulfilled ambitions, financial problems, and studio treachery.

He followed *Kane* with *The Magnificent Ambersons* (1942). Though many critics consider the film a masterpiece, RKO eliminated about one-third of its running time while Welles was away in Brazil and Mexico working on another project. His next three films—*The Stranger* (1946), *The Lady from Shanghai* (1947), and *Macbeth* (1948)—all suffered the same fate of being shortened against his wishes.

Welles took on acting roles—notably in Carol Reed's *The Third Man* (1949)—to fund his often ill-fated directorial pursuits.

His final Hollywood movie, *Touch of Evil* (1958), is considered the last great work of the film noir era. But it was a box office bust and did not reflect Welles's original vision until it was reedited in 1998. The rest of his career was marked by minor acting roles and directorial efforts abroad until his death at age seventy.

ADDITIONAL FACTS

1. *Welles was married to fellow screen legend Rita Hayworth from 1943 until their divorce in 1948. Hayworth costarred with Welles in* The Lady from Shanghai.

2. *Because of financial problems, his adaptation of* Othello *(1952) took years to complete. It was finally released in 1952, winning the Palme d'Or at the Cannes Film Festival, but was not released in the United States until 1955.*

3. *Welles became a national celebrity for his 1938 Halloween Eve radio broadcast of the H. G. Wells novel* The War of the Worlds, *which convinced many listeners that Martians had landed in New Jersey.*

•••••

Suburbanization

After World War II, millions of Americans seeking a house and a yard of their own moved out of cities and into newly built suburban towns, a trend that soon led to profound social and environmental consequences. With the sudden departure of so many residents, many older urban areas were thrown into crisis. Meanwhile, millions of acres of rural farmland were lost to so-called sprawl as the suburbs grew inexorably outward.

The major housing crunch that emerged after World War II helped trigger suburbanization. Few new houses had been built during the Great Depression of the 1930s. As a result, many returning war veterans were unable to find a place to live. In cities such as New York, some families were forced to double up in tiny apartments. In congressional testimony in 1947, housing advocates said, "Veterans and civilians alike are seeing the ruins of their postwar dream homes."

In response, developers began to build new communities from scratch. The first and most famous postwar suburb, Levittown, New York, opened in 1947. Thousands of others sprang up over the next decades. Amid the economic growth of the 1950s, the suburbs became symbols of the nation's postwar prosperity.

The departure of middle-class residents, however, left many cities in decay. Urban unrest in the 1960s exacerbated this trend by sparking another exodus to suburbia (sometimes known as white flight).

Suburbanization also made millions of Americans completely dependent on their automobiles for transportation, a trend that some economists and social scientists blame for rising air pollution, increasing dependence on imported oil, and even the nation's staggering obesity rate.

ADDITIONAL FACTS

1. *Some demographers and city planners have coined a new term—exurbs—to name the developments now forming outside the ring of suburbs directly surrounding a city.*

2. *The demographics of many American cities changed drastically in a very short time, with the white populations of cities such as Detroit; Newark, New Jersey; and Washington, DC, declining precipitously in the space of about two decades.*

3. *Levittown was named after Levitt and Sons, the construction firm that built the suburb.*

John Wooden

Other college basketball coaches have won more games than John Wooden (1910–), but no other coach has won as many championships or left as renowned an outline for success in life as he did. Wooden considered himself a molder of men first and a basketball coach second. His legacy at the University of California, Los Angeles, in the 1960s and 1970s is an unmatched run of success: ten college basketball championships, including seven consecutive titles from 1967 through 1973, and the deep respect and admiration of generations of former players.

He arrived at UCLA in 1948 after successful coaching stints at the high-school level and at Indiana Teachers College (later known as Indiana State University). He built his program on the tenets of his Pyramid of Success, which stressed such virtues as loyalty, friendship, and enthusiasm, all leading to "competitive greatness."

On the first day of practice each year, he showed players the proper way to put on their socks and tie their shoelaces. Many of his players were surprised by his old-fashioned approach, which some considered corny—but it worked.

Wooden spent twenty-seven seasons at UCLA, compiling a 620-147 record, and his teams won ten NCAA titles in his final twelve years as coach. His Bruins also racked up streaks of eighty-eight consecutive victories (1971–1973) and thirty-eight straight NCAA tournament wins (1964–1974), and four of his teams finished with perfect 30-0 records. Among his players were two of the greatest in college basketball history: Lew Alcindor (later Kareem Abdul-Jabbar, 1947–) and Bill Walton (1952–).

Before he became a successful coach, Wooden was an all-American guard at Purdue University. He led the Boilermakers to the national championship in 1932 and later became the first man inducted into the Basketball Hall of Fame as both a player and a coach.

ADDITIONAL FACTS

1. *As a player, Wooden was known as the Indiana Rubber Man for diving all over the court. At UCLA, he was dubbed the Wizard of Westwood.*

2. *Bobby Knight (1940–), who retired from Texas Tech University in 2008, is the overall winningest coach in Division I men's basketball history, with 902 victories. Tennessee women's coach Pat Summitt (1952–) has even more: 981 wins through 2007.*

3. *During World War II, Wooden served as a lieutenant in the US Navy.*

••●••

American Bandstand

American Bandstand was one of the first televised music programs in the United States and helped introduce hundreds of rock bands to the public during its thirty-year run on the airwaves. The show also inspired programs such as *Soul Train* and *Solid Gold,* which served as launchpads for the careers of countless musical acts.

Dick Clark

Originally called *Bandstand,* the show premiered on a Philadelphia TV station on October 7, 1952, with local disc jockey Bob Horn (1916–1966) serving as host. The format was simple. Horn played music, teenagers danced, and toward the end of the show, a live act came onstage to play a few songs. Dion and the Belmonts, Bill Haley and the Comets, and Buddy Holly (1936–1959) all performed during *Bandstand*'s early years.

In 1956, Horn was arrested for driving while intoxicated, and a young Dick Clark (1929–), a radio DJ, took over as host. Clark recognized the show's potential and over the next year regularly pitched it as a nationwide program to ABC network executives. Clark's persistence paid off, and on August 5, 1957, *American Bandstand* began airing nationally.

Clark made a number of other important changes. He pushed for audience participation whenever possible, regularly asking dancing teenagers their opinions of the music and occasionally having them introduce live acts.

He also insisted on racially integrating the acts that were brought on the show, noting that a number of African-American performers were not getting their due respect. Clark's efforts boosted the careers of Sam Cooke (1931–1964), Chuck Berry (1926–), and Fats Domino (1928–).

After more than thirty years, ABC dropped *American Bandstand* from its program schedule in 1989. By then, more than 10,000 performers had appeared on the show, and an estimated 600,000 teenagers had danced along. The program remains one of the longest-running US television shows aimed at youth culture.

ADDITIONAL FACTS

1. *Barry Manilow (1943–) sang the show's theme song from 1977 to 1987.*

2. *From 2002 to 2005,* American Bandstand *was featured in NBC's* American Dreams, *a drama series about the 1960s produced by Dick Clark.*

3. *A fictional show called* National Bandstand, *a takeoff on* American Bandstand, *was featured in the movie* Grease *(1978).*

••••

Lenny Bruce

Before Lenny Bruce (1925–1966), stand-up comedians got onstage and told jokes. But Bruce did something else—he stood in front of an audience and unleashed caustic, obscenity-laced social commentary, exploring issues of race, sex, drugs, politics, religion, and whatever else came to mind.

He influenced generations of comedians, particularly Richard Pryor (1940–2005) and George Carlin (1937–), but he paid a price for his work. He was first arrested for obscenity in 1961, touching off five years of battles with law enforcement over obscenity and drug charges. He was convicted of obscenity in New York City in 1964 and pardoned in 2003.

Bruce was born Leonard Schneider and began performing in and around New York City in 1947, after serving in the US Navy during World War II. He started to gain national notoriety in the late 1950s and made his first album, *The Sick Humor of Lenny Bruce* (1959), with the help of *Playboy* magazine publisher Hugh Hefner (1926–), who was an early fan.

Bruce's performances both shocked and amused audiences as he sought to expose the hypocrisy of modern life. And once he began to get in trouble with the law, he often worked his experiences with police officers, lawyers, and judges into his act.

After his first arrest, local authorities routinely attended his nightclub appearances, listening for obscenities and arresting him after his sets. Club owners themselves were threatened with being shut down or jailed if they allowed him to take the stage.

Bruce was arrested in San Francisco, New York, Philadelphia, Los Angeles, and other cities. He became paranoid and obsessed with the law, and after years of fighting (some have called him a martyr for the First Amendment), the legal battles bankrupted him by 1965. A year later, he was dead of a morphine overdose at age forty.

ADDITIONAL FACTS

1. *Bruce received the Hollywood biopic treatment in* Lenny *(1974), directed by Bob Fosse (1927–1987) and starring Dustin Hoffman (1937–). The film was nominated for six Academy Awards and followed the 1971 Broadway play.*

2. *More recently, a documentary,* Lenny Bruce: Swear to Tell the Truth *(1998), directed by Robert B. Weide (1959–), and an off-Broadway show,* Lenny Bruce: In His Own Words, *have brought Bruce's work to modern audiences.*

3. *Bruce is one of the people featured on the cover of the Beatles album* Sgt. Pepper's Lonely Hearts Club Band *(1967).*

•••••

All the King's Men

Many canonical novels of the American South, from William Faulkner's *The Sound and the Fury* (1929) to Carson McCullers's *The Heart Is a Lonely Hunter* (1940), have focused on the hidden lives of the region's private citizens. But Robert Penn Warren's *All the King's Men* (1946) tells a very public story: the rise and fall of a flamboyant southern politician. Based partly on real events, it was one of the most prominent American political novels of the past century.

Robert Penn Warren

Warren (1905–1989) grew up in Kentucky and Tennessee but spent much of his life away from his home turf, studying and serving in teaching posts at universities from Berkeley to Yale to Oxford. By his thirties, he was an accomplished poet and also a significant literary critic—one of the founding members of the so-called New Criticism school, which dominated Western literary criticism until the 1960s.

Upon his appointment to a teaching post at Louisiana State University in 1933, Warren witnessed the local politics of Baton Rouge firsthand—particularly the career of the state's showy, controversial governor, Huey Long (1893–1935). An infamous Depression-era politician, Long attained enormous popularity with his populist stances but was criticized for his autocratic style and possible involvement in corruption. His meteoric rise ended abruptly when he was assassinated in 1935.

Though Warren insistently played down any link between Long and Willie Stark, the main character of *All the King's Men*, the parallels are too numerous to be coincidental. Like Long, Stark rises from humble origins to great fame as the governor of a southern state. Using bullying and often illegal techniques, he forces his policies into place, endearing himself to the public but corrupting himself both professionally and personally—with ultimately tragic consequences. Warren's novel remains a gripping read and a relevant parable about the fine line between corruptness and effectiveness in politics.

ADDITIONAL FACTS

1. *Though best known for* All the King's Men, *Warren was far more prolific as a poet. He was also the first person to be named poet laureate of the United States, in 1986.*

2. *Warren derived the title of his novel from the children's nursery rhyme about Humpty Dumpty: "All the king's horses and all the king's men / Couldn't put Humpty together again."*

3. *A new film version of* All the King's Men *appeared in 2006, starring Sean Penn (1960–) and Jude Law (1972–). It was ravaged by critics, who saw it as a pointless remake of the novel's original, Oscar-winning film adaptation from 1949.*

••●••

Dizzy Gillespie

With his pouched cheeks and bent trumpet, John Birks "Dizzy" Gillespie (1917–1993) was one of the most recognizable figures in modern jazz. Gillespie performed with many of the biggest names in twentieth-century music and helped create bebop, a style that became popular after World War II.

Born in South Carolina, Gillespie began his career as a player in big-band groups of the 1930s and 1940s, backing stars such as Cab Calloway (1907–1994) and Duke Ellington (1899–1974). Gillespie wasn't successful in these venues, however, because his unique, fast-paced soloing style didn't fit in with the conventions of traditional big-band music.

By the mid-1940s, Gillespie had moved on to smaller, less mainstream groups that allowed him to showcase his unique talents and develop bebop, which he pioneered along with saxophonist Charlie "Bird" Parker (1920–1955).

Before bebop, the most popular form of jazz was swing. Swing jazz is characterized by a strong and steady rhythm, a prominent melody, and a medium, danceable tempo—but little improvisation.

Bebop differs radically from swing in nearly every respect. The tempo is considerably faster, giving the musicians an opportunity to demonstrate their skills but keeping audiences listening in their seats rather than dancing on their feet. The rhythm section is far more prominent and is no longer confined to keeping time— drum and bass sections are much more complex. And melodies serve as jumping-off points for elaborate improvisations: Rather than being carried throughout a tune, melodies are stated early on and musicians riff on them as inventively as possible.

Onstage, Gillespie was an inventive improviser and an affable performer who was extremely well liked by his audiences. He was introduced to a younger generation with appearances on *The Cosby Show* and *Sesame Street* before his death in 1993.

ADDITIONAL FACTS

1. *In 1964, Gillespie ran for president, promising to rename the White House "the Blues House" and appoint Ray Charles (1930–2004) librarian of Congress, Miles Davis (1926–1991) head of the CIA, and Malcolm X (1925–1965) attorney general.*

2. *One of Gillespie's last jobs was as leader of the United Nations Orchestra.*

3. *Gillespie never completed his college education, but he received fourteen honorary degrees over the course of his lifetime.*

••••

Citizen Kane (1941)

No film in the history of cinema has been more discussed, more praised, or more influential than *Citizen Kane* (1941), the first movie ever directed by Orson Welles (1915–1985). The film was a landmark in its blending of new methods of storytelling with a sophisticated visual style, modern sound, and the use of technical innovations, and many critics consider it the greatest movie ever made.

As film historian Robert Sklar writes, "No single aspect of *Citizen Kane* was entirely original or previously unknown to filmmakers, but the work's startling impact came from its total effect, the concentration, comprehensiveness, and unity of its stylistic effort."

The plot centers on a reporter's investigation into the life and death of Charles Foster Kane (played by Welles), a complex, larger-than-life American who rose from nothing to become a world-famous publishing tycoon. Most of the story is told in flashbacks by those who knew Kane best, turning the film into a jigsaw puzzle. The reporter, Jerry Thompson, must put together the often contradictory pieces to get a sense of the man. And throughout, Thompson believes that an explanation of "Rosebud," the last word Kane utters before dying, is the key that will unlock the mystery of Kane's life.

The jigsaw puzzle aspect of the film makes it cinema's most noteworthy example of nonlinear storytelling. Unlike most Hollywood films of the time, *Citizen Kane* is not told chronologically, and as Thompson discovers, the pieces do not make a complete puzzle.

Citizen Kane sparked controversy even before its release by RKO Pictures. When the publishing magnate William Randolph Hearst (1863–1951) learned that some of the film was based on his life, he attempted to suppress the project. When he was unsuccessful, Hearst instead used intimidation, blackmail, and newspaper smears, among other tactics, to discredit Welles and RKO.

The film's visual style was jarring for filmgoers in 1941 and still astounds modern viewers. Welles's use of deep-focus photography; exaggerated, expressionistic lighting; long takes; low- and high-angle shots; and layered sound has kept film students occupied for decades.

ADDITIONAL FACTS

1. *In 2007, the American Film Institute named* Citizen Kane *the greatest American film ever made.*

2. *The film was one of the first in which the ceilings of sets could be seen, thanks to Gregg Toland's low-angle camera shots.*

3. *Welles shared the screenwriting Oscar with Herman Mankiewicz (1897–1953), though which man was more responsible for the actual shooting script is a subject of much controversy.*

•• • ••

Containment

In 1946, an American diplomat stationed in Moscow named George Kennan (1904–2005) sent a cable to Washington outlining a proposed strategy for dealing with the Soviet Union. The United States and the USSR had been uneasy allies against Nazi Germany during World War II, but tensions had risen sharply since the end of the war.

In the so-called Long Telegram, Kennan argued that while it was impossible to confront the Soviet Union directly, the United States could still prevent further communist expansion. In a later article he wrote elaborating on his recommendations, Kennan advocated "a policy of firm containment, designed to confront the Russians with unalterable counter-force at every point where they show signs of encroaching upon the interests of a peaceful and stable world."

Kennan's recommendations steered a middle course between that of the hawks who hoped the United States would go on an immediate military offensive to reverse the spread of communism in Eastern Europe and the tactics advocated by former vice president Henry Wallace (1888–1965), who favored a more conciliatory approach to the Soviets.

President Harry Truman (1884–1972) soon endorsed Kennan's strategy of containment, which became the basis for American foreign policy for the remaining forty-five years of the Cold War.

Truman unveiled the policy—soon dubbed the Truman Doctrine—to the public in 1947, when he announced that the United States would intervene, if necessary, to prevent the spread of Communism in Greece and Turkey.

The goal of containing Communist expansion, an aim endorsed by successive presidents from both political parties, would form the rationale for American involvement in wars in Korea and Vietnam.

Ironically, Kennan later regretted many of his recommendations and emerged as a critic of American foreign policy during the Cold War and afterward. He died at age 101, shortly after giving interviews criticizing the 2003 American invasion of Iraq.

ADDITIONAL FACTS

1. *Wallace had served as vice president under Franklin D. Roosevelt (1882–1945) from 1941 to 1945. He ran against Truman on a peace platform as a third-party candidate in the 1948 presidential election.*

2. *The term* cold war *was coined by the British writer George Orwell (1903–1950), the author of* Animal Farm *(1945) and* 1984 *(1949).*

3. *Part of Truman's containment policy called for a massive program of aid to Europe to strengthen American allies; the Marshall Plan was launched in 1947.*

••●••

Arnold Palmer

Before Arnold Palmer, golf in the United States was purely for the moneyed country-club set. But Palmer took the game in a more populist direction with his success in the late 1950s and early 1960s. With his good looks and his aggressive play, Palmer (1929–) hastened the game's popularity boom in the second half of the twentieth century and earned a legion of fans known as Arnie's Army.

The son of a greenskeeper and golf pro at Latrobe Country Club in Pennsylvania, Palmer won sixty-two times on the Professional Golfers' Association of America Tour, including seven major championship victories. He was the first golfer to win $1 million on tour and played on six Ryder Cup teams (serving as US captain twice). He translated his immense popularity into a hugely successful business career that spanned golf course design, auto dealerships, clothing companies, and cable television. (He was a founding member of the Golf Channel.)

Palmer's prime years on the golf course were 1960 to 1963, when he won twenty-nine times on tour. In 1960, he claimed victories in the Masters and the US Open—in which he came back from seven strokes behind in the final round—and was named Sportsman of the Year by *Sports Illustrated*. The Associated Press named him the top athlete of the 1960s. He benefited from the growth of televised golf, and his success in turn helped create new fans for the game.

Although he would not win another major after 1964, Palmer remained "the King"—a champion of the people and one of the most popular players in the world—for another four decades.

ADDITIONAL FACTS

1. *In 1950, Palmer dropped out of Wake Forest University during his senior year, after the death of his friend Bud Worsham. Palmer enlisted in the US Coast Guard and did not play golf seriously until 1953. In 1954, he won the US Amateur Championship, and a year later, he turned professional.*

2. *Palmer won the Masters four times, the US Open once, and the British Open twice. Before his British Open victories, few Americans entered the tournament.*

3. *Another component of golf's growing popularity in the 1960s was Palmer's rivalry with Jack Nicklaus (1940–). The rivalry was born at the 1962 US Open, where Nicklaus upset the heavily favored Palmer for the first win of his career and the first of his eighteen major championships.*

••●••

Hula Hoops

In the spring of 1958, a toy company in California called Wham-O introduced its newest novelty: the Hula Hoop. Based on an age-old toy with origins stretching back to ancient Greece and Rome, Wham-O's plastic version of the hoop sold for $1.98 and became an overnight sensation. In the first four months, the company sold an astonishing 25 million hoops in the United States; within two years, the figure reached 100 million.

At the height of the Hula Hoop's popularity in the summer of 1958, hooping was an omnipresent national fad. Imitators like the Hooper Dooper and Whoop-de-Doo also quickly appeared around the nation's waists.

But the fad died almost as quickly as it had begun; indeed, Wham-O actually lost money in 1958 because sales plummeted after kids went back to school in September, causing unwanted hoops to pile up in the company's warehouses.

By the early 1960s, sales had stabilized. Stores continue to sell the hoops, which have enjoyed periodic revivals—albeit never at the level of the initial craze.

With its brief, overwhelming popularity, the Hula Hoop has been described as the prototype for later consumer fads. "No sensation has ever swept the country like the Hula Hoop," wrote Richard Johnson (1953–) in the book *American Fads;* the hoop "remains the one standard against which all national crazes are measured."

Recently, hooping has shown some signs of a resurgence, in part because of a jam band called the String Cheese Incident, which threw hoops into the crowd at its concerts in the mid-1990s. Some regulars at the show—the "Friends of Cheese"—took to the hoops, and a new, if smaller, trend was born.

ADDITIONAL FACTS

1. *Wham-O also introduced the first Frisbee in 1958.*

2. *Hooping was also a widespread fad in fourteenth-century England.*

3. *Enthusiasts have declared September 9, 2009, World Hoop Day. Mark your calendars!*

• • ● • •

Julia Child

Julia Child (1912–2004) broke new ground as America's first celebrity chef. Beginning with the 1963 debut of her public-television show, *The French Chef*, Child demystified sophisticated French cooking for the American viewing audience and became immensely popular in the process. During her four-decade television career, she hosted several shows and wrote a dozen cookbooks, including some of the finest ever published on French cuisine.

Child's first true exposure to French cooking came in 1948, when she and her husband moved to Paris. She enrolled at le Cordon Bleu cooking school and soon befriended fellow enthusiasts Simone Beck and Louisette Bertholle. Together, they founded a cooking school (l'École des Trois Gourmandes) and wrote *Mastering the Art of French Cooking*, which was published in 1961.

After Child appeared on a book show on Boston's WGBH, the station invited her to create her own program, and *The French Chef* was born. Child's no-nonsense yet relaxed approach was an immediate sensation with viewers, and PBS affiliates across the country soon picked up the show.

She was a fixture on public television for forty years, earning generations of fans and accumulating scores of honors. In 1966, she became the first PBS personality to win an Emmy Award. Child was also the first woman inducted into the Culinary Institute of America's hall of fame, and she received the prestigious Légion d'honneur from the French government in 2000.

Child died of complications from kidney failure at age ninety-one.

ADDITIONAL FACTS

1. *Child's signature sign-off from her television programs was "Bon appétit!"*

2. *During World War II, Child served as a file clerk with the Office of Strategic Services (the precursor to the Central Intelligence Agency) in Washington, DC, and in Ceylon (now Sri Lanka) and China.*

3. *She was a breast cancer survivor.*

•••••

1984

After frightening an entire generation of readers in the mid-twentieth century, George Orwell's nightmare political novel *1984*, first published in 1949, has lost none of its power or prescience today. Its effects on the English language are still felt sixty years after its publication, and its depictions of totalitarianism, government invasion of privacy, and other oppressions are still disturbingly relevant.

Orwell (1903–1950) set *1984* in a fictional, futuristic Great Britain that has become part of an enormous totalitarian state called Oceania. Virtually all aspects of society are dominated by the government—an omniscient, intrusive police organization that monitors all of its citizens constantly, even in their private moments. Ubiquitous propaganda touts the greatness of Oceania's ruling party and its leader—a mysterious, mustachioed figure known as Big Brother. Giant posters throughout London remind everyone, "Big Brother is watching you."

The novel's protagonist, Winston Smith, is a low-ranking clerk at the government's Ministry of Truth, where he is responsible for altering historical records so that they always match the party's current stance. Smith secretly hates the party, though, and puts his career and life at risk by embarking on an illegal affair with a female colleague and joining an underground revolutionary organization.

Orwell's masterpiece is one of the best-known dystopian novels ever written. Rather than depicting an ideal, utopian world, dystopian works portray the opposite—a nightmare society, often one that is brutal and oppressive. In the years since *1984* was published, the genre of dystopian fiction has burgeoned, not only in literature but also in films such as *Blade Runner* (1982), *The Matrix* (1999), and *Children of Men* (2006).

ADDITIONAL FACTS

1. *Orwell based many aspects of the society in 1984 on the Soviet Union under the totalitarian regime of Joseph Stalin (1879–1953). The novel's physical descriptions of Big Brother even resemble Stalin himself.*

2. *The book contributed many words and phrases to modern English. Invasive or oppressive policies are often described as Orwellian, and the idea of Big Brother intruding in everyday citizens' lives is still commonly cited.*

3. *Apple Inc. drew on 1984 and the image of Big Brother in a now-famous TV commercial announcing the launch of the Macintosh computer line in 1984. That commercial, in turn, was parodied in an anti–Hillary Clinton ad that appeared on the Internet during the 2008 US presidential campaign.*

•••••

Hank Williams

The country musician Hank Williams (1923–1953) established a tragic pattern that would become all too common in the history of American popular music: a difficult and impoverished childhood, early success through hard work and dedication, decline as a result of alcoholism and drug addiction, redemption and superstardom, and, finally, a relapse into old habits and a tragically early death.

Hiram King "Hank" Williams was born in a small town in Alabama, with a spinal cord disorder that would cause him lifelong pain. His father was hospitalized with a brain aneurysm for much of Williams's young life, and his mother was forced to move across the South looking for work during the Great Depression.

When the family settled in Montgomery, Alabama, Williams took the first step toward his dream of becoming a country star by playing guitar outside the local radio station. The station eventually invited him inside to play on the air, and "the Singing Kid" was so successful that he was given a twice-weekly radio show. Soon thereafter, he started his first band, the Drifting Cowboys, which broke up in 1941. Williams's alcoholism became a problem at this time, eventually causing him to lose his radio show.

By the late 1940s and early 1950s, however, Williams had recovered his health and become one of the nation's biggest stars. He was the most popular performer at the Grand Ole Opry—the famed country-music radio show broadcast live from Nashville, Tennessee—and had eleven number one hits, starting with "Lovesick Blues" in 1949. Other hits included the classics "Cold, Cold Heart" (1951), "Hey Good Lookin'" (1951), and "Your Cheatin' Heart" (1953). Nonetheless, Williams's problems with alcohol, morphine, and painkillers returned, and he was kicked out of the Grand Ole Opry in October 1952. This time, there was no comeback: The great star of country music was found dead in the back of his car on January 1, 1953, at age twenty-nine.

ADDITIONAL FACTS

1. *Hank Williams's last single was called "I'll Never Get Out of This World Alive" (1952).*

2. *Using the pseudonym "Luke the Drifter," Williams recorded fourteen tracks of storytelling and blues that were very different in style from anything else he did.*

3. *Tony Bennett (1926–) made Williams's song "Cold, Cold Heart" a crossover hit when he covered it in 1951.*

•••••

Humphrey Bogart

Humphrey Bogart (1899–1957) emerged from a privileged upbringing on Manhattan's Upper West Side to become the archetypal Hollywood tough guy of the 1940s and 1950s. Playing some of the silver screen's most enduring characters, including Rick Blaine in *Casablanca* (1942), Bogart delivered an almost endless number of memorable lines, appearing in an array of classic films that made him a worldwide icon.

Bogart began his acting career portraying romantic leads onstage in the 1920s and made a few minor film appearances in the early 1930s. His breakthrough stage role as gangster Duke Mantee came in Robert Sherwood's 1935 play *The Petrified Forest,* which was a smash hit that year on Broadway. Bogart reprised the role in the 1936 film version of the play, which set him on course to play a string of villains in mostly low-budget B movies.

His Hollywood breakthrough came in Raoul Walsh's *High Sierra* (1941), in which he played the complex antihero Roy "Mad Dog" Earle. Later that year, in John Huston's *The Maltese Falcon,* Bogart ascended to Hollywood stardom as hard-bitten detective Sam Spade, honing the acerbic on-screen persona that would define the rest of his career.

In 1942, he appeared in his most celebrated film, Michael Curtiz's *Casablanca.* As saloon keeper Rick Blaine, Bogart uttered such classic lines as "Here's looking at you, kid"; "We'll always have Paris"; and "Louis, I think this is the beginning of a beautiful friendship." In that film, he also perfected the role of the tough, caustic loner who was, deep down, a true romantic.

His appearance in the 1944 film *To Have and Have Not,* based on the novel by Ernest Hemingway, was particularly notable because of his costar: a nineteen-year-old starlet named Lauren Bacall. They married in 1945, when Bogart, who'd had three previous marriages, was forty-five. Together, they starred in Howard Hawks's *The Big Sleep* (1946), one of the best detective films ever made.

Over the last decade of his career, his notable films included *The Treasure of the Sierra Madre* (1948); *In a Lonely Place* (1950); *The African Queen* (1951), for which he won his only Academy Award for Best Actor; *The Caine Mutiny* (1954); and his final film, *The Harder They Fall* (1956). He died of throat cancer at age fifty-seven.

ADDITIONAL FACTS

1. *Bogart appeared in seventy-six films from 1930 to 1956.*

2. *His persona has inspired several films of tribute, from Jean-Luc Godard's* À bout de soufle *(Breathless, 1960) to Woody Allen's* Play It Again, Sam *(1972) and beyond.*

3. *In 1999, the American Film Institute named Bogart the screen's top male legend of the twentieth century, and* Entertainment Weekly *picked him as the top movie legend of all time in 1993.*

· · ● · ·

Television

Today, television is one of the most ubiquitous parts of American life. The average American watches more than four hours of television a day, and more than half the homes in the United States have three or more television sets. All told, Americans watch 250 billion hours of TV every year.

Only sixty years ago, however, television was an expensive, cumbersome novelty that was found in only a handful of homes.

Television technology developed incrementally, beginning with the first primitive models, invented in 1920. Major radio networks soon developed television affiliates to reach the tiny number of TV owners. CBS went on the air in 1931. NBC broadcast its first black-and-white television images in 1939.

Still, the viewership for the fledgling networks was extremely limited. For instance, only about 1,000 homes in the New York area had televisions in 1939, when NBC began transmitting from an antenna atop the Empire State Building.

World War II temporarily halted the growth of television, as the government shut down commercial broadcasting and factories that made TV components were switched to wartime production.

With the end of the war, however, the networks went back on the air. In the late 1940s and early 1950s, the price of TV sets plummeted, and Americans began buying them in droves to see television pioneers such as the comedian Milton Berle (1908–2002) and the newsman Edward R. Murrow (1908–1965).

The cultural impact of television was controversial from its inception. TV's more idealistic backers hoped the newfangled invention would spread knowledge with news and educational programming. But critics feared it was draining the life out of American culture. Newton Minow (1926–), in a famous 1961 speech called Television and the Public Interest, called the medium a "vast wasteland" of shallow comedies, violence, and cartoons.

In the speech, Minow described television's cultural impact in terms that have not changed greatly in the four decades since: "When television is good, nothing—not the theater, not the magazines or newspapers—nothing is better," he said. "But when television is bad, nothing is worse."

ADDITIONAL FACTS

1. *The great American inventor Thomas Edison (1847–1931) and telephone inventor Alexander Graham Bell (1847–1922) both contributed important work toward the development of TV technology.*

2. *The first new network since the early days of television was the Fox Broadcasting Company, which began transmitting in 1986.*

3. *Cable television was originally introduced to bring TV to rural areas that could not receive broadcast signals.*

•• • ••

Johnny Unitas

Johnny Unitas (1933–2002) was one of the most unlikely success stories in the history of American professional sports. Unwanted by the Pittsburgh Steelers after the team drafted him in 1955, he spent the ensuing season working construction and earning $6 a game playing quarterback for a semiprofessional team in Pittsburgh. He signed with the Baltimore Colts in 1956 and went on to become arguably the greatest quarterback in National Football League (NFL) history.

Over Unitas's eighteen-year career, he set just about every NFL passing record, including yards (40,239), touchdowns (290), and consecutive games with a touchdown (47, a mark that still stands). But Unitas was always about more than statistics—he was about leadership, poise, and competitiveness. Said Colts teammate John Mackey (1941–) of the quarterback, "It's like being in the huddle with God."

Unitas spent seventeen seasons with the Colts, leading the team to NFL championships in 1958 and 1959 and contributing to a victory in Super Bowl V. (He was injured in the second quarter and missed the game's second half.) Three times, he was named league Most Valuable Player, and he was a ten-time Pro Bowl selection.

Unitas's signature performance came in the 1958 NFL Championship game against the New York Giants. He engineered a drive that resulted in the game-tying field goal with seven seconds left in regulation play, then led a thirteen-play drive in overtime that culminated in Alan Ameche's (1933–1988) one-yard touchdown plunge to give the Colts the title, 23–17. It is commonly known as the Greatest Game Ever Played.

Unitas played his last season with the San Diego Chargers before retiring in 1973. In his later years, his body showed the effects of the physical abuse he took on the field—he had both knees replaced and lost most of the use of his celebrated right arm and three fingers on his right hand. He died of a heart attack at age sixty-nine.

ADDITIONAL FACTS

1. *After graduating from high school in Pittsburgh, Unitas hoped to play for Notre Dame, but the Irish did not want a 138-pound quarterback. He attended the University of Louisville instead.*

2. *Unitas was elected to the Pro Football Hall of Fame in 1979.*

3. *He was the first quarterback in NFL history to pass for 40,000 career yards.*

• • • • •

Barbie

Cultural icon, fashion plate, toy, muse—Mattel's Barbie doll has been many things to many people. However, one thing has been clear since her debut in 1959: Barbie is nearly as controversial as she is beloved.

Creator and Mattel cofounder Ruth Handler (1916–2002) got the idea for Barbie from Bild Lilli, an adult-bodied German fashion doll that was originally intended for adults but became popular with young girls as well. In a market glutted with baby dolls and stuffed animals, Handler recognized the overwhelming demand for a doll that would let children play at grown-up dramas. Handler was right, and Mattel sold 350,000 Barbie dolls in the first year alone.

The doll's high-profile success has brought with it an equal measure of scrutiny. Among other things, Barbie's unrealistic figure has been criticized for promoting an unhealthy self-image in young girls. (A real woman with Barbie's shape would be unable to menstruate because of her extremely low body-fat percentage.) Further, by some estimates, Barbie's abnormally small waist and curved feet might render her physically incapable of standing up. The release of Teen Talk Barbie (1992) only made critics roar louder, with each doll spouting four out of 270 possible ditzy phrases, such as "Will we ever have enough clothes?" and "Math class is tough!" Hubbub over the latter prompted Mattel's offer to exchange any Teen Talk Barbie programmed with the offending exclamation.

Barbie has evolved over the years to reflect societal changes, both in America and internationally. Not only has the doll explored multiple careers (among them, astronaut, race-car driver, doctor, and flight attendant), Barbie has also introduced friends of diverse backgrounds and ethnicities, and even taken on different cultural identities. For example, Mattel offered a Colored Francie doll in 1965 and an African-American doll named Christie in 1968, but it wasn't until 1980 that a black Barbie and a Hispanic Barbie came on the market.

ADDITIONAL FACTS

1. *Barbie and her male counterpart, Ken, are named for Ruth Handler's children, Barbara and Kenneth.*

2. *It has been estimated that more than a billion Barbie dolls have been sold worldwide.*

3. *Barbie became the first toy marketed directly to children and not to their parents when Handler paid $500,000 to become the sole sponsor of* The Mickey Mouse Club.

•••••

Barry Goldwater

Barry Goldwater (1909–1998) served as an outspoken and controversial US senator from Arizona for five terms and was the Republican nominee for president in 1964. But his most significant impact was as the leader of the modern conservative movement, pulling the center of the Republican Party to the right, away from its liberal eastern wing.

Goldwater's political philosophy rested on reducing the role of government at home and fighting Communism abroad. He was opposed to federally funded social programs created by the New Deal in the 1930s and criticized the Modern Republicanism policies of President Dwight D. Eisenhower (1890–1969) as a "dime store New Deal."

In the Senate, Goldwater advocated the repeal of the income tax, welfare programs, and the nuclear test ban treaty; he also opposed foreign aid, and federal aid to education. He assailed the landmark Supreme Court ruling in *Brown v. Board of Education* (1954), calling it outside the Court's jurisdiction to decide on desegregation of schools. He also voted against the 1964 Civil Rights Act, a decision he later regretted.

Goldwater criticized politicians (including Eisenhower) who sought peace with the Soviets rather than victory over them. He believed the United States needed to build up its military, withdraw diplomatic recognition of the Soviet Union, and encourage the people living under communist rule to rebel against their leaders.

His 1960 book *Conscience of a Conservative* was a bestseller and an important statement in the development of modern conservatism.

After serving two terms in the Senate, he ran for the White House in 1964 and was handily defeated by President Lyndon B. Johnson (1908–1973). Though Goldwater carried just six states, his campaign laid the foundation for the presidential triumph of Ronald Reagan (1911–2004) in 1980.

Goldwater returned to the Senate in 1969 and served three more terms, though over the years, he lost touch with the conservative movement. He clashed with other conservatives on various issues, including abortion (he was pro-choice) and whether to allow homosexuals in the military (he supported it). Health problems hindered his effectiveness in his final years in the Senate, and he retired in 1987. He died at age eighty-nine.

ADDITIONAL FACTS

1. *Goldwater is widely credited with convincing President Richard M. Nixon (1913–1994) to resign during the Watergate scandal in 1974.*

2. *Reagan's compelling 1964 speech supporting Goldwater turned the former actor into a major political player and contributed to his 1966 election as governor of California.*

3. *In 1986, Goldwater championed a bill that reorganized the top levels of the Pentagon, establishing the chairman of the Joint Chiefs of Staff as the principal military advisor to the president. Goldwater later called it "the only goddamn thing I've done in the Senate that's worth a damn."*

••••

Pablo Neruda

As active in politics as he was in literature, Chilean poet Pablo Neruda (1904–1973) lived a globe-trotting life marked by heights of fame and dark periods of exile. Though Neruda was a controversial figure for some of the political stances he took during his lifetime, he was an immense talent and produced some of the richest lyrical poetry in recent memory.

Neruda wrote poems as early as age ten, despite his father's discouragement. He was first published in his midteens, and he first attracted significant attention for *Twenty Love Poems and a Song of Despair* (1924). Notable for its explicit sensuality, the collection stunned readers all the more because that the poet was only nineteen.

Over the next decade, Neruda became a beloved public figure in Chile and was appointed to a succession of diplomatic posts abroad, from Burma to Mexico to Spain. The widespread poverty he witnessed during these travels turned his sympathies leftward and spurred him toward political involvement. After becoming embroiled on the leftist side of the Spanish civil war, he returned home and was elected to the Chilean senate.

Neruda's South American travels during the 1940s inspired his *Canto General* (1950), an epic poem celebrating the history, land, and people of his native continent. Around this time, Neruda fell so severely out of favor with the Chilean government that he had to go into hiding and flee Chile in 1949. In exile, he remained a polarizing figure due to his outspoken praise for the Soviet dictator Joseph Stalin (1879–1953). After a safe return to Chile and remarkable poetic output over two more decades, Neruda once again fell into political disfavor in 1973 when a right-wing coup overthrew Chile's government. He died of cancer just days later, and the new regime denied him a state funeral, despite his popularity with the Chilean people.

ADDITIONAL FACTS

1. *Neruda's birth name was Neftalí Ricardo Reyes Basoalto. Borrowing from the Czech writer Jan Neruda (1834–1891), he adopted a pseudonym so that his published poems would escape his disapproving father's eye.*

2. *The CIA viewed Neruda as a Communist agitator and a threat; during the 1960s, it even launched several covert propaganda operations in an attempt to discredit his reputation.*

3. *Because of Neruda's vocal support for Stalin, the decision to award him the 1971 Nobel Prize in Literature was one of the most contentious in the prize's history.*

4. *Neruda is a major character in the Italian film* Il Postino *(1994), in which he teaches a rustic postman to appreciate poetry. Most of the film's events, though, are fictional.*

•••••

Frank Sinatra

Before Elvis and the Beatles became pop sensations surrounded by adoring teenage fans, Frank Sinatra (1915–1998) almost single-handedly created the teen market for popular music in the 1940s. In the six decades after his first brush with fame, Sinatra endured as one of the most famous musical performers of the twentieth century and a cultural icon on stage and on screen.

Sinatra first rose to prominence as a member of the Dorsey Brothers Orchestra, a big-band group. Thanks to his smooth singing voice and appealing looks, Sinatra attracted a particular breed of fans: bobby-soxers, the teenage girls who flocked to Sinatra's shows in poodle skirts and socks rolled down to their ankles. When Sinatra eventually left the Dorsey Brothers, his fame grew, culminating in a 1943 show at the Hollywood Bowl before a crowd of 10,000 shrieking adolescents.

In the 1950s, however, Sinatra's success with the bobby-soxers waned. He made some false starts in his search for a new audience but soon reclaimed his stardom with his Academy Award–winning performance in the 1953 film *From Here to Eternity*. He then released a string of now-classic albums, including *In the Wee Small Hours* (1954), *Songs for Swingin' Lovers* (1956), and *Come Fly with Me* (1958). On these albums Sinatra first performed the songs with which he will always be associated: "I've Got You under My Skin," "Autumn in New York," "Come Fly with Me," and many others.

His career revived, Sinatra remained successful for the rest of his life. His television specials won high ratings, especially his show welcoming Elvis Presley (1935–1977) back home from the army; the 1960 film *Oceans 11* was the most successful of that year; and Sinatra's albums in collaboration with big-band leader Count Basie (1904–1984) and Brazilian composer Antonio Carlos Jobim (1927–1994) were some of the most well received of his career. In 1969, more than three decades after Sinatra began his singing career, he recorded his signature song, "My Way."

ADDITIONAL FACTS

1. *The sequence in* The Godfather *(1972) in which mobsters threaten a Hollywood producer for failing to hire singer Johnny Fontaine (most famously by putting a horse's head in his bed) was reportedly based on unsubstantiated rumors about mob involvement in Sinatra's early contract negotiations.*

2. *Sinatra's 1943 Hollywood Bowl show was so successful that it wiped out the venue's significant debts in a single evening.*

3. *Dissatisfied with his treatment at Columbia Records, Sinatra started Reprise Records in 1960. Reprise is still in business and has recorded artists as varied as Fleetwood Mac, Depeche Mode, and the Smashing Pumpkins.*

• • ● • •

Ingrid Bergman

The Swedish-born screen legend Ingrid Bergman (1915–1982) is best known for her portrayals of tormented, fragile women, particularly in *Casablanca* (1942), *Gaslight* (1944), and *Notorious* (1946).

In real life, her affair with the director Roberto Rossellini, which became public in 1949, caused an international scandal and led to a seven-year exile from Hollywood.

Bergman starred in films in Sweden and Germany before the Hollywood producer David O. Selznick saw her in *Intermezzo* (1936) and brought her to the United States. She made four Hollywood movies before *Casablanca,* her most memorable film. Bergman played Ilsa Lund, a woman caught in a love triangle between the man to whom she's devoted (played by Paul Henreid) and the man she loves (played by Humphrey Bogart).

Two years later, she received her first Academy Award nomination for best actress for her performance in a film adaptation of Ernest Hemingway's *For Whom the Bell Tolls* (1943). And a year after that, she won her first Oscar for *Gaslight,* playing a woman slowly driven mad by her criminal husband (Charles Boyer).

Bergman appeared in two more critical and box office hits, *Spellbound* (1945) and *The Bells of St. Mary's* (1945), before filming her second signature performance, in Alfred Hitchcock's *Notorious* (1946). In it, she again portrayed a character in a love triangle—a story that would soon play out for her in real life.

When her affair with Rossellini became public in 1949, both she and the noted Italian director were married and had children. In 1950, she gave birth to an out-of-wedlock child (son Roberto) after working with Rossellini on the film *Stromboli* (1950).

The scandal was devastating. Reverberations even reached the floor of the US Senate, where Bergman was publicly condemned. She divorced her husband, Petter Lindström, moved to Italy, and married Rossellini in 1950.

Until her divorce from Rossellini in 1957, Bergman made four more films with him and had two more children.

She made her triumphant return to Hollywood with *Anastasia* (1956), for which she won her second Academy Award. Her film career tailed off from there, although she returned to prominence in *Murder on the Orient Express* (1974), winning a best supporting actress Academy Award. She died of cancer on her sixty-seventh birthday.

ADDITIONAL FACTS

1. *Bergman is considered one of cinema's true natural beauties, renowned for using little or no makeup in her films.*

2. Casablanca *is the only film in which both Bergman and Bogart starred.*

3. *Two of Bergman's children became famous in their own right—daughter Pia Lindström (1938–) as an actress and television anchorwoman, and Isabella Rossellini (1952–) as an actress and model.*

• • ● ● •

Organ Transplants

The first successful organ transplant took place in 1954, when an American surgeon named Joseph Murray (1919–) transplanted a living kidney from one identical twin to another. The operation, which took about four hours, was immediately hailed as a milestone in medical history, setting the stage for some of the major medical advances of the late twentieth century.

Moving an organ from one human body to another posed a daunting array of medical challenges. The biggest worry was that the patient's immune system would reject the new organ. Before Murray's surgery, previous transplants had failed because the patient's body treated the new organ as a foreign parasite and immediately attacked it.

Because identical twins have identical genes, however, Murray was able to circumvent the rejection problem. His operation proved that a transplant was possible and inspired scientists to tackle the problem of organ rejection.

In the 1950s and 1960s, pharmaceutical companies rushed to develop drugs that would suppress the immune system's rejection of foreign tissue. When these drugs became available, transplants of organs from unrelated donors became possible for the first time.

In 1963, the Mississippi physician James D. Hardy (1918–2003) performed the first lung transplant, and in 1967, the South African doctor Christiaan Barnard (1922–2001) performed the first heart transplant.

In the decades since, the success of organ transplants has increased considerably. Today, more than 80 percent of patients live for up to one year after receiving a new heart, and more than 70 percent survive for five years or longer.

ADDITIONAL FACTS

1. *The oldest surviving heart transplant patient is Tony Huesman (1956–), who received his new heart in 1978.*

2. *Murray was a corecipient of the Nobel Prize in Medicine in 1990, along with the Seattle doctor E. Donnall Thomas (1920–).*

3. *Richard Herrick, the recipient of the first kidney transplant, lived for another eight years after the operation.*

· · ● ● · ·

Bill Russell

In the history of basketball, no player has been as synonymous with defense, team play, and winning as Bill Russell (1934–). He was the cornerstone of the midcentury Boston Celtics dynasty, playing on each of the franchise's eleven championship teams from 1956 to 1969. He also served as player-coach for the final two of those title runs, succeeding his mentor, Red Auerbach (1917–2006).

Russell, a six-foot-ten center, revolutionized the game by proving that a player could dominate without being a prolific scorer. Even though he averaged only 15.1 points for his career, he was still voted the National Basketball Association's Most Valuable Player (MVP) five times and was a twelve-time all-star in his thirteen-year career.

He was the most feared shot blocker of his era and was a rebounding wizard, averaging 22.5 rebounds for his career. He was not as imposing a physical presence as his great rival, Wilt Chamberlain (1936–1999), but he was a terrific athlete with unparalleled instincts, body position, and intelligence. In most years, Chamberlain posted the better statistics, but Russell won the championships.

Russell came to the Celtics after winning two college basketball titles at the University of San Francisco and claiming a gold medal at the 1956 Olympics. Before his arrival, the Celtics had never won an NBA title; by the time he retired in 1969, they were a symbol of success.

Despite his achievements, Russell faced racism in Boston and had a difficult relationship with the city's fans and media. He famously refuses to sign autographs, and he chose not to attend when the Celtics retired his number, 6, in 1972. He also passed when he was inducted into the Basketball Hall of Fame in 1974.

Some of Russell's hard feelings toward the city have softened in recent years, and he attended the ceremony when the Celtics reretired his number in 1999.

ADDITIONAL FACTS

1. *In 1961–1962, Russell averaged 18.9 points to Chamberlain's 50.4—but Russell was still voted the league's MVP by his fellow players.*

2. *In 1968, he was named Sportsman of the Year by* Sports Illustrated *and was tabbed as the top athlete of the 1960s by the* Sporting News.

3. *Russell received an honorary doctorate from Harvard in 2007 in recognition of his accomplishments and for "revolutionizing basketball by elevating defensive play."*

•• • ••

Marilyn Monroe

Norma Jeane Mortenson was born to a single mother on June 1, 1926, raised by a series of foster parents (with a brief stint at an orphanage), and married at age sixteen to a merchant marine sailor named James Dougherty (1921–2005), with whom she lived near Los Angeles, California.

When Dougherty was sent to the South Pacific during World War II, Norma Jeane worked at a munitions factory in Hollywood. She was noticed by an army photographer, who took pictures of the young brunette for *Yank,* a magazine distributed to service members, and referred her to a modeling agency. It was while she was there that Norma Jeane had plastic surgery on her nose, straightened and dyed her hair, and changed her name to Marilyn Monroe.

Monroe's modeling career soon led to film stardom. She began by acting in small pictures for Fox studios but soon moved on to the more serious role of Miss Caswell in the 1950 film *All About Eve.* As successful as that film was, it was her performance in the 1953 film *Niagara* that made her an international star and led to her most famous roles, in films such as *Gentlemen Prefer Blondes* (1953), *How to Marry a Millionaire* (1953), and *Some Like It Hot* (1959).

Monroe's public success was a stark contrast to her tumultuous private life. She left her first husband after beginning her modeling career and went through a succession of dramatic and short-lived relationships thereafter. She wedded Yankee center fielder Joe DiMaggio (1914–1999) in 1954, a union that lasted less than a year, and married playwright Arthur Miller (1915–2005) in 1956. Her public image and private demons collided during a televised celebration in May 1962, when she sang an infamously sultry "Happy Birthday" to President John F. Kennedy (1917–1963), with whom she allegedly had an affair.

She was fired from the film *Something's Got to Give* the following month and died of a drug overdose on August 5, 1962.

ADDITIONAL FACTS

1. *In 1999,* Playboy *magazine named Monroe the number one sex star of the century.*

2. *After she had become famous, Monroe's agents tried to cover up the fact that she had posed nude for a calendar in 1947, but Monroe refused to play along and admitted the fact to her fans.*

3. *Before being fired from* Something's Got to Give, *Monroe shot the first nude scene by a major Hollywood actress for the film.*

••●••

Walter Cronkite

In 1972, one poll called him the most trusted figure in American life. As anchor and managing editor of the *CBS Evening News* from 1962 to 1981, Walter Cronkite (1916–) delivered the news to America in a straightforward, objective manner, and in many ways spoke for America as well.

When President John F. Kennedy (1917–1963) was assassinated, it was Cronkite who told the country that its young president had died. When Cronkite returned from a trip to Vietnam following the Tet Offensive in 1968, he told viewers, "It seems more certain than ever that the bloody experience of Vietnam is a stalemate." That comment prompted President Lyndon Johnson (1908–1973) to say, "If I've lost Cronkite, I've lost America." And when *Apollo 11* rocketed toward the moon, Cronkite echoed the thoughts of many Americans, crying out, "Go, baby, go!"

Cronkite got his start in the news business working for newspapers and small radio stations in the Midwest. After the United States entered World War II, he took a job as a war correspondent for United Press. He went ashore on D-day, parachuted with the 101st Airborne, flew bombing missions over Germany, and covered the Nuremberg trials.

In 1950, he joined CBS, first at its Washington affiliate, then working for the national news operation. He hosted a series of CBS news shows and anchored the network's presidential election coverage beginning in 1952.

In 1962, Cronkite succeeded Douglas Edwards (1917–1990) as the anchor of the *CBS Evening News*, a post he held until 1981, when he retired in accordance with CBS policies. Within a year of taking over, he expanded the show from fifteen minutes to thirty minutes, which remains the network news standard.

When he retired at age sixty-five, he gave up the anchor chair and managing editor duties to Dan Rather (1931–), who served in those roles until 2005. In retirement, Cronkite has continued to report, covering stories for CBS, PBS, CNN, and the Discovery Channel, among other activities.

ADDITIONAL FACTS

1. *Cronkite's tagline at the end of the* CBS Evening News *was "And that's the way it is."*

2. *In 1972, the* CBS Evening News *picked up on reporting by the* Washington Post *and produced a two-part series on Watergate that helped make it a national story.*

3. *In 1977, Cronkite asked the Egyptian president Anwar el-Sādāt (1918–1981) if he would go to Jerusalem to talk to the Israelis. Sādāt said he would, and the next day, Israeli prime minister Menachem Begin (1913–1992) invited Sādāt to Jerusalem, a step that eventually led to the Camp David Accords and an Israeli-Egyptian peace treaty.*

• • • •

The Catcher in the Rye (1951)

The Catcher in the Rye, by J. D. Salinger (1919–), became a cultural phenomenon upon its publication in 1951 and has remained one of the best-selling American novels of the twentieth century. Though the work has been especially popular among readers in high school and college, its exploration of adolescent angst has resonated with readers of all ages.

J. D. Salinger

The protagonist of *The Catcher in the Rye* is Holden Caulfield, a disgruntled, antiauthoritarian sixteen-year-old who has failed out of several prep schools. When he receives notice at the end of the semester that he is once again about to be expelled from school for poor performance, he decides to return home to Manhattan a few days early and get a hotel room without telling his parents he has arrived.

Most of Holden's experiences during his free days in Manhattan are aimless and abortive: He walks around the city, drinks, flirts halfheartedly with girls, calls acquaintances, and meets various strangers. Throughout, the cranky and jaded Holden complains endlessly about the hypocrisy he sees in the world of adults, dismissing most of the people he meets as "phonies." Although Holden is perceptive and his observations frequently ring true, he is judgmental, self-absorbed, and often naïve, which undermines his reliability as a narrator.

The Catcher in the Rye was a shock for 1950s readers, many of whom were unprepared for such a brazen assault on the social conformity of the postwar decade. The novel's use of slang and occasional profanity, as well as its frankness about sex, continues to offend some readers. Nonetheless, it is exactly this irreverent, casual quality that has kept the novel a bestseller and a perennial staple of high-school reading lists. All told, the novel has sold more than 10 million copies worldwide.

ADDITIONAL FACTS

1. *The infamously reclusive Salinger disappeared entirely from public view in 1965, after moving to rural New Hampshire. His last public interview was in 1980.*

2. *Despite its popularity,* The Catcher in the Rye *has never been adapted for stage or screen, because Salinger has never granted permission.*

3. The Catcher in the Rye *is the only full-length novel Salinger has published. He is believed to have written at least two more novels since he disappeared from public life, but they have yet to appear in print.*

•••••

Ella Fitzgerald

Singer Ella Fitzgerald (1917–1996), the First Lady of Song, was renowned for her near-perfect performances. Her vocal range was so wide that she could sing almost anything with incredible clarity, and her voice was so much her instrument that she perfected a style known as scat singing, in which the performer improvises entirely in nonsense words or vocal sounds. A prolific performer, Fitzgerald recorded many of the most beloved renditions of canonical tunes from the Great American Songbook.

The *Great American Songbook* refers to a collection of songs that were mostly written between 1920 and 1960, an era that extends from the end of Tin Pan Alley to the advent of rock and roll. In jazz, these tunes are often referred to as standards. Contributors include songwriters Irving Berlin (1888–1989) ("White Christmas," "Blue Skies") and Hoagy Carmichael (1899–1981) ("Stardust," "Georgia on My Mind"), Broadway composers George (1898–1937) and Ira (1896–1983) Gershwin ("I Got Rhythm," "Embraceable You"), and performers and bandleaders such as Duke Ellington (1899–1974) ("In a Sentimental Mood").

Over the course of a career that lasted more than half a century, Fitzgerald recorded all these songs and many others. She got her start in 1934, at the age of seventeen, when she won an amateur-night competition at the Apollo Theater in Harlem. She began performing with a big band soon after, and by 1939 she was leading Ella Fitzgerald and Her Famous Orchestra. Fitzgerald achieved her greatest success, however, as a solo artist. While at Verve Records in the 1950s, she released her eight songbook albums, including *Ella Fitzgerald Sings the Cole Porter Song Book* and *Ella Fitzgerald Sings the Irving Berlin Song Book*. She was also famous for her collaborations with Louis Armstrong (1901–1971), with whom she recorded three records, including a version of the Gershwin musical *Porgy and Bess*.

ADDITIONAL FACTS

1. *Songwriter Ira Gershwin gave Fitzgerald one of the biggest compliments of her life when he said, "I didn't realize our songs were so good until Ella sang them."*

2. *Even after the era of the Great American Songbook came to an end, many artists returned to standards as the basis for their avant-garde experiments. A particularly famous example is a recording of "My Favorite Things" by the saxophonist John Coltrane (1926–1967).*

3. *Out of respect for Fitzgerald's songbook series, Frank Sinatra (1915–1998) did not allow his record label to repackage his performances into composer-based albums.*

••●••

Casablanca (1942)

Casablanca's combination of mystery, suspense, romance, and comedy has made Michael Curtiz's (1886–1962) film one of the most beloved movies in history. Featuring a cast headed by the legendary Hollywood actors Humphrey Bogart and Ingrid Bergman, and taking World War II as its historical backdrop, the film tackles honor, duty, self-sacrifice, and lost love—and does so in a way that moviegoing audiences have found hugely entertaining for decades.

The film went on to win Academy Awards for Best Picture, Best Director, and Best Screenplay for 1943. (Although the film was originally released in 1942, it did not go into wide release until 1943.) And in 2007, the American Film Institute ranked *Casablanca* at number three on its list of the best American films ever made, behind only *Citizen Kane* (1941) and *The Godfather* (1972).

Critics have credited several aspects of *Casablanca* for its enduring popularity, including the chemistry between stars Bogart and Bergman; the performance of the strong supporting cast; the witty dialogue, much of which was penned by brothers Philip and Julius Epstein; the sweeping score, written by Max Steiner; and the romance and intrigue of the plot. In truth, *Casablanca* would not have been *Casablanca* without any one of those parts.

The story of the film's production itself could only have been dreamed up in Hollywood. It began as an unproduced play called *Everybody Comes to Rick's,* by Murray Burnett and Joan Alison. Warner Bros. paid $20,000 for the rights to the script, a record at the time for an unproduced play.

The screenwriters wrote and rewrote the script throughout shooting—indeed, nobody, not even the writers themselves, knew exactly how the story would end.

The plot itself revolves around European refugees trying to escape the Nazis in French-occupied Morocco, as well as a love triangle involving the three lead characters. (The third was played by Paul Henreid [1905–1992].) But the plot itself pales in comparison to the film's overall themes of self-sacrifice and patriotism. As Bogart's Rick Blaine says, with war breaking out all over Europe, "It doesn't take much to see that the problems of three little people don't amount to a hill of beans in this crazy world."

ADDITIONAL FACTS

1. *The film popularized the song "As Time Goes By," which had been a minor hit when it was originally released in 1931.*

2. *The line "Round up the usual suspects," spoken by Claude Rains (1889–1967) as Captain Renault, was the inspiration for the title of the 1995 Hollywood hit* The Usual Suspects.

3. *The film's last line, delivered by Bogart—"Louis, I think this is the beginning of a beautiful friendship"—was dubbed in three weeks after shooting ended. The line is said to have been written by Warner Bros. executive Hal Wallis, who was the driving force behind the film's production.*

•••••

Jet Travel

On May 2, 1952, the first commercial passenger jet flew from London to Johannesburg, inaugurating the age of jet travel. The development of jet engine technology made traveling between distant continents much quicker and more practical than it was on ships or in older types of airplanes, bringing people and cultures together like never before.

Both the Allies and Nazi Germany deployed planes with jet engines during World War II. In contrast to propeller-driven aircraft, jets flew about 50 percent faster and reached altitudes of 40,000 feet or more.

The first jet for commercial service, the De Havilland Comet, was made in the United Kingdom and put into service by British Overseas Airways Corporation (BOAC), the predecessor to British Airways, on its 6,724-mile route to the South African capital. Flying at about 490 miles per hour, it made the trip in just under twenty-four hours—about ten hours faster than the old propeller planes managed for the same route.

Within months of their debut, jets had captured the imagination of people across the world; a *New York Times* reporter rode one of BOAC's jets and pronounced it "a unique and exhilarating experience." Airlines rushed to order jets, and by the 1960s, the faster planes accounted for nearly all long-distance flights.

In practical terms, jets had the effect of making international travel cheaper, more dependable, and faster, enabling millions of people to visit once-inaccessible parts of the world. In 1952, at the dawn of the jet age, airlines carried about 800,000 passengers a week. Today, that number is about 14 million every week in the United States alone.

ADDITIONAL FACTS

1. *The first trip to Johannesburg carried thirty-two passengers and stopped five times en route.*

2. *The Queen Mother, Elizabeth (1900–2002), flew in a jet later in May of 1952, giving jet travel the royal blessing.*

3. *Jet travel put a swift end to ocean liner companies. Currently, the* Queen Mary 2 *is the only passenger ship that still routinely makes the trip from Europe to North America.*

•••••

Hank Aaron

Over his twenty-three-year major-league baseball career, Hank Aaron (1934–) defined consistency. For twenty consecutive seasons, he hit at least twenty home runs (1955–1974), and he is the only player to have hit at least thirty home runs fifteen times. With his sustained excellence, Aaron broke one of baseball's hallowed records—the career home runs mark set by Babe Ruth (1895–1948)—to become one of the sport's immortals.

Aaron's statistics are staggering. In addition to his 755 career home runs, he also owns career records for runs batted in (2,297), extra-base hits (1,477), and total bases (6,856), while ranking second in runs (2,174) and third in hits (3,771). In 1957, he won his only National League Most Valuable Player award with a .322 batting average, 44 home runs, and 132 runs batted in, leading the Milwaukee Braves to a World Series crown.

Statistics aside, the legacy of Hammerin' Hank will always be his successful pursuit of Babe Ruth's record of 714 home runs, and the racist abuse Aaron endured during the 1973 season, as Aaron edged closer to 714, he received upwards of 3,000 pieces of mail daily—much of it containing hateful, threatening messages. Playing for the Atlanta Braves, he finished that year with 40 home runs (in just 392 at bats), pushing his career total to 713.

Aaron endured death threats during the off-season, but in his first at bat of the 1974 season, he tied the Babe. Four days later, in the fourth inning of the home opener at Atlanta-Fulton County Stadium, Aaron hit a high fastball thrown by Los Angeles Dodgers pitcher Al Downing (1941–) over the left center field fence to take the record.

Aaron added forty more home runs in the rest of his career. He retired after the 1976 season at age forty-two and was inducted into the Baseball Hall of Fame in 1982.

ADDITIONAL FACTS

1. *Aaron began his professional career in 1952, when he joined the Indianapolis Clowns of the Negro League.*

2. *He played for two franchises in the major leagues—the Milwaukee Braves, which moved to Atlanta in 1966, and the Milwaukee Brewers.*

3. *He was a twenty-four-time all-star selection and the first player to reach both 500 home runs and 3,000 hits.*

•••••

Drag Racing

A sport with corporate sponsorship and televised races today, drag racing has its roots in the badlands of Southern California in the 1930s, when drivers of hot rods, or dragsters—cars stripped of all but the essential parts—competed in breakneck acceleration contests across barren lake beds, reaching speeds of over 100 miles per hour.

The danger and noise of these competitions, which were also sometimes held on empty airfields or even on a town's "main drag" after dark, earned the sport a notoriety associated with street gangs, leather jackets, and switchblades, an image captured in films such as 1955's *Rebel Without a Cause.*

In the early 1950s, however, racing pioneers such as Wally Parks (1913–2007) and C. J. Hart (1911–2004) sought to distance the sport from its outlaw roots. Hart is generally credited with creating the first commercial strip when he charged admission to a race on the runway of the Orange County Airport in Santa Ana, California. This became the first commercial drag strip on June 19, 1950. Parks, the editor of *Hot Rod* magazine in the 1950s, used his clout to form the National Hot Rod Association (NHRA) in 1951, to "create order from chaos" and draw up rules and safety regulations. Today the NHRA has 80,000 members and more than 35,000 licensed competitors, and it sponsors elimination contests lasting for up to three days.

Changes have helped push drag racing into the mainstream, but the illegal street racing that gave birth to the sport is not dead, prompting many communities to form programs like San Diego's RaceLegal to get wannabe racers off the public roads. As Hart said, "there's been drag racing since cars were invented," and drivers will always answer the call to "drag their car out of the garage and race."

ADDITIONAL FACTS

1. *Drag racing taxes an engine so severely that one run, or "pass," can cause damage requiring up to $5,000 worth of replacement parts.*

2. *The National Electric Drag Racing Association was formed in 1997 to race electric cars, which were accepted under NHRA rules beginning in 1999.*

3. *Winston cigarettes was the first to sponsor an NHRA series.*

•••••

Billy Graham

Billy Graham (1918–) has been called "America's pastor" and "the pope of Protestant America." Widely regarded as the world's foremost evangelist, Graham has preached the Gospel to nearly 215 million people on six continents and has been a spiritual advisor to each of the past eleven US presidents.

A significant part of Graham's appeal has been his welcoming approach, eschewing strict religious doctrine and partisan politics in recent years to focus instead on world peace and Gospel love. He also harnessed the power of the media—particularly radio, television, and film—taking his preaching from the revival tent directly into his followers' homes.

Graham grew up on a dairy farm in Charlotte, North Carolina. He experienced his personal religious awakening at age sixteen after seeing a revival meeting led by the traveling evangelist Mordecai Ham (1877–1961). Graham was ordained a Southern Baptist minister in 1939 and was soon preaching around the country and in Europe.

In the late 1940s, possibly because of Graham's strong anticommunist stance, he caught the eye of the newspaper magnate William Randolph Hearst (1863–1951), who used his array of media outlets to promote Graham's 1949 revival meetings in Los Angeles. Originally scheduled for three weeks, Graham's stand in Los Angeles lasted for more than eight weeks, and he was soon a national figure.

Through the decades, Graham continued to preach about world peace and sought US reconciliation with China and the Soviet Union. He was the first major evangelist to preach behind the Iron Curtain, visiting Hungary in 1977 and later speaking four times in the Soviet Union. In 2007, President George H. W. Bush (1924–) praised Graham for helping to "tip the balance of history in freedom's favor."

ADDITIONAL FACTS

1. *Graham has not been without his serious missteps. He staunchly supported the controversial (and ultimately discredited) communist hunt by Senator Joseph McCarthy (1908–1957) in the 1950s and was recorded making anti-Semitic comments to President Richard M. Nixon (1913–1994) at the White House.*

2. *Graham has prayed with every president in the Oval Office since Harry Truman (1884–1972).*

3. *Graham's early revival meetings were among the first public functions in the South where seating was not segregated.*

••••

Waiting for Godot

Waiting for Godot (1952) is the most famous, and arguably most accessible, play by the wildly experimental Irish-French writer Samuel Beckett (1906–1989). Though critics and audiences have expressed divided opinions about the play, it holds an indisputably central place in twentieth-century drama. A landmark in the so-called theater of the absurd, Beckett's play has endured as a widely read and frequently performed work worldwide.

Samuel Beckett

In *Waiting for Godot,* words and ideas take precedence over events—in fact, very little action transpires over the course of the play. In Act I, two men named Vladimir and Estragon simply wait by a roadside for a mysterious person named Godot. Several odd characters pass by, and a number of strange conversations ensue. Later, a boy shows up and informs them that Godot will not be coming until the next day. Act II takes place that next day, when Vladimir and Estragon have returned to the same roadside. They continue to argue and converse and see some of the same people from the previous day, although these strangers inexplicably do not remember meeting them. Finally, the same boy arrives and announces that Godot is no longer coming. Though Vladimir and Estragon talk of leaving for home, they remain waiting by the roadside even in the play's last moments.

Perhaps more than any other work, *Waiting for Godot* influenced the development of absurdist theater—a major movement in drama during the mid-twentieth century, particularly in France. Along with Eugène Ionesco (1909–1994), Jean Genet (1910–1986), and other playwrights, Beckett pushed the theatrical envelope aggressively in terms of both style and content. Absurdist plays often feature empty or minimalist sets, bizarre dialogue or monologues, and seemingly meaningless plots with many unresolved questions. Indeed, in *Waiting for Godot,* Beckett leaves the biggest question—who is Godot?—unanswered.

ADDITIONAL FACTS

1. *One critic, Vivian Mercier (1919–1989), encapsulated* Waiting for Godot *by calling the two-act work "a play in which nothing happens, twice."*

2. *Beckett wrote* Waiting for Godot *in French but later translated it into English himself. Though he completed the original version of the play in the late 1940s, it was not published until 1952 and not performed until 1953.*

3. *Many of Beckett's other plays are even more experimental than* Waiting for Godot. Play *(1963) features three characters trapped in urns onstage. In* Not I *(1972), a lone actress delivers a lengthy, jumbled monologue in pitch blackness, with only her mouth visible to the audience.*

••••

Chuck Berry

Singer and guitarist Chuck Berry (1926–) is widely considered one of the founders of rock and roll. So great has been his influence on other musicians that John Lennon (1940–1980) of the Beatles once said, "If you were going to give rock and roll another name, you might as well call it 'Chuck Berry.'"

Berry debuted in the early 1950s, playing before mostly black audiences in East St. Louis. His sound was highly distinctive: Berry combined elements of traditionally black music, such as the blues, with the rhyme schemes and jolting guitars of white "hillbilly" music. His breakthrough came when he moved to Chicago in 1955. At the prompting of the Chicago blues legend Muddy Waters (1915–1983), Berry gave a demo tape to Leonard Chess (1917–1969) of Chess Records. They rerecorded one song from the tape and released it as "Maybellene." The record was a hit, and a star was born.

Berry went on to record many of rock and roll's greatest early hits, including "Roll Over Beethoven" (1956), "Brown Eyed Handsome Man" (1956), the anthem "Rock and Roll Music" (1957), and "Johnny B. Goode" (1958). His music, blaring out of radios and jukeboxes around the world, was an inspiration to aspiring teenage musicians such as Bob Dylan (1941–) in Minnesota and John Lennon in Liverpool, who would both cite Berry as an influence after they become famous.

Berry's success came to an abrupt end in 1959, however, when he was convicted of transporting a minor over state lines for purposes of prostitution. Remarkably, Berry's star continued to climb while he was in prison. As the Aerosmith guitarist Joe Perry (1950–) wrote in *Rolling Stone*, "Like a lot of guitarists of my generation, I first heard Chuck Berry because of the Beatles and the Rolling Stones." The year that Berry was released from prison—1963—marked the beginning of the British Invasion. When Berry was released, it was to a new audience and new opportunities.

ADDITIONAL FACTS

1. *Although he produced a number of hits, Berry's only number one single was a live recording from 1972 of a raunchy New Orleans tune called "My Ding-a-Ling."*

2. *Though in his eighties, Berry still plays one Wednesday every month at Blueberry Hill, a club in his old St. Louis neighborhood.*

3. *Berry went to prison one more time in his life: in 1979, for tax evasion. He played for President Jimmy Carter (1924–) at the White House that same year.*

•••••

Cary Grant

Born Archibald Alexander Leach in Bristol, England, Cary Grant (1904–1986) came to represent the epitome of debonair sophistication through his performances in a series of wildly successful romantic comedies. Though Grant never won an Academy Award (he was given a special Oscar in 1970 for lifetime achievement), he is regarded as one of the finest actors in Hollywood history. In 2004, *Premiere* magazine named Grant the Greatest Movie Star of All Time; film historian David Thomson (1941–) has called him "the best and most important actor in the history of the cinema"; and the American Film Institute ranked him second on its list of male screen legends, behind only Humphrey Bogart (1889–1957).

Grant arrived in Hollywood in 1931 after having a career as an acrobat, vaudevillian, and stage actor. He appeared in twenty-nine films of varying quality before the urbane, witty persona that would define his life emerged in the romantic comedy *The Awful Truth* (1937).

He continued to display his brilliant comic timing, verbal wit, and romantic screen appeal in a series of screwball comedies, including the landmark *Bringing Up Baby* (1938), *Holiday* (1938), *His Girl Friday* (1940), and *The Philadelphia Story* (1940). In three of those films (all but *His Girl Friday*), he sparred with Katharine Hepburn (1907–2003)—who became Hollywood's leading lady.

In general, Grant's films were successful regardless of the director and costar. But two actor-director relationships proved fruitful—he made five films with Howard Hawks (1896–1977) (including *Bringing Up Baby* and *His Girl Friday*) and four thrillers with Alfred Hitchcock (1899–1980) (including *Notorious* in 1946 and *North by Northwest* in 1959).

In all, Grant made seventy-three films before retiring in 1966. Many producers and directors tried to lure him out of retirement, but he never returned before his death at age eighty-two.

ADDITIONAL FACTS

1. *Grant was nominated for two Academy Awards for Best Actor—for* Penny Serenade *(1941) and* None but the Lonely Heart *(1944).*

2. *Tony Curtis (1925–) parodied Grant's accent in the Billy Wilder (1906–2002) comedy classic* Some Like It Hot *(1959).*

3. *Author Ian Fleming (1908–1964) has said that Grant was an inspiration for his James Bond character. Grant was reportedly offered the part but turned it down because he considered himself too old to play the British spy.*

•••••

McCarthyism

In 1953, Senator Joseph McCarthy (1908–1957) of Wisconsin launched a series of investigations to identify communist sympathizers he believed had infiltrated the United States government. Before the Senate ended his high-profile crusade a year later, McCarthy had convened dozens of hearings carried on national television and accused hundreds of government and military officials of communist leanings, fostering a climate of fear and suspicion in the early years of the Cold War.

McCarthy, a former marine who was first elected to the Senate in 1946, rose to the chairmanship of the Senate Committee on Government Operations when the Republicans took control of the Senate after the 1952 election. He arranged his first hearings to investigate alleged communist influence at the Voice of America radio network.

Joseph McCarthy

Initially, McCarthy's hearings enjoyed bipartisan support, since political leaders of both parties regarded communism as a mortal threat. One of his early staffers was Democrat Robert F. Kennedy (1925–1968), the brother of future president John F. Kennedy (1917–1963).

But criticism of McCarthy's tactics mounted in 1954 as the senator and his senior staff member, Roy Cohn (1927–1986), lodged a series of wild accusations against witnesses, often with little or no evidence. His targets included authors, lawyers, and high-ranking military officers.

Critics accused McCarthy of conducting a witch hunt, and even former allies complained he had gone too far with his baseless accusations. Opposition to McCarthyism was voiced most famously by a lawyer for the army, Joseph Welch (1890–1960), who asked McCarthy during a heated hearing in 1954, "Have you no sense of decency, sir, at long last? Have you left no sense of decency?"

By the end of 1954, the Senate had halted the hearings and voted to censure the senator. McCarthy died of alcoholism three years later, at age forty-eight.

ADDITIONAL FACTS

1. *The playwright Arthur Miller (1915–2005) wrote the 1953 drama* The Crucible *in response to the hearings, comparing them to the 1692 witch hunt in Salem, Massachusetts.*

2. *In addition to his quest for communists, McCarthy also attacked alleged homosexuals in government; ironically, his loyal sidekick Cohn was later unmasked as a closeted gay man.*

3. *The McCarthy hearings formed the basis for the 2005 film* Good Night, and Good Luck.

•••••

Jim Brown

If there was one thing that every football player and fan knew from 1957 to 1965, it was this: You did not mess with Jim Brown. At six foot two and 232 pounds, the Cleveland Browns fullback was the roughest, toughest offensive player in the National Football League, with a reputation for meanness off the field as well as on. Such was his power that one defender could rarely tackle him alone; it took a gang of men to bring him down. After such a tackle, Brown (1936–) famously would rise slowly, return to the huddle, then smash his way into the heart of the defense again.

Many consider him the greatest football player in history. In 2002, the *Sporting News* named him the top player in National Football League (NFL) history, and in 1999, ESPN anointed him the top football player of the twentieth century.

When he retired after the 1965 season, Brown held almost every rushing record in NFL history, including career marks for yards (12,312), touchdowns (126), and rushing touchdowns (106), as well as the single-season yardage record (1,863). His statistics were particularly remarkable considering that he played only nine seasons, retiring at his peak to devote his time to social activism and acting in movies such as *The Dirty Dozen* (1967) and *Any Given Sunday* (1999). He never played a down after age twenty-nine.

Brown packed a lot of success into those nine seasons, leading the NFL in rushing eight times, becoming league Most Valuable Player twice (1958, 1965), earning Rookie of the Year honors (1957), winning an NFL championship (1964), and playing in nine Pro Bowls—all while never missing a game.

ADDITIONAL FACTS

1. *At Syracuse University, Brown was an all-American in football and lacrosse, and some say he was even better at lacrosse than at football. He also lettered in basketball, track, and baseball in college.*

2. *He is the only person inducted into the Halls of Fame for pro football, college football, and lacrosse.*

3. *Brown spends a significant part of his time working to help gang members become productive members of society through his Amer-I-Can Program, which he founded in 1988.*

•••••

Gidget

The story of a spunky blonde tomboy who joins the California surfer scene, *Gidget* was a popular book, movie, and television series in the 1950s and 1960s. Originally conceived by screenwriter Frederick Kohner (1905–1986), the series captured the carefree innocence of youth and helped popularize surfing.

In the 1957 novel, young Frances Lawrence, less buxom than the other beach girls, doesn't seem to fit in anywhere. Bored and lonely, she goes for a swim in the ocean and gets caught in a tangle of seaweed. She's rescued by a local surfer, Jeffrey Matthews, a.k.a. Moondoggie, and soon becomes part of the surfing subculture. After some hazing, she acquires the nickname "Gidget" (short for "girl midget") and is accepted into the clique, where she takes on the task of winning Moondoggie's heart.

Gidget was brought to the screen in 1959 by director Paul Wendkos (1922–) and starred Sandra Dee (1942–2005) as Gidget and James Darren (1936–) as Moondoggie. The film was a commercial success and spawned a sequel film, *Gidget Goes Hawaiian* (1961), with Deborah Walley (1943–2001) replacing Dee in the title role. Yet another sequel was made, *Gidget Goes to Rome* (1963), featuring Cindy Carol (1944–) as the sprightly teen. Then, in 1965, ABC brought the *Gidget* franchise to the small screen, casting a perky, button-nosed young actress named Sally Field (1946–).

After a single season, ABC canceled the series. However, after airing in reruns, the show gained more popularity and eventually spawned a new version, *The New Gidget,* in the 1980s.

ADDITIONAL FACTS

1. *Novelist Kohner based Gidget on his then-sixteen-year-old daughter, Kathy, and dreamed up Kathy's beach-shack adventures.*

2. *Originally, Elvis Presley (1935–1977) was intended to play the role of Moondoggie, but the studio declined because he was too expensive.*

3. *The names* Gidget *and* Moondoggie *were used for characters in the anime science-fiction series* Eureka Seven, *about a teenage boy enchanted by "lifting" on particle waves—a sport similar to surfing.*

Robert F. Kennedy

Throughout his life, Robert F. Kennedy (1925–1968) always seemed to be following his older brother, John F. Kennedy (1917–1963). The younger Kennedy ran JFK's successful 1952 US Senate campaign and eventually served in the Senate himself. He also helped his brother win the White House in 1960 and followed him to Washington, DC, to serve as arguably the most influential attorney general in American history.

In 1968, five years after President Kennedy's assassination, Robert appeared poised to continue his brother's unfinished legacy in the White House. But, like his older brother, he was tragically murdered, assassinated as his presidential campaign gathered momentum, leaving the country to wonder what might have been.

Robert Kennedy was the seventh of nine children and said that growing up with so many older siblings forced him to develop internal strength to survive. He lacked the charisma and rhetorical skills of his more celebrated brother, but his determination and toughness offset some of his deficiencies. His critics later called him overly ambitious, ruthless, and calculating, but those characteristics helped him in the service of his older brother.

A year after completing law school at the University of Virginia, Kennedy successfully managed his brother's campaign for the US Senate in Massachusetts.

Once he became attorney general in 1961, Kennedy battled organized crime, defended new civil rights laws, and played a key role in defusing the Cuban missile crisis. Most important, he acted as the president's most trusted advisor.

After his brother's death, Robert Kennedy ran for the US Senate for New York in 1964 and won, committing himself to helping the nation's poor and advancing human rights abroad. Four years into his term, when President Lyndon B. Johnson (1908–1973) opted not to run for reelection, Kennedy entered the race for the White House, promising to end the Vietnam War.

After winning a key primary in California, Kennedy was gunned down at the Ambassador Hotel in Los Angeles. He died at age forty-two.

ADDITIONAL FACTS

1. *Kennedy and his wife, Ethel (1928–), had eleven children, the last of whom was born after Kennedy's death. His eldest son, Joseph (1952–), served six terms for Massachusetts in the US House of Representatives.*

2. *One of Robert Kennedy's most noteworthy acts as attorney general was sending US marshals and troops to the campus of the University of Mississippi to ensure that the first African-American student there, James Meredith (1933–), was admitted to the school.*

3. *Kennedy's assassin, Sirhan Sirhan (1944–), was sentenced to death in 1969. The death sentence was later commuted to life imprisonment, and Sirhan remains in a California prison today.*

• • • • •

Truman Capote

The novelist and short-story writer Truman Capote (1924–1984) was one of the most prominent pop culture figures of the mid-twentieth century: a quiet young southerner turned infamous Manhattan socialite, flamboyant media personality, and pioneer in the genre of journalistic fiction.

Born in New Orleans and raised in Alabama, Capote endured a lonely and sensitive childhood by writing incessantly. In 1933, his family relocated to New York City, where he eventually got a number of short stories published in the *New Yorker, Harper's,* the *Atlantic Monthly,* and other magazines. His first major novel, *Other Voices, Other Rooms* (1948), about a young boy's struggle with homosexuality while growing up in the South, caused controversy not only for its subject matter but also for the author photo on its book jacket—a provocative shot of Capote lounging on a couch and staring directly into the camera. The novel and the photo made Capote a media sensation; by the time he wrote *Breakfast at Tiffany's* (1958), about a Manhattan call girl, he'd become a full-fledged celebrity.

Capote enjoyed the limelight: He was a staple at the parties of New York's rich and famous, and his reedy, high-pitched drawl made him a memorable storyteller. By the 1960s, he had grown increasingly interested in journalism—an interest that culminated in his greatest work, the groundbreaking "nonfiction novel" *In Cold Blood* (1966). The idea for the novel originated in 1959, when Capote read a news item about a family that was murdered in a small Kansas town. He became obsessed with the story, traveled to Kansas to research it, and ended up developing a close, ethically ambiguous relationship with the killers themselves. The novel was unprecedented in its blending of novelistic and journalistic techniques and was the forerunner of virtually every subsequent novel in the now-commonplace true-crime genre.

ADDITIONAL FACTS

1. *Capote grew up in the same town as novelist Harper Lee (1926–), the author of* To Kill a Mockingbird *(1960), and the two remained close lifelong friends.*

2. *Though the film adaptation of* Breakfast at Tiffany's *is now considered a classic, Capote objected both to the casting of Audrey Hepburn (1929–1993) and to the studio's heavy sanitization of her character, Holly Golightly.*

3. *The story behind Capote's writing of* In Cold Blood *formed the basis for the Oscar-winning film* Capote *(2005).*

·•●•·

Johnny Cash

Johnny Cash (1932–2003) was the original outlaw of country music. Before his debut, country tended to be a genteel affair, epitomized by the professionalism of Nashville recording artists. Cash, with his hard-charging lyrics and rocky personal life, changed everything.

Born in Arkansas, Cash began his career in 1955 at Sun Records, the legendary Memphis label that also signed Elvis Presley (1935–1977). Cash and his backup band recorded several hits, including two songs that would be associated with him for his entire career: "Folsom Prison Blues" (1956) and "I Walk the Line" (1956).

Even in the 1950s, Cash was already cultivating his image as the Man in Black, trading in the fancy suits and cowboy boots of Nashville for an all-black uniform. He soon left behind most of his connections with Memphis, signing a deal with Columbia Records in 1958 and leaving his first wife in 1966.

It was during the 1960s that Cash's outlaw image—and outlaw behavior—reached their peak. His substance abuse problem and stormy relationship with folksinger June Carter (1929–2003), whom he eventually married in 1968, was captured in one of Cash's biggest hits, "Ring of Fire" (1963). Carter cowrote the song, which referred to Cash's struggles with alcohol and pills. He was arrested several times, but often for quite odd offenses, including picking flowers on private property.

Eventually, though, Cash did go to prison—but not to serve time. He went to play a concert. Inmates at Folsom Prison had long idolized Cash and adopted his "Folsom Prison Blues" as their anthem. In 1968, he played a concert inside the prison walls that was recorded for his classic album *Johnny Cash at Folsom Prison*. He followed it the next year with another hit live album from California's San Quentin prison. But Cash's outlaw image came to a halt in the early 1970s, when he gave up drinking and traded in his pills for a rediscovered Christian faith.

ADDITIONAL FACTS

1. *Cash faded from view in the years after his San Quentin concert, but rose to prominence again in the 1990s after releasing a series of records under the direction of producer Rick Rubin (1963–).*

2. *The oddball 1969 hit "A Boy Named Sue," from* Live at San Quentin, *was written by the children's poet Shel Silverstein (1930–1999).*

3. *In 1990, Cash released an audiobook of his reading of the entire New Testament, amounting to nineteen hours and sixteen compact discs.*

•••••

John Huston

John Huston (1906–1987) is remembered almost as much for his outsize personality—he was a gambler, painter, boxer, sculptor, pilot, and womanizer—as for his contributions to film. He worked in several different genres and was nominated for fifteen Academy Awards in three categories (Best Director, Best Screenplay, and Best Supporting Actor).

He won two Oscars, both for the 1948 hit *The Treasure of the Sierra Madre* (director and screenplay). His father, Walter, won an Oscar in that film as well, for supporting actor. The lead role of Fred C. Dobbs was played by Humphrey Bogart (1899–1957), with whom Huston collaborated on six films.

In fact, Huston played a pivotal role in launching Bogart's legendary career. Huston was the screenwriter of *High Sierra* (1941), Bogart's breakthrough film, and also directed Bogey in the gritty detective movie *The Maltese Falcon* (1941), which was Huston's directorial debut.

The two also collaborated on *The African Queen* (1951), for which Bogart won his only Academy Award, as well as *Across the Pacific* (1942), *Key Largo* (1948), and *Beat the Devil* (1953).

Among the hallmarks of Huston's films are toughness, manliness, and adventure. Some critics consider the gritty and downbeat masterpiece *The Asphalt Jungle* (1950) the definitive heist film. He also worked successfully in the western genre with *The Misfits* (1961)—the last film in which Clark Gable (1901–1960) and Marilyn Monroe (1926–1962) each appeared—and in adventure pictures with *The Man Who Would Be King* (1975).

Huston directed his daughter, Anjelica, to an Academy Award for Best Supporting Actress in *Prizzi's Honor* (1985), which made him the first to direct both a parent and a child to Oscar wins.

An ex-boxer and an imposing figure at six foot two, Huston appeared in several films as well, notably Otto Preminger's *The Cardinal* (1963), for which he received an Oscar nomination, and Roman Polanski's *Chinatown* (1974). A heavy smoker, Huston died of emphysema at age eighty-one.

ADDITIONAL FACTS

1. *Many film historians consider* The Maltese Falcon, *which was adapted from Dashiell Hammett's 1930 novel, the first example of film noir.*

2. The African Queen *was the first color picture Huston directed.*

3. *Huston made three documentaries for the army during World War II*: Report from the Aleutians *(1943),* The Battle of San Pietro *(1945), and* Let There Be Light *(1946).* Let There Be Light, *which examined the treatment of US servicemen suffering from emotional trauma and depression, was suppressed by the US military until 1980.*

•••••

The Third World

In the early stages of the Cold War, political theorists divided the globe into three sections—the democratic First World, the communist Second World, and the poor, developing countries that belonged to neither bloc: the Third World.

The term was invented in 1952 by a French writer, Alfred Sauvy (1898–1990), to describe the vast stretches of Africa, Asia, and Latin America whose citizens lived in dire poverty. Many of these countries were former outposts of the European empires that had collapsed after World War II.

For instance, India, one of the largest Third World countries, gained its independence from the United Kingdom in 1947. The Netherlands recognized the independence of Indonesia in 1949, and France decolonized Morocco in 1956.

Since Third World countries were, by definition, aligned with neither the United States nor the Soviet Union, both superpowers tried to woo them during the Cold War with promises of economic aid and military support. Indeed, the Third World was often a major battleground between the two superpowers; the Vietnam War and the bloody civil war in Angola were two prominent examples of such "proxy wars" in the Third World.

Caught between two superpowers, leaders of many Third World nations joined the Non-Aligned Movement, a group that was founded by the Indian prime minister Jawaharlal Nehru (1889–1964) to promote cooperation between neutral powers. In addition, some artists and intellectuals adopted the term *Third World* to describe the common history of imperialism and decolonization shared by many countries in the group.

After the end of the Cold War, the original meaning of the phrase *Third World* became obsolete. Though some now regard the term as insensitive, it remains in use to describe impoverished parts of the globe.

ADDITIONAL FACTS

1. *Although it was a communist country, Yugoslavia was a founding member of the Non-Aligned Movement because its leader, Josip Tito (1892–1980), refused to take orders from Soviet leader Joseph Stalin (1879–1953).*

2. *Among academic economists, the term* Third World *has been replaced by* developing countries *to describe the poor nations of Asia, Africa, and Latin America.*

3. *The Non-Aligned Movement still exists, despite the end of the Cold War, and claims 115 member countries.*

••◉••

Wilt Chamberlain

Wilt Chamberlain (1936–1999) was one of the most dominant offensive players in basketball history. The seven-foot-one, 275-pound center was the National Basketball Association's Most Valuable Player (MVP) four times, led the league in scoring seven times and in rebounding eleven times, and retired with countless records—including career scoring (31,419 points, now fourth of all time) and career rebounding (23,924, still the record). He is perhaps best remembered for scoring a record 100 points in a single NBA game, in 1962. For his career, he averaged 30.1 points and 22.9 rebounds.

Chamberlain's fourteen-year NBA career will always be compared with that of his rival, Bill Russell (1934–) of the Boston Celtics. While Chamberlain—nicknamed Wilt the Stilt and the Big Dipper—was known for his awesome scoring totals (he averaged 50.4 points during the 1961–1962 season), Russell is remembered for his overall team play and for helping the Celtics to eleven championships. Chamberlain, by comparison, won just two NBA titles and lost to Russell's Celtics in seven of eight playoff series.

Chamberlain was an all-American at the University of Kansas, where he played two varsity seasons before joining the Harlem Globetrotters for a season. He then entered the NBA with the Philadelphia Warriors for the 1959–1960 season and became the first player to be named both Rookie of the Year and MVP in the same year.

He played on two NBA championship teams—the 1967 Philadelphia 76ers, who ended the Celtics' streak of eight consecutive titles, and the 1972 Los Angeles Lakers.

Chamberlain retired after the 1972–1973 season, but he frequently remained in the public eye. He was a coach in the American Basketball Association for one season, challenged heavyweight champion Muhammad Ali (1942–) to a boxing match, played professional volleyball, ran marathons, and, most notoriously, bragged in an autobiography that he'd had sexual relations with more than 20,000 women.

He died at age sixty-three of heart failure, with many of his NBA records intact.

ADDITIONAL FACTS

1. *Chamberlain was a hugely prolific scorer, topping the fifty-point mark an astounding 118 times in the NBA. Even more remarkable is how poorly he shot free throws—just .511 for his career.*

2. *In addition to his amazing point totals, Chamberlain was also a great passer—he's the only center in NBA history to lead the league in assists (1967–1968).*

3. *Unlike many centers, Chamberlain was in terrific shape—in the 1961–1962 season, he played all but eight of his team's 3,890 total minutes. He also never fouled out in his NBA career, which some say is an indication that he was too nice a player.*

·•●•·

Paparazzi

For a photo of celebrities Brad Pitt (1963–) and Jennifer Aniston (1969–) just after their wedding, *People* magazine paid almost $100,000. Immediately after their divorce, pictures of the pair fetched $150,000. A photo of troubled pop tart Britney Spears (1981–) with one of her children goes for up to $2 million, according to some estimates.

The pursuit of candid celebrity photos by photographers known as paparazzi has grown into big business, fed by voracious demand from high-circulation magazines such as *People* and *Us Weekly* and supermarket tabloids like the *National Enquirer.*

The term *paparazzi* originated with the 1960 movie *La dolce vita* (*The Sweet Life*), by Italian director Federico Fellini (1920–1993). The film revolves around the life of a tabloid journalist named Marcello, played by Marcello Mastroianni (1924–1996). One of the minor characters in the film is a photographer named Paparazzo, and celebrity photographers have been referred to as paparazzi ever since.

At their most innocuous, paparazzi stand behind the velvet ropes at red-carpet events, from awards ceremonies to movie premieres. Indeed, lesser-known celebrities often court photographers to increase their exposure.

However, the dark side of celebrity photography became a major news item in 1997, when a car carrying Diana, Princess of Wales (1961–1997), and her lover, Dodi Al-Fayed (1955–1997), crashed while trying to escape from paparazzi. Many continue to blame paparazzi for her death, and celebrities often complain that overly aggressive photographers invade their privacy.

Nevertheless, the public continues to fuel the paparazzi boom: *People* alone boasts more than 3.7 million subscribers.

ADDITIONAL FACTS

1. *Fellini took Paparazzo's name from the Italian word for a noisy mosquito.*

2. *With the proliferation of digital and cell-phone cameras, many amateurs are beginning to shoot candid celebrity photographs when the chance arises. These amateurs have earned the new name* snaparazzi.

3. *The official report on the causes of Diana's death found that her driver was under the influence of alcohol at the time of the accident.*

••●●••

Yasir Arafat

Yasir Arafat (1929–2004) was one of the most recognizable and polarizing figures of the twentieth century. Proponents called him the father of Palestinian nationalism and saw him as a statesman, leader, and martyr. Opponents deemed him a terrorist who did little to improve the lot of his people.

In 1959, Arafat cofounded Fatah (or Al Fatah, "the Conquest"), an underground network of secret cells dedicated to Palestinian nationalism. Five years later, he became a full-time revolutionary, organizing Fatah raids into Israel from Jordan.

In 1964, the Palestinian Liberation Organization (PLO) formed and Arafat brought Fatah into the group. After Israel's victory over its Arab opponents in the Six Days' War of 1967, Fatah emerged as the most powerful faction in the battered PLO. Within two years, Arafat was chairman of the PLO's executive committee, and he set about turning the group into an independent nationalist organization based in Jordan.

While in Jordan and later Lebanon and Tunisia, the PLO became known for its violent revolutionary methods, most of which were aimed at dismantling the Israeli state. Among the attacks rumored to have been endorsed by Arafat was the infamous massacre of eleven Israeli athletes at the 1972 Munich Olympics.

But by 1988, at least publicly, Arafat had changed his position on Israel. At a United Nations session in Switzerland that year, he announced that the PLO would renounce terrorism and support "the right of all parties concerned in the Middle East conflict to live in peace and security, including the state of Palestine, Israel and other neighbors."

In 1993, the Oslo Accords represented a major step forward in the Israeli-Palestinian peace process, and Arafat was the cowinner of the 1994 Nobel Peace Prize.

Two years later, he was elected president of the Palestinian Authority, but in 2000, the peace process came to an abrupt halt. Arafat rejected Israel's land-for-peace offer, touching off a renewal of guerrilla warfare and terrorism against Israel.

Arafat died at age seventy-five, spending most of the last three years of his life in confinement, held by Israel at his headquarters in Ramallah. He died without achieving any of his stated goals—the destruction of Israel, peace with Israel, or the creation of a Palestinian state.

ADDITIONAL FACTS

1. *The duality of Arafat's character and his politics—particularly after 1988—is perhaps best encapsulated in a speech he gave before the United Nations in 1974. He said he had come "bearing an olive branch and a freedom fighter's gun."*

2. *Arafat was instantly recognizable by his trademark checked head scarf and light beard. He also always carried a silver-plated .357 Magnum handgun.*

3. *Arafat claimed to have survived as many as forty attacks on his life—from Israelis and Arabs alike—as well as a 1992 airplane crash.*

Lolita

Since its publication in 1955, Vladimir Nabokov's *Lolita* has fascinated and repelled readers in equal measure. Simultaneously a daring work of literary innovation and a piercing psychological study of obsession and delusion, the novel enjoys rare status as a landmark of both pop culture and serious literature.

Vladimir Nabokov

The Russian-born, English-educated Nabokov (1899–1977) became a published author, translator, and academic at a relatively young age. In his early works, he honed a distinctive style that was erudite, clever, and technically brilliant, whether in Russian or English—he published novels in both. Though some of Nabokov's early efforts were critical successes, none attained nearly the notice, or the notoriety, of *Lolita*.

Probably the most candid literary study of pedophilia yet published in its day, *Lolita* focuses on a middle-aged professor, Humbert Humbert, who falls into a disturbing sexual infatuation with a young girl. Humbert stumbles upon twelve-year-old Lolita by chance and from then on reorganizes his entire life to remain as close to her as possible. The pair's relationship eventually does become sexual; though the novel avoids any explicit or pornographic depictions, the subject matter shocked many readers and publishers and led the novel to be widely banned.

Humbert epitomizes the concept of the unreliable narrator that became a staple of postmodern literature in the late twentieth century. Having long ago convinced himself that his attraction to young girls is socially and morally acceptable, Humbert eloquently twists the facts to try to justify his actions to the reader. Just as Humbert comes across as alternately charming and chilling, the novel as a whole walks a tightrope between cheeky humor and serious depiction of a disturbed and tortured soul.

ADDITIONAL FACTS

1. *Lolita has been adapted into two major films: one by Stanley Kubrick (1928–1999) in 1962 and one by Adrian Lyne (1941–) in 1997.*

2. *Though Nabokov finished* Lolita *in 1955, US publishers initially were reluctant to associate themselves with such a controversial work. When Putnam finally agreed to publish the novel in 1958, it was a runaway bestseller.*

3. *Nabokov's primary intellectual pursuit aside from literature was lepidopterology, the study of butterflies and moths. His knowledge of the field was extensive, and he even discovered and named several new species.*

••••

Leonard Bernstein's *Young People's Concerts*

A generation of American children were introduced to classical music by a famous television program called *Young People's Concerts*, which was directed by the renowned composer Leonard Bernstein (1918–1990) and appeared on CBS between 1958 and 1972.

Bernstein, the charismatic maestro of the New York Philharmonic Orchestra and the composer of *Candide* (1956) and *West Side Story* (1957), taped the show for the first time at a concert at New York's Carnegie Hall in 1958. Previously, CBS had broadcast concerts for children on its radio network only; Bernstein's performance was the first to appear on television.

The first program was simply titled "What Does Music Mean?" To explain the basics of music theory, Bernstein drew examples not only from the classical canon, but also from jazz and Latin American music.

In total, Bernstein led fifty-three concerts, and they were eventually broadcast worldwide. Some programs focused on specific musical concepts, such as intervals, modes, the sonata form, and the concerto, but Bernstein also highlighted specific composers, including Gustav Mahler (1860–1911), Jean Sibelius (1865–1957), and Aaron Copland (1900–1990), who was honored on his birthday. In addition, Bernstein directed several theme concerts, such as "Jazz in the Concert Hall" and "The Latin American Spirit."

As a primer on music from one of the masters, the *Young People's Concerts* are unsurpassed. Many of the shows were eventually transcribed, and the collected scripts are still in print; they're also available on DVD.

ADDITIONAL FACTS

1. *CBS broadcast the* Young People's Concerts *on Saturday mornings beginning in 1962.*

2. *The New York Philharmonic began performing* Young People's Concerts *in 1924. They were originally led by Ernest Schelling (1876–1939).*

3. *Bernstein's program was so popular that it was eventually translated into multiple languages and syndicated in forty different countries.*

•• • ••

John Wayne

Few people in twentieth-century American pop culture reached the iconic status of John Wayne (1907–1979) in American cinema. He was the quintessential western star, tough guy, leader, and war hero (although, unlike some of his acting contemporaries, Wayne never fought in any actual wars). After his rise to fame in 1939, he was an almost-certain box office winner for the rest of his life.

At the start of his career, the Duke was nothing but a B-movie player, appearing in more than seventy generally low-budget films until he starred as the Ringo Kid in John Ford's (1894–1973) landmark western *Stagecoach* (1939). It was the first of fourteen major collaborations between Wayne and Ford, and this particular picture, the story of a dangerous stagecoach trip through hostile Apache territory, revitalized the western genre and made Wayne a leading man.

Indeed, for the rest of his career Wayne would be best known for his westerns. In addition to *Stagecoach,* he carried Ford's so-called cavalry series of *Fort Apache* (1948), *She Wore a Yellow Ribbon* (1949), and *Rio Grande* (1950), as well as *The Man Who Shot Liberty Valance* (1962).

The films widely considered Wayne's best are Howard Hawks's (1896–1977) *Red River* (1948) and Ford's *The Searchers* (1956). Both pictures feature Wayne in complex roles.

In *Red River,* he played Tom Dunson, a tough, bitter father in conflict with his adopted son, played by Montgomery Clift (1920–1966). The story revolves around a cattle drive of epic proportions, and Wayne's Dunson is both hero and villain.

He played the similarly complex Ethan Edwards in *The Searchers,* which many critics consider the finest western ever made. Edwards is a study of obsession as he goes on a five-year quest to reclaim his niece, kidnapped by Comanches.

Wayne also starred in war movies, particularly those depicting World War II battles, including *They Were Expendable* (1945), *Sands of Iwo Jima* (1949), and *The Longest Day* (1962). The Duke played somewhat against type as a reformed boxer who falls in love with Ireland and Maureen O'Hara (1920–) in Ford's *The Quiet Man* (1952).

Wayne was twice nominated for Academy Awards for Best Actor, winning for *True Grit* (1969). The film is not considered one of his finer pictures or performances, and the award was seen as more of an unofficial lifetime achievement award. Wayne died of cancer at age seventy-two.

ADDITIONAL FACTS

1. *Wayne's given name was Marion Robert Morrison.*

2. *He attended the University of Southern California on a football scholarship.*

3. *Wayne directed two films—*The Alamo *(1960) and* The Green Berets *(1968).*

• ● ● •

Apartheid

Apartheid, a term that means "apartness" in Afrikaans, was a system of strict racial segregation that was enforced in South Africa between 1948 and 1994. The apartheid regime was the target of intense international opposition in the 1980s from activists across the world, leading to the system's eventual downfall and replacement with a democratic, multiracial government.

South Africa is a former British colony with a sizable proportion of Afrikaners, who are the descendants of Dutch settlers. Apartheid became the country's official national policy after the Afrikaner National Party won a general election in 1948 on a platform of white supremacy.

The system was designed to keep the white minority in a position of power over the much larger black population. Under the apartheid system, people were categorized into racial groups: white, black, Indian, or colored. The rights of South Africans in the last two categories were severely curtailed.

In 1951, the government created "homelands" called *Bantustans* for blacks, herded blacks into the territories, and required them to carry passbooks if they wanted to travel elsewhere within South Africa.

Uprisings against the apartheid system were dealt with harshly. Nelson Mandela (1918–), a leader of the antiapartheid African National Congress, was accused of terrorism and convicted of treason in 1964.

International disapproval mounted, and South Africa was forced to leave the British Commonwealth in 1961. Because the nation was an ally of the United States in the Cold War, however, some Western leaders shied away from direct confrontation with South Africa's leaders.

Soon after the end of the Cold War, though, external and internal pressure to end apartheid swelled, and the country was increasingly treated as a pariah state on the world stage. President F. W. de Klerk (1936–), the leader of the Afrikaner National Party, eventually gave in to pressure to release imprisoned black leaders, including Mandela.

In 1994, the apartheid system collapsed, and Mandela won the first-ever general election as South Africa's first black president.

ADDITIONAL FACTS

1. *The word* bantustan *has come to be a pejorative term meaning an illegitimate or powerless country—a mockery of a state.*

2. *By the 1980s, the international community was boycotting South Africa's participation in international sports, and certain countries were refusing to sell television programming to the country. South Africa was barred from the Olympics from 1964 until 1992.*

3. *Mandela and de Klerk were jointly awarded the Nobel Peace Prize in 1993.*

• • • • •

Rod Laver

Although there are several candidates for the title of the greatest men's tennis player of all time, one thing is certain: No one managed to twice win the Grand Slam—claiming the Australian, French, Wimbledon, and US championship singles titles in the same year—besides Australian Rod Laver (1938–).

The left-hander known as the Rocket won the Grand Slam as an amateur in 1962 and again as a professional in 1969. And he would have had more shots at it, except that he turned professional after the 1962 season, and pros were not permitted to enter the Grand Slam tournaments until the so-called Open era began in 1968.

Laver therefore missed five years of playing the major events but still managed to end his career with eleven Grand Slam tournament titles—tied for fourth of all-time behind Pete Sampras (1971–), who won fourteen titles, and Roy Emerson (1936–) and Roger Federer (1981–) with twelve each.

During his five professional years before the Open era, Laver won sixty-three tournaments, including ten of the fifteen "professional majors" held during that period.

Laver was the consummate all-around player, able to serve and volley effectively and hit hard ground strokes from the baseline. His aggressive, attacking style set him apart from many of his contemporaries, and he is credited with popularizing the topspin forehand, a staple of the modern game.

He was the first player to win $1 million in prize money and also helped Australia to five Davis Cup titles.

ADDITIONAL FACTS

1. *There is some dispute about how many tournaments Laver won in his career, taking into account his amateur and professional status. Jimmy Connors (1952–) is considered the all-time record holder with 109 titles, but Laver is believed to have won at least 188 crowns.*

2. *Laver was inducted into the International Tennis Hall of Fame in 1981.*

3. *In 2000, center court at Melbourne Park—home of the Australian Open—was named in Laver's honor.*

•••••

Ken Kesey

It is debatable whether author Ken Kesey (1935–2001) is better known for his critically acclaimed writing or for his role in popularizing psychedelic drugs during the 1960s.

Born in La Junta, Colorado, in 1935, Kesey set a course for fame in both realms when he enrolled in Stanford University's creative writing program in 1958. In order to make extra money, he participated in psychedelic-drug trials at the Menlo Park Veterans Hospital, experiments that would greatly influence the rest of his life.

Shortly after starting these experiments, Kesey found work in the hospital's psychiatric ward. His acclaimed novel *One Flew Over the Cuckoo's Nest* (1962) arose from the time he spent working the night shift in the ward while using psychedelics such as LSD. Published when he was just twenty-seven years old, the book eventually spawned a widely celebrated movie starring Jack Nicholson (1937–).

Kesey went to great lengths to get the word out about the alleged benefits of hallucinogens. In 1964, he gathered a group that became known as the Merry Pranksters and headed east from California in a wildly decorated bus for the World's Fair in New York. The bus was packed with not only Kesey's friends, but also a large amount of LSD that he encouraged riders to sample along the way.

Kesey also achieved fame for organizing the Acid Tests, parties at which he would supply LSD-laced Kool-Aid to the general public. These parties were equally famous for serving as the launchpad for the band that would eventually become the Grateful Dead.

Kesey continued to appear occasionally at rock concerts and political events until his death at age sixty-six.

ADDITIONAL FACTS

1. *Kesey, upset with both the script and the choice of Nicholson for the lead role, sued the producers of the film version of* One Flew Over the Cuckoo's Nest *and never actually watched the movie.*

2. *Kesey was a main character in* The Electric Kool-Aid Acid Test, *a nonfiction bestseller by Tom Wolfe (1931–) that chronicled the Prankster tour.*

3. *In 1966, Kesey fled to Mexico to avoid going to trial for possession of marijuana.*

•••••

Neil Armstrong

In 1961, President John F. Kennedy (1917–1963) challenged Americans to land a man on the moon and return him safely to Earth before the end of the decade. Eight years later, that dream turned into a reality when Neil Armstrong (1930–) lowered himself down a ladder from the lunar module onto the surface of the moon.

His first words after reaching the lunar surface are some of the most famous of the twentieth century: "That's one small step for man, one giant leap for mankind."

Armstrong, the commander of the *Apollo 11* mission, and pilot Buzz Aldrin (1930–) spent 2½ hours on the surface of the moon, conducting experiments and collecting data. They returned home, along with command module pilot Michael Collins (1930–), as national heroes.

Before becoming an astronaut, Armstrong served as a naval aviator in the Korean War, flying seventy-eight combat missions, and was later a test pilot for, among other aircraft, the X-15 (which traveled at speeds of up to 4,000 miles per hour).

In 1962, he was elevated to astronaut status, and he completed his first space mission in 1966 with the *Gemini 8* mission.

But Armstrong is forever remembered for the first moonwalk, on July 20, 1969. The trip to the lunar surface took four days but was the culmination of nearly a decade of work by 400,000 people, costing $24 billion.

The mission was jeopardized as the ship neared the lunar surface when the onboard guidance system appeared to be taking the spaceship into a large crater. Armstrong overrode the autopilot to find a new place to land as the ship came perilously close to burning all its fuel.

More than 500 million television viewers held their breath until they heard Armstrong's words, "Houston, Tranquility Base here. The *Eagle* has landed."

In 1970, the laconic Armstrong resigned from the astronaut program. He has since lived a quiet life as a teacher and board member for several corporations.

ADDITIONAL FACTS

1. *Armstrong received the Presidential Medal of Freedom in 1969 and the Congressional Space Medal of Honor in 1978.*

2. *Armstrong's love of aviation began at age six, when he took his first flight in a Ford Tri-Motor airplane. He earned his pilot's license at age sixteen, before he earned his driver's license.*

3. *A word was lost from his famous quote. He actually said, "That's one small step for a man, one giant leap for mankind," but the "a" was inaudible because of an audio transmission problem.*

Long Day's Journey into Night

Long Day's Journey into Night is the crowning achievement of Eugene O'Neill (1888–1953), widely considered one of the greatest American playwrights of the past century. This gut-wrenching play is derived so transparently from O'Neill's own family history that he refused to let it be performed, or even published, until after his death.

O'Neill grew up amid a tumultuous family life, traveling incessantly as a result of his father's stage-acting career. The playwright's neurotic, unstable mother struggled with a lifelong morphine addiction, his underachieving older brother died of alcoholism, and the sickly O'Neill himself drank heavily. Nonetheless, he mined these experiences to create a remarkable run of plays throughout the 1920s. By 1930, he had won three Pulitzer Prizes and scored major successes with *Anna Christie* (1922), *Desire Under the Elms* (1924), and *Strange Interlude* (1928), among others.

After the deaths of his parents and older brother, O'Neill felt freer to include autobiographical elements in his works. This tendency culminated in *Long Day's Journey into Night* (1941), which depicts the crises that tear apart the allegedly fictional Tyrone family over the course of a single day. The Tyrones' hard-drinking, former-matinee-idol father; morphine-addicted mother; and two sons—one a dissipated alcoholic, the other an ailing, sensitive writer—are so clearly based on O'Neill's family that he required his publisher to promise not to release the play until twenty-five years after his death. Nonetheless, in 1956, just three years after O'Neill died, his widow sidestepped this arrangement by taking the play directly to Yale University Press, which published it that year.

Like much of his earlier work, *Long Day's Journey into Night* confirmed O'Neill as the heir to Anton Chekhov (1860–1904), Henrik Ibsen (1828–1906), August Strindberg (1849–1912), and other nineteenth-century European masters of realist drama. The play opened on Broadway to rave reviews in late 1956 and has since been revived four times.

ADDITIONAL FACTS

1. *The most recent Broadway production of* Long Day's Journey into Night, *in 2003, starred Vanessa Redgrave (1937–), Brian Dennehy (1938–), Philip Seymour Hoffman (1967–), and Robert Sean Leonard (1969–).*

2. *The alcoholic son in* Long Day's Journey into Night, *Jamie Tyrone, also appears as a major character in O'Neill's final play,* A Moon for the Misbegotten *(1947).*

3. *O'Neill literally was born into the theater world: His mother gave birth to him in a hotel room on Broadway, near Times Square. Oddly, he also died in a hotel room in Boston after a long illness.*

• • • • •

Ray Charles

Ray Charles (1930–2004) lost his vision to glaucoma at the age of seven and was sent to a special school for the blind in Florida, where he first learned to play musical instruments. Despite his disability, Charles would become one of the most versatile and prolific musicians of the twentieth century, with his works spanning genres and earning him the nickname the Genius.

In his first years of performing, Charles was a devoted admirer of the songwriter Nat King Cole (1919–1965), a popular jazz singer. Charles's first big hit was a version of the soul classic "I Got a Woman" (1954). He followed this success with other soul and R & B hits, including "Hit the Road Jack" (1961), "Drown in My Own Tears" (1957), and "What'd I Say" (1959), which crossed over to the pop music charts.

As eclectic as Charles's tastes were, he still surprised his producers and his fans when he decided to cut a country record in 1962. To the amazement of many music critics, the album became one of his biggest hits. His version of "I Can't Stop Loving You" (1962), originally by Don Gibson (1928–2003), rose to number one on both the R & B and pop charts, and he also had top-ten hits with versions of "Born to Lose" (1962) and "You Don't Know Me" (1962). The record was such a hit that it played a significant role in bringing country music in general into the pop mainstream.

Charles struggled with drug addiction for years, and his production of hits tailed off after the 1960s. However, his popularity enjoyed a resurgence in the 1980s, and he was the subject of a critically acclaimed biopic, *Ray,* that was released just after his death in 2004.

ADDITIONAL FACTS

1. *In 1979, Charles's version of "Georgia on My Mind" was named the official state song of Georgia.*

2. *"What'd I Say," Charles's first song that was both an R & B and a pop hit, almost went unreleased because his label found it "too long" and "too risqué" owing to its implied sexual content.*

3. *In the 1990s, Charles was introduced to a new generation of listeners when he performed in a series of nationally broadcast commercials for Diet Pepsi.*

••●••

Billy Wilder

Born and raised in Austria, Billy Wilder (1906–2002) became one of Hollywood's most successful writer-directors. During his illustrious career, he was nominated for twenty-one Academy Awards in various categories, winning six statues (including a lifetime achievement award in 1988). Writing is at the heart of his work, and his films are renowned for their witty, cynical, often dark wit.

Even though comedy often formed the foundation of Wilder's work, he was not limited by genre. Consider that he cowrote and directed *Double Indemnity* (1944), arguably the quintessential film noir; *The Lost Weekend* (1945), Hollywood's first treatment of alcoholism as a modern illness; *Sunset Boulevard* (1950), considered by many critics the finest Hollywood film about Hollywood; and *Some Like It Hot* (1959), a screwball comedy that an American Film Institute ranking in 2000 rated as the funniest movie ever made.

His movies have some of the smartest (and often sexiest) dialogue ever written, and the final line of *Some Like It Hot* is often considered the best closing line in movie history.

Wilder began his career as a journalist before transitioning to screenwriting in Germany. The rise of Hitler prompted Wilder to leave Berlin in 1933, first for Paris, then for Hollywood. For the first decade of his time in Hollywood, he worked exclusively as a screenwriter—he earned his first Academy Award nomination for cowriting the screenplay to *Ninotchka* (1939).

In 1942, he made his Hollywood directorial debut with *The Major and the Minor*. His third picture was *Double Indemnity*, which quickly established him as an elite director. Over his forty-year directing career, he made twenty-six Hollywood films and had a particularly successful working relationship with the actor Jack Lemmon (1925–2001)—together, they collaborated on seven films.

Wilder retired from directing after the Lemmon–and–Walter Matthau (1920–2000) black comedy *Buddy, Buddy* (1981). He died at age ninety-five.

ADDITIONAL FACTS

1. *One of the trademarks of Wilder's stories is voice-over narration—two of his greatest films,* Double Indemnity *and* Sunset Boulevard, *are told in the past tense by narrators.*

2. *Wilder directed two films that won Academy Awards for Best Picture—*The Lost Weekend *and* The Apartment *(1960). He is one of four Hollywood figures to have won Oscars for best picture, best screenplay, and best director for the same film. (He took home all three for* The Apartment.*)*

3. *Wilder garnered twenty-one Academy Award nominations, winning six. He was nominated for screenwriting twelve times (and won three) and directing eight times (and won two).*

•••••

DNA

On April 25, 1953, biologists James D. Watson (1928–) and Francis Crick (1916–2004) published an article titled "Molecular Structure of Nucleic Acids: A Structure for Deoxyribose Nucleic Acid" in the scientific journal *Nature*. The article was only one page long, but by explaining the structure of a substance called DNA, Watson and Crick solved one of the greatest mysteries of human evolution—how traits are passed on from one generation to the next—and ushered in the era of molecular biology.

Scientific exploration of genetics dated back to the nineteenth century, when an Austrian priest named Gregor Mendel (1822–1884) performed a series of experiments in his garden with thousands of pea plants, hoping to understand how individual plants of the same species ended up with different characteristics. In his experiments, he carefully noted several traits of the plants, including the shape and color of the seeds, flowers, and pods. He then crossbred strains of the plant to observe the effects.

According to theories of inheritance prevalent at the time, the result should have been a blend of the two parent strains. So, if a plant with white flowers was crossed with a plant that had violet flowers, the result should have been a plant with light violet flowers. This was known as blending inheritance—but it wasn't what Mendel found. Instead, he observed that one of the traits would be dominant, and the other recessive. When a new plant was born, it would have either white or violet flowers (for instance), and one of these (the dominant trait) was more common.

But Mendel was unable to show exactly how traits were passed along. With their discovery of the structure of DNA, which is found within every cell in the body, Watson and Crick provided the explanation. They ascertained that DNA is a double helix filled with the genetic instructions that result in hereditary traits. They also suggested a way to copy this structure and pass it down to future generations: When a strand of DNA was split, it was able to replicate itself. The replication would never be perfect, however, which accounts for the subtle changes from one generation to the next. With little more than a drawing and some accompanying text, Watson and Crick solved one of the major scientific mysteries of the century.

ADDITIONAL FACTS

1. *A set of nucleotide pairs is called a* gene, *and a collection of genes is called a* chromosome.

2. *The next step after the discovery of DNA's structure was to identify and map all the specific information that it contained. The Human Genome Project was launched in 1990 to undertake this mapping and completed its work in 2003.*

3. *Watson, Crick, and the biologist Maurice Wilkins (1916–2004) shared the 1962 Nobel Prize in Medicine for their DNA research.*

••●••

Vince Lombardi

Though many consider him to be the greatest coach of all time, few people realize that Vince Lombardi (1913–1970) was a National Football League (NFL) head coach for only ten years. But in that decade, he won five NFL championships (including the first two Super Bowls), never had a losing season, and became one of the most commonly quoted sports figures in history. In 2000, ESPN named him the top coach of the twentieth century.

Lombardi did not become an NFL head coach until 1959, when, at age forty-five, he took on the roles of coach and general manager of the Green Bay Packers. The team had finished its previous season with a record of one win, ten losses, and one tie, and it had not had a winning year since 1947. But through his intensive training sessions, his demand for total dedication from his players, and his inspirational leadership, Lombardi turned the franchise around.

Within three years, the Packers were NFL champions. They won consecutive titles in 1961 and 1962, added another NFL championship in 1965, then won Super Bowl I and Super Bowl II to complete an unprecedented run of three consecutive NFL crowns.

Lombardi retired from coaching the Packers after Super Bowl II but stayed on as general manager for one season. In 1969, he came out of coaching retirement to take over the Washington Redskins and led that team to its first winning season in fourteen years.

The 1969 season would be his last—he died of cancer the following year, at age fifty-seven.

Though he did not coin the phrase, Lombardi will forever be associated with the maxim that summed up his approach to football: "Winning isn't everything; it's the only thing."

ADDITIONAL FACTS

1. *Lombardi finished his NFL career with a record of 105-35-6. He was named the NFL's Man of the Decade for the 1960s.*

2. *He was inducted into the Pro Football Hall of Fame in 1971, the same year the Super Bowl trophy was named in his honor.*

3. *Before taking the Green Bay coaching job, Lombardi served as an assistant coach at Fordham University (his alma mater), at the US Military Academy at West Point, and for the New York Giants.*

••●••

James Bond

The suave, martini-sipping spy James Bond debuted in 1953 as the main character in *Casino Royale,* a thriller by the British author Ian Fleming (1908–1964). Since then, the Bond character has starred in twenty-one movies, including blockbusters *Thunderball* (1965) and *Live and Let Die* (1973), making Fleming's creation one of the most popular movie franchises of the past four decades.

Ian Fleming

Fleming used his own experiences as a British intelligence official during World War II for inspiration. He had directed an espionage unit that specialized in infiltrating German defenses, and he based his Bond characters on several British spies he'd encountered during the war.

The first Bond novels drew heavily from American pulp fiction and the crime writer Raymond Chandler (1888–1959). Like Chandler's hard-boiled detectives, Bond smoked, drank, gambled, and broke the rules to catch his foes.

Fleming published *Live and Let Die* in 1954, *Moonraker* in 1955, and eleven other Bond books before his death. His novels, set in the midst of the Cold War, often pitted Bond against communist villains aligned with SMERSH, a fictional Soviet counterintelligence agency based on the KGB.

The popularity of the series received a huge boost when President John F. Kennedy (1917–1963) named *From Russia with Love* as one of his favorite books in 1961.

Dr. No, the first Bond film, was released in 1962 and starred the Scottish actor Sean Connery (1930–) in the lead role. *From Russia with Love* (1963), *Goldfinger* (1964), and *Thunderball* (1965) soon followed.

Since then, a succession of actors have filled the Bond role, including George Lazenby (1939–), Roger Moore (1927–), Timothy Dalton (1946–), and Pierce Brosnan (1953–). Daniel Craig (1968–), the current Bond, was introduced in *Casino Royale* (2006), which finally brought Fleming's first Bond novel to the big screen.

ADDITIONAL FACTS

1. *Fleming also wrote the children's classic* Chitty Chitty Bang Bang *(1964).*

2. *Bond's most frequent antagonist was the bald, cat-scratching supervillain Ernst Stavro Blofeld, who was parodied in the character Dr. Evil in the Austin Powers movies.*

3. *Countless Bond parody films have been produced, including a 1967 version of* Casino Royale *starring David Niven (1910–1983).*

••●●••

Abbie Hoffman

A countercultural icon in the 1960s and 1970s, Abbie Hoffman (1936–1989) rose to national fame for his use of witty political stunts to agitate for social change. He achieved his greatest measure of attention when he was arrested as one of the Chicago Seven—a group of radicals charged with conspiring to disrupt the 1968 Democratic National Convention in Chicago.

Born in Massachusetts and a graduate of Brandeis University, Hoffman was a cofounder of the Youth International Party, a radical, youth-oriented movement popularly known as the yippies.

In 1967, Hoffman spearheaded two political stunts that made national headlines. He led a group of anticapitalists to the New York Stock Exchange, where they dropped dollar bills from the balcony onto the floor as traders scrambled to retrieve the cash.

He also led a demonstration in which a crowd of 50,000 people tried to levitate the Pentagon with their combined psychic power—an attempt to end the Vietnam War. (It failed.)

But it was the trial of the Chicago Seven that truly captured the attention of the nation. Hoffman and fellow yippie Jerry Rubin (1938–1994) turned the five-month court proceedings into a virtual circus. Among other stunts, they wore judicial robes, brought a birthday cake into the court, blew kisses to the jury, bared their chests, and generally made a mess of the defense table.

In the end, all seven members of the group were acquitted of conspiracy, but Hoffman and four others were convicted of crossing state lines with intent to riot (a conviction that was later overturned).

Hoffman's activist days largely ended in the 1960s, though he remained a symbol of youth culture and rebellion through the 1970s. He returned briefly to radical protests in the mid-1980s before committing suicide at age fifty-two.

ADDITIONAL FACTS

1. *Hoffman was largely absent from the political scene in the 1970s because he was on the run from the police from 1974 to 1980 following his arrest for selling cocaine to an undercover officer. He finally emerged from hiding in 1980 when he sat down for an interview with ABC's Barbara Walters (1931–).*

2. *While in hiding, Hoffman lived in upstate New York under the name Barry Freed.*

3. *In 1987, Hoffman was arrested (along with President Jimmy Carter's daughter, Amy) at an anti-CIA protest. It was the last major public attention he received before his death.*

·•••·

On the Road

Jack Kerouac's *On the Road* (1957) was the defining literary work of the Beat generation, a rebellious, bohemian artistic movement that arose in the United States during the 1950s. A tale of several friends crisscrossing the country by car, it remains a classic of American road fiction.

Jack Kerouac

Although the 1950s in America are remembered as a time of social conformity, by the middle of the decade, elements of artistic society had begun to rebel against this conformity. In the coffee shops and bookstores of three urban neighborhoods in particular—San Francisco's North Beach, Los Angeles' Venice West, and New York City's Greenwich Village—writers and poets formed a new literary undercurrent that came to be labeled the Beat movement. Led by Kerouac (1922–1969), novelist William S. Burroughs (1914–1997), and poet Allen Ginsberg (1926–1997), they sent a shock wave through the American literary system.

The central figure of the movement, Kerouac spent the years after World War II wandering around North America and writing. The more he wrote, the more he grew to favor a free-flowing, unpolished writing technique that he termed *spontaneous prose*—the polar opposite of the meticulous craftsmanship that most traditional novelists employed. Indeed, Kerouac completed the original manuscript of *On the Road* in just three weeks.

On the Road follows two young men—based on Kerouac and his friend Neal Cassady (1926–1968)—back and forth on a series of aimless road trips across the United States. Along the way, they muse formlessly about jazz, Buddhism, drinking, women, and their dislike of society's constraints. The novel's style is frantic, featuring high-speed, stream-of-consciousness conversations and dense imagery. Eventually, the two men grow apart, and the road loses its allure—a fitting illustration of the earthly transience that the Beat writers both celebrated and lamented in their works.

ADDITIONAL FACTS

1. *Kerouac typed the entire first draft of* On the Road *on one enormous, 120-foot-long scroll—single-spaced, with tiny margins, and without any paragraph breaks.*

2. *Kerouac himself coined the term* Beat *to denote his generation's weariness of social norms. Later, though, the term became associated with musical beats, as well as the "beatific," or spiritual, nature of some of the movement's beliefs.*

3. *Many critics disdained Kerouac's work and his contempt for traditional methods. Truman Capote (1924–1984), for one, bluntly dismissed* On the Road *by saying, "That's not writing, it's typing."*

Phil Spector

The music producer Phil Spector (1940–) created the Wall of Sound, an innovative technique for recording pop music that was used on many hits of the early 1960s. Thanks to his groundbreaking technical work—and his personal eccentricities and fondness for guns—Spector is one of the few rock producers whose fame rivals and even exceeds that of many performers.

Though most famous as a producer, Spector started out as a member of the Teddy Bears, a pop band he formed with a group of high-school friends. Their first record, written by Spector when he was seventeen years old, was "To Know Him Is to Love Him." It rose to number one in 1958 and stayed on the charts for weeks. The group was never able to replicate its early success, however, and Spector soon switched his focus to producing.

Spector's Wall of Sound technique, which was first used in the early 1960s on recordings by "girl groups" such as the Crystals and the Ronettes, was tailored specifically to the needs of jukeboxes and radios. Because the primitive speakers of early jukeboxes and the poor quality of AM radio couldn't transmit the subtleties of a recording, Spector decided to go in the opposite direction. He recorded numerous musicians, including many playing the same instrument, in a relatively small space. This method echoed and amplified an already big sound. With a backdrop this elaborate, pop songs began to sound nearly epic, even on a simple AM radio. As Spector put it, he took "a Wagnerian approach to rock & roll: little symphonies for the kids."

While many critics disparaged his techniques, Spector had more than fifty top-100 hits. These included many classics of the era, from "Da Doo Ron Ron" in 1963 to the classic John Lennon (1940–1980) single "Imagine" in 1971.

More recently, Spector was arrested for allegedly murdering a California waitress. His 2007 trial ended in a mistrial.

ADDITIONAL FACTS

1. *"You've Lost That Lovin' Feelin'," cowritten by Spector and first performed by the Righteous Brothers in 1964, has received more airplay on radio and television than any other song in the past century.*

2. *Spector has perfect pitch, the ability to identify a musical note or other sound without referring to a score.*

3. *Beatles songwriter and bassist Paul McCartney (1942–) was dissatisfied with Spector's work on the ballad "The Long and Winding Road" (1970) and unsuccessfully tried to release it without the producer's overdubs.*

••●••

Marlon Brando

Many film historians consider Marlon Brando (1924–2004) to be one of the most influential movie actors of all time. He was the first major star to bring Method acting (in which a performer tries to replicate the emotional state of his character) to Hollywood, imbuing his performances with a more naturalistic style. Using this approach, Brando inhabited some of the most iconic characters in the history of American cinema.

He brought his intense, raw style from Broadway to Hollywood, causing a sensation in just his second film, as the violent Stanley Kowalski in *A Streetcar Named Desire* (1951). After successful turns in *¡Viva Zapata!* (1952) and *Julius Caesar* (1953), Brando starred in *The Wild One* (1953), a landmark and influential film of 1950s rebellion. In *On the Waterfront* (1954), Brando played the brutish and inarticulate ex-boxer Terry Malloy ("I coulda been a contender," he mumbles) and won his first Academy Award for Best Actor on his fourth nomination.

For the rest of the 1950s and the 1960s, Brando settled into something of a mid-career slump. By most accounts, he took on roles in lesser films for the money, becoming bored with acting and revolted by Hollywood.

He resurrected his career with his portrayal of Vito Corleone in *The Godfather* (1972), directed by Francis Ford Coppola (1939–). Brando had to submit to a screen test, and Paramount executives were wary of hiring the star because of his eccentricities. In the end, he was the only actor then considered a star to be cast in the film, and his performance won him a second Academy Award for Best Actor.

Brando began the 1970s with the sexually explicit *Last Tango in Paris* (1972), considered his most daring film. Through the rest of the decade, Brando worked sparingly and put on weight dramatically. In Coppola's *Apocalypse Now* (1979), playing Colonel Walter E. Kurtz, he was cloaked in darkness and shadows because of his obesity (but his impact on the film was still powerful).

For the rest his life, Brando was more a curiosity than an actor. His later films, by and large, were unsuccessful, and he became an enigmatic and increasingly reclusive figure, living at times on his own island near Tahiti. He died at age eighty.

ADDITIONAL FACTS

1. *Brando refused his Academy Award for* The Godfather *and instead used the ceremony to protest Hollywood's mistreatment of Native Americans. In his place, he sent an actress named Sacheen Littlefeather to speak from the podium on his behalf.*

2. *Brando was paid $3.7 million and a percentage of the profits for twelve shooting days to play Jor-El, Superman's father, in the hit superhero flick* Superman *(1978). For ten minutes of screen time, Brando ended up earning about $14 million.*

3. *His character in* The Wild One, *juvenile delinquent Johnny Strabler, is the leader of an outlaw motorcycle gang—and the sale of leather jackets and motorcycles across America skyrocketed after the film's release.*

••••

The John Birch Society

In 1958, a group of anticommunist activists founded an organization called the John Birch Society that was dedicated to finding and destroying all traces of communism in the United States. Within several years, the society had grown to more than 50,000 members, forming one of the foundations of the so-called New Right, a resurgence in political conservatism that began in the 1950s and 1960s.

Initially led by the retired Boston candy manufacturer Robert H. W. Welch Jr. (1899–1985), the group took its name from John Birch (1918–1945), an American intelligence officer who had been killed in China. They considered him a martyr— the first casualty of the Cold War against worldwide communism.

At its peak in the early 1960s, the organization counted business leaders, congress-men, and military generals among its members. Society members formed a base of support for 1964 Republican presidential candidate Barry Goldwater (1909–1998).

In an effort to unearth the communist menace they believed lurked in their midst, the group's adherents supported anticommunist politicians, sponsored investiga-tions, and lobbed wild, often baseless accusations of communist sympathies against political figures.

Although their period of prominence was brief, the John Birch Society attracted an enormous amount of attention in the early 1960s and was a significant force within the Republican Party. Birchers were attacked in newspapers and lampooned by singer Bob Dylan (1941–) in his 1964 song "Talkin' John Birch Paranoid Blues," which poked fun at a member of the group's belief that communists lurked every-where—even "deep inside my toilet bowl."

The group's stridency and paranoia also attracted the attention of the historian Richard Hofstadter (1916–1970), who argued in a famous 1964 essay in *Harper's* magazine that the John Birch Society's conspiratorial rhetoric followed a long tradi-tion in American politics—what he called the "paranoid style."

After 1965, the Republican Party began to distance itself from the extremism and increasing zaniness of the society's leaders. Although the group still exists today as an anti-United Nations and antitax association, its sway is far diminished.

ADDITIONAL FACTS

1. *Birch's parents were given honorary lifetime membership in the organization.*

2. *Despite its ostensible concern for protecting freedom, the John Birch Society opposed the civil rights movement, fearing it was a front group for communists.*

3. *The Birchers were particularly opposed to President Dwight D. Eisenhower (1890–1969), who some members suspected was a secret communist operative.*

•• • ••

Sandy Koufax

On the strength of one dazzling five-year period, Sandy Koufax (1935–) may have been the most dominating pitcher who ever lived. From 1962 to 1966, the Los Angeles Dodgers lefty compiled a record of 111 wins and 34 losses, along with an earned run average (ERA) of 2.02. During the span, Koufax won one National League Most Valuable Player (MVP) award, received three Cy Young Awards, reached 25 victories in three different seasons, helped his team to two World Series crowns, and threw four no-hitters, including a perfect game in 1965.

Said Pittsburgh Pirates slugger Willie Stargell (1940–2001), "Hitting against him is like eating soup with a fork."

Little in Koufax's first six seasons in the majors portended his unsurpassed success during the 1960s. From 1955 to 1960, he compiled a 36-40 record with a 4.10 ERA, struggling with his control. But once he focused more on throwing strikes than on the velocity of his fastball, he became an immortal.

His most dominant season was 1965, which he finished with a 26-8 record, a 2.04 ERA, and a record 382 strikeouts. He won the Cy Young and was the MVP of the World Series, helping the Dodgers to victory over the Minnesota Twins. He also became a tremendous hero in the Jewish community when he refused to pitch in Game 1 of the World Series, which fell on Yom Kippur, the holiest day of the Jewish calendar.

His achievements were particularly remarkable considering the amount of pain Koufax endured during his final two seasons. Suffering from a case of traumatic arthritis in his left elbow, he still led the majors in wins, ERA, and strikeouts in both seasons. But by the end of 1966, doctors told Koufax his arthritis was so severe that he could lose his arm if he continued pitching. So at the height of his powers, he walked away from the game.

Koufax was a reluctant celebrity in his later years, keeping out of the public eye aside from a short-lived television commentary career. He has worked as an instructor for the Dodgers and New York Mets.

ADDITIONAL FACTS

1. *He was born Sanford Braun but changed his name when his divorced mother married Irving Koufax when Sandy was nine.*

2. *Though it is widely believed that Koufax attended Yom Kippur religious services instead of pitching Game 1 of the 1965 World Series, biographer Jane Leavy reported that he actually spent the night alone in his hotel room.*

3. *He was inducted into the Baseball Hall of Fame in 1972, the youngest player ever elected, at age thirty-six.*

••●••

Ed Sullivan

As host and producer of his long-running television variety show, Ed Sullivan (1901–1974) enjoyed a two-decade run as America's premier star-maker. A sharp-eyed talent scout, Sullivan remained finely attuned to the whims of a fickle audience and introduced many top acts, including the Beatles, to American audiences.

Sullivan began his career as a newspaper reporter in 1919, first as a sportswriter for the *Hartford Post* and then, after 1927, at New York City's *Evening Graphic*. After becoming a Broadway columnist two years later, Sullivan eventually came to rival Walter Winchell (1897–1972) as a top entertainment and gossip writer.

In 1948, CBS tapped Sullivan to host a new televised variety show, *Toast of the Town*. Soon renamed *The Ed Sullivan Show*, this Sunday-night fixture hosted the American television debuts of countless performers, including the opera singer Maria Callas (1923–1977), the dancer Rudolf Nureyev (1938–1993), and the ventriloquist-comedian Señor Wences (1896–1999). The Beatles' 1964 debut attracted a record audience of more than 70 million.

Well aware of his own lack of charisma, Sullivan often invited impersonators onto the show to lampoon his stiff posture and stilted phrasing. He also paid generously to secure top performers, occasionally dipping into his own salary to do so. Ever confident in his own eye for talent, Sullivan also disregarded southern advertisers' early concerns about African-American performers appearing on the show. In his first years on the air, Sullivan booked Cab Calloway (1907–1994), Count Basie (1904–1984), and Nat King Cole (1919–1965), and later noted that his show remained popular in the South, as he had predicted.

The Ed Sullivan Show was abruptly canceled in 1971, the victim of its own high budget and an aging audience that was slowly shrinking in numbers. The program's role as nationwide cultural arbiter, showcasing high and pop culture to an audience spanning generations, has remained unrivaled ever since.

ADDITIONAL FACTS

1. *Sullivan's bumbling, uneasy manner on stage and the show's focus on his guests earned him critical barbs and amiable mockery. The columnist Harriet Van Horne (1920–1998) observed that Sullivan had gained his success "not by having a personality, but by having no personality." Fred Allen (1894–1956), a comedian who frequently appeared on the show, said that Sullivan's success would last "as long as someone else has talent."*

2. *Before playing their hit "Light My Fire" in a 1967 appearance, the Doors agreed to censors' demands that they change the line "Girl, we couldn't get much higher" to remove any possible drug implications. The band earned a lifetime ban from the show when they instead performed the original lyrics on live television. The Rolling Stones' performance the same year went more smoothly. When asked to change the chorus of "Let's Spend the Night Together" to "Let's spend some time together," singer Mick Jagger (1943–) confined his protests to rolling his eyes on camera.*

3. *Late-night TV host David Letterman (1947–) now uses the Ed Sullivan Theater in New York City for his show.*

•••••

Charles Manson

Although he did not actually kill anyone, Charles Manson (1934–) is considered one of the most notorious mass murderers of the twentieth century. He was the charismatic, messianic leader of a cult known as the Manson Family, largely made up of young women. In August 1969, he directed several members of the group to commit a series of grisly murders known as the Tate-LaBianca killings.

In all, his disciples killed seven people, including actress Sharon Tate (1943–1969), the wife of noted film director Roman Polanski (1933–). Manson and three members of his "family" were convicted of murder and conspiracy in 1971 and sentenced to death. Their bizarre trial captivated the nation and was the longest and most expensive in California history. In February 1972, the Supreme Court of California abolished the death penalty, automatically reducing the convicts' sentences to life in prison.

Manson came from a troubled background. He was born to an unwed mother and never knew his father. He spent seventeen of his first thirty-two years in reformatories and prisons. In 1967, following a release from prison, he moved to San Francisco, where he immersed himself in hippie culture.

Spouting philosophy and strumming a guitar, he soon developed a following of around twelve young women and six young men, who were generally lonely outcasts like him. Manson was said to believe that a race war—what he termed *Helter Skelter*, after the 1968 Beatles song of the same name—was imminent.

He believed that blacks would be blamed for the murders his family commited, touching off the race war. Having moved the family to the Nevada desert in 1968 to prepare for the coming war, he was instead arrested there in October 1969 for possession of stolen property. Two months later, he was charged for the Tate-LaBianca killings.

ADDITIONAL FACTS

1. *Part of the public's fascination with the trial stemmed from the circumstances of the murders. Five of the victims were stabbed at least sixteen times, with Polanski's friend Wojciech Frykowski (1936–1969) receiving fifty-one stab wounds. (He was also shot twice and struck thirteen times on the head.)*

2. *The killers scrawled several references to Beatles songs in blood on walls and appliances at the murder scene, including "healter skelter" [sic] and "pig," for the 1968 song "Piggies." Manson was obsessed with the Beatles, particularly the 1968 album* The Beatles *(commonly known as* The White Album*).*

3. *Manson's trial was nothing short of bizarre. At one point, brandishing a sharpened pencil, he lunged across the defense table at Judge Charles Herman Older (1917–2006). At another point, Manson flashed the jurors a newspaper headline that said that President Nixon believed Manson was guilty.*

•••••

Ayn Rand

Though Ayn Rand (1905–1982) had as many detractors as devotees, she was indisputably one of the most influential figures in twentieth-century fiction. Also an important popular philosopher, she promoted an achievement-oriented worldview that, while controversial, resonated with many among her legions of readers.

Rand was born and educated in St. Petersburg, Russia, where as a university student she read voraciously and developed strong opinions about the writings of Aristotle (384–322 BC), Thomas Aquinas (c. 1225–1274), Fyodor Dostoyevsky (1821–1881), Friedrich Nietzsche (1844–1900), and other major Western thinkers. In 1926, she immigrated to the United States. After a brief stint as a Hollywood script reader, she turned her attention to writing—first a screenplay, then a stage play, and then the first of several novels.

Rand's reputation rests primarily on two giant works—*The Fountainhead* (1943) and *Atlas Shrugged* (1957)—that set out the tenets of her personal philosophy, which she called objectivism. *The Fountainhead* focuses on a young, capable architect whose refusal to conform to expectations or lower his standards brings him initial hardship but ultimate triumph. *Atlas Shrugged,* meanwhile, depicts the crumbling of America after its inventors, artists, and industrialists stage a "strike of the mind," withdrawing from society because of its failure to recognize and adequately reward their efforts.

Both works, but particularly *Atlas Shrugged,* articulate the principles of objectivism. In short, Rand believed that humankind's capacity for reason could lead to enormous achievements, and that each individual had the obligation to use his or her gifts to strive toward accomplishment, profit, and self-improvement, and thereby personal happiness. Although countless readers found Rand's teachings inspiring, many were turned off by her aggressive egoism and her seeming opposition to traditional Judeo-Christian values of charity and selflessness. In any case, Rand's novels have remained enormously widely read—all told, they have sold more than 22 million copies worldwide.

ADDITIONAL FACTS

1. *When the Modern Library asked readers to vote for the 100 greatest novels of the twentieth century,* Atlas Shrugged *and* The Fountainhead *placed first and second, respectively.*

2. *Twelve publishers rejected* The Fountainhead *before Indiana-based Bobbs-Merrill finally accepted it in 1943. It has since sold more than six million copies.*

3. *Rand summed up objectivism as "the concept of man as a heroic being, with his own happiness as the moral purpose of his life, with productive achievement as his noblest activity, and reason as his only absolute."*

••●••

Beatlemania

At the beginning of December 1963, few Americans had ever heard of a British pop group called the Beatles. Early that month, however, Marsha Albert (1948–), a ninth-grader in Washington, DC, wrote to a local AM radio station and requested a song by the group titled "I Want to Hold Your Hand." A disc jockey at the station obtained an imported copy from Great Britain and played the song on December 17, 1963.

Within a few days of that first, fateful broadcast in Washington, the United States was firmly in the grip of Beatlemania. Amid thousands of requests from fans and other radio stations for copies of the single, the band's record label was forced to release "I Want to Hold Your Hand" in the United States on December 26; within three days, it had sold 250,000 copies nationwide.

The Beatles' sudden, overwhelming popularity, coming barely a month after the assassination of President John F. Kennedy (1917–1963), was unprecedented. When the band began its American tour in February 1964, the Beatles were mobbed by thousands of shrieking teenagers at the newly renamed John F. Kennedy Airport in New York; their debut performance on *The Ed Sullivan Show* two days later was drowned out by cheers.

The Beatles had formed in the British city of Liverpool in the late 1950s. The band starred John Lennon (1940–1980) and George Harrison (1943–2001) on guitar, Paul McCartney (1942–) on bass, and Ringo Starr (1940–) on drums. Influenced by American rock acts such as Elvis Presley (1935–1977) and Chuck Berry (1926–), the band's first albums featured upbeat love songs that thrilled teenage audiences. Their success in the United States sparked the so-called British Invasion period in American culture as more British groups, including the Rolling Stones, crossed the Atlantic.

Within three years, however, the Beatles had quit touring for good, weary of their crazed fans. In the late 1960s, the band's sound changed drastically on a series of studio albums, with groundbreaking psychedelic songs such as "Lucy in the Sky with Diamonds" (1967) and dark ballads like "While My Guitar Gently Weeps" (1968) replacing the exuberant love songs of the Beatlemania period.

ADDITIONAL FACTS

1. *In 2004,* Rolling Stone *magazine ranked the Beatles first on its list of the greatest rock artists of all time.*

2. *When Decca Records A&R executive Dick Rowe turned down the Beatles for a record deal in 1962, he reportedly told their manager, "Guitar groups are on the way out." He made up for the mistake by signing the Rolling Stones the next year.*

3. *The Beatles' first appearance on CBS's* Ed Sullivan Show *was watched by about 73 million viewers— 40 percent of the American population at the time.*

•••••

Sidney Poitier

No actor had a greater impact on the acceptance of black actors in Hollywood than Sidney Poitier (1927–). Through his roles in several films that addressed racism head-on, Poitier was able to establish himself—and, by extension, African-American men—as successful Hollywood stars. He was the first black male actor to be nominated for a competitive Academy Award (for *The Defiant Ones,* 1958) and the first to win an Oscar for best actor (for *Lilies of the Field,* 1963).

Born on a boat en route from his parents' home in the Bahamas to Miami, Poitier grew up in the Bahamas and came to the United States as a teenager. He began his career on the stage before landing his first film job for *No Way Out* (1950).

His breakthrough performance was as a troubled high-school student in *Blackboard Jungle* (1955), and he received his first major acclaim for *The Defiant Ones.* In that film, he played a fugitive convict shackled to Tony Curtis (1925–); the two must learn to accept one another to survive.

In his Oscar-winning turn in *Lilies of the Field,* Poitier portrayed Homer Smith, an out-of-work construction worker who befriends a group of East German nuns and helps them build a church.

Poitier's most successful year was 1967, when he starred in *To Sir, with Love; In the Heat of the Night;* and *Guess Who's Coming to Dinner.*

Most critics agree that *In the Heat of the Night* is Poitier's finest film. In it, he played Virgil Tibbs, a Philadelphia homicide detective who investigates a murder in a small Mississippi town. Tibbs must join forces with police chief Bill Gillespie (played by Rod Steiger), causing both men to reexamine their views on race. The film won five Academy Awards, including Best Picture and Best Actor (Steiger), though Poitier was not nominated.

Poitier starred alongside the Hollywood legends Spencer Tracy (1900–1967) and Katharine Hepburn (1907–2003) in *Guess Who's Coming to Dinner,* an exploration of interracial relationships.

Poitier spent much of the 1970s focusing more on directing than acting, and since 1977, he has appeared in only a handful of feature films.

ADDITIONAL FACTS

1. *Poitier has directed nine films, including* Stir Crazy *(1980), starring Richard Pryor (1940–2005) and Gene Wilder (1933–). For twenty years, it was the highest-grossing film by a black director ($101 million at the box office).*

2. *After* In the Heat of the Night, *he reprised the role of Virgil Tibbs in two films:* They Call Me Mister Tibbs! *(1970) and* The Organization *(1971).*

3. *In 2002, Poitier received an honorary Academy Award "for his extraordinary performances and unique presence on the screen."*

•• • ••

Nonviolent Resistance

In 1959, the civil rights activist Martin Luther King Jr. (1929–1968) traveled to India to meet with the family of the late independence leader Mohandas Gandhi (1869–1948). King was deeply moved by the trip, which reinforced many of his own beliefs about the power of an idea: nonviolent resistance against injustice.

Back in the United States, King applied many of Gandhi's methods of civil disobedience to the struggle for equal rights for blacks and made nonviolence one of the ideological foundations of the American civil rights movement.

In addition to Gandhi, King also found inspiration in the ideas of the nineteenth-century American author Henry David Thoreau (1817–1862), who had written the essay "Civil Disobedience" in 1849 to protest American involvement in the Mexican War.

In essence, Gandhi and King believed that nonviolent resistance was ultimately a more effective strategy than resorting to arms to try to force social change. By calling attention to injustice through symbolic, nonviolent means, King believed he could turn public sympathies against discrimination. Gandhi's successful use of fasts, peaceful marches, and boycotts during the struggle against the British was an inspiration to King and other civil rights leaders.

Many of the most well-known tactics embraced by the civil rights movement, such as the Montgomery bus boycott of 1955 and the march on Washington in 1963, reflected the commitment to nonviolent protest. One major civil rights group, the Student Nonviolent Coordinating Committee (SNCC), was formed in 1960 to organize sit-ins, demonstrations, and freedom rides in the segregated South.

True to King's prediction, televised images of nonviolent protestors in Alabama being savagely beaten by white police officers and attacked by police dogs in 1963 outraged viewers and helped turn the tide of public opinion against Jim Crow segregation.

ADDITIONAL FACTS

1. *Gandhi's birthday, October 2, is the United Nations–approved International Day of Non-Violence.*

2. *King was awarded the Nobel Peace Prize in 1964.*

3. *SNCC activists included John Lewis (1940–), who was later elected to Congress representing Atlanta, Georgia.*

· · ● · ·

Pelé

Pelé (1940–) is widely considered the greatest soccer player of all time. He scored an amazing seventy-seven goals in the ninety-two games he played for Brazil's national team, contributing to the country's first three World Cup championships. Perhaps most improbably, Pelé also helped make soccer a popular spectator sport in the United States when he moved to a New York team in the mid-1970s.

Born to a poor family, Edson Arantes do Nascimento, or Pelé, joined the Brazilian club team Santos in 1956, at age sixteen. He turned it into one of the most famous soccer teams in the world, taking on all comers.

But Pelé established true global greatness as a member of the Brazilian national squad at the 1958 World Cup. In the elimination round, the seventeen-year-old was spectacular, scoring once in the quarterfinals, three times in the semifinals, and twice more in the final to help Brazil to its first World Cup title.

After two personally disappointing World Cups in 1962 and 1966, the 1970 edition was Pelé's last to prove himself as the greatest player of all time. He did not disappoint, leading arguably the best team ever assembled to another World Cup crown and scoring a goal in the championship game victory over Italy.

At the height of Pelé's fame, only the boxer Muhammad Ali (1942–) was as popular an athlete around the globe. Pelé was known for his acrobatic and graceful moves on the pitch, which seemed to defy both gravity and age.

He retired from Santos in 1974 but shocked the soccer community when he came out of retirement to sign a three-year contract with the New York Cosmos of the North American Soccer League (NASL). Because of Pelé's arrival, attendance at NASL games increased by 80 percent in 1975. Two years later, he led the Cosmos to the league championship before retiring for good.

Since then, Pelé has been a goodwill ambassador for soccer, has served as Brazil's minister of sport, and has been a global pitchman for various corporations. In 1999, the International Olympic Committee named him the Athlete of the Century, and in 2000, the Fédération Internationale de Football Association, the international soccer governing body, named him Footballer of the Century.

ADDITIONAL FACTS

1. *Pelé acquired his nickname as a poor boy playing soccer in southeastern Brazil, though the exact origin of the moniker is not known.*

2. *Pelé was the first player to contribute to three World Cup championship teams. (He played in two games in 1962 before suffering a leg injury and missing the rest of the tournament.)*

3. *He finished his World Cup career with twelve goals in the tournament.*

•••••

Miniskirts

In 1968, police in the Congo Republic, a former French colony in Africa, launched a series of raids in and around the capital city of Brazzaville. Their target: 300 girls who had worn a banned garment known as the miniskirt.

First introduced in 1964, the miniskirt swept the world in the mid-1960s, scandalizing conservatives and, to some, signaling the rapidly changing mores of the decade. Miniskirts end six to seven inches above the knee, exposing territory on the body that had previously been considered indecent.

The fashion designers André Courrèges (1923–) and Mary Quant (1934–) are credited with designing the first miniskirts. Quant's version of the garment was especially popular in the United Kingdom, where it was known as the Chelsea Look, in honor of what was then one of London's hippest neighborhoods.

Many feminists, including Germaine Greer (1939–) and Gloria Steinem (1934–), embraced the miniskirt as a symbol of youth and women's liberation. Indeed, a Gallup poll in 1970 found that 51 percent of young women preferred miniskirts—compared with 5 percent of women over fifty.

Not surprisingly, however, the miniskirt provoked a ferocious backlash. In addition to the raids in the Congo, a Roman Catholic cardinal denounced miniskirts as "provocatory and shameless." In Malawi, the government approved an order to deport foreign women who wore miniskirts "before they corrupt the local population." Churches in Venezuela warned women to wear more modest dresses "or be condemned to hell." Iraq banned the skirts completely.

As a symbol of rebellion, however, the miniskirt faded as it eventually became more established. Indeed, Quant herself proclaimed the miniskirt passé while unveiling a new clothing line in 1970. "The mini has served its purpose of proving that woman is emancipated; that's now accepted," she said. "We can get back to normal."

ADDITIONAL FACTS

1. *Miniskirts got a major leg up when Jean Shrimpton (1942–), a British supermodel of the time, began wearing them herself.*

2. *In the late 1960s and early 1970s, miniskirts were followed by micro skirts, often only a few inches long.*

3. *Former president Dwight D. Eisenhower (1890–1969) criticized miniskirts on aesthetic grounds in a 1967 graduation speech. "Ankles are nearly always neat and good-looking, but knees are nearly always not," he said.*

••••

Howard Cosell

At his peak, Howard Cosell (1918–1995) was both the most loved and the most hated sports broadcaster in the country, as well as the most outspoken and most famous. Unlike the majority of sportscasters of the 1960s and 1970s, he was acid tongued, erudite, and arrogant on and off the air. As he put it, "I tell it like it is."

And it wasn't just what he said, but how he said it: In his distinctively nasal Brooklyn staccato, he emphasized every syllable of every word as if reciting Shakespeare.

During his thirty-year television career, Cosell rose to prominence calling boxing matches, covering the Olympics, and providing analysis on *Monday Night Football.* He was also known for his close on-air relationship with heavyweight boxing champion Muhammad Ali (1942–). Cosell was often a lightning rod for criticism because, in addition to his sarcastic comments, he also took moral stands on controversial issues, particularly when he perceived injustice or racism.

He was once quoted as saying, "Arrogant, pompous, obnoxious, vain, cruel, verbose, a showoff. I have been called all of these. Of course, I am."

Cosell was trained as a lawyer but left his practice to do sports commentary for ABC full-time in 1956. At ABC, Cosell covered boxing for *Wide World of Sports,* frequently interviewing Ali. Despite their obvious cultural differences, the two developed a successful chemistry and became friends. In 1967, when Ali was stripped of his title for refusing entry to the draft on religious grounds, Cosell defended him.

In 1970, ABC Sports executive Roone Arledge (1931–2002) made the controversial decision to add Cosell to the *Monday Night Football* commentating team. The choice was an enormous success and Cosell helped draw a huge audience, turning professional sports into a prime-time television attraction.

Disgusted by the violence and corruption of boxing, Cosell stopped calling bouts in 1982. A year later, he left *Monday Night Football* after a fourteen-year run. In 1985, ABC dropped him altogether following the publication of his book *I Never Played the Game,* which was critical of his colleagues at the network.

He left the air for good in 1992 when he retired from his last two radio shows. He died at age seventy-seven of a heart embolism.

ADDITIONAL FACTS

1. *Cosell made several cameos in movies—including two Woody Allen (1935–) films—and on television, where he once hosted an episode of* Saturday Night Live.

2. *A TV Guide poll once simultaneously named him the country's most liked and most disliked sportscaster.*

3. *Before entering the sports world, Cosell was the editor of the law review at New York University Law School.*

• • ● • •

J. R. R. Tolkien

The epic fantasy novels *The Hobbit* (1937) and *The Lord of the Rings* (1954–1955) made J. R. R. Tolkien (1892–1973) a household name and one of the most beloved fiction writers of modern times. Though some literary critics have derided Tolkien's works as clunky and overlong, his novels rank among the biggest popular successes of the twentieth century and did much to spawn the growth of the fantasy genre in literature.

Born in South Africa in 1892, Tolkien grew up in England and attended Oxford, where he became a professor of Anglo-Saxon languages and literature. While on the faculty, he indulged his creative side by inventing several complete languages from scratch. He then created and populated an entire fictional world—which he called Middle-earth—based around those languages and wrote a comprehensive, thorough mythological history for it. It was from these whimsies that Tolkien's novels were born.

Tolkien intended *The Hobbit* primarily as a children's work, a tale about a race of small, friendly creatures who live in a pastoral region of Middle-earth called the Shire. The novel's irresistible landscape of hobbits, elves, dwarves, dragons, and wizards was a hit with readers and convinced Tolkien's publisher that a sequel would be viable. This follow-up came in the form of *The Lord of the Rings*, a sprawling, complex, three-part novel that was much more serious and adult in tone than *The Hobbit*.

The Lord of the Rings stands apart from other fantasy writing not merely in the depth and imaginativeness of its fictional world but also in the earnestness and resonance of its themes—fellowship, cooperation, tolerance, and respect for the environment, among others. The novel was reintroduced to a new generation between 2001 and 2003, when director Peter Jackson's (1961–) three-part film adaptation won numerous Academy Awards and became the highest-grossing motion picture trilogy of all time.

ADDITIONAL FACTS

1. *Tolkien came up with the word* hobbit *while scribbling aimlessly on a sheet of paper one day while grading exams.*

2. *Never particularly comfortable with his fame, Tolkien fled to the English seacoast and kept an unlisted telephone number after* The Lord of the Rings *became a runaway success.*

3. *The hard-rock band Led Zeppelin found inspiration in Tolkien's works and included references to Middle-earth in several of its songs.*

•• • ••

The Rolling Stones

The Rolling Stones formed in London in the early 1960s. Within a decade, the five British teenagers had become multimillionaires, sex symbols, and international cultural icons as "the Greatest Rock and Roll Band in the World."

Initially, the Stones mostly covered songs by American artists such as Chuck Berry (1926–) and Sam Cooke (1931–1964). The band's founders, singer Mick Jagger (1943–), guitarist Keith Richards (1943–), and guitarist Brian Jones (1942–1969), were heavily influenced by American rhythm and blues music.

After the Beatles kicked off the British Invasion in early 1964, the Stones quickly joined the migration of British bands across the Atlantic, staging their first United States tour in 1964. Their first major hit, "(I Can't Get No) Satisfaction," was released in 1965. In contrast to the Beatles, the Stones cultivated a bad-boy image with their unkempt appearance and suggestive lyrics, such as those of the 1967 single "Let's Spend the Night Together."

Despite their success, the Stones grew tired of the constant comparisons to the Beatles, and a friendly rivalry between the two British bands developed. The song-writing duo of Jagger and Richards took on a more prominent role to compete with the Beatles duo of John Lennon (1940–1980) and Paul McCartney (1942–). The fourth Stones album—*Aftermath,* in 1966—was made up exclusively of original songs. Nonetheless, the album still owed a great deal to American popular music, especially bluesy tracks like "Going Home."

In the late 1960s, as their songwriting matured, the Stones released harder-edged albums such as *Between the Buttons* (1967), *Beggars Banquet* (1968), and *Let It Bleed* (1969), which contained the hit single "Gimme Shelter."

The Beatles broke up in 1970, but the Stones kept going, even after Jones was found dead in a swimming pool in 1969. The album that many critics consider their best, *Exile on Main Street,* came out in 1972, and many classic Stones tracks, including "Tumbling Dice" (1972), "Moonlight Mile" (1971), and "Angie" (1973), were also released in the 1970s. The band had late successes with *Some Girls* in 1978 and *Emotional Rescue,* which rose to number one in both the United Kingdom and the United States in 1980. The band continues to tour and record new music today.

ADDITIONAL FACTS

1. *The band's famous tongue-and-lips logo was designed by pop artist Andy Warhol (1928–1987).*

2. *In 2005, the Stones sparked controversy once again with the release of "Sweet Neo Con," a critique of American foreign policy, on the album* A Bigger Bang.

3. *The band lived in the south of France while recording* Exile on Main Street *in order to avoid penalties for unpaid income taxes in the United Kingdom.*

• • ● • •

Paul Newman

Paul Newman's piercing blue eyes and famously handsome face have made him a screen icon for more than five decades. But he has always seemed to seek out roles that are not about looks, often playing tough, troubled men—antiheroes and outlaws.

Newman (1925–) studied at the Yale Drama School and in the Method technique under Lee Strasberg at the Actors' Studio. He made his film debut in *The Silver Chalice* (1954) and broke through in 1958 with his performances in *The Long, Hot Summer; The Left Handed Gun;* and *Cat on a Hot Tin Roof*—for which he received his first Academy Award nomination.

He emerged as a major star when he played conflicted pool shark "Fast" Eddie Felson in *The Hustler* (1961) opposite Piper Laurie, George C. Scott, and Jackie Gleason. (All four received Oscar nominations.) Through the 1960s and into the following decade, Newman's best roles were as outsiders or nonconformists, including the amoral title character in *Hud* (1963) and the leader of a chain gang in *Cool Hand Luke* (1967). He was nominated for Academy Awards for both films.

Two of his most beloved films were collaborations with costar Robert Redford and director George Roy Hill—*Butch Cassidy and the Sundance Kid* (1969), one of the most successful westerns of all time, and *The Sting* (1973), which won the Academy Award for Best Picture.

Newman successfully transitioned into more mature roles in *Slap Shot* (1977), *Absence of Malice* (1981), and *The Verdict* (1982) before reprising his role as "Fast" Eddie Felson in Martin Scorsese's *The Color of Money* (1986). For his second turn as Fast Eddie, Newman received his first Academy Award for acting (he received an honorary Oscar in 1986), though most observers believe it was not the finest performance of his career.

In the two decades since, Newman has appeared in films sparingly and usually in strong supporting roles, as in *The Hudsucker Proxy* (1994) and *Road to Perdition* (2002).

ADDITIONAL FACTS

1. *Newman married actress Joanne Woodward (1930–) in 1958. They have costarred in ten features together, and Newman directed his wife four times, including in* Rachel, Rachel *(1968), which was nominated for an Academy Award for Best Picture.*

2. *Newman is known for his philanthropic endeavors. His Newman's Own company, which produces salad dressing, popcorn, salsa, lemonade, and other items, has raised more than $200 million for charity. Newman also founded the Hole in the Wall Gang, a summer camp in Connecticut for sick children.*

3. *Newman has competed in professional auto races since 1972 and is part-owner of a Champ Car series team.*

··●··

The Birth Control Pill

In 1960, the Food and Drug Administration (FDA) approved the first birth control pill for public use. The pill, which safely prevents pregnancy when taken daily, swiftly led to profound changes in many women's lives by giving them far more control over when and whether they became pregnant.

The search for an effective birth control pill was largely driven by one woman, activist Margaret Sanger (1879–1966). Sanger opened her first birth control clinic in 1916, the same year she published a book on basic sexuality titled *What Every Girl Should Know*.

By 1950, Sanger had already founded the influential American Birth Control League and was continuing her campaign for the full legalization of birth control devices such as condoms and diaphragms.

Still, Sanger hoped to find a more effective form of contraception—one that did not depend on a man's cooperation. That year, she joined with wealthy heiress Katharine McCormick (1875–1967) to hire biologist Gregory Pincus (1903–1967) to develop an oral contraceptive pill.

The notion of a hormonal contraceptive was first proposed by Harvard endocrinologist Fuller Albright (1900–1969) in 1945. He never followed through on his idea, but it formed the starting point for Pincus's research.

After years of experimentation and clinical trials, Pincus finally developed a pill that met FDA approval. For Sanger and McCormick, the discovery represented the realization of lifelong dreams.

However, contraception would not become generally available in the United States until six years later, because many states had laws prohibiting contraception. One of the strictest was Connecticut, where "the use of any drug, medicinal article, or instrument for the purpose of preventing conception" was illegal. In the 1965 case *Griswold v. Connecticut*, the Supreme Court struck down this law, making birth control legal for all married couples—a right that was expanded to unmarried couples in 1972.

Having achieved her life's ambition, Sanger died a few months after *Griswold* was decided, at the age of eighty-six.

ADDITIONAL FACTS

1. *As well as legalizing contraception for married couples,* Griswold v. Connecticut *was the first case to establish a constitutional right to privacy.*

2. *The American Birth Control League that Sanger founded later became Planned Parenthood.*

3. *In addition to being an advocate for contraception, Sanger was a supporter of eugenics, a movement that advocated selective breeding among human beings to promote "superior" traits and races.*

•••••

Muhammad Ali

Around the world, he is known as the Greatest. Muhammad Ali (1942–) gave himself that moniker, but he backed it up in the boxing ring by winning the world heavyweight championship three times and defending the title against some of the greatest boxers of the twentieth century. Before Ali, the world had never seen an athlete with such skills and charisma who was also willing to share—loudly—his controversial political and religious views during a tumultuous time in American history.

Ali was born Cassius Clay in Louisville, Kentucky, and began boxing as a child. He qualified for the US Olympic team in 1960 and won a gold medal in Rome. He went pro soon afterward and steadily rose through the ranks of the heavyweight division. Still, his victory over heavyweight champion Sonny Liston (c. 1932–1970) in 1964 was a stunning upset that, as Ali himself put it, "shook up the world." The next day, he announced that he had become a member of the black nationalist Nation of Islam and changed his name to Muhammad Ali.

Ali spent the rest of the decade defending his heavyweight title and his controversial views on major issues. In 1967, in the midst of the Vietnam War, he refused induction into the armed forces on religious grounds and suffered terrible consequences— he was stripped of his title, faced up to 5 years in prison, and was exiled from boxing for 3½ years while no state would grant him a boxing license. His case eventually reached the US Supreme Court, which ruled in his favor.

Ali returned to the ring in 1970. In an attempt to regain his belt, he faced Joe Frazier (1944–) in 1971, the first of three bouts with Frazier. Ali lost the fight—his first professional defeat—but eventually regained the title. In 1978, Ali lost and won back his title in a pair of fights with Leon Spinks (1953–), becoming the first to win the heavyweight title three times. Ali retired in 1979 but returned for two more fights, both of which he lost.

In 1984, he learned he had Parkinson's disease, a condition that causes the deterioration of motor skills. The world has watched while Ali's illness has robbed him of the physical and verbal skills that were his trademarks. But he still travels the globe on humanitarian missions and provided one of the singular moments of the 1996 Atlanta Olympics when he lit the Olympic Cauldron to start the Games.

ADDITIONAL FACTS

1. *Ali's boxing career began at age twelve, when his bicycle was stolen. He found a policeman at a local gym and told the cop he wanted to "whup" whomever had stolen the bike. The policeman, Joe Martin, told young Cassius that before he could whup anyone, he needed to learn how to box.*

2. *Some of Ali's fights have memorable nicknames—the Fight of the Century for his 1971 bout with Frazier in New York City; the Rumble in the Jungle for his 1974 fight with George Foreman in Kinshasa, Zaire; and the Thrilla in Manila for his 1975 rematch with Frazier in Quezon City, Philippines.*

3. *Ali's daughter, Laila Ali, is a professional boxer in the women's super middleweight division.*

•••••

Johnny Carson

When Johnny Carson (1925–2005) bid viewers "a very heartfelt goodnight" on May 22, 1992, many felt as if they had lost a family member instead of a late-night host. For thirty years, Carson had entertained Americans in the privacy of their homes as the longtime host of *The Tonight Show* on NBC.

While growing up in Iowa and Nebraska, Carson was drawn to magic and performed under the name "the Great Carsoni"—a harbinger of one of the *Tonight Show* characters he would later create—at age fourteen. After serving in the navy and graduating from the University of Nebraska in 1949, Carson worked at radio and TV stations in Omaha and Los Angeles. In 1954, he got his big break when the comedian Red Skelton (1913–1997), for whom Carson was a writer, was injured right before his show went on the air; Carson took the stage instead. When Jack Paar (1918–2004) quit *The Tonight Show* in 1962, Carson was tapped for the job.

With Carson at the helm, joined by sidekick and announcer Ed McMahon (1923–), *The Tonight Show* became the model for subsequent late-night talk shows, including that of successor Jay Leno (1950–). Each night began with music from the Tonight Show Band, followed by Carson's monologue, comedy sketches, interviews, stand-up, and more music. Many performers, including Leno, David Letterman (1947–), and Joan Rivers (1933–), launched their careers on *The Tonight Show;* getting the green light from Johnny to come sit in the guest chair after a stand-up performance opened huge doors.

Carson delighted audiences with his coterie of alter egos, including crotchety Aunt Blabby, right-wing extremist Floyd R. Turbo, and his best-known character, Carnac the Magnificent. As Carnac, a turban-wearing Carson would "divine" the answer to a question contained within a sealed envelope, then rip open the envelope and read the question, usually resulting in a corny, ironic pun. On one episode, for example, Carson announced, "Green acres." McMahon replied, "Green acres?" Ripping open the envelope, Carson read the question: "What Kermit has after Miss Piggy kicks him in the groin."

Carson died of emphysema at age seventy-nine.

ADDITIONAL FACTS

1. *Carson was considered for the role of TV writer Rob Petrie on a planned show titled* Head of the Family, *but he lost out to Dick Van Dyke (1925–), for whom the series was subsequently renamed.*

2. *The 2005 film* The Aristocrats, *a documentary in which various comedians tell their own version of a purportedly offensive joke, was dedicated to Carson, as he was apparently a fan of the joke.*

3. *After a ferocious competition between Leno and Letterman, Leno was named to replace Carson on* The Tonight Show *in 1992.*

•••••

Bob Woodward and Carl Bernstein

Theirs is one of the most improbable stories in the history of journalism. In June 1972, Bob Woodward (1943–) and Carl Bernstein (1944–)—two lowly metro desk reporters at the *Washington Post* who were barely acquainted with one another—were assigned to cover a seemingly innocuous break-in at the Democratic National Committee's headquarters at the Watergate office complex in Washington, DC.

Over the next two years, their reporting on this "third-rate burglary" would help unravel a scandal that led to the unprecedented resignation of President Richard M. Nixon (1913–1994) and made them the most famous journalists of the twentieth century.

The impact of their dogged Watergate reporting went well beyond the downfall of a president and his administration. Their success led to the rise and importance of investigative journalism, popularized the use of anonymous sources (a key player in the Watergate investigation was a shadowy figure known as Deep Throat), and inspired a generation of young writers to seek the truth through journalism.

Their work, coinciding with the late stages of the Vietnam War, also fed the national mood of cynicism and distrust of the country's leaders.

Woodward and Bernstein's 1974 book about their Watergate reporting, *All the President's Men,* became a bestseller and was adapted in 1976 into an Academy Award–winning film. After they collaborated on a second book, *The Final Days* (1976), their careers diverged.

Woodward went on to become one of the most successful nonfiction authors in American history, turning his attention to the CIA, the Supreme Court, and the presidencies of Bill Clinton (1946) and George W. Bush (1946–), among other subjects. He has remained at the *Post* as assistant managing editor.

Bernstein left the *Post* in 1976 to pursue an independent writing career, though he has published sporadically since then. His most recent work, a biography of Hillary Rodham Clinton (1947–) released in 2007, was ten years in the making.

ADDITIONAL FACTS

1. *The identity of Deep Throat was one of the great secrets in modern American history. It lasted for more than three decades before former FBI associate director Mark Felt (1913–) announced in May 2005 that he was Woodward's shadowy source.*

2. *In the Hollywood version of* All the President's Men, *Woodward was portrayed by Robert Redford (1937–) and Bernstein was played by Dustin Hoffman (1937–).*

3. *In 2003, Woodward and Bernstein sold their papers from between 1972 and 1976 to the University of Texas for $5 million.*

•••••

Night

Elie Wiesel's brief but devastating memoir *Night* (1958) stands among the great autobiographical novels of the past century and the most powerful literary works about the Holocaust. The work brought Wiesel (1928–) to international prominence as a spokesman for pacifism and nonviolence.

Night recounts Wiesel's experiences during his youth in a Romanian Orthodox Jewish family through the end of World War II in 1945. Though Wiesel's hometown was spared Nazi persecution for much of the war, in March 1944 the Nazis finally arrived and began deporting local Jews to concentration camps. Wiesel and his family were sent to Auschwitz, one of the most notorious camps, where he and his father were separated from his mother and sister, never to see them again. Alongside his father, Wiesel endured months of hard labor and inhuman conditions before his father died of disease and exhaustion in January 1945. Wiesel was sixteen at the time.

Elie Wiesel

Just months later, Allied forces defeated Germany and liberated the camps. Wiesel relocated to France and became a journalist but refused for years to write about what he had witnessed at Auschwitz. Finally, in 1954, he began a sprawling, 800-page memoir; in 1958, he significantly abridged the work and translated it into the novel that is now *Night*.

Night is both a retelling of real-life events and a work of religious thought. Throughout, Wiesel struggles to reconcile his profound Jewish faith with his conviction that a benevolent God could not exist in a world that included the horrors of the Nazi concentration camps. All the while, he attempts to answer two of the great ethical questions of the modern era: What allowed humankind to bring about the Holocaust in the first place, and why did humankind fail to realize what was happening until it was too late?

ADDITIONAL FACTS

1. *Wiesel did not know definitively what had happened to his mother and sister until years after the war, when he learned that both had been sent almost immediately to the gas chambers upon their arrival at Auschwitz.*

2. *For his efforts to speak out against genocide and promote nonviolence, Wiesel was awarded the Nobel Peace Prize in 1986.*

3. *Wiesel followed* Night *with the novels* Dawn *(1961) and* Day *(1962), which, though fictional, contain a number of autobiographical elements.*

••●••

Motown Records

Motown Records, one of the most successful record labels of the 1960s and a launchpad for the careers of many African-American performers, was founded by Detroit songwriter Berry Gordy (1929–) in 1959, taking its name from the city's nickname, Motor City. Many of the label's biggest stars, such as Smokey Robinson (1940–) and Stevie Wonder (1950–), originally hailed from the Detroit area.

Gordy, who controlled almost every aspect of record production at Motown, instituted a strict system for producing singles in his studio, which came to be known as the Hit Factory. Young Motown artists were given lessons in everything from dancing to dressing and were expected to hone their skills in the touring Motortown Revue before releasing records on their own. Songs were written by professionals employed by the label—most famously the trio of Lamont Dozier (1941–), Brian Holland (1941–), and Edward Holland Jr. (1939–)—and were approved for release by Gordy in a weekly quality-control meeting.

The boss wasn't always right: Gordy initially rejected the classic Marvin Gaye (1939–1984) tracks "I Heard It Through the Grapevine" (1968) and "What's Going On" (1971).

For the most part, though, the system worked: Motown produced more than one hundred number one singles.

Some artists, most famously Wonder and Gaye, resented Gordy's strict controls, but other acts such as the Supremes were disciplined members of the team. The Supremes, an all-female trio that was one of the most successful acts of the 1960s, had no hits for their first two years at the label. Eventually, Gordy fixed the lineup by making Diana Ross (1944–) the lead and settling on Florence Ballard (1943–1976) and Mary Wilson (1944–) as her backups. Their first number one was "Where Did Our Love Go?" (1964). A string of hits followed, including "Baby Love" (1964), "Stop! In the Name of Love" (1965), and "You Can't Hurry Love" (1966).

However, when songwriters Holland, Dozier, and Holland left Motown in 1967, the label went into decline. The Supremes had two more number one hits—"Love Child" in 1968 and "Someday We'll Be Together" in 1969—but disbanded a few years after Ross left the group in 1970 to pursue her solo career.

Its glory days fading, the Motown label was sold to MCA in 1988.

ADDITIONAL FACTS

1. *The 1981 musical and 2006 film* Dreamgirls *were based loosely on the story of the Supremes.*

2. *In addition to carving out a successful solo music career, Ross became an accomplished actress, winning a Golden Globe award for her portrayal of Billie Holiday (1915–1959) in the 1972 film* Lady Sings the Blues.

3. *The Supremes had a cameo as a group of nuns in the television series* Tarzan.

•••••

Audrey Hepburn

Born in Belgium, raised in the Netherlands, and educated in England, Audrey Hepburn (1929–1993) came to represent European elegance and sophistication in 1950s and 1960s Hollywood, and her natural femininity and cosmopolitan fashion still resonate with fans today. As *New York Times* critic Bosley Crowther wrote, she was "a slender, elfin and wistful beauty, alternately regal and childlike."

As a child, Hepburn overcame hardships in the Netherlands during the German occupation in World War II. (Hepburn talked at length about her connection to the young diarist Anne Frank; they were the same age and both lived in the Netherlands during the privations of the Nazi occupation.)

After the war, Hepburn was a ballet student in London before turning to acting. She appeared in a few British films, and in 1951, she moved to Broadway to star in the musical *Gigi*. A year later, she was in Hollywood.

Her American film debut, *Roman Holiday* (1953), made her an overnight star. Appearing opposite Gregory Peck (1916–2003), she played a princess in disguise who falls in love with an American journalist. Her impact on the American viewing public was immediate, and she received an Academy Award for Best Actress.

Her most beloved roles were as Holly Golightly, the humble girl–turned–Manhattan socialite in *Breakfast at Tiffany's* (1961), and as Eliza Doolittle in *My Fair Lady* (1964), which won eight Academy Awards, including Best Picture.

The casting of Hepburn in *My Fair Lady* was controversial at the time. She was chosen over Julie Andrews (1935–), who had completed a successful run as Eliza Doolittle on Broadway but was considered too much of an unknown for the film. For the film's songs, Hepburn's voice was overdubbed by Marni Nixon, and Hepburn was subsequently not granted an Academy Award nomination. Ironically, Andrews won the Oscar that year for best actress for her performance in *Mary Poppins*.

Hepburn left full-time acting in 1967, living mostly in Switzerland and devoting herself to philanthropic causes. From 1988 until her death, she traveled the world as a UNICEF Goodwill Ambassador. She died at age sixty-three of colon cancer.

ADDITIONAL FACTS

1. *Throughout her film career, Hepburn costarred with older men, most of them Hollywood megastars— Humphrey Bogart and William Holden (Sabrina, 1954), Fred Astaire (Funny Face, 1957), Maurice Chevalier and Gary Cooper (Love in the Afternoon, 1957), Cary Grant (Charade, 1963), and Rex Harrison (My Fair Lady).*

2. *Hepburn has remained a fashion icon in Europe and the United States. One of the black sleeveless gowns she wore in Breakfast at Tiffany's was auctioned off in 2006, fetching $920,000 (the proceeds of which benefited disadvantaged children in India).*

3. *In 1954, Hepburn won an Academy Award (for Roman Holiday) and a Tony Award (for Ondine). She is one of three women to win both awards in the same year. (Shirley Booth and Ellen Burstyn are the others.)*

•••••

Silent Spring and the Environmental Movement

Environmentalism, one of the most influential political movements to emerge in the late twentieth century, is in no small part the legacy of author and journalist Rachel Carson (1907–1964), who first alerted millions of Americans to the deadly dangers of pollution in her 1962 book *Silent Spring.*

The book, which documented the harmful effects of the chemical pesticide DDT on natural ecosystems, takes its name from the "silent spring" that Carson warned would soon arrive if the government allowed unimpeded chemical use to kill off songbirds and other wildlife.

In the short term, Carson's book outraged readers and convinced the federal government to ban DDT in 1972.

Over the long term, however, *Silent Spring* inspired many to think more carefully about how human activity affects the earth. During the 1960s, the United States and other countries adopted several of the first pieces of environmental legislation, such as the Clean Air Act of 1970 and the Endangered Species Act of 1973. The first Earth Day was celebrated in 1970; President Richard M. Nixon (1913–1994) created the Environmental Protection Agency in the same year.

Before the publication of *Silent Spring,* many environmental groups focused on land conservation, hoping to preserve scenic vistas. After the 1960s, however, the environmental movement pursued a broader agenda of fighting pollution, protecting endangered species, and, more recently, seeking to reduce the carbon emissions that cause global warming.

Carson, however, did not live to see the flourishing of the movement she helped create. She died of cancer shortly after the book's publication.

ADDITIONAL FACTS

1. *Most of* Silent Spring *was originally published as a series of articles in the* New Yorker *magazine, as was her 1951 bestseller* The Sea Around Us.

2. *Carson originally planned to write only an introduction and conclusion to* Silent Spring *and coauthor the rest of the book with scientists.*

3. *In 1980, Carson was posthumously awarded the Presidential Medal of Freedom.*

••●••

1966 NCAA Men's Basketball Championship

It was not the most exciting game in college basketball history, but it may have been the most consequential. What thirty-six-year-old Texas Western head coach Don Haskins (1930–) did on the night of March 19, 1966, was an act that revolutionized college basketball, particularly in the South: He started five black players.

At the time, the conventional wisdom was that a team must have at least one white player on the court at all times in order to provide a steadying influence over the supposedly undisciplined black players.

Never in history had a major college team started five blacks in a National Collegiate Athletic Association (NCAA) championship game. And before Haskins had done so earlier in the season, no major college team had ever started five blacks in *any* college basketball game.

Not only did Haskins start five black players in the tournament, he also faced a Kentucky team coached by the legendary Adolph Rupp (1901–1977), who refused to dress a single black player. Rupp, sixty-four, had notched four NCAA championships with a then-record 749 career wins, and his top-ranked Wildcats were expected to claim his fifth title. Rupp himself said that a team starting five blacks would never beat a team of his, heightening the racial drama of a matchup that came in the midst of the civil rights movement.

Almost from the start of the game, Texas Western's stifling defense stymied the usually high-scoring Wildcats. And center David Lattin's powerful dunk on Texas Western's second possession of the game set the tone for the upset 72–65 victory.

The game had a dramatic impact on college athletics and race, particularly in the South. The following season, the Southeastern Conference integrated for the first time, though it would not be until 1970 that Rupp would dress a black player in Kentucky blue and white.

ADDITIONAL FACTS

1. *The five starters for Texas Western were Lattin, Harry Flournoy, Bobby Joe Hill, Orsten Artis, and Willie Worsley.*

2. *The game was played at the Cole Field House at the University of Maryland. Tip-off was at 10 p.m., and there was no live or national television coverage—only tape-delayed coverage to select cities.*

3. *Texas Western is now known as the University of Texas at El Paso.*

•••••

The Monkees

Hoping to capitalize on the popularity of pop-rock bands such as the Beatles and the Rolling Stones, NBC created the Monkees in 1965, a band that enjoyed brief popularity among teenagers in the late 1960s but also became synonymous with vapid, corporate rock.

Indeed, *The Monkees* was a TV show before it was a group. A pair of American television producers—Bob Rafelson (1933–) and Bert Schneider (1934–)—developed the series as a show about a struggling pop group based on the model of the early Beatles films *A Hard Day's Night* (1964) and *Help!* (1965).

Originally, the producers attempted to use existing groups, but they eventually decided to create the Monkees from scratch, using musicians and actors with musical backgrounds. The final lineup included musicians Michael Nesmith (1942–) on guitar and Peter Tork (1942–) on bass, as well as two actors—Davy Jones (1945–) on vocals and Mickey Dolenz (1945–) on drums.

Just as each of the Beatles earned a reputation for one trait or another, the Monkees were consciously trained to fit specific roles: the smart one (Nesmith), the naïve one (Tork), the cute one (Jones), and the funny one (Dolenz).

After some basic music training and lessons in acting and comedy, the group's first episode aired on September 12, 1966, and the show soon gained in popularity in the United States and abroad.

The television success of *The Monkees* was matched by musical success. The group had two number one hits with "Last Train to Clarksville" and "I'm a Believer" (the latter penned by singer-songwriter Neil Diamond), and their self-titled debut album sold more than a million copies.

Fans began to demand live performances, but there was a problem: The Monkees didn't play on their albums. Nonetheless, they went on tour in late 1966, and they were a hit. The show's last episode aired in 1968 and the group broke up in 1971, but members of the Monkees continue to tour today.

ADDITIONAL FACTS

1. *One musician who failed to make the cut in the original Monkees auditions was Stephen Stills (1945–), who went on to become a member of the late-1960s supergroup Crosby, Stills, Nash and Young.*

2. *Many episodes of* The Monkees *were shot on stages that had been used for* The Three Stooges.

3. *In some episodes of* The Monkees, *the editors employed jump cuts, a technique involving an abrupt change from one scene to another that was first used in 1960 by the French director Jean-Luc Godard (1930–) in his New Wave classic* Breathless.

•••••

Deng Xiaoping

Though he was never officially head of state, Deng Xiaoping (1904–1997) transformed China, enacting revolutionary reforms in the 1970s and 1980s to direct the nation toward a market economy while still maintaining the authoritarian presence of the Communist Party.

He is responsible for turning China into a giant on the global economic stage by giving individuals the right to improve their own financial well-being. But he also developed a reputation for crushing prodemocracy forces and suppressing dissent, as he did with his approval of the brutal massacre of hundreds of Chinese prodemocracy demonstrators in Beijing's Tiananmen Square in 1989.

Deng loyally served the communist cause during the civil war era in China, joining the famed Long March in 1934 and helping to lead the military campaign of 1948–1949 that delivered Mao Zedong (1893–1976) and the communists to power.

Deng became general secretary of the Chinese Communist Party in 1954, but his economic theories clashed with Mao's doctrinal communism. When Deng suggested that China undertake capitalist-style market reforms in 1966 to overcome Mao's disastrous Great Leap Forward program, Deng was denounced as a "capitalist roader," placed under house arrest, and ultimately sent into exile in southeast China.

Deng made a comeback in 1973 and survived another purge three years later, ultimately outmaneuvering his opponents to gain control of the Communist Party by 1978. Once in office, he unveiled a series of dramatic reforms that spurred economic growth and set China on a course to become the world's dominant producer of textiles and other goods. Most notably, he abolished rural communes, allowing peasants to cultivate their own plots, and permitted city dwellers to open small businesses.

Critics point to the negative consequences of Deng's economic policies: the emergence of sweatshops and the use of child labor, as well as the production of cheap, sometimes unsafe products, a legacy that continues today.

Internationally, Deng established full relations with the United States in 1979, successfully negotiated the return of Hong Kong from British rule in 1984, and improved China's relationship with Japan. He officially retired from government in 1989 but retained political influence for years afterward. He died at age ninety-two.

ADDITIONAL FACTS

1. *Deng's most famous aphorism, "It doesn't matter whether a cat is black or white, as long as it catches mice," reflects his preference for pragmatism over ideology.*

2. *By the end of his life, Deng had been credited with lifting 170 million peasants out of extreme poverty through his economic reforms.*

3. *Deng, who stood about four foot eleven, was twice named* Time *magazine's Man of the Year—in 1978 and 1985.*

•••••

Catch-22

Although it remains Joseph Heller's only well-known work, *Catch-22* (1961) holds a place among the greatest war novels of all time. Its mix of black comedy, surrealist whimsy, and visceral violence portrays the madness and illogicality of war in a manner unlike that of any literary work that came before it.

Joseph Heller

Heller (1923–1999) set *Catch-22* during World War II, amid a US Air Force squadron stationed on an island near the Italian coast. The unit is stuffed to the gills with quirky, oddball characters, including a bumbling colonel obsessed with his own reputation, a shameless war profiteer who bombs his fellow airmen, an enigmatic and godlike major who plays horseshoes all day and dabbles in real estate, and a soldier so covered in bandages that it becomes unclear whether anyone is still alive underneath.

Especially in its early chapters, *Catch-22* is a confusing novel to read. Mimicking the haphazardness of the war, the story unfolds erratically and out of chronological order. Gradually, pieces begin to fall into place; as details emerge, scenarios that initially seemed funny turn out to be grave and tragic. Cartoonish pranks give way to real violence, and the life-and-death consequences of the squadron commanders' petty lies and deceptions become evident.

The novel's title, which has become firmly implanted in the English language, refers to a bureaucratic paradox hidden in the squadron's rule book. The rule states that any airman who is deemed insane can be excused from further combat missions, but if he actually asks to be excused, he clearly is too sane to qualify for the exemption. True to the spirit of Heller's novel, the phrase *catch-22* has since come to signify any situation or bureaucratic regulation that is paradoxical or inescapable—a perfect encapsulation of the absurdity that Heller discerned in the modern world.

ADDITIONAL FACTS

1. *Although* Catch-22 *is nominally about World War II, it was written during the early stages of the Vietnam War, and Heller saw it as a protest against war and bureaucracy in general.*

2. Catch-22 *was not a unanimous critical darling when it was published.* The New Yorker *called it "a debris of sour jokes" that "gives the impression of having been shouted onto paper."*

3. *The novel's nonlinear structure proved so confusing that Heller himself had to use hundreds of index cards to keep track of its events while he was writing.*

James Brown

James Brown (1933–2006) recorded his first hit, "Please, Please, Please," in 1956 as a member of a band called the Flames, a rhythm and blues group led by the vocalist Bobby Byrd (1934–2007). It was an impassioned soul track, not surprisingly from an artist who has been nicknamed the Godfather of Soul and Soul Brother Number One.

But while Brown's best soul tracks are comparable to those by Sam Cooke (1931–1964) or Ray Charles (1930–2004), his greatest contribution was to the musical form that he invented and pioneered a decade later: funk.

Funk was born February 1, 1965, when Brown, already a veteran performer, entered Arthur Smith Studios in Charlotte, North Carolina. He brought along a band of eight musicians, including the famous saxophonist Maceo Parker (1943–). Brown had lyrics as well, but there wasn't much to them. He wanted a song to encompass every style of dance popular at the time, so he shouted out their names one by one: "the jerk," "the fly," "the monkey," "the mashed potato," "the twist," "the boomerang."

While Brown sang, his musicians shot out notes all around him, each one a quick, staccato burst. Every note sounded percussive. As Brown wrote in his autobiography, "I was hearing everything, even the guitars, like they were drums." The song Brown and his band recorded in a single take that day—"Papa's Got a Brand New Bag"—was the perfect prototype for funk, a style that values rhythm above all else.

Over the next four decades, Brown would earn another of his nicknames: the Hardest-Working Man in Show Business. His output included classic singles such as "I Got You (I Feel Good)" (1965), "Say It Loud—I'm Black and I'm Proud" (1968), and "Mother Popcorn" (1969). He also performed elaborate live shows, including his 1963 *Live at the Apollo*, which some critics regard as one of the greatest live performances ever recorded on tape. Brown died in 2006, but his funk revolution is carried on to this day by nearly every pop artist in the world.

ADDITIONAL FACTS

1. *Steve Binder, who directed Brown's famous appearance on* The T.A.M.I. Show *in 1964, went on to produce Elvis Presley's famous Christmas special in 1968.*

2. *Samples from numerous records that Brown recorded, including "Sex Machine" (1970), "The Payback" (1974), and "Get on the Good Foot" (1972), were used as the basis for some of the first hip-hop tracks of the 1970s and 1980s.*

3. *A trademark of his live act was for the master of ceremonies to drape a cape over Brown's shoulders while escorting him offstage at the end of the show, only to have Brown to throw it off and return for an encore.*

•••••

James Dean

Although—or perhaps because—he starred in just three films, James Dean (1931–1955) achieved iconic status in the United States and around the world. His death in a two-car accident while he was driving his Porsche Spyder outside Bakersfield, California, froze his persona in time forever at age twenty-four. Never had the mantra "Live fast, die young" been felt so keenly in American pop culture.

Dean took on a series of small movie and television roles in the early 1950s before moving to Broadway, where he achieved his first major acclaim. Returning to Hollywood as a star, he landed his first leading role in *East of Eden* (1955), an adaptation of the John Steinbeck novel directed by Elia Kazan (1909–2003). Dean beat out fellow up-and-comer Paul Newman for the role of Cal, the emotionally bruised son of a lettuce farmer who is destined to forever live in his twin brother's shadow.

Though some critics disparaged Dean's performance as an obvious imitation of his idol, Marlon Brando, Dean received a nomination for an Academy Award for Best Actor. But he would not live to learn of the honor.

He died on September 30, 1955, less than a month before the release of his second major film, Nicholas Ray's *Rebel Without a Cause*.

In what would be regarded as his signature role, Dean played Jim Stark, a seventeen-year-old who moves to a new town and soon runs afoul of his parents, the police, and his peers. He became a symbol of teen angst to which kids then—including twenty-year-old Elvis Presley, who worshipped Dean—and now still relate. His ambiguous sexuality (many who knew Dean, including Ray, say he was bisexual) also comes through in the film and helped make him an icon of the gay community.

Dean's final film, *Giant* (1956), a sprawling epic about a Texas oil family, was completed shortly after his death. *Giant* was nominated for ten Academy Awards (winning for best director) and earned Dean his second consecutive posthumous nomination for best actor.

ADDITIONAL FACTS

1. *Dean was engaged to the actress Liz Sheridan, who later played Helen Seinfeld, Jerry's mother, on the hit television series* Seinfeld.

2. *Dean was the first to receive a posthumous Academy Award nomination for acting and is the only actor to receive two such nominations.*

3. *The last name of his character in* Rebel Without a Cause, *Stark, is an anagram of the last name of his character in* East of Eden, *Trask. It was no accident—director Nicholas Ray (1911–1979) knew Dean was destined to play Jim Stark.*

•••••

Second-Wave Feminism

Beginning in the early 1960s, a revitalized women's rights movement in the United States launched "second-wave feminism," a renewed push to end discriminatory laws and social practices. Building on the legacy of the "first wave" of the women's rights movement, which culminated in the ratification of the nineteenth amendment in 1920, granting women the right to vote, feminists of the 1960s broadened their agenda to include abortion rights, equal pay in the workplace, and laws against sexual harassment.

Although the second wave had many roots, two major events in 1963 are credited with sparking the movement. The first was the publication of a report by the Presidential Commission on the Status of Women, which found that women were discriminated against in many realms of American life, especially in the workplace. A year later, a provision outlawing employment discrimination on the basis of sex was incorporated into the Civil Rights Act of 1964.

The second catalyst was the publication of *The Feminine Mystique,* by Betty Friedan (1921–2006), which criticized the notion that women have "no greater destiny than to glory in their own femininity" and argued that many women were unfulfilled by a life exclusively dedicated to housekeeping and child rearing. Friedan's book, which proved enormously influential for a generation of women, demonstrated how the leaders of second-wave feminism expanded their focus to the overall place of women in society, rather than exclusively focusing on their legal status.

Other milestones of the movement included Title IX, which was passed in 1972 and forbade discrimination in higher education, and the 1973 Supreme Court decision *Roe v. Wade,* which guaranteed women the right to choose an abortion.

ADDITIONAL FACTS

1. *The National Organization for Women (NOW) was founded in 1966 by former members of the Presidential Commission on the Status of Women.*

2. *The chair of the commission was former first lady Eleanor Roosevelt (1884–1962), who died before the report's completion.*

3. *In 1972, Congress approved an amendment to the Constitution banning sex discrimination, known as the Equal Rights Amendment (ERA), but in a significant setback for the feminist movement, it failed to win ratification from the required thirty-eight states to become law.*

••●••

Super Bowl III

"We're gonna win the game. I guarantee it."

So said twenty-five-year-old Joe Namath (1943–), the quarterback of the New York Jets, three days before Super Bowl III. At the time, the statement was laughable. Few gave the Jets a chance against the Baltimore Colts, who were heavy favorites and considered by some observers to be the greatest football team ever assembled.

But the Jets backed up the boast, pulling off a monumental upset on January 12, 1969, that turned Namath into a legendary figure and gave credibility to the upstart American Football League (AFL). The stunning victory also helped solidify the growing popularity of football on the American sports scene.

In 1966, the established National Football League (NFL) and the rival AFL, founded in 1960, had agreed to a merger (which would be completed in 1970), but many observers saw the AFL as a vastly inferior league of teams that could not hope to compete with the NFL's more experienced teams.

The first two Super Bowls reinforced this belief. Under coach Vince Lombardi (1913–1970), the NFL's Green Bay Packers had easily handled the AFL's champions in 1967 (the Kansas City Chiefs) and 1968 (the Oakland Raiders).

Few believed Super Bowl III would be any different. The Colts had finished the regular season 13-1 and had avenged their only defeat with a 34–0 drubbing of the Cleveland Browns in the NFL title game. The Jets, meanwhile, had squeaked past the Oakland Raiders for the AFL championship.

But on the field at Miami's Orange Bowl, the Jets' defense intercepted three passes by Baltimore quarterback Earl Morrall (1934–) in the first half, and a touchdown by fullback Matt Snell (1941–) gave the Jets a 7–0 halftime lead. The Jets added two field goals in the third quarter, and not even Baltimore hero Johnny Unitas (1933–2002), who had missed most of the season with a sore throwing arm and replaced Morrall in the third quarter, could rally the Colts late in the game.

After the Jets' 16–7 victory, Namath was awarded the Super Bowl Most Valuable Player award—even though the quarterback had not thrown for a touchdown in the game or even attempted a pass in the fourth quarter of the legendary upset.

ADDITIONAL FACTS

1. *The 1969 clash was the first AFL-versus-NFL championship game to be dubbed the Super Bowl. The first two were retroactively referred to as Super Bowls I and II.*

2. *Namath won the MVP award having completed seventeen of twenty-eight passes for 206 yards and no touchdowns. He is the only quarterback to win Super Bowl MVP without throwing for a score.*

3. *Snell rushed for 121 yards and scored the Jets' only touchdown.*

••●••

Woodstock

A four-day music festival held at a muddy farm in rural New York in 1969, Woodstock has achieved near-mythic status as the defining event of the baby boomer generation and one of the greatest collections of rock-and-roll talent ever assembled. About 500,000 fans braved rain, traffic, and bad acid to hear acts such as the Grateful Dead, Janis Joplin (1943–1970), and Jimi Hendrix (1942–1970) perform at the epic concert.

The festival was originally planned for Woodstock, New York, but was moved to the town of Bethel, about 100 miles northwest of New York City, when organizers couldn't find a venue large enough to hold the crowds. At virtually the last minute, a local farmer, Max Yasgur (1919–1973), agreed to rent out his dairy farm, which allowed the concert to go on (and ensured Yasgur a place in rock history).

The show's lineup included Creedence Clearwater Revival, sitar player Ravi Shankar (1920–), Joan Baez (1941–), Carlos Santana (1947–), Joe Cocker (1944–), and the Band. All told, Woodstock lasted four days, a day longer than planned, to accommodate the dozens of musicians who shared the stage.

Afterward, the event was immortalized in a 1970 documentary, *Woodstock*, directed by Michael Wadleigh (1941–), and in the song "Woodstock," by Joni Mitchell (1943–). (Mitchell, ironically, was not actually at Woodstock.)

More than just a music festival, to its attendees Woodstock represented a generational symbol of liberation. Or, as the lyrics to Mitchell's song put it:

> *I'm going to get back to the land*
> *And get my soul free . . .*

Anniversary concerts have been staged several times since 1969, each with progressively greater levels of commercialism and declining levels of peace, love, and understanding. A museum and performing-arts center has been built at the original concert site, which was sold by the Yasgur family in 1971.

ADDITIONAL FACTS

1. *Congress came under criticism in 2007 for providing $1 million in federal money for a Woodstock museum in Bethel. The funding was later withdrawn.*

2. *"Woodstock" became a hit single after Crosby, Stills, Nash and Young recorded it in 1970 for their album* Déjà Vu.

3. *Cartoonist Charles M. Schulz (1922–2000) named the* Peanuts *character Woodstock in honor of the festival.*

•••••

Margaret Thatcher

As the first woman ever to become prime minister of Great Britain and one of the first women to rule a major world power, Margaret Thatcher (1925–) had one of the most unlikely political careers of the twentieth century. During her 11½ years as the leader of Britain, the country rebounded from economic strife, won a war over Argentina, and enjoyed more than a decade of political stability.

Known as the Iron Lady, Thatcher rose from humble beginnings as the daughter of a grocer and local politician to become a member of Parliament by age thirty-four. She worked her way up through the Conservative Party ranks to the cabinet, where she was secretary of education under prime minister Edward Heath (1916–2005) from 1970 to 1974.

In 1975, she pulled off a shocking upset to become the leader of the Conservative Party, and four years later, when the Conservatives won the general election, she became prime minister.

While in office, Thatcher championed free markets and privatized several major industries, including airlines and steel production. Her success at deregulation set off a wave of privatization across the globe; by the end of the 1980s, more than fifty countries had followed Great Britain's lead.

Also on the domestic front, Thatcher dramatically reduced the power of trade unions and cut income tax rates, correctly believing that emphasizing self-reliance and personal accountability would stimulate the British economy.

She scored a major victory in 1982, after Argentina invaded the Falkland Islands, a British colony in the South Atlantic Ocean. Thatcher sent a naval force, which retook the island and forced the Argentinean forces to withdraw.

She also played a role in the downfall of the Soviet Union, persuading friend and ally President Ronald Reagan (1911–2004) that Soviet general secretary Mikhail Gorbachev (1931–) was willing to take a more open approach with the West.

With support of her party waning, Thatcher resigned in November 1990, ending her tenure as the longest-serving prime minister in 150 years. She was succeeded by John Major (1943–), a former chancellor of the exchequer.

ADDITIONAL FACTS

1. *In 1987, Thatcher became the first British prime minister of the twentieth century to win three consecutive elections.*

2. *The Irish Republican Army bombed the hotel Thatcher was staying at during a Conservative Party conference in 1984. She was unhurt, but five others were killed and thirty-four were wounded.*

3. *In 2007, Thatcher became the first living ex–prime minister to be honored with a bronze statue at the House of Commons.*

••●••

Sylvia Plath

Though her famously tragic, untimely death has sometimes stolen the spotlight from her literary achievements, Sylvia Plath (1932–1963) remains a poet of extraordinary originality and power. Her intense, bracing, and often dark works illuminate the mind of a brilliant woman who battled with mental illness all her life.

A native of Massachusetts, Plath got an early artistic start: Her first published poem appeared when she was eight, and she won numerous awards for her writings throughout secondary school. As a student at Smith College during the early 1950s, she developed into an accomplished poet, achieving significant critical recognition. Despite her outward success, though, she struggled with severe depression; after a mental breakdown and suicide attempt in 1953, she had to be hospitalized—an experience she adapted into her later, autobiographical novel, *The Bell Jar* (1963).

After her recovery and graduation from Smith, Plath accepted an academic fellowship in England, where she met the British poet Ted Hughes (1930–1998). They married in 1956 and had two children, but their relationship quickly became tumultuous. Splitting her time between England and Massachusetts, Plath released her first poetry collection, *The Colossus* (1960), to positive reviews.

By 1962, Plath's depression had worsened, and she had separated from Hughes. Despite her condition, she became exceptionally prolific, writing a large body of visceral, ruthlessly confessional poems that expressed her alienation, depression, and growing fascination with death. After a final mad rush of productivity, Plath committed suicide in February 1963. Her last works are regarded as her finest—though very dark and often morbid, they display a shocking immediacy and an uncommon wisdom for a writer barely out of her twenties. These later works were published in 1965 as the collection *Ariel*. Later collections appeared throughout the 1970s and 1980s, and Plath won a posthumous Pulitzer Prize in 1982.

ADDITIONAL FACTS

1. *Despite her suicide attempt and subsequent hospitalization during her junior year, Plath returned to Smith College and graduated just a few months late, summa cum laude.*

2. *Plath originally published* The Bell Jar *under the pseudonym Victoria Lucas, but after her death the novel was republished in her own name.*

3. *Plath kept many journals that are now publicly available—except for the last volume, detailing her final months, which Hughes destroyed. Literary historians criticized this decision, but Hughes insisted that it was necessary to protect his and Plath's children.*

••••

Bob Dylan's Switch to Electric

Singer Bob Dylan (born Robert Allen Zimmerman in 1941) initially achieved critical acclaim and commercial success with his recordings of folk music, a genre that was popular in the early 1960s. Folk music during the period was usually played on the acoustic guitar, and its lyrics often dealt with serious political themes such as war and racism. Dylan's austere antiwar anthems "Blowin' in the Wind" (1963) and "Masters of War" (1963) are widely considered masterpieces of the genre.

But Dylan, whose first musical love as a teenager in Minnesota had been rock and roll, chafed against the staid conventions of folk music. In 1965, at the height of his popularity as a folksinger, he abruptly shifted gears. To the horror of folk aficionados, Dylan started adding rock rhythms and instruments to records such as *Bringing It All Back Home* (1965) and *Highway 61 Revisited* (1965). Dylan, the critics complained, had reinvented himself; he had "gone electric."

As an artist who was often referred to as the voice of his generation because of his politically charged folk songs, Dylan's makeover caused an enormous uproar in the music world. Folk purists regarded his use of electric organs and guitars as apostasy. After releasing "Like a Rolling Stone," one of his most famous rock singles, in early 1965, Dylan performed at the Newport Folk Festival in Rhode Island. He came onstage with an electric band, and the reaction was immediate. After playing three songs over a chorus of boos, Dylan and his band abruptly left the stage. When the master of ceremonies urged him to come back with an acoustic guitar, Dylan obliged. Appropriately enough, he played "It's All Over Now, Baby Blue."

When Dylan toured England the following year, the reactions were even harsher. Most of his shows featured two sets. In the first, Dylan would play an acoustic guitar to a docile crowd. In the second, he would bring out his backing band for a searing electric set. Members of the audience would jeer, boo, or applaud through songs to drown out the band. In one famous moment, an audience member summed up the feelings of the folk community by shouting, "Judas!" Enraged, Dylan told his band to crank up the volume and launched into a raucous rendition of "Like a Rolling Stone."

ADDITIONAL FACTS

1. *A bootleg recording containing the famous "Judas!" incident is often referred to as* The Royal Albert Hall Concert, *referring to the final shows on the 1966 tour, on May 26 and 27. The recording was actually made in Manchester, England, on May 17.*

2. *After the negative response he got in 1965, Dylan didn't return to the Newport Folk Festival until 2002.*

3. *A film clip of the rock single "Subterranean Homesick Blues," from* Bringing It All Back Home, *directed by D. A. Pennebaker (1925–) in 1965, was one of the first music "videos" ever made.*

••◆••

Stanley Kubrick

Stanley Kubrick's directing career spanned nearly fifty years but resulted in just thirteen feature films. His perfectionism, extreme care in film production, and reputation for shooting an uncommonly high number of takes kept him from a more prolific career. But of the thirteen, several are considered classics, including a pair of hugely influential works—the black comedy *Dr. Strangelove or: How I Learned to Stop Worrying and Love the Bomb* (1964) and the groundbreaking science-fiction movie *2001: A Space Odyssey* (1968).

Kubrick (1928–1999) began his professional life as a still photographer before making the transition to film directing in 1951. Two years later, he made his feature debut with *Fear and Desire*. And by his fourth film, the antiwar classic *Paths of Glory* (1957), he had established himself as an elite director.

Paths of Glory, which tells the cynical story of a fruitless French battle plan during World War I, is the first of an antiwar trilogy that took Kubrick three decades to complete. It continued with *Dr. Strangelove* (which centers on the Cold War) and ended with *Full Metal Jacket* (1987), which turns its lens on Vietnam.

Dr. Strangelove was the first commercially successful political satire of nuclear war, and through his darkly comedic script, Kubrick shows the absurdity of the US government's approach to nuclear deterrence. The film is also notable for the impressive performance of comic actor Peter Sellers in three separate roles, including the title character, a demented scientist.

Though *2001* was not initially a critical success, its significance has grown as the science-fiction genre has become more sophisticated and mainstream. The film is a study of visual imagery and musical evocations rather than a classic, straightforward science-fiction narrative. Through innovative special effects, Kubrick spectacularly shows viewers the vastness of space.

Kubrick's other noteworthy films include the historical epic *Spartacus* (1960); an adaptation of Vladimir Nabokov's (1899–1977) novel *Lolita* (1962); the hugely controversial, futuristic *A Clockwork Orange* (1971); the horror cult classic *The Shining* (1980); and his final film, *Eyes Wide Shut* (1999).

ADDITIONAL FACTS

1. *Kubrick made films in the United States only until 1962; disliking the Hollywood system, he worked in Great Britain for the rest of his career.*

2. *A Clockwork Orange initially received an X rating before it was reedited and rereleased in 1972. It is one of two movies originally rated X to receive an Academy Award nomination for best picture. (The other was 1969's* Midnight Cowboy.*)*

3. *Eyes Wide Shut was also nearly rated NC-17, the modern equivalent of the X rating, but an orgy scene was digitally altered to help secure an R rating.*

• • • •

Tobacco and Cancer

On July 12, 1957, scientists announced a medical discovery that would eventually upend American society: Smoking cigarettes, they claimed, caused lung cancer.

Until that day, the 1950s had been a golden age for American tobacco companies. About 45 percent of adults smoked cigarettes in 1954, according to a Gallup survey, and celebrities such as Frank Sinatra (1915–1998) and Ronald Reagan (1911–2004) happily endorsed Lucky Strikes and Chesterfields.

At first, the study linking tobacco to cancer had little impact on the public. Tobacco companies furiously denied the link and hired scientists to produce bogus reports attacking the findings. Even smokers worried by the study soon found that it was surprisingly hard to quit the habit.

Under pressure from health advocates, however, Congress required tobacco companies to add health warnings to packs of cigarettes in 1965. In 1971, television ads for cigarettes were banned from the airwaves.

By 1981, the number of Americans who smoked was down to 33 percent.

Then, in 1982, Reagan—having become president of the United States—appointed C. Everett Koop (1916–) as his surgeon general, the nation's chief public health official. Koop revised the warnings, making them more explicit.

Koop also released a report in 1988 that proved what many smokers already knew: Cigarettes were highly addictive. In fact, he said, they were as addictive as cocaine and heroin.

The growing body of evidence triggered a major cultural shift, with smoking becoming less socially acceptable. During the 1990s, many state and local governments banned smoking in restaurants and hotels, and tobacco companies lost multibillion-dollar lawsuits filed by cancer-stricken customers.

In 2007, Gallup found that the proportion of adult smokers had declined to 24 percent—roughly half the level in the 1950s.

ADDITIONAL FACTS

1. *In 1997, Camel was forced to discontinue the use of its advertising mascot Joe Camel, which anti-smoking activists argued was intended to market cigarettes to children.*

2. *Cigarette smoking kills about 440,000 Americans annually, according to the American Cancer Society—more than alcohol, car accidents, suicide, AIDS, murder, and illegal drugs combined.*

3. *Smoking has also been linked to cancers of the throat, pancreas, liver, uterine cervix, kidneys, bladder, stomach, colon, and rectum.*

•••••

Jack Nicklaus

Jack Nicklaus's accomplishments on the golf course are staggering. During his illustrious career, he won seventy-three times on the PGA Tour, including a record eighteen major championships. From 1962 to 1978, he won at least two PGA events every year. And, perhaps most significantly, he won each of the four majors at least three times—an unprecedented achievement.

Nicklaus (1940–), born in Columbus, Ohio, was a golfing prodigy from an early age. At age twenty, while still an amateur, he finished second to Arnold Palmer (1929–) at the 1960 US Open, losing by two strokes. Two years later, he turned professional and beat Palmer in an eighteen-hole playoff at the 1962 US Open. It was a stunning upset that had the upstart coming from five strokes down with eleven holes remaining to defeat the King. Their rivalry would help fuel golf's surging popularity in the 1960s and 1970s.

By age twenty-six, Nicklaus had won the career grand slam. By age thirty-one, he had become the first player to win each major twice.

The Golden Bear dominated golf in the 1970s like few others dominated their sports in the twentieth century. Of his forty starts in major championships that decade, he won eight times and finished in the top ten a staggering thirty-five times.

Perhaps his most memorable victory came in 1986, when he was considered a washed-up forty-six-year-old. At that year's Masters, he shot a stunning six-under-par thirty in the final-round back nine to claim his sixth and final Masters title—and the final victory of his PGA Tour career.

Nicklaus now manages a golfing business empire that includes equipment and apparel. He has also designed more than 200 renowned golf courses and is the founder and host of the Memorial, a PGA Tour event.

ADDITIONAL FACTS

1. *In 1999,* Sports Illustrated *named Nicklaus the twentieth century's top male athlete in an individual sport.*

2. *All told, Nicklaus won the Masters six times, the US Open four times, the British Open three times, and the PGA Championship five times.*

3. *In addition to his eighteen wins, Nicklaus also had a remarkable number of near misses in major tournaments: He finished second nineteen times and third on nine occasions.*

•••••

Sesame Street

Getting kids to watch more television has never been a high priority for parents. But *Sesame Street*, a mainstay of educational programming on public television for four decades, has been a long-standing exception to the rule.

Jim Henson

The most famous member of the team that created *Sesame Street* was the puppeteer Jim Henson (1936–1990). Henson began making and performing with puppets in high school, and from 1955 until 1961, he produced an NBC show featuring his creations, which he called Muppets.

Henson was approached by Children's Television Workshop, a nonprofit organization, about using his Muppets in an educational program for preschool children. It was while working on the series that Henson introduced some of his most memorable characters, including Cookie Monster, Oscar the Grouch, Bert and Ernie, Elmo, and, of course, Big Bird. The first episode of *Sesame Street* aired on November 10, 1969.

Along with the Muppets, *Sesame Street* features many live actors, especially in the more explicitly educational portions. Children who watch the show are introduced to the alphabet and basic reading, as well as mathematical concepts such as counting, arithmetic, and shape recognition.

The show also helps children with weightier issues. In a famous 1983 episode, children learned about death and dying after Will Lee (1908–1982), who played Mr. Hooper on the program, passed away.

Despite its success—regional versions of the show are now broadcast in 140 countries—many critics maintain that it has a detrimental effect. The show was originally conceived as a way to use the flashy, attention-grabbing effects of television commercials to educate children—each episode is "sponsored" by a letter—but some critics contend that this has led to further deterioration of children's attention spans.

ADDITIONAL FACTS

1. *In 2004, Palestinian and Israeli stations broadcast a short-lived series based on* Sesame Street *called* Sesame Stories, *with the goal of promoting cultural understanding between Arab and Israeli youth.*

2. *In addition to general education programs,* Sesame Street *has made efforts to help children deal with difficult issues in the news, as in episodes that focused on the aftermath of the September 11, 2001, attacks.*

3. *The consumer advocate Ralph Nader (1934–) has criticized PBS for allowing McDonald's to sponsor* Sesame Street *despite the connection between fast food and childhood obesity.*

•◦•◦•

Pope John Paul II

The election of Karol Wojtyla (1920–2005) to the papacy in 1978 left many across the Catholic world scratching their heads. Wojtyla, who took the name John Paul II, was an unusual selection in several respects. He was the first non-Italian pope in 455 years, the first Slav to take the papacy, and, at fifty-eight, the youngest pope to serve in 132 years.

He was selected in the eighth round of balloting, and although he was a surprise candidate, he would go on to have a lasting impact in his nearly twenty-seven years as pope. John Paul II was an athlete, poet, dramatist, and linguist, but most of all, he was a man of the people. During his pontificate, he made 104 trips outside of Italy, visiting 129 countries, including historic voyages to Israel and Cuba.

John Paul II sought to stabilize the church after the tumultuous post–Vatican II reforms, and wherever he went, his dynamism, charisma, and personal magnetism brought huge crowds, prompting some to call him the "rock star" pope. He preached the importance of human rights, and the dangers of materialism, secularism, and selfishness. Although he apologized for many of the Catholic Church's errors over the previous two millennia, he was strictly conservative, particularly in his opposition to artificial birth control, the ordination of women, and gay marriage.

John Paul II was born in Wadowice, Poland, and spent many of his early years in Kraków. During the Nazi occupation of Poland, he secretly studied at an underground seminary while taking jobs in a stone quarry and a factory.

His experience living under totalitarian rule informed some of his later positions and played a role in what many historians believe to be his contribution to the fall of communism in the Soviet realm. Specifically, his emotional visit to Poland in 1979 is often regarded as a catalyst for the downfall of communist rule there.

Slowed by Parkinson's disease and other health ailments, John Paul II curtailed his travels in his final years and died at age eighty-four.

ADDITIONAL FACTS

1. *John Paul II survived an assassination attempt in 1981. A gunman shot him in the abdomen, right arm, and left hand in St. Peter's Square, forcing him to undergo five hours of surgery in which part of his intestine was removed.*

2. *He and the Vatican were criticized for their handling of the American sexual molestation scandal that exploded in 2002. The pope offered sorrow for the victims but enacted no sweeping changes to church policy.*

3. *John Paul II spoke eight languages, learning Spanish after becoming the pope.*

••••

A Clockwork Orange

A Clockwork Orange (1962) is the best-known work by the British novelist Anthony Burgess (1917–1993). This disturbing comic novel, about a vicious but charismatic teenage hoodlum, gained attention for its candid depictions of violence, its creative use of invented language, and its controversial 1971 film adaptation.

In 1961, with a half-dozen novels already under his belt, Burgess visited the Soviet Union on vacation. During the trip, he noted the Soviet state's total control over its people, but also, paradoxically, the presence of seemingly uncontrollable, violent youth gangs in St. Petersburg (then called Leningrad). These observations directly influenced *A Clockwork Orange*, which Burgess finished upon returning home.

The novel is narrated by a young thug named Alex who lives in a vaguely futuristic, oppressed society of indeterminate setting. He and his pals habitually get high on drugged milk at a local bar, roam the streets, and terrorize citizens with brutal crimes—ranging from armed robbery to sadistic rape—all the while talking in a bizarre dialect that blends Russian words with Cockney rhyming slang. But Alex is no ordinary thug: Despite his fondness for ultraviolence, he is a sensitive youth and has a passion for classical music, particularly that of Beethoven.

After one of Alex's rape victims dies, Alex is arrested, imprisoned, and subjected to brainwashing treatments as the government attempts to reform his violent ways. But beyond curing Alex's brutal tendencies, these mind-control techniques also rob him entirely of his free will—which the ardently individualistic Burgess sees as unacceptable.

In 1971, Stanley Kubrick (1928–1999) released a brazen, graphic film adaptation of *A Clockwork Orange* that received an X rating and generated a storm of controversy. Although the film became an instant cult classic, Burgess lamented that it omitted the final chapter of his novel, completely changing the meaning of its ending.

ADDITIONAL FACTS

1. *The novel's title stems from a Cockney slang expression, "as queer as a clockwork orange." Burgess felt that this was an apt descriptor for a story about a living organism—Alex—being treated or modified by artificial, mechanical forces.*

2. *In a later interview, Burgess said that* A Clockwork Orange *was so disturbing that he wrote the book "in a state of near drunkenness in order to deal with material that upset me very much."*

3. *Burgess believed that* A Clockwork Orange *was not nearly his best work, and he expressed consternation that it was the novel for which he would be most remembered.*

•••••

Aretha Franklin

If Aretha Franklin (1942–) has a signature song, it is undoubtedly "Respect," her number one hit from 1967. She succeeded so completely in making the song her own that many listeners didn't realize she was covering a 1965 hit by soul singer Otis Redding (1941–1967). But even Redding was ready to concede defeat when he heard Franklin's electrifying version of his work: "I just lost my song," he said. "That girl took it away from me."

By the time Franklin came out with her string of hits in the late 1960s, she was already a minor star. Born in Memphis, Tennessee, she began singing on the gospel circuit at a very young age and switched to pop music following the example of legendary singer Sam Cooke (1931–1964).

While Franklin had some success after signing with Columbia Records, she attained superstardom only after moving to Atlantic Records in 1966. In quick succession, she released a string of classic records including *I Never Loved a Man the Way I Love You* (1967), *Lady Soul* (1968), and *Soul '69* (1969). She recorded songs in almost every style, from gospel numbers to standards such as "Over the Rainbow," from *The Wizard of Oz* (1939).

Still, the genre she is best known for is the one that earned her the nickname the Queen of Soul. Soul music blends two genres that were previously kept separate: rhythm and blues and gospel. Rhythm and blues is a personal style that combines the standard twelve-bar blues with a clearly defined beat, while gospel is a form of confessional church music. The result is a style that mixes the driving tempo of R & B with the exalted hymns of gospel. Franklin is one of the most acclaimed soul performers, alongside other greats such as Redding, Cooke, and Ray Charles (1930–2004).

ADDITIONAL FACTS

1. *Because the Grammy for Best Female R & B Vocal Performance went to Franklin so often—including an unbroken eight-year stretch from 1967 to 1974—it was once nicknamed the Aretha Award.*

2. *After a lull in the late 1970s, Franklin's career was revitalized after her cameo in the classic 1980 film* The Blues Brothers.

3. *In 1987, Franklin became the first woman inducted into the Rock and Roll Hall of Fame.*

• • • • •

Elizabeth Taylor

For decades, Elizabeth Taylor (1932–) was an enormous star whose off-screen life received even more attention than her hugely successful acting career. Her eight marriages—including two to fellow megastar Richard Burton (1925–1984)—have been fodder for movie magazines and tabloids since she was a teenager, though in recent years health problems have kept her out of the public eye.

Taylor emerged as a child star with her performance in *National Velvet* (1944). She embarked on a series of juvenile roles until she appeared in *Father of the Bride* in 1950—which also happened to be the year of her first marriage. A year later, she established her adult on-screen persona as a beautiful, passionate woman in the tragic *A Place in the Sun* (1951).

She received Academy Award nominations for four consecutive years—including for performances in adaptations of two smoldering Tennessee Williams plays, *Cat on a Hot Tin Roof* (1958) and *Suddenly, Last Summer* (1959)—and won on the fourth try for *BUtterfield 8* (1960).

After *BUtterfield 8*, an adaptation of a novel by John O'Hara, she was not in a film for three tumultuous years. During that period, she had a series of health problems and worked on the disastrous production of *Cleopatra* (1963) that ultimately cost $44 million to make and lost more than $10 million for 20th Century Fox.

During the filming of *Cleopatra*, Taylor, who was married, had a highly publicized affair with her married costar, Burton. Their romance elicited a rebuke from the Vatican and led to the end of her fourth marriage (to entertainer Eddie Fisher), as well as to the first of two marriages to Burton, in 1964. (They divorced in 1974, remarried in 1975, and divorced again in 1976.)

Taylor picked up her second Academy Award for costarring with Burton in an adaptation of playwright Edward Albee's *Who's Afraid of Virginia Woolf?* (1966), a performance that many critics consider the high point of Taylor's career. After a string of unremarkable films in the 1970s, she has appeared in relatively few movies since 1980.

ADDITIONAL FACTS

1. *In recent years, Taylor has been known more for her close friendship with Michael Jackson, her love of jewelry, and her passionate dedication to the fight against HIV/AIDS than for her acting.*

2. *For appearing in* Cleopatra, *Taylor was paid $1 million plus 10 percent of the film's gross, making her the highest-paid actress to that point.*

3. Who's Afraid of Virginia Woolf? *was the first film to be released with a "Suggested for Mature Audiences" warning because of its groundbreaking use of words such as* bugger *and* screw.

•••••

The Space Race

On October 4, 1957, a small aluminum satellite called *Sputnik 1* entered orbit high above the earth's atmosphere. Launched by the Soviet Union from a remote base in Kazakhstan, the tiny satellite was the opening salvo of the "space race" between the United States and the USSR.

Over the next three decades, the two Cold War superpowers spent billions of dollars on space exploration. For both countries, the space race was a matter of national pride, but it also yielded significant scientific gains and a deeper understanding of the universe beyond our skies.

After the launch of *Sputnik,* the United States accelerated its own fledgling space program. Congress swiftly established the National Aeronautics and Space Administration (NASA) to spearhead the effort.

Initially, however, the Soviet program was much more successful. Less than a month after sending off *Sputnik 1,* the Soviet Union put a dog named Laika into space, while NASA's first attempts at launching a simple satellite were dismal failures. Four years later, the Russian pilot Yury Gagarin (1934–1968) became the first human in space and the first to orbit the earth.

NASA was behind, and it needed to do something spectacular to make up for it.

What that something would be was announced by President John F. Kennedy (1917–1963) in 1961: "I believe that this nation should commit itself to achieving the goal, before this decade is out, of landing a man on the Moon and returning him safely to Earth."

Kennedy's promise was fulfilled by the *Apollo 11* mission in 1969, when astronauts Neil Armstrong (1930–) and Buzz Aldrin (1930–) walked on the moon. In the years that followed, NASA introduced reusable shuttles, unmanned exploration of Mars, space stations, and spacecraft such as *Voyager 1* that probed the farthest reaches of the solar system and transmitted brilliant images of the moons of Jupiter and the rings of Saturn.

ADDITIONAL FACTS

1. *The Apollo program got off to a tragic start: In the first manned mission,* Apollo 1, *the rocket never made it off the launchpad. An accidental fire killed the entire crew.*

2. *NASA placed a solid gold phonograph record in the* Voyager *satellite, in case the aircraft was ever found by extraterrestrial life. The disc included songs by artists ranging from Johann Sebastian Bach (1685–1750) to Louis Armstrong (1901–1971) to Chuck Berry (1926–).*

3. *Many common inventions were first developed for use in space, or as a result of discoveries made in space, including the TV satellite dish, smoke detectors, and ski boots, the latter of which are modifications of space suit designs.*

· · ● ● · ·

Joe Namath

Though he may not have had the greatest statistics or the longest career, "Broadway" Joe Namath (1943–) was synonymous with football in the tumultuous 1960s. When he left the University of Alabama in 1965, he carried with him a rocket right arm, a gimpy right knee, and an abundance of charisma.

As quarterback of the New York Jets, Namath first guaranteed, then executed, a victory over the heavily favored Baltimore Colts in Super Bowl III in 1969—the greatest upset in Super Bowl history. Most observers consider that game the birth of modern American professional football, hastening the emergence of the National Football League as the country's most popular sports league.

Namath spent twelve years with the Jets (1965–1976) and one with the Los Angeles Rams (1977), racking up 27,663 passing yards and 173 touchdowns. His first contract with the Jets was reportedly for more than $400,000, which was a pro football record at the time.

The Jets' investment immediately proved fruitful. In 1965, Namath was the league's top rookie; in 1967, he became the first quarterback to throw for more than 4,000 yards in a season; and in the 1968 season, he led the Jets to a Super Bowl title and was named the league's Player of the Year.

With his long brown hair and Fu Manchu mustache, Namath was an icon of the late-1960s youth culture that embraced antiheroes. He was a cocky and rebellious sex symbol but also accessible and fun loving—as evidenced by his famous appearance in a television ad for Beautymist panty hose.

After his initial success in pro football, Namath's knee injuries limited his effectiveness. He ended up with a losing career record, a completion rate of 50 percent, and forty-seven more interceptions than touchdowns.

But his impact on professional football and American culture was no less profound, and he was inducted into the Pro Football Hall of Fame in 1985.

ADDITIONAL FACTS

1. *Namath was also a budding baseball star, receiving interest from six major-league teams—including the Chicago Cubs, who reportedly offered him a $50,000 bonus. But Namath decided to play football at Alabama instead.*

2. *At Alabama, the legendary head coach Bear Bryant (1913–1983) called Namath "the greatest athlete I ever coached."*

3. *Namath's flamboyance was not limited to his off-field appearances—he also frequently wore full-length fur coats on the sidelines during games.*

•••••

Mary Tyler Moore

When Brooklyn-born actress Mary Tyler Moore (1936–) began her career as a dancing kitchen appliance in a 1955 TV commercial, she could never have known that she would play two famous TV characters that would mirror the changing role of American women in the 1960s and 1970s.

In 1961, Moore's face became synonymous with that of the happy homemaker when she was cast as Laura Petrie, the wife of TV writer Rob Petrie in *The Dick Van Dyke Show*. Moore won two Emmys for her portrayal of the flighty but lovable wife and mother in the CBS series, but after its finale in 1966—and a rocky period in the movies—Moore returned to television in 1970 to play Laura Petrie's opposite: an independent career woman, Mary Richards, in *The Mary Tyler Moore Show*.

In the series, Mary Richards moves to Minneapolis following a breakup with a live-in boyfriend of many years. As the theme song states, she's "going to make it after all" and "make it on her own," a first at a time when female TV characters existed almost exclusively as wives or girlfriends. Richards lands a job as an associate producer at a struggling television newsroom and takes an apartment in a house occupied by a New York City transplant (Rhoda Morgenstern) and their landlady.

In another television first, Moore's character on occasion spends the night with some of the men she dates in the course of the show, but her dating life is always secondary to her relationship with her "workplace family."

Mary Richards, modeled after the "new woman" of the era, put a friendly spin on feminism, and the show set the standard for the working-woman genre on TV. When the series ended in 1977, it was one of the first to bring closure to the story: Ironically, everyone but the station's dim-witted anchorman, Ted Baxter, is fired, and Mary Richards turns out the newsroom light for the last time.

ADDITIONAL FACTS

1. The Mary Tyler Moore Show *is called* Oh, Mary *in Germany.*

2. *A Mary Richards statue was erected in Minneapolis in 2002 on the spot where Moore famously throws her hat in the air in the opening credits.*

3. *Originally, the character of Mary Richards was intended to be divorced, but producers feared the controversy and thought viewers might think she had divorced Rob Petrie from* The Dick Van Dyke Show.

•••••

Ayatollah Khomeini

With his long white beard, black turban, and glowering countenance, Ayatollah Ruhollah Khomeini (c. 1900–1989) came to symbolize Iran's Islamic revolution and its outright hostility toward the West.

Khomeini took control of Iran in February 1979, following the abdication of the country's autocratic, Western-backed leader, Mohammad Reza Shah Pahlavi (1919–1980). Khomeini soon established Iran as an Islamic state, with himself as its supreme leader.

Under Khomeini, Iran became more fundamentalist and anti-West, as new laws forced women to wear the chador (a full-length gown) and a veil. Criticism of his rule was not permitted, and music and alcohol were banned. Thousands were publicly executed after the revolution, while others were purged from government and military posts as Khomeini consolidated his power.

Meanwhile, Khomeini often referred to the United States as "the Great Satan," railed against Israel and Zionists at every opportunity, and sought to foment revolution in other Middle Eastern countries.

Before rising to be Iran's leader, Khomeini was a Shi'ite Muslim scholar and teacher who focused on Islamic philosophy, law, and ethics. He did not become a political figure until 1941, when he published *Unveiling the Mysteries,* a book that criticized the shah for destroying Islamic culture and laid out his vision of an Islamic state.

In 1964, Khomeini was banished into exile for advocating the overthrow of the shah. From his base in Iraq, he continued to undermine the Iranian regime and became a source of inspiration for dissidents within Iran. By 1978, while still in exile, he had become a symbol of public rage against the shah. When he returned to Iran in February 1979, he was welcomed as a conquering hero.

During his rule, he promoted a nationalist agenda, rallying public support throughout the Iranian hostage crisis (1979–1981) and the costly war with Iraq (1980–1988). Upon his death at age eighty-nine, the Islamic revolution in Iran remained firmly in place and now lives on under the leadership of his successor, Ayatollah Ali Khamenei (1939–).

ADDITIONAL FACTS

1. *Khomeini received the title* ayatollah *("reflection of Allah") in the late 1950s. In 1962, he was given the honorific grand ayatollah, a title held by only six other mullahs in Iran at the time.*

2. *The year of Khomeini's birth is disputed. Some sources list him as being born in 1900, others in 1901, and still others in 1902. According to the* New York Times, *the most accepted date of his birth is May 27, 1900.*

3. *One of Khomeini's most publicized public statements was in 1989, when he issued a fatwa (a religious edict) calling for the British author Salman Rushdie (1947–) to be killed. Rushdie's book* The Satanic Verses *was deemed "blasphemous against Islam," and the fatwa forced him to live with increased security protection.*

•••••

Who's Afraid of Virginia Woolf?

Who's Afraid of Virginia Woolf? (1962), by the playwright Edward Albee (1928–), is hailed as one of the great American dramas of the twentieth century. Profane, absurd, and cutting-edge for its time, it did much to undermine the rosy picture of domestic life that had dominated American popular culture during the 1950s.

Edward Albee

Albee's play centers on a hard-drinking middle-aged couple named George and Martha: He is a history professor at a small university and she is the daughter of the university president. Late one night, they come home from a faculty party, drunk and hurling insults at each other. To George's annoyance, the brash, intimidating Martha announces that she has invited another couple from the party—a young biology professor named Nick and his wife, Honey—over for even more drinks.

When Nick and Honey arrive, Martha goes on the warpath, airing out dirty laundry about her marriage and taunting George mercilessly in front of the handsome, overconfident Nick. The evening escalates into a long night of verbal abuse, sexual frankness, and elaborately choreographed mind games—all propelled by Albee's brilliant, brutal dialogue, in which George and Martha exchange near-constant insults and humiliations.

Despite their efforts to remain merely bystanders, Nick and Honey get embroiled in George and Martha's battle, and several painful secrets that both couples have tried to keep under wraps end up being dragged out into the open. Ultimately, it becomes clear that George and Martha's bitter arguments are all a facade, covering both their deep love for each other and their profound sadness at the frustrations and disappointments they have experienced in their marriage. Once all the verbal brutality has subsided, George and Martha come across not as a pair of larger-than-life monsters but as a very human couple wearied by the fears and challenges of married life.

ADDITIONAL FACTS

1. *The 1966 film version of* Who's Afraid of Virginia Woolf? *starring Elizabeth Taylor (1932–) and Richard Burton (1925–1984) had only four principal cast members, and all four were nominated for Oscars.*

2. *Albee got the idea for the play's title from some graffiti he saw scrawled on a barroom mirror in the Greenwich Village neighborhood in New York City.*

3. Who's Afraid of Virginia Woolf? *was Albee's first full-length play. His first few works were one-act plays, the best-known of which is* The Zoo Story *(1959).*

• • • •

Jimi Hendrix

In June of 1967, Brian Jones (1942–1969) of the Rolling Stones introduced a relatively unknown guitarist from Seattle named Jimi Hendrix (1942–1970) at the Monterey Pop Festival, a three-day concert in California. "He's the most exciting performer I've ever heard," Jones declared. Hendrix's performance at Monterey created a sensation. In an epic set, he played with the guitar behind his back, plucked at the strings of his Fender Stratocaster with his teeth, and ultimately lit the guitar on fire to end the show.

Hendrix's Monterey act sent the sales of his debut album, *Are You Experienced?* soaring. *Are You Experienced?* and the two studio albums that followed in his short career are considered cornerstones of the psychedelic movement in the late 1960s. But the albums, and Hendrix, were far more than simply psychedelic. Jimi Hendrix invoked rhythm and blues, jazz, folk, rock, and funk with his wailing electric guitar.

Hendrix, more than any artist before him, made use of the unique sonic capabilities of an electric guitar, rather than simply playing it like a plugged-in acoustic. He pioneered techniques such as the use of guitar feedback, distortion, and wah-wah pedals to make the instrument sing. Hendrix is still regarded by many as the greatest rock guitarist of all time.

Two years after his performance at Monterey, Hendrix was one of the biggest music stars in the world. His third album, *Electric Ladyland,* peaked at number one on the US album charts, and he was named the headliner of the famous Woodstock festival in 1969. At 7:30 a.m. on a wet Monday morning during the festival, Hendrix roused the sleeping concertgoers with a solo electric-guitar rendition of "The Star-Spangled Banner." Full of distortion and improvisation, the performance became a symbol of the hippie generation and the changing mood of America.

Less than a year later, Jimi Hendrix died of complications following a drug overdose in a London hotel room. Only twenty-seven, he had already changed the face of rock music and furthered the development of hard rock, heavy metal, and funk.

ADDITIONAL FACTS

1. *In 1992, Hendrix won a posthumous Grammy award for lifetime achievement.*

2. *Hendrix's performance at the Monterey Pop Festival is featured in D. A. Pennebaker's documentary film* Monterey Pop.

3. *Hendrix's first North American tour was in support of the made-for-TV band the Monkees.*

•••••

Bonnie and Clyde (1967)

"We rob banks."
—Faye Dunaway as Bonnie Parker

When director Arthur Penn's feature film on the murderous Depression-era bank robbers Bonnie Parker and Clyde Barrow came out, most film critics didn't understand what they were seeing—but they knew they didn't like it. Upon its release in the summer of 1967, *Bonnie and Clyde* was almost universally panned for glamorizing violence and for blending killings with comedy. The movie quickly left theaters and appeared to be a disaster for Penn (1922–) and Warren Beatty (1937–), the producer and star.

But in its short initial release, the film made an impact on America's youth culture. A bluegrass song by Flatt and Scruggs on the sound track went to the top of the charts; fashions influenced by the film started catching on; and a twenty-five-year-old critic named Roger Ebert, representing a new generation of filmgoers, championed the picture as "a milestone in the history of American movies, a work of truth and brilliance."

Soon enough, attitudes changed, and *Bonnie and Clyde* went on to revolutionize American cinema—and gross $50 million.

Along with *The Graduate* (1967), *Bonnie and Clyde* tapped into a disaffection with American society that many young people in the 1960s were feeling; the film historian Robert Sklar writes that American kids saw in *Bonnie and Clyde* a "doomed lawlessness as a metaphor for their own social alienation."

As the film's tagline says, Bonnie and Clyde rob banks and kill people. Borrowing a nihilistic sensibility from films of the French New Wave (particularly the work of Francois Truffaut and Jean-Luc Godard), they rob and kill because they can, because they're bored, and because they don't care about anything.

Penn's overt use of sex and violence, which may seem tame by today's standards, shocked audiences in 1967. It also ushered in an era known as the New Hollywood, in which a young generation of writers, directors, and actors—many of them film-school educated—pulled Hollywood away from old-fashioned studio pictures, such as musicals and historical epics, toward more personal and modern films.

ADDITIONAL FACTS

1. Bonnie and Clyde *received ten Academy Award nominations, with wins for Estelle Parsons (best supporting actress) and Burnett Guffey (best cinematography).*

2. *Among the fashion trends set by the film were berets and maxiskirts for women and 1930s gangster outfits (fedoras, double-breasted suits) for men.*

3. *The film helped launch the careers of principal players Faye Dunaway, Gene Hackman, and Parsons, as well as Gene Wilder, who had a small role.*

•••••

Affirmative Action

Affirmative action has been one of the most contentious political issues in American life since its widespread implementation in the 1960s and 1970s to give racial minorities and women an advantage in hiring and university admissions.

In one indication of the continuing discord on the issue, a 2005 Gallup poll found that 50 percent of Americans favored affirmative action programs as a means of undoing past race and gender discrimination, while 42 percent opposed them.

Affirmative action stemmed from a growing concern over the inequality in American society exposed by the civil rights and women's rights movements of the 1960s. Civil rights advocates such as Martin Luther King Jr. (1929–1968) argued that "a society that has done something special against the Negro for hundreds of years must now do something special for the Negro."

In 1965, President Lyndon B. Johnson (1908–1973) issued an affirmative action order that required government contractors to actively recruit minority workers. Many public and private universities, as well as local government agencies such as fire and police departments, followed suit.

From their inception, however, such programs have proved enormously controversial. To its critics, affirmative action amounts to reverse racial discrimination against whites.

Indeed, voters in some states have rejected affirmative action, most famously in California, where the use of racial preferences in university admissions was banned in a 1996 referendum.

As recently as 2003, however, the Supreme Court has upheld the legality of affirmative action. That year, the court ruled that the University of Michigan Law School could use race as a factor in admissions, turning aside a complaint from a woman who claimed that she had been denied admission in favor of less-qualified minority candidates.

ADDITIONAL FACTS

1. *In 2005, a poll showed that 61 percent of men believed that women now enjoy equal opportunities in the workplace. Only 45 percent of women agreed.*

2. *After the Michigan case, voters passed a referendum in 2006 outlawing affirmative action in the state's universities.*

3. *Affirmative action is practiced in a handful of foreign countries, including India, where such laws have been used to benefit members of the country's* dalit, *or "untouchable," caste.*

•••••

Mark Spitz

Over an eight-day span in 1972, the swimmer Mark Spitz (1950–) achieved what no other Olympic athlete has ever done—he entered seven events, won seven gold medals, and broke seven world records. Many consider Spitz's performance at the Munich Games to be the greatest feat in Olympic history and one of the greatest individual athletic accomplishments ever.

Four years earlier, at the 1968 Mexico City Games, eighteen-year-old Spitz had brashly predicted that he would win six gold medals. By that standard, his accomplishments at those Games were disappointing: He won two gold medals as a member of relay teams, a silver in the 100-meter butterfly, and a bronze in the 100-meter freestyle.

Determined to improve, Spitz then went to Indiana University to train under famed coach Doc Counsilman (1920–2004). There, Spitz won eight individual college swimming titles and helped the Hoosiers to four consecutive team championships.

He entered the Munich Games having twice been named World Swimmer of the Year (1969, 1971) and having won the Sullivan Award in 1971 as the top American amateur athlete. The pressure was unrelenting, but unlike in 1968, Spitz thrived and won every race he entered (the 100- and 200-meter freestyle, the 100- and 200-meter butterfly, and all three relays).

Spitz, who is Jewish, filled the members of the international Jewish community with great pride, particularly since the Olympics were held in Germany less than three decades after the Holocaust. But their pride turned to horror when members of the Palestinian militant group Black September killed eleven Israeli athletes during the Games. For his own protection, Spitz left Munich before the closing ceremony.

Spitz retired from the sport at age twenty-two and hoped to parlay his swimming success and sex-symbol status into Hollywood stardom. He made a reported $7 million the first two years after the Games as a celebrity pitchman, but his Hollywood career soon fizzled. He later went into real estate in California.

ADDITIONAL FACTS

1. *During his competitive career, Spitz lived by the mantra of his father, Arnold: "Swimming isn't everything; winning is." By age ten, he was already the world's best ten-and-under swimmer, having set seventeen national age-group records and one world record.*

2. *Spitz is tied for the most career Olympic gold medals (nine) with American track-and-field athlete Carl Lewis (1961–), Soviet gymnast Larissa Latynina (1934–), and Finnish distance runner Paavo Nurmi (1897–1973).*

3. *In 1977, Spitz was inducted into the International Swimming Hall of Fame, and in 1983 he became a charter member of the US Olympic Hall of Fame.*

• • • • •

Doonesbury

The comic strip *Doonesbury*, penned by Garry Trudeau (1948–), debuted on October 26, 1970, in twenty-eight newspapers. Thirty-eight years later, the comic is syndicated in 1,400 papers and is one of the most influential—and most controversial—comics in American history.

Trudeau began drawing a strip called *Bull Tales* for the college newspaper at Yale University in 1968. Steeped in college life and 1960s youth counterculture, the strip depicted characters smoking marijuana, worrying about the draft, and, in one series of comics, waking up next to a stranger in bed. After Trudeau graduated, the strip was renamed *Doonesbury* after its main character, Mike Doonesbury, and went into national syndication.

Almost from the beginning, the strip was controversial for its drug references and left-wing political barbs. But it was enormously popular among readers of the baby boomer generation, and dozens of papers

Garry Trudeau

added the strip in its first year. *Doonesbury* was also much more literate and featured more-developed characters than many of its competitors, pioneering a more sophisticated style of daily cartoons.

During the Watergate scandal, Trudeau penned dozens of strips taking aim at President Richard M. Nixon (1913–1994). In recognition of his Watergate cartoons, Trudeau won a Pulitzer Prize in 1975 for editorial cartooning—the first ever awarded to a comic strip.

Since then, Trudeau's highly political cartoons, and his frank depictions of homosexuality, AIDS, and racism, have made the strip both controversial and beloved. In a testament to the strip's cultural weight, when a fictional *Doonesbury* character died of AIDS in 1990, the *San Francisco Chronicle* ran an obituary in its news pages.

ADDITIONAL FACTS

1. *The character BD was named after the former Yale and New England Patriots quarterback Brian Dowling (1947–).*

2. *Trudeau is married to Jane Pauley (1950–), a former cohost of NBC's* Today Show.

3. *Trudeau was nominated for an Academy Award in 1977 for an animated* Doonesbury *special.*

••◦••

Ronald Reagan

With his eternally optimistic attitude, President Ronald Reagan (1911–2004) is credited with restoring American confidence at home and abroad during his eight years in the White House. During his tenure, the country emerged from recession to experience economic expansion, though the financial gap between rich and poor increased. Meanwhile, some historians credit Reagan's anti-communist rhetoric and massive increases in defense spending as contributing to the collapse of the Soviet Union in 1991.

Reagan was born in Illinois and enjoyed a successful career as a Hollywood actor, radio broadcaster, and public relations pitchman before turning to politics. Originally a Democrat, he joined the Republicans in 1962.

Reagan was elected governor of California in 1966 and served two terms. He then nearly unseated the incumbent president, Gerald R. Ford (1913–2006), in the race for the Republican presidential nomination in 1976. In 1980, Reagan handily won the nomination by campaigning on promises of smaller government, lower taxes, and a balanced budget. He easily defeated Democrat President Jimmy Carter (1924–).

But while Reagan did lower taxes and cut federal programs, the federal deficit almost tripled as the government spent billions on defense, seeking to intimidate Soviet leaders into believing that they could not compete with the United States in an arms race. He also fought the Cold War with rhetoric, dubbing the Soviet Union the "evil empire."

Scandal nearly overwhelmed Reagan's presidency in his second term, when he was forced to take personal responsibility for the 1986 Iran-contra affair, in which his subordinates had sold arms to Iran and then used some of the profits to fund guerrillas battling the Cuban-backed Sandinista regime in Nicaragua. In the subsequent congressional hearings, Reagan was often depicted as an uninformed leader who operated more as a delegator than as a primary actor.

But the scandal did little to damage Reagan's high approval ratings, and he left office in 1989 as one of the most popular presidents in history. In 1994, he announced that he was suffering from Alzheimer's disease, and he lived privately in California until his death at age ninety-three.

ADDITIONAL FACTS

1. *Just sixty-nine days into his first term, Reagan survived an assassination attempt when a gunman's bullet pierced his left lung. Though he suffered a life-threatening loss of blood, he reportedly retained his good humor, telling his wife, "Honey, I forgot to duck."*

2. *Reagan appeared in more than fifty Hollywood films, including his most famous role as the legendary Notre Dame football player George Gipp (1895–1920) in* Knute Rockne All-American *(1940).*

3. *Before moving to Hollywood, Reagan worked as a radio sports announcer in Iowa. He would call baseball games for WHO in Des Moines by recreating the play-by-play based on telegraph reports from Chicago. In one oft-told story, the wire went dead in the ninth inning of a game, forcing Reagan to give a detailed description of a long series of foul balls.*

•••••

Kurt Vonnegut

Though he never won a major literary prize, Kurt Vonnegut (1922–2007) was one of the most widely appreciated American writers of the past century. His quirky, unconventional novels are studies in contradiction: funny yet pessimistic, cartoonish yet grave, and simple to read yet complex to understand. They brought a dose of science fiction to "serious" literature, and their pacifist bent made Vonnegut a hero of the antiwar counterculture during the Vietnam era.

A native of Indiana, Vonnegut attended college briefly before enlisting in the army in 1943, at the height of World War II. This decision led him to arguably the single most significant formative experience of his life—witnessing the Allied bombing of Dresden, Germany, in February 1945, which destroyed one of the great historic cities of Europe and is estimated to have killed at least 35,000 people in a single night. Vonnegut, who had been taken prisoner by the Nazis in 1944, was one of only a handful of American POWs to survive the bombing, and the sight of the utter destruction and loss of life was burned in his memory.

After the war, Vonnegut returned to the United States to embark on a writing career. Following a handful of novels—including the well-received *Cat's Cradle* (1963), about the destructive potential of science—Vonnegut finally wrote about his wartime experience in *Slaughterhouse-Five* (1969). The work exemplifies Vonnegut's style, with harrowing autobiographical episodes sharing the stage with aliens, time warps, and other science-fiction elements. The novel's protagonist lives through the firebombing of Dresden and becomes "unstuck in time," forced to live and relive different moments of his life out of chronological order, in a manner beyond his control. The novel's antiwar message resonated with Vietnam-era protesters, particularly on college campuses, where Vonnegut held cult-figure status for virtually the rest of his life.

ADDITIONAL FACTS

1. In 1947, the University of Chicago faculty rejected Vonnegut's master's thesis in anthropology, labeling it "unprofessional." In 1971, they finally awarded him the degree, claiming that his novel Cat's Cradle qualified as a thesis.

2. In the early 1950s, Vonnegut started a Saab dealership in Massachusetts but quickly drove it bankrupt. He later joked that this debacle was the reason the Sweden-based Nobel Foundation never awarded him the Nobel Prize.

3. Vonnegut remained an ardent antiwar activist in his later years, speaking and writing vehemently against the US invasion of Iraq in 2003.

••●••

The Velvet Underground

The Velvet Underground never had a hit during its brief existence and never performed before adoring crowds in packed stadiums. Nonetheless, the group was highly influential. As rock producer Brian Eno (1948–) supposedly put it, only a few thousand people bought Velvet Underground records when they came out—but all of them started bands.

The group was founded by singer and guitarist Lou Reed (1942–) and classical musician John Cale (1942–), who met in New York City in 1964. At the time, Reed was writing pop songs professionally and Cale, a Welshman, was writing experimental classical compositions. The duo recruited guitarist Sterling Morrison (1942–1995) and drummer Angus MacLise (1938–1979) to round out the group. The band played a few small shows, but its real breakthrough occurred when it was discovered by pop artist Andy Warhol (c. 1928–1987).

By the time Warhol found the Velvet Underground, he was already a major figure in the art world. Within months of taking the band under his wing, Warhol had secured it a record deal. He gave the band free rein, but only on the condition that it take on a German-born model and singer named Nico (1938–1988) to perform on some of its tracks. The band agreed and in 1967 released *The Velvet Underground and Nico,* with the famous "peel slowly and see" banana cover art by Warhol. The album contained some of the group's best-known songs, including "Heroin," "I'm Waiting for the Man," and "All Tomorrow's Parties." Nico soon left the band, and the group released *White Light/White Heat* without her in 1968. Cale was the next to leave, and the group's final albums—*The Velvet Underground* (1969) and *Loaded* (1970)—were released without him.

The Velvet Underground's albums sold poorly, but the lo-fi sound it pioneered had a deep and lasting influence. Today, many successful bands began as self-produced "indie rock" groups. Each of them owes a debt to the Velvet Underground, the original indie band.

ADDITIONAL FACTS

1. *The band's name comes from the title of a book about sadomasochism.*

2. *In the 1996 film* I Shot Andy Warhol, *the Velvet Underground is portrayed by indie rock group Yo La Tengo.*

3. *The group named its final album* Loaded *because its label asked it to produce a record "loaded with hits."*

••●••

The Graduate (1967)

"Mrs. Robinson, you're trying to seduce me."
—Dustin Hoffman as Benjamin Braddock

Mike Nichols's black comedy *The Graduate* tapped into the growing turbulence of America in the late 1960s. The film deals with themes of alienation, confusion, and ennui in American suburban culture, and some critics have deemed it the defining film of the baby boomer generation.

Dustin Hoffman (in his first major screen role) stars as Benjamin Braddock, an awkward, twenty-one-year-old recent college graduate who grows bored and disaffected upon returning to his upper-middle-class home. He spends his days floating aimlessly in his parents' pool, a symbol of uncertainty during the time of the country's dramatic upheaval, especially on college campuses.

Campus culture versus suburban life and the clash of generations are two of the film's most powerful themes, and both play out in Benjamin's relationships with women. In suburbia, he has an affair with Mrs. Robinson (played by Anne Bancroft), the wife of his father's business partner, essentially because he has nothing else to do. Living with his parents, he lacks purpose and passion, and he allows himself to be seduced.

On the college campus of Mrs. Robinson's daughter, Elaine (played by Katharine Ross), Benjamin is passionate and determined to win the woman he loves. But once he does, the uncertainty that permeates their generation returns for both Benjamin and Elaine.

The film was a surprise hit, grossing $104 million at the box office to become the decade's most successful comedy. It also achieved critical success, particularly from younger reviewers, revitalizing an interest in cinema on college campuses across the country. The sound track by Simon and Garfunkel, including the iconic songs "The Sound of Silence" and "Mrs. Robinson," also tapped into the youth culture of the period.

The Graduate was nominated for seven Academy Awards and garnered one Oscar—Nichols (1931–) won for best director for just the second feature of his career.

ADDITIONAL FACTS

1. *Although the film indicates that there is a significant age gap between Mrs. Robinson and Benjamin, there was only a six-year difference between Anne Bancroft (born in September 1931) and Dustin Hoffman (August 1937).*

2. *The film made Dustin Hoffman a star and helped move Hollywood away from the conventional leading man in favor of quirkier actors.*

3. *Hoffman had already signed on to costar in the Mel Brooks film* The Producers *(1968) when he was invited to read for* The Graduate. *Brooks, who was familiar with the film because his wife, Bancroft, had already been cast as Mrs. Robinson, allowed Hoffman to audition—he never thought Hoffman would get the part. He was wrong.*

•• ● ● ••

Black Power

A radical offshoot of the mainstream civil rights movement, the black power movement of the 1960s and 1970s used more aggressive and confrontational tactics to fight for political power for African-Americans. Black power's most famous representatives, the Black Panthers, eschewed the nonviolent principles of mainstream rights advocates such as Martin Luther King Jr. (1929–1968) and were involved in several high-profile clashes with authorities before the movement faded in the 1970s.

Established leaders such as King and the NAACP believed that marching alongside whites and encouraging desegregation was the best way to achieve racial equality. Black power advocates like Stokely Carmichael (1941–1998), however, felt that blacks needed to take charge of their own movement and rely less on support from whites. In a famous 1966 speech, Carmichael said, "It is a call for black people in this country to unite, to recognize their heritage, to build a sense of community. It is a call for black people to define their own goals, to lead their own organizations."

The black power movement enjoyed its greatest popularity in the 1960s, after King's assassination caused many blacks to become disillusioned with the civil rights movement and its insistence on nonviolence and integration. In an effort directed toward black self-reliance, members organized medical and food relief programs in African-American communities. They also amassed weapons stockpiles and, in a famous case in Connecticut, murdered one of their own members who was suspected of collaborating with the police.

The movement soon had its critics, including some from within the black community who argued that the Black Panthers served only to isolate and marginalize the black population, especially when they indulged in the sort of violence that caused blacks to be vilified.

The black power movement dissipated during the 1970s, but some of its tenets were subsumed under the umbrella of later, more positively focused efforts such as the black arts movement.

ADDITIONAL FACTS

1. *The earliest documented use of the term* black power *was in the 1954 book of that name by the African-American author Richard Wright (1908–1960).*

2. *The 1969 black power anthem "Say It Loud—I'm Black and I'm Proud" by James Brown (1933–2006) appeared on* Rolling Stone *magazine's 2004 list of the 500 greatest songs of all time.*

3. *Two American sprinters, Tommie Smith (1944–) and John Carlos (1945–), were suspended after giving the black power salute—an upraised fist—during the medal ceremony at the 1968 Olympics in Mexico City.*

• • • •

Secretariat

Secretariat is widely considered the most dominant Thoroughbred in the history of horse racing. In 1973, he became the first horse in twenty-five years to win the sport's Triple Crown—the Kentucky Derby, Preakness Stakes, and Belmont Stakes—and he still owns the track record in two of the three races.

Big Red, as Secretariat was known, was foaled in 1970, the offspring of 1957 Preakness winner Bold Ruler and Somethingroyal. He was trained by Lucien Laurin (1912–2000).

Secretariat's signature race was the 1973 Belmont. Only four horses, including Kentucky Derby and Preakness runner-up Sham, challenged Secretariat, who went off as an overwhelming favorite. After an early test from Sham, Secretariat surged ahead of the field—and kept surging until he had won by an incredible thirty-one lengths in a 1½-mile world record of two minutes, twenty-four seconds.

Race announcer Chic Anderson (1931–1979) famously called, "He is moving like a *tremendous machine!*" Late in the race, jockey Ron Turcotte (1941–) peeked behind him to see where the other horses were—and they were nowhere near the new Triple Crown winner. Turcotte later said that he did virtually nothing atop Secretariat; he just let the horse shift into "high gear."

Secretariat was such a sensation that he was featured on the covers of *Time, Newsweek,* and *Sports Illustrated* simultaneously in June 1973.

He won sixteen of the twenty-one races he entered in his two-year career, earning $1.3 million, and won Horse of the Year honors as a two-year-old and three-year-old.

Secretariat spent sixteen years at stud before he was euthanized in 1989 after suffering from the hoof disease laminitis. An autopsy revealed that he had a heart twice the size of that of the average horse.

ADDITIONAL FACTS

1. *The previous Triple Crown winner was Citation in 1948. Seven subsequent horses won the Kentucky Derby and Preakness, only to lose the Belmont.*

2. *In 1973, owner Penny Chenery (1922–) sold Secretariat to a breeding syndicate for a then-record $6.08 million.*

3. *Secretariat sired 1988 Preakness and Belmont winner Risen Star and 1986 Horse of the Year Lady's Secret. His bloodline also includes 2004 Kentucky Derby and Preakness winner Smarty Jones.*

• • ● ● •

Archie Bunker

On January 12, 1971, CBS doubled the staff at its switchboards to field a flood of viewer complaints as America was introduced to the sitcom *All in the Family* and its bigoted patriarch, Archie Bunker. After a lackluster debut (and only twenty calls) the show went on to garner an audience of 50 million and become the top-rated television series for five years. In 2004, *TV Guide* named Archie Bunker one of the fifty greatest TV dads of all time.

A dock foreman, taxi driver, and eventual bar owner, the outspoken and conservative Archie Bunker, played by Carroll O'Connor (1924–2001), railed against minorities and mourned the changing state of the nation "ruined by Franklin Delano Roosevelt." From his trademark wing chair in the living room of 704 Houser Street in Queens, New York, he tangled with his liberal son-in-law, Michael Stivik, played by Rob Reiner (1947–), and his "women's lib" daughter, Gloria, played by Sally Struthers (1948–). Jean Stapleton (1923–) played Archie's wife, Edith, whom he referred to as a "dingbat." (His line "Stifle, Edith!" made *TV Guide*'s 2005 list of TV's twenty top catchphrases.)

In an era of frothy domestic comedies, *All in the Family* grappled with socially relevant topics such as racism, sexuality, and the Vietnam War in a true-to-life setting where families squabbled and toilets flushed for the first time on American television. Equal parts offensive and sympathetic, Bunker became an American everyman and icon, albeit a polarizing one seen by some as combating bigotry and by others as advancing it. In the early 1970s, the phrase *the Bunker vote* came to describe dissatisfied, lower-middle-class whites.

The show opened the door for subsequent portrayals of the blue-collar family man in shows such as *Married with Children*. Still, few TV characters have touched a nerve in the same way Archie Bunker did. As one current sitcom actor noted, "Archie was saying things that no one on TV has said since."

ADDITIONAL FACTS

1. *The character Archie Bunker was inspired by the father of the show's producer, Norman Lear (1922–). The elder Lear was a salesman and second-generation Russian Jew who would call his son "the laziest white kid I ever saw" and tell his wife to "stifle."*

2. *The actor Mickey Rooney (1920–) turned down the role of Archie Bunker, fearing it was too controversial.*

3. *Archie and Edith's wing chairs were donated to the Smithsonian.*

4. *Archie was almost killed off in the fifth season when star Carroll O'Connor missed four tapings over a contract dispute.*

•••••

Sandra Day O'Connor

From a young age, Sandra Day O'Connor (1930–) was determined to be a trail-blazer. As a child growing up on a remote ranch in Arizona, she aspired to be a cattle rancher—a rare job indeed for a woman.

Instead, O'Connor became one of the most powerful women in American history as the first female justice ever to serve on the US Supreme Court.

O'Connor graduated from Stanford University in 1950 and from Stanford Law School two years later. After finishing law school, she was repeatedly turned down for jobs at firms because she was a woman. She eventually earned a position as deputy county attorney in San Mateo, California.

She later served as an assistant state attorney general in Arizona, as a member of the Arizona State Senate (where she became the first woman in US history to be majority leader of a state senate), on the Maricopa County Superior Court, and on the Arizona Court of Appeals.

Fulfilling a campaign promise to nominate a woman to the Court, President Ronald Reagan (1911–2004) chose O'Connor to replace Potter Stewart (1915–1985) in 1981.

O'Connor was confirmed by a vote of 99–0 in the Senate, and she served until her retirement in July 2005. During her twenty-four years on the bench, she often cast the deciding vote on such contentious issues as abortion, affirmative action, and capital punishment.

Though she was nominated by a Republican, O'Connor did not follow a conservative ideology and was considered a moderate member of the Court. She was replaced by a justice regarded as more conservative, Samuel Alito Jr. (1950–).

Arguably her most important votes were on the subject of abortion. She chose in 1992 to affirm *Roe v. Wade* with her deciding vote in *Planned Parenthood v. Casey*, which challenged a woman's right to an abortion.

Her critics thought that her lack of a broad judicial philosophy created instability on the Court, while her supporters said her case-by-case approach showed pragmatism. In 2004, she summed up her attitude in this way: "If indeed the choice is between adopting a balanced case-by-case approach ... and adopting a rigid rule that destroys everything in its path, I will choose the former."

ADDITIONAL FACTS

1. *O'Connor is a breast cancer survivor, having received successful treatment for the illness in 1988.*

2. *She finished third in her law-school graduating class; William H. Rehnquist (1924–2005), who later became O'Connor's colleague as chief justice of the Supreme Court, finished first.*

3. *In April 2006, Arizona State University named its law school in O'Connor's honor.*

•••••

John Updike

In an era in which the voices of women and minorities have assumed ever more prominent positions in American literature, novelist John Updike (1932–) has remained an incisive communicator of the late-twentieth-century American male experience. He is particularly known for his depictions of white, Protestant, middle-class men who feel trapped in the doldrums of married life.

Updike's upbringing mirrors those of many of his protagonists: He grew up in suburban Pennsylvania, went to Harvard, and lived briefly in Manhattan before settling in a small town in northeastern Massachusetts. Following a steady path toward a writing career, he cut his humor-writing teeth at Harvard, majoring in English, and afterward landed a spot as a contributor to the *New Yorker*.

Over the course of several highly regarded short stories and nonfiction pieces, Updike honed a detailed, realistic writing style that he employed in his first major novel, *Rabbit, Run* (1960). This book and its four sequels—*Rabbit Redux* (1971), *Rabbit Is Rich* (1981), *Rabbit at Rest* (1990), and *Rabbit Remembered* (2000)—follow the life of the character Harry "Rabbit" Angstrom, a former star basketball player who, after the glory days of his youth, has difficulty settling into the responsibilities and routines of faithful marriage. Building on the success of the Rabbit novels, Updike experimented with different genres later in his career, including fantasy, in *The Witches of Eastwick* (1984), and metafiction, in *Brazil* (1994) and *Gertrude and Claudius* (2000).

Updike's central subject matter—the domestic and sexual angst of American men—has earned him both praise and derision. Devotees assert that he is an important chronicler of the American mainstream, while critics have lambasted his works as juvenile and misogynist—one 1997 essay famously labeled Updike as simply "a penis with a thesaurus." Indisputably, though, Updike ranks among the most widely read and widely praised American novelists of recent years.

ADDITIONAL FACTS

1. *In addition to novels, Updike has also produced children's books, poetry, and a large body of essays about everything from art to golf.*

2. *Several of Updike's works have been adapted into film, most notably* The Witches of Eastwick, *which became a 1987 movie starring Jack Nicholson (1937–), Cher (1946–), Susan Sarandon (1946–), and Michelle Pfeiffer (1958–).*

3. *Updike's publisher, Knopf, fearing an obscenity lawsuit, requested that he tone down several sexually explicit passages in* Rabbit, Run. *The passages were restored to their original form in a reissue edition published in the 1980s.*

•••••

Elvis Presley's 1968 Comeback Special

By the late 1960s, Elvis Presley (1935–1977) had gone years without a major hit. His classic recordings with Sun Records were more than a decade old, and he hadn't made a song like "Heartbreak Hotel" (1956) in years. After a brief stint with the US Army in Germany, he had returned to the United States with a new focus: Largely abandoning the recording studio and the concert hall, Presley restarted his career in Hollywood. His musicals were popular at the box office and even contained an occasional gem like "Viva Las Vegas," but most critics and rock fans had written him off as a pudgy has-been.

This was the situation in 1968 when a television producer approached Elvis about taping a Christmas special for NBC. The end result was different than anybody had expected. There was a version of "Blue Christmas" thrown in for good measure, but that was the only part of the show that had anything to do with Christmas.

Instead, the producers assembled Elvis's old band from his Memphis days, including guitarists Scotty Moore (1931–) and Charlie Hodge (1934–2006) and drummer D. J. Fontana (1931–), and dressed the singer up in an all-leather suit (mistakenly assuming that it was the uniform he wore in his first concerts).

With an audience assembled at the last minute huddled around a tiny stage, the group gave one of the greatest rock and blues performances of all time. They played some of the songs that had made Elvis famous, including "Heartbreak Hotel," "One Night" (1958), "Blue Suede Shoes" (1956), and his first commercial recording, "That's All Right, Mama" (1954). They also performed astonishing versions of classics like "Lawdy Miss Clawdy" (1956) and "Trying to Get to You" (1956). The show was a huge hit, and Elvis was back in the limelight. The mammoth productions and rhinestone suits of Las Vegas were still to come.

ADDITIONAL FACTS

1. *The group performed "One Night" twice, and Elvis often slipped back into the original lyrics. The cover Presley released in 1956 included the lines "One night with you / Is what I'm now praying for / The things that we two could plan / Would make my dreams come true." The chorus of the Smiley Lewis original, which was about a night in a brothel, went "One night of sin / Is what I'm now paying for / The things I did and I saw / would make the Earth stand still."*

2. *Presley's manager, Colonel Tom Parker (1909–1997), had originally wanted Elvis to perform twenty Christmas songs in a tuxedo for the special.*

3. *Because there was no space for a drum kit on the stage, drummer Fontana kept time on the back of a guitar case.*

•••••

Robert Altman

Robert Altman (1925–2006) did not become a major Hollywood director until age forty-five, but his career was still marked by his youthful resistance to convention and genre. He was an uncompromising artist who detested Hollywood rules and Hollywood producers. And his films are a testament to improvisation, innovation, and naturalism, creating a mosaic of characters, images, and sounds.

Altman graduated from commercial short films to features in 1957 with the film *The Delinquents*. But his film career languished for more than a decade as he directed television and unsuccessful features until he agreed to direct a film called *M*A*S*H* (1970). At age forty-five, Altman took on the antiwar black comedy set during the Korean War after more than fifteen other directors had passed on the project.

M*A*S*H tapped into Vietnam-era disillusionment and Hollywood's more liberal attitudes toward sex and violence to reinvent the war genre. Altman's overlapping, blurred sound and long takes would become trademarks of his idiosyncratic style.

He continued his genre-redefining work as the 1970s continued. In *McCabe & Mrs. Miller* (1971), which the critic Roger Ebert has called "a perfect film," Altman rejected the glamour of previous westerns, showing the grit and grime of the turn-of-the-century West. In *The Long Goodbye* (1973), he took on film noir, making his detective character goofy and lost rather than tough and hard-boiled.

Nashville (1975), which is arguably Altman's masterpiece, features improvised, overlapping dialogue, long takes, and an experimental narrative in which the focus is not on one protagonist but on a collection of twenty-four characters who are examined over a five-day period. The film is a tapestry of American society as it embarked on the post-Watergate, post-Vietnam era.

Altman struggled through the 1980s without a successful film, but he returned to form with his scathing satire of Hollywood, *The Player* (1992). A year later, he directed *Short Cuts* (1993), an adaptation of several Raymond Carver stories.

Altman earned his fifth and final Academy Award nomination for best director for *Gosford Park* (2001), though his only career Oscar was an honorary statue he received in 2006. He died later that year of leukemia at age eighty-one.

ADDITIONAL FACTS

1. *Though Altman never won a competitive Academy Award, he was successful at the Cannes Film Festival, where M*A*S*H won Best Picture honors in 1970 and he was named best director for* The Player *in 1992.*

2. *When he received his honorary Oscar in 2006, Altman revealed that he had received a heart transplant in the mid-1990s and had kept it a secret so that he could continue to get work.*

3. M*A*S*H, *which was set during the Korean War, spawned the popular television series.*

•••••

The Generation of '68

The year 1968 marked the peak of a student protest movement that crossed international boundaries and symbolized a growing disillusionment among members of the baby boomer generation. That year, massive demonstrations were staged in cities including Paris, Prague, Chicago, and New York City, attracting thousands of angry young people to the streets.

Although the circumstances in each country differed dramatically, the common factors were the youth of the protestors and their determination to challenge what they regarded as authoritarian, unfair, and outdated rules.

In New York, students at Columbia University launched sit-ins and a takeover of university buildings to protest the school's collaboration with the military during the Vietnam War. They were also upset by plans to expand the university's campus into poor neighborhoods in Harlem; the plans were eventually scrapped as a result of the protest.

In Chicago, antiwar demonstrators clashed with police on the streets outside the Democratic National Convention to protest the nomination of the pro-war candidate Hubert Humphrey (1911–1978).

In Paris, students launched protests against censorship on campuses, prohibitions on coed dormitories, and limited employment prospects after graduation. Labor unions eventually joined the demonstrations, which paralyzed France for weeks.

In Prague, students formed the bedrock of support for Alexander Dubček (1921–1992), who attempted to liberalize the country, to the displeasure of the Soviet Union. In one famous incident in 1969, student Jan Palach (1948–1969) set himself on fire in protest, symbolizing the frustrations of Czechoslovakian students, whose government had even banned rock-and-roll music as "subversive."

In Mexico City, a protest ended tragically when between 200 and 300 students were killed by police on October 2, 1968.

The demonstrations fed off of a sense of alienation and unrest among baby boomers—a trend that crossed global lines. Although the protests had mixed results, they became a badge of generational identity and were later seen as the first signs of a major cultural shift away from the values of the World War II generation.

ADDITIONAL FACTS

1. *Protests also broke out in Pakistan, Italy, and other countries.*

2. *French president Charles de Gaulle (1890–1970) was one of the targets of the Paris protests; the World War II military hero was portrayed as the out-of-touch embodiment of conservative France.*

3. *The Unbearable Lightness of Being, a 1984 novel by the Czech writer Milan Kundera (1929–), which was later made into a film staring Daniel Day-Lewis (1957–), takes place during the Prague Spring. The film includes real archival footage of Soviet tanks rolling through Old Town Square.*

•• • ••

The Battle of the Sexes

What began as a publicity stunt by two tennis stars in 1973 unexpectedly turned into an important cultural moment in the history of American women's sports.

At the time, women's sports were struggling for public acceptance. The women's professional tennis tour was just three years into its existence. Title IX, the federal legislation barring discrimination on the basis of sex—which would eventually have a profound impact on girls' and women's athletics in schools and colleges—had been enacted only a year before.

Into this environment stepped twenty-nine-year-old Billie Jean King (1943–), one of the era's top players. King was an outspoken champion of women's rights and had helped found the women's tennis tour. By September 1973, she had won ten Grand Slam singles titles, including Wimbledon five times.

She would go on to win thirty-nine Grand Slam titles—singles, doubles, and mixed doubles—but her most memorable victory came over a fifty-five-year-old, self-proclaimed "male chauvinist pig" named Bobby Riggs (1918–1995).

Riggs, the 1939 Wimbledon champion, had already defeated Margaret Court (1942–), the top women's player in the world, in an exhibition match on Mother's Day 1973.

After Riggs defeated Court, King believed she had no choice but to take him on in order to defend the honor of her gender. They agreed to a $100,000, winner-take-all match to take place at the Astrodome, a giant domed stadium in Houston.

Said King, "I thought it would set us back fifty years if I didn't win that match. It would ruin the women's tour and affect all women's self-esteem."

King was carried onto the court like Cleopatra by four muscular men. Riggs was wheeled in on a chariot by scantily clad models dubbed Bobby's Bosom Buddies.

A crowd of 30,492 at the Astrodome—the largest ever to see a tennis match—and a worldwide television audience estimated at 50 million saw King run Riggs ragged to claim a 6–4, 6–3, 6–3 victory.

Even though her win came over a middle-aged man, it still gave public credibility to women's tennis, and the overwhelming interest in the match brought an enormous new audience to the sport.

ADDITIONAL FACTS

1. *King's celebrated status in American tennis culminated on August 28, 2006, when the United States Tennis Association (USTA) National Tennis Center in Flushing Meadows, New York—the site of the US Open—was rededicated as the USTA Billie Jean King National Tennis Center.*

2. *Riggs and King became close friends after their Battle of the Sexes, and King spoke to Riggs on the telephone the night before he died of cancer in 1995.*

3. *King's brother, Randy Moffitt (1948–), was a major-league baseball pitcher, primarily for the San Francisco Giants.*

•••••

Pong

Before there was *Halo 3, Tiger Woods PGA Tour,* or *Super Mario Brothers,* there was *Pong.*

Regarded as the first legitimate arcade video game to achieve widespread popularity, *Pong* was created by Atari, a California computer company, in November 1972. The game is a rudimentary electronic version of table tennis in which players hit a ball back and forth between two paddles on opposite sides of a court. Much like in tennis, the object is to hit the ball past your opponent.

To test its viability, Atari installed the first arcade version of *Pong* at a local bar called Andy Capp's in Sunnyvale, California, near the Atari headquarters. According to *Zap! The Rise and Fall of Atari,* by Scott Cohen (1946–), the game was literally an overnight sensation, and by 10 a.m. the following day, customers were lining up outside the bar to play. One day later, the game was broken because the milk carton that had been placed inside to catch quarters had overflowed and jammed the machine.

Atari went on to sell approximately 38,000 coin-operated *Pong* machines.

Pong spawned a number of different versions, including *Pong Doubles, Quadrapong, Super Pong,* and *Doctor Pong.* However, none of the offshoots achieved the popularity of the 1976 version called *Breakout.* A one-player game in which the object is to hit the ball against a wall and eliminate as many bricks as possible, *Breakout* eventually was updated to the game *Arkanoid* in the 1980s.

By the early 1980s, however, *Pong* had been surpassed by more sophisticated video games such as *Pac-Man.* But *Pong* is still available for nostalgia buffs on most modern computer operating systems.

ADDITIONAL FACTS

1. *Tennis star Andy Roddick (1982–) appeared in an American Express commercial in 2006 in which he is playing against a* Pong-*like opponent.*

2. *Frank Black (1965–), lead singer for the Pixies, wrote a song for his album* Teenager of the Year *(1994) entitled "Whatever Happened to Pong?" an ode to* Pong *competition in bars across the United States.*

3. *To produce* Pong *games on a large scale, Atari rented an abandoned roller rink and hired Sunnyvale locals to build consoles.*

•••••

Tom Wolfe

Tom Wolfe (1930–) is widely considered the father of New Journalism, a literary style that emerged in the 1960s in an effort to liberate nonfiction writing from older conventions of journalistic prose. Though its foundation is still reportage, this style is considered to have more in common with fiction writing than with classic newspaper reporting.

Wolfe's style tends to include realistic dialogue, first-person accounts of experiences, and unconventional use of exclamation points, repetition, and italics. His most celebrated examples are two nonfiction books, *The Electric Kool-Aid Acid Test*, published in 1968, and *The Right Stuff*, published in 1979.

Wolfe ushered in this new era with an article about cars published in *Esquire* magazine in 1965 entitled "The Kandy-Kolored Tangerine-Flake Streamline Baby." The article was originally a letter that Wolfe had written to his editor, Byron Dobell, stringing together all of Wolfe's notes and thoughts for the article. Dobell was so struck by the letter that he removed the words "Dear Byron" and published the rest of it. The story later provided the title for a collection of Wolfe's magazine stories.

In 1968, Wolfe published both *The Electric Kool-Aid Acid Test*, a book about LSD and hippies that some view as one of the definitive accounts of the 1960s, and *The Pump House Gang*, a collection of articles. Both went on to become bestsellers.

The Right Stuff, his chronicle of rocket airplane experiments after World War II and the early days of the US space program, achieved significant critical and commercial success. The book earned Wolfe several honors, including the American Book Award for nonfiction, and was adapted into a successful Hollywood film, released in 1983, that won four Academy Awards.

He has since written three best-selling novels: *The Bonfire of the Vanities* (which was released in serial form in *Rolling Stone* magazine beginning in 1984), *A Man in Full* (1998), and *I Am Charlotte Simmons* (2004).

A Man in Full received poor reviews from three giants of American fiction, John Irving (1942–), Norman Mailer (1923–2007), and John Updike (1932–), and Wolfe returned the criticism, referring to them as "three stooges."

ADDITIONAL FACTS

1. *One of Wolfe's trademarks is his attire—he is almost always seen wearing a cream-colored suit, a bold tie-and-pocket-square combination, and old-fashioned shoes.*

2. *Wolfe was born in Virginia and began his writing career as a newspaper reporter, with stints at the* Springfield (Massachusetts) Union, Washington Post, *and* New York Herald Tribune.

3. *Other writers considered part of the New Journalism movement include Mailer, Hunter S. Thompson (1937–2005), Gay Talese (1932–), Joan Didion (1934–), and Truman Capote (1924–1984).*

•••••

Maya Angelou

A poet, memoirist, orator, and teacher for much of the past half century, Maya Angelou is one of the most recognizable faces of contemporary American literature. Her powerful reflections on her struggles with childhood trauma, poverty, and racial discrimination have inspired and empowered countless readers of her works.

Born in Missouri in 1928, Angelou was sent, upon her parents' divorce, to live with her grandmother in rural Arkansas. At age eight, she was raped by her mother's boyfriend and was further scarred when her public admission of the incident resulted in the rapist's death at the hands of a lynch mob. In the years following, Angelou's life remained unstable: She lived in San Francisco with her mother, then endured a period of homelessness in Los Angeles, gave birth to a child out of wedlock at age sixteen, and finally ended up in New York City.

By the early 1960s, Angelou had begun to write, supported by the nonprofit Harlem Writers' Guild. At the end of that decade, her first major work, *I Know Why the Caged Bird Sings* (1970), appeared. This autobiographical novel chronicles Angelou's early years, from her childhood in Arkansas to her time spent in Los Angeles as a young teen. The memoir was hailed as a surging testament to female and black empowerment and established Angelou as a major literary voice.

Over the next two decades, Angelou produced several more volumes of her memoir, continuing where she left off. She also began to write significant amounts of poetry—including the collections *Just Give Me a Cool Drink of Water 'fore I Diiie* (1971) and *And Still I Rise* (1978). Her notable later poems include "On the Pulse of Morning," which she delivered at the presidential inauguration of Bill Clinton (1946–) in 1993.

ADDITIONAL FACTS

1. *Angelou speaks at least six languages and has traveled extensively throughout her career, including extended periods when she lived in Egypt and Ghana.*

2. *Angelou's name is frequently mispronounced with an oo sound at the end, when in fact her name ends with a long o, as if it were spelled "Angelo."*

3. *Some critics faulted Angelou for "selling out" when she signed a contract with Hallmark in 2002 to write greeting cards. She countered, "[M]y work should be in the people's hands. There are many people who will never buy a book, but who would buy a card."*

•••••

Miles Davis and Fusion Jazz

The trumpeter and composer Miles Davis (1926–1991) played a major role in almost every phase of jazz's history. He was an early performer of bebop, as well as its slower cousin, cool jazz. His 1959 record *Kind of Blue* is considered a classic of modal jazz, and his 1982 album *We Want Miles* even includes rap lyrics. But perhaps Davis's most lasting contribution was his decision to go electric, creating a new style known as jazz fusion.

In 1967, Davis recorded "Circle in the Round," his first song to include a prominent electric guitar, and it was a sign of things to come. In the years that followed, Davis was introduced to Jimi Hendrix (1942–1970), and Hendrix's music, along with that of Sly Stone (1943–) and James Brown (1933–2006), became a major influence. By 1969, Davis was working almost exclusively with electric guitars, electric organs, and the pedals and devices that had become such a big part of rock music.

The first major work to come out of this period was *In a Silent Way* (1969), a mysterious and quiet album that lives up to its title. Rather than a live recording, like most of Davis's previous jazz records, the album was largely constructed in the studio and owes almost as much to producer Teo Macero (1925–2008) as it does to the musicians who played on it.

The most famous work from this period is *Bitches Brew,* from 1969. Largely owing to the performance of the guitarist John McLaughlin (1942–), the record was as much of a hit with rock audiences as with jazz aficionados.

The last major album from this era is 1972's *On the Corner,* which incorporates funk influences just as the earlier albums had incorporated rock. After this record, Davis began to focus on live performance. Unfortunately, his heroin addiction grew worse in this period and in 1975, Davis took a five-year break from performing while the fusion style he pioneered moved into the musical mainstream.

ADDITIONAL FACTS

1. *Davis made his debt to rock and roll explicit by opening for acts such as the Grateful Dead and Carlos Santana (1947–).*

2. *A Tribute to Jack Johnson was not the only sound track that Davis recorded. In 1957, he provided the sound track for the first film by the French director Louis Malle (1932–1995),* Ascenseur pour l'échafaud *(Elevator to the Gallows).*

3. *When guitarist McLaughlin played his famous solo for* In a Silent Way, *he thought he was only doing a rehearsal take. He was shocked to hear it on the final album.*

•••••

2001: A Space Odyssey (1968)

When most people think about science-fiction movies, they picture a strong narrative featuring good guys, bad guys, aliens, ray guns, explosions, and fighter planes. Stanley Kubrick's *2001: A Space Odyssey,* which many fans consider the greatest science-fiction film of all time, has none of these.

Director Kubrick (1928–1999) set out to make a film that would break the rules of narrative cinema, presenting human history from the beginning of man into the near future—and, in the process, exploring the vastness of space. Kubrick presents the film with relatively little dialogue, a classical music sound track, and ground-breaking special effects, for which the effects pioneer Douglas Trumbull (1942–) was largely responsible.

Many films—not just those in the science-fiction genre—owe a debt to *2001,* from George Lucas's *Star Wars* (1977) to Martin Scorsese's *Gangs of New York* (2002).

Kubrick was inspired by the writings of Arthur C. Clarke (1917–2008), particularly his 1948 short story "The Sentinel." The two collaborated on the film's script, but the brilliance of *2001* is in its visual imagery and its use of music and sound.

The film breaks with narrative form in several ways, particularly in its use—or lack—of dialogue. It is divided into four acts (which is also unusual), and there is no dialogue in the first and fourth acts. Words are not uttered for the first twenty-five minutes of the film. And when there is dialogue, most of it seems to serve no narrative purpose—it does not advance the "story" but is a realistic portrayal of what people in various situations would say.

Because of the lack of dialogue and the often slow-moving shots in space, may critics and viewers found the film boring and confusing; they were expecting a classic Hollywood story, which Kubrick never intended the film to be.

Other critics saw the film for what it was: a landmark in special effects wizardry with an open-ended narrative that leaves interpretations of human history and of the vastness of space up to the individual viewer. As the critic Roger Ebert (1942–) writes, *2001* "is not concerned with thrilling us, but with inspiring our awe."

ADDITIONAL FACTS

1. *The film's most memorable character is actually a supercomputer, HAL 9000, who is considered a member of a spaceship crew. HAL signals a future in which technology is so powerful that it's capable of destroying its human creators.*

2. *Kubrick originally commissioned a musical score but ended up using classical music that was not written for the film. The piece of music most associated with the film is Richard Strauss's* Also Sprach Zarathustra, *which plays behind a lunar eclipse early in the film.*

3. *There are fewer than 40 minutes of dialogue in the film, which runs 141 minutes. The original cut ran 160 minutes, but Kubrick trimmed 19 minutes after the premiere screening when viewers complained that it was too long.*

•••••

Coeducation

Beginning in the 1960s, many universities began admitting both male and female students, instantly making college far more compelling for millions of Americans. Known as coeducation, the switch was largely complete by 1980; today, only a handful of institutions of higher education enroll only men or only women.

Many private schools, especially those in the top tier of American universities, were traditionally limited to men. Critics charged that by turning away females, elite colleges were perpetuating an "old boys' club" that kept women out of the halls of power.

Under pressure, Yale began admitting women in 1969. Dartmouth followed in 1972.

The transition also affected many all-women's schools. Vassar began accepting men in 1969, and Radcliffe was absorbed by neighboring Harvard beginning in the 1970s after Harvard started accepting women.

In general, proponents of coeducation argued that mixing the sexes would lead to a better educational environment for everyone. The student newspaper at Princeton, for instance, argued in 1965 that admitting women "is the solution for Princeton's illness. . . . There is good reason to believe that the development of a young man's mind is not only not impeded but is enhanced by normal contact with women."

However, some schools, especially traditionally all-women's schools such as Wellesley and Smith, resisted coeducation, claiming that an environment free of men helped some women educationally. In 2007, fifty-four all-women colleges remained in operation, although the number continues to shrink.

ADDITIONAL FACTS

1. *The military academies went coed in 1976.*

2. *Columbia was the last Ivy League university to go coed, in 1983.*

3. *Only a handful of all-men's colleges remain, including Hampden-Sydney College in Virginia and Wabash College in Indiana.*

•••••

The Thrilla in Manila

Joe Frazier and Muhammad Ali

The third and final bout between the boxers Muhammad Ali (1942–) and Joe Frazier (1944–) was terrifying in its brutality, inspiring in the courage and will shown by its two combatants, and a sad harbinger of Ali's eventual decline into ill health.

The two men had split their first two fights, in 1971 and 1974. Entering their third match on October 1, 1975, the conventional wisdom was that Ali, the champion, would have little trouble with Frazier, whom many considered to be past his prime.

Nobody believed the conventional wisdom more than Ali, who was overconfident and undertrained for the fight. Frazier, meanwhile, was driven by Ali's public taunts—among other epithets, Ali had called Frazier "ugly," "ignorant," "a gorilla," and an "Uncle Tom" since their first fight in 1971.

When their final matchup began, 28,000 fans had filled Araneta Coliseum in Quezon City, Philippines. It would turn into a bout in three acts. In Act I, Ali outboxed and outscored Frazier in the first four rounds, battering the former champion with powerful jabs. But beginning in the fifth round, Frazier—who fought with a relentless style that punished Ali with body blows—began to take control.

By the seventh round, Ali is reported to have said, "Joe, they told me you was all washed up." Frazier replied, "They lied." Frazier later said, "Man, I hit him with punches that'd bring down the walls of a city."

But Ali withstood Frazier's onslaught and somehow summoned the energy to muster a comeback in the middle of the tenth round. In the eleventh, Ali's barrage of shots to the head caused both of Frazier's eyes to swell nearly shut. By the fourteenth round, both men were exhausted, but Ali held the advantage—Frazier was essentially blind. Frazier's trainer, Eddie Futch (1911–2001), finally stopped the fight after that round. When his fighter protested, Futch told him, "No one will forget what you did here today."

After the fight, a battered and exhausted Ali ominously said, "It was like death. Closest thing to dying that I know of."

ADDITIONAL FACTS

1. *Said Ali later, "We went to Manila as champions, Joe and me, and we came back as old men."*

2. *Frazier would fight only twice more. He lost one bout and earned a draw in the other.*

3. *Ali would fight until 1981, losing the heavyweight title to Leon Spinks (1953–) in 1978, winning it back from Spinks later that year, then surrendering it for the final time to Larry Holmes (1949–) in 1980. But many believe that Ali was never the same after his third bout with Frazier.*

•••••

Free to Be . . . You and Me

Many children raised in the 1960s and 1970s, especially those from liberal-minded families, grew up humming the tunes of *Free to Be . . . You and Me,* a 1972 children's album that aimed to challenge gender stereotypes. Steeped in the feminist movement, the record imbued children with the notion that they could be whatever they wanted to be, regardless of whether they were born a boy or a girl.

Marlo Thomas (1937–), an actress, spearheaded the *Free to Be . . . You and Me* project in order to teach her young niece, Dionne, about individuality and self-confidence. Other participants included actor Alan Alda (1936–), actress Carol Channing (1921–), and singer Harry Belafonte (1927–).

In the song "Parents Are People," Thomas and Belafonte tell kids that mommies can be doctors and daddies can be bakers. In another sketch, director Mel Brooks (1926–) and Thomas give voice to newborn babies in a hospital nursery who are going through the gender stereotypes to figure out which one of them is a boy and which is a girl. Former New York Giants defensive tackle Rosey Grier (1932–) challenges the tough-guy image in his ballad "It's Alright to Cry." And in "William's Doll," Alda and Thomas tell the story of young William, a boy who yearns for a doll to love despite his friends' teasing him and urging him to play with balls and bats.

The album was a huge hit and became a cult classic. In 1974, *Free to Be . . . You and Me* was made into a successful television special.

ADDITIONAL FACTS

1. *The original proceeds from the* Free to Be . . . You and Me *album went to the Ms. Foundation for Women.*

2. *The feminist author Gloria Steinem (1934–) contributed to the record's liner notes.*

3. *Celebrities featured on the album and the TV special included Michael Jackson (1958–), Kris Kristofferson (1936–), Dionne Warwick (1940–), and Roberta Flack (1939–).*

•••••

Bruce Springsteen

One of the best-selling singer-songwriters in music history, Bruce Springsteen (1949–) has cultivated a devoted international fan base through his introspective yet accessible songs about the struggles and triumphs of working-class life, and through his marathon concert performances with the E Street Band.

Signed in 1972 by the legendary Columbia Records executive John Hammond (1910–1987), Springsteen was quickly marketed as a "new Dylan" because of his kaleidoscopic lyrics and folk-rock sound, which reminded some listeners of another Hammond discovery, Bob Dylan (1941–).

Springsteen's first two albums, both released in 1973, offered hints of the Dylan sound, and neither was a commercial success. But with the release of *Born to Run* (1975), Springsteen emerged with a unique style and, in the eyes of many critics, saved rock music from the self-indulgent era of disco and glam.

Born to Run changed Springsteen's life and career forever. He delivered on the enormous hype Columbia had created before the album's release and managed to translate the intensity of his live performances to the studio. The result was a record that many critics cite as one of the greatest in rock-and-roll history and that landed him on the covers of *Time* and *Newsweek* simultaneously in October 1975.

Since *Born to Run,* Springsteen has recorded albums alternating between a classic rock sound with the E Street Band—from *Darkness on the Edge of Town* (1978) to *Magic* (2007)—and more folk-inspired songs, either solo or with other musicians—from *Nebraska* (1982) to *We Shall Overcome: The Seeger Sessions* (2006).

He is perhaps best known to mainstream audiences for *Born in the U.S.A.* (1984), his massive hit album that spawned seven top-ten songs and sold 15 million copies. The record made him one of the touchstone cultural icons of the 1980s.

Springsteen was also one of the first major artists to address the September 11, 2001, terrorist attacks with his critically and commercially successful album *The Rising* (2002).

ADDITIONAL FACTS

1. *Springsteen has won fifteen Grammy Awards and picked up an Academy Award for Best Original Song for "Streets of Philadelphia," from the movie* Philadelphia *(1993). He has sold more than 60 million albums and was inducted into the Rock and Roll Hall of Fame in 1999.*

2. *The anthemic title track of* Born in the U.S.A., *which focused on the shattered dreams of Americans in the post-Vietnam era, was—and still is—widely misinterpreted as a song of patriotism, most famously by President Ronald Reagan (1911–2004).*

3. *Springsteen has never had a number one hit on the pop charts. His highest chart climber was "Dancing in the Dark," which reached number two in 1984.*

•••••

Philip Roth

For the past four decades, Philip Roth has been both a major figure in American fiction and—along with Norman Mailer (1923–2007), Saul Bellow (1915–2005), and others—one of the standard-bearers of modern Jewish-American literature. His novels, often partly autobiographical in nature, balance bawdy comedy with weighty inquiry into issues of cultural and personal identity.

Born in 1933, Roth grew up in a predominantly Jewish, middle-class community in Newark, New Jersey. This community has served as the setting, or at least the inspiration, for many of his works—a specificity that has sharpened Roth's eye for detail over the years but also opened him to criticism that he is a "narrowly focused" writer.

Roth first established his name with *Goodbye, Columbus* (1959), a short-story collection that explores what would become a perennial theme for him: the struggle of American Jews to reconcile their upbringings with the cultural, social, and sexual demands of mainstream American life. Although *Goodbye, Columbus* won acclaim, it was not until ten years later, with *Portnoy's Complaint* (1969), that Roth cemented his reputation. This comic novel concerns a young Jewish man from New Jersey who, with the help of his therapist, struggles with sexual guilt and his relationship with his overbearing mother. Although much of its subject matter has since become archetypal, *Portnoy's Complaint* broke substantial new ground at the time. Its racy, explicit content—a series of monologues delivered from a therapist's couch—led many people to label it obscene.

Roth has continued to churn out notable novels, from *Zuckerman Bound* (1985) to *American Pastoral* (1997) to *The Human Stain* (2000). Though some critics dismiss him as misogynist and sexually obsessed, many regard him as the foremost American novelist writing today. Indeed, the tensions that he explores in the context of the Jewish community—between tradition and modernity, identity and assimilation, parents and children—are, arguably, universal.

ADDITIONAL FACTS

1. *Roth often uses recurring characters who appear as either narrators or observers in multiple novels. One such character, Nathan Zuckerman, has appeared in nine of Roth's works to date.*

2. *Perhaps Roth's most outlandish novel,* The Breast *(1972), concerns a man who awakens one day to discover that he has turned into a giant female breast.*

3. *In recent years, Roth has tackled more-serious political topics in his novels, from the rise of terrorism to American Jews' relationship with Israel.*

•••••

Led Zeppelin

Like many great rock-and-roll bands of the 1960s, the British group Led Zeppelin found its inspiration in American blues music. But its sound was much harder and heavier than that of other groups such as the Rolling Stones, who drew on the same set of influences.

Led Zeppelin was a four-piece group: guitarist Jimmy Page (1944–), singer Robert Plant (1948–), bassist John Paul Jones (1946–), and drummer John Bonham (1948–1980). When the group released its self-titled debut album in 1969, the blues influence was apparent in songs like "You Shook Me" and "I Can't Quit You Baby." But Led Zeppelin turned the volume up louder than anybody had before, earning the group its reputation as one of the first heavy-metal bands.

Despite the lack of a hit single, the group's debut album was a success. Its second album, *Led Zeppelin II* (1969), reached number one in both the United Kingdom and the United States. The influences on the group's second album were somewhat broader than the first, this time including references to Celtic myths and fantasy novels. *Led Zeppelin III* (1970) contained powerful numbers such as "Immigrant Song," but also quieter acoustic tracks like "Bron-Y-Aur Stomp."

Annoyed by accusations that they were all hype, the band members released their next album in 1971 with no title and no mention of the group's name, only four meaningless symbols. This did nothing to harm sales, and one track on the album— "Stairway to Heaven"—is considered by many fans to be the group's signature song.

Led Zeppelin would continue to record hit albums through the end of the decade with *Houses of the Holy* (1973), *Physical Graffiti* (1975), and *In Through the Out Door* (1979). But Led Zeppelin came to an abrupt and tragic end. In 1980, drummer Bonham died at the age of thirty-two after a day of heavy drinking, and the remaining members immediately disbanded. The group has reunited for benefit concerts several times since then, often with Bonham's son, Jason (1966–), on drums.

ADDITIONAL FACTS

1. *The 1984 mockumentary* This Is Spinal Tap *is largely a spoof of Led Zeppelin.*

2. *The use of the flaming airship* Hindenburg *on the cover of the band's first album almost resulted in legal action from Eva von Zeppelin, a relative of the aircraft's creator.*

3. *Led Zeppelin released the concert film* The Song Remains the Same *in 1976 and a two-DVD set of live performances in 2003.*

•• • ••

Clint Eastwood

Clint Eastwood (1930–) has fashioned a remarkable career in which he has evolved from a tough-guy television star and Hollywood outsider to a film legend as actor, director, and producer of both war movies and emotional dramas.

From 1959 to 1965, Eastwood played Rowdy Yates on the television western *Rawhide,* one of the most popular series of the era. Despite his TV success, Eastwood found that Hollywood producers did not believe a television actor could make the transition to serious films.

Avoiding Hollywood, Eastwood joined Italian director Sergio Leone (1929–1989) to make a series of what would become known as spaghetti westerns—films set in the American West but shot in Italy. The first, *A Fistful of Dollars* (1964), debuted Eastwood's steely-eyed, laconic character, popularly known as the Man with No Name. The role helped make Eastwood what he so desired to be: a film star.

He made two more such films with Leone, *For a Few Dollars More* (1965) and *The Good, the Bad and the Ugly* (1966), which many critics consider a masterpiece.

The year 1971 was an important one for Eastwood. He directed his first film, *Play Misty for Me,* and created another iconic film role as the title character in *Dirty Harry.* Directed by Don Siegel (1912–1991), one of Eastwood's mentors, *Dirty Harry* is something of an outgrowth of Leone's films, changing the detached antihero gunslinger into the detached antihero rogue cop.

Eastwood starred in most of the films he directed in the 1980s, with the noteworthy exception of *Bird* (1988), his acclaimed biopic of the legendary jazz saxophonist Charlie Parker (1920–1955), which starred Forest Whitaker (1961–) in the title role.

As he has matured, Eastwood has developed an increasingly spare directing style that critics and audiences have found deeply emotional and affecting. In this vein, he achieved his first major success with *Unforgiven* (1992), a return to the western genre that won four Academy Awards, including Best Picture and Best Director (Eastwood's first two Oscars).

During this decade, Eastwood has cemented his reputation as one of his generation's major directors with *Mystic River* (2003), *Million Dollar Baby* (2004), and the World War II dramas *Flags of Our Fathers* (2006) and *Letters from Iwo Jima* (2006). Like *Unforgiven, Million Dollar Baby* earned Eastwood Oscars for best director and best picture.

ADDITIONAL FACTS

1. *In 1986, Eastwood was elected mayor of Carmel-by-the-Sea, California. He served for two years and still managed to make two films,* Heartbreak Ridge *(1986) and* Bird, *during his term in office.*

2. Dirty Harry, *which the critic Tim Dirks calls "the seminal vigilante film of the decade," inspired an array of imitators—as well as four sequels with Eastwood.*

3. *Eastwood received the Irving G. Thalberg Memorial Award at the Academy Awards in 1995, and the American Film Institute gave him its Life Achievement Award in 1996.*

••••

Busing

In an effort to achieve racial balance in public schools, beginning in the early 1970s federal courts ordered many school districts to bus black children to schools in white neighborhoods and vice versa. *Busing,* as the policy was known, sparked strident opposition and even riots in some cities, particularly Boston. Always controversial, busing had mixed results and has largely been abandoned.

Busing emerged from a series of Supreme Court decisions in the 1950s and 1960s that required racial desegregation in schools. The most important of the cases, *Brown v. Board of Education* in 1954, made it illegal for school districts to assign blacks and whites to separate schools.

However, civil rights advocates argued that *Brown* didn't go far enough to ensure an equal education. Merely outlawing segregation, they said, wouldn't provide a racially balanced school. Since school assignments were based on geography and city neighborhoods were often segregated, even a city with no official policy of racial discrimination could end up with de facto segregation in its schools. And without access to the same schools as white children, busing advocates argued, blacks would inevitably receive an inferior education, since schools in white neighborhoods tended to be richer.

The first busing order was issued in Charlotte, North Carolina, in 1969. Tens of thousands of white parents signed a petition protesting the mandate, and the case quickly went to the Supreme Court. In 1971, the court upheld the order, a ruling that opened the door to busing orders in other cities. The same year, busing began in Richmond, Virginia. It was ordered in Indianapolis, Indiana, in 1981. Dozens of other cities were also tasked with creating racially balanced schools.

But it was the busing drama in Boston that captured the nation's attention. In 1974, a federal judge determined that the city's schools had an impermissible pattern of racial segregation and mandated busing as a solution. Parents were livid; in one protest, a white protestor famously tried to impale a black attorney with a flagpole.

Schools began abandoning busing in the 1990s. Then, in 2007, the Supreme Court made it illegal to reference race in school assignments to achieve racial balance except in an attempt to redress past discrimination, a ruling that has prevented some school districts from pursuing cases to fix "accidental" racial segregation. Critics charge that the Court is allowing segregation to return.

ADDITIONAL FACTS

1. *A photographer in Boston, Stanley Forman (1945–), won a Pulitzer Prize for his pictures of a violent antibusing rally at Boston City Hall in 1976.*

2. *Busing ended in Charlotte in 2001 after a judge ordered an end to the thirty-year program. Boston dropped its busing program in 2000.*

3. *According to USA Today, about 43 percent of white public school students in the United States attend schools that are more than 90 percent white.*

··●●··

Dale Earnhardt

The man known as the Intimidator and Ironhead died doing what he was best known for—aggressive, fearless driving. On the final turn of the 2001 Daytona 500 NASCAR race, Dale Earnhardt (1951–2001) made a gutsy passing attempt and collided with another car before crashing head-on into the wall at 160 miles per hour.

Because of his reputation as a tough competitor, few believed that Earnhardt wouldn't be racing again a week later. But just hours after the crash, he was pronounced dead of a fractured skull.

It was a stunning end to a marvelous career. Earnhardt compiled seventy-six NASCAR victories and won the Winston Cup crown seven times, tying Richard Petty (1937–) for the most championships. Driving his trademark number 3 Chevrolet Monte Carlo for most of his career, he accumulated more than $41 million in career earnings for his racing victories and helped turn stock car racing from a regional sport into a national entertainment powerhouse.

In addition to his achievements on the track, he also was a successful owner with his Dale Earnhardt Inc. racing team. In the race in which he was killed, two of his drivers finished first and second: Michael Waltrip (1963–) won, while Dale Earnhardt Jr. (1974–) placed second.

The elder Earnhardt was also immensely popular, which allowed him, by the late 1990s, to earn an estimated $40 million annually through endorsement and memorabilia deals in addition to race purses. After Earnhardt's death, President George W. Bush (1946–) called him "a national icon," and Earnhardt's fans exhibited numerous tributes—including holding up three fingers on the third lap of every NASCAR race.

His most memorable victory came at the 1998 Daytona 500. Though he had won more races than anyone else on the Daytona International Speedway, he had never won NASCAR's Super Bowl. But on his twentieth attempt, he finally claimed victory, ending a fifty-nine-race winless streak.

ADDITIONAL FACTS

1. *Earnhardt is the only driver to be named NASCAR's Rookie of the Year (1979) and take home the Winston Cup title (1980) in successive years.*

2. *In the first race at Daytona after Earnhardt's death, his son won the Pepsi 400. Earnhardt Jr. would later claim a victory in the Daytona 500 in 2004, six years to the day after his father won in 1998.*

3. *Earnhardt's best season was 1987, when he won eleven races and had twenty-one top-five finishes in twenty-nine starts. His prize money that year totaled more than $2 million.*

•••••

Richard Pryor

Richard Pryor (1940–2005) was a trailblazing African-American comedian whose direct commentary on racism and other societal ills—along with his vulgarity and explicit drug humor—made him one of the most popular stand-up comics of his day.

Pryor was born in Peoria, Illinois, the son of a prostitute and a pimp. He was raped by a neighbor at the age of six, molested by a Catholic priest a few years later, abandoned by his mother at ten, and expelled from school at fourteen.

Very early in his life, Pryor learned to cope with hardship by turning to comedy. He performed his first "routine" in a production of *Rumpelstiltskin* at the age of twelve. Inspired by the example of Bill Cosby (1937–), one of the first successful mainstream African-American comedians, Pryor moved to New York City in 1963 and quickly established himself as a major presence. A few years after starting out, he was making appearances on major television programs such as the *Ed Sullivan Show*. He appeared in his first film—*The Busy Body*—in 1967.

In the 1970s, his act became much more controversial, departing from Cosby's unthreatening fare. Pryor spoke openly about racial tensions in the United States, used profanity and discussed such taboo topics as his cocaine abuse, once claiming that he had, in effect, "snorted Peru" at the height of his addiction. (He once reportedly set himself on fire while free-basing cocaine.) Pryor continued to work in this vein for many years, releasing widely praised records and films of his routines and starring in a number of movies.

In 1986, however, Pryor was diagnosed with multiple sclerosis. He continued to perform for a few years thereafter but was soon forced to retire. He died at age sixty-five.

ADDITIONAL FACTS

1. *After an inspirational trip to Kenya in 1979, Pryor never again used the word "nigger."*

2. *Pryor cowrote the 1974 film* Blazing Saddles *with Mel Brooks (1926–).*

3. *In 1997, Pryor made a cameo appearance in the David Lynch (1946–) film* Lost Highway, *though he was confined to a wheelchair and severely debilitated by his illness by that time.*

•••••

Mikhail Gorbachev

In his quest to revitalize and reform the basic foundations of the ailing Soviet Union, Mikhail Gorbachev (1931–) instead presided over the country's death in 1991 when his belief that glasnost (openness) and perestroika (restructuring) would invigorate and modernize the communist system turned out to be false.

When Gorbachev took over as general secretary of the Soviet Communist Party in 1985, the USSR was already in steady decline and facing economic stagnation. He believed that through greater government efficiency and more democracy, the country could overcome its problems.

Through glasnost, he gave Soviets more freedom of speech and relaxed restrictions on the press. Through perestroika, he began a slow transition toward a market economy, allowing private ownership of small businesses, profitability in industries, and fewer centralized government controls over the economy.

But his reforms did not revitalize the country and instead resulted in unintended consequences. Soviet hardliners criticized him for being too liberal, while liberals used their new freedoms to argue that his reforms did not go far enough.

Meanwhile, on the international front, Gorbachev pushed for a halt to the arms race with the United States and announced the end of the Soviet Union's war with Afghanistan in 1988. Also that year, he declared that other Eastern bloc countries would be allowed to decide their own political futures. That decision subsequently led to the collapse of communist regimes across Europe in 1989, including those in East Germany, Czechoslovakia, and Poland. Dominoes continued to fall in the Soviet republics, where glasnost first led to stronger cries for independence, then to freedom in places like Estonia, Latvia, and Lithuania.

With the country crumbling around him, Gorbachev watched his political life come to an end in August 1991, when a coup led by Soviet hardliners briefly removed him from power. He returned a few days later but was fatally weakened politically; four months later, the Soviet Union was gone.

Gorbachev's legacy is decidedly mixed. In the West, he was hailed as *Time* magazine's Man of the Decade for the 1980s, a visionary leader who dismantled the Soviet model and ended the Cold War. In Russia, his leadership led to long lines for the basic necessities, new avenues for corruption, a widening gap between rich and poor, and the shocking and embarrassing collapse of an empire.

ADDITIONAL FACTS

1. *Gorbachev was born into a peasant family in the Stavropol region of the Soviet Union. He joined the Communist Party in 1952, was elected to the Central Committee in 1971, and became a full Politburo member in 1980.*

2. *Gorbachev won the Nobel Peace Prize in 1990.*

3. *His most recognizable feature is the port-wine birthmark on his forehead.*

●●●●●

One Hundred Years of Solitude

If one single work opened the world's eyes to the richness of Latin American literature, it was undoubtedly *One Hundred Years of Solitude* (1967). This magnum opus of the Colombian novelist Gabriel García Márquez (1928–) encapsulates nearly the entire sweep of Latin American history—from indigenous roots to European conquest to modern-day dictatorship—in just one novel, through the lens of one town.

Gabriel García Márquez

One Hundred Years of Solitude takes place in the fictional village of Macondo, based loosely on García Márquez's hometown of Aracataca, Colombia. The sprawling arc of the novel follows the town's fate from its founding—by the patriarch of the Buendía family, José Arcadio Buendía—through five subsequent generations.

Over the years, the events that befall Macondo mirror the history of Colombia and Latin America as a whole. The town grows from a tiny village into a prosperous trading hub, attracting outside attention and later becoming a flash point in a lengthy, brutal civil war between liberals and conservatives. The ever-proliferating Buendía family remains at the center of these political and economic events, and their house becomes a concentrated symbol of Colombia itself, from its construction to its renovation and even its decor—red or blue paint, depending on characters' leftist or rightist political tendencies.

The novel is a masterpiece of magic realism, a genre in which detailed, realistic descriptions blend seamlessly with fantastical elements. Throughout, García Márquez's main theme is the cyclicality of history, which he emphasizes by repeating characters' names from generation to generation of the Buendía family. Characters and names fall into predictable patterns: Men named José Arcadio tend to be forceful and rash, for example, whereas those named Aureliano tend to be sensitive and thoughtful. This mass of repeated names—one generation has no less than seventeen Aurelianos—makes the novel a confusing read, but one eased by the clarity and beauty of García Márquez's writing.

ADDITIONAL FACTS

1. *García Márquez's novel first appeared in English in 1970 and became an international bestseller. It has since appeared in more than thirty languages and sold more than 30 million copies.*

2. *García Márquez is known for backing leftist political causes, including his controversial support of the Fidel Castro (1926–) regime in Cuba.*

3. *García Márquez's works often blur the boundary between fact and fiction, notably his novel* Love in the Time of Cholera *(1985), which is based on the romance between his mother and father.*

• • • • •

Black Sabbath

In the late 1960s, four childhood friends in the British industrial city of Birmingham formed a jazz-blues band. Inspired by heavier guitar-driven acts such as Cream and Led Zeppelin, these boys turned their guitar volume way up and adopted the title of an occult novel as their band's moniker: Black Sabbath. Sabbath combined screaming vocals, sinister themes, and a sludgy, heavy bass, and, with the release of its self-titled debut album in 1970, the band invented the heavy-metal genre.

There is much folklore about how Sabbath's sound got so heavy and its lyrics so sinister. Bassist Terence "Geezer" Butler (1949–) was a fan of dark fantasy and black-magic books. Because of an accident that severed his fingertips, guitarist Tony Iommi (1948–) had to tune his guitar to a lower setting to make it more comfortable to play. The gloomy lyrics and heavy sound made for a perfect match for the onstage antics of lead singer Ozzy Osbourne (1948–), who wailed and thrashed about without much regard for actual singing.

Black Sabbath didn't write complicated or overly intellectual songs. Although perpetually unpopular with both critics and discriminating musicians, the band had no shortage of fans. Teenagers loved it, because Sabbath spoke to the dark side of adolescence: drugs, mental illness, and macabre fantasy. Perhaps a new generation of teens was burnt out on the peace and love of the 1960s, or perhaps Sabbath touched a previously taboo nerve. The band encouraged its fans to be loud, raucous, provocative, and messy, and inspired the founders of heavy-metal bands such as Metallica, Pantera, and Slayer.

ADDITIONAL FACTS

1. *Ozzy Osbourne was fired from Black Sabbath in 1979 as a result of an overpowering drug problem. He then married Sharon Arden (1952–), the daughter of Black Sabbath's manager.*

2. *Black Sabbath was the band's third name. First they were Polka Tulk Blues Company, and then they were Earth. Because there was another touring band with the name Earth, they switched to Black Sabbath.*

3. *From 2002 to 2005, the television network MTV aired a reality show,* The Osbournes, *that chronicled the life of Ozzy Osbourne and his family.*

•••••

Woody Allen

Woody Allen (1935–) is the most prolific major modern American director, having churned out a feature a year for most of the past four decades. His best films combine drama and comedy, romance and relationship angst, life, death, and a love of New York City—all written with unparalleled wit and sophistication.

Allen (born Allen Konigsberg) transitioned from being a comedy writer and stand-up comedian into a playwright, a screenwriter, and finally a movie director. His early directorial period, which began with the fake documentary *Take the Money and Run* (1969), is marked by zany, often absurdist comedies that owe a debt to the Marx Brothers, including *Bananas* (1971), *Sleeper* (1973), and *Love and Death* (1975).

Those movies gave way to his most fertile period, in which he created some of the most cerebral and bittersweet romantic comedies ever captured on film. His most celebrated is *Annie Hall* (1977), which was a critical and commercial success and earned Academy Awards for Best Picture, Best Director, Best Original Screenplay (Allen and Marshall Brickman), and Best Actress (Diane Keaton).

Annie Hall provides a snapshot of what was valued in Hollywood in the late 1970s. Allen's film, about a neurotic, Jewish New Yorker who falls in love with an equally neurotic midwestern WASP, is essentially just about people in their thirties and forties talking and living. It is filled with intellectual and pop cultural references and grossed around $40 million—a far cry from the blockbuster performance of *Star Wars* (1977), which lost the Best Picture Oscar to *Annie Hall* that year.

Allen scored another critical success with *Manhattan* (1979), which is at once an elegy of lost love and a paean to his beloved New York. *Zelig* (1983) is a special effects marvel that paved the way for the technological breakthroughs of *Forrest Gump* (1994) a decade later.

After almost four decades in Hollywood, Allen continues to direct about one film a year, most of them comedies—some more celebrated than others. He scored his most recent success with a noirish thriller, *Match Point* (2005).

ADDITIONAL FACTS

1. *Allen is the most-often-nominated screenwriter (fourteen times) in Academy Awards history. He has been nominated for a total of twenty-one Oscars (fourteen for screenwriting, six for directing, and one for acting). He has won three times (twice for writing, once for directing).*

2. *With Annie Hall, Allen became only the second person to be nominated for Academy Awards for Best Director, Best Actor, and Best Original Screenplay for the same film—Orson Welles was the first, for Citizen Kane (1941).*

3. *Allen is known for his romantic relationships with some of his leading ladies, particularly Mia Farrow (1945–) and Diane Keaton (1946–). Farrow and Allen were together for twelve years before their relationship degenerated into a bitter custody battle that played out in the New York tabloids. Allen later married Soon-Yi Previn, Farrow's adopted daughter from her marriage to the pianist Andre Previn (1929–).*

●●●●

Détente

Détente, a French word meaning "relaxing," refers to a shift in American foreign policy that began in the 1960s and led policymakers to embrace a less confrontational stance toward the Soviet Union and its communist allies. In the United States, détente ended in 1980 with the election of President Ronald Reagan (1911–2004), who resumed taking a harder line against Soviet power.

Two of the most significant events of the détente period were the establishment of US diplomatic ties with communist China, which occurred in 1972, and the negotiation of arms control treaties to reduce the size of the American and Soviet nuclear arsenals.

Détente emerged in the early 1960s, as leaders on both sides of the Cold War sought a way to lessen tensions that had almost led to nuclear war during the Cuban missile crisis of 1962.

For both sides, economics also played a role: Soviet leader Leonid Brezhnev (1906–1982) feared that keeping pace with the American military would bankrupt his country, while the American economy stumbled in the early 1970s.

The establishment of ties with communist China occurred after more than six months of secret negotiations conducted by national security advisor Henry Kissinger (1923–) and Chinese leaders. In 1972, President Richard M. Nixon (1913–1994) traveled to Beijing, toured the Great Wall of China, and met with the country's ruler, Mao Zedong (1893–1976).

Later the same year, US and Soviet negotiators reached accord on the Strategic Arms Limitation Treaty (SALT), an agreement to cap the number of strategic nuclear missile launchers on both sides. The agreement is credited with relieving tensions during the Cold War.

However, to some Americans, détente seemed to represent a form of capitulation to communism. Reagan campaigned in 1980 on a platform of instituting a more aggressive foreign policy, and after taking office, he turned up the heat on the Soviet Union both in his rhetoric—calling the USSR an "evil empire"—and with his massive military budgets.

ADDITIONAL FACTS

1. *The United States and the Soviet Union also agreed to ban biological weapons in 1972.*

2. *In a tangible sign of improved relations, the United States and the Soviet Union cooperated on a space mission in 1975, the Apollo-Soyuz project.*

3. *One key event that helped end détente was the Soviet invasion of Afghanistan, which began on Christmas Day in 1979.*

Martina Navratilova

The tennis player Martina Navratilova (1956–), who excelled with her superb volleying skills at the net, compiled an unsurpassed résumé in her remarkable career. She won 59 career Grand Slam tournament titles—18 singles, 31 women's doubles, and 10 mixed doubles—from her first major crown, in 1978, to her final one, in 2006.

Among her record are nine Wimbledon singles championships, 167 overall singles titles, and 178 doubles crowns. Some consider her to be the greatest women's singles and doubles player in history, having won the career Grand Slam in singles, women's doubles, and mixed doubles. She also achieved fame and the admiration of millions by becoming one of the first active professional athletes to announce that she was homosexual.

Navratilova was born in Prague, in communist Czechoslovakia, and joined the professional women's tour at age sixteen. Two years later, in 1975, she had professional and personal breakthroughs—she reached the finals of the Australian Open and French Open and defected to the United States.

She struggled with her weight early in her career as she adjusted to a fast-food lifestyle in the United States. But she dedicated herself to fitness and became the most dominant women's player of the 1980s. During that decade, she won fifteen of her eighteen major singles titles, including at least two every year from 1982 to 1987.

Another outcome of her improved fitness—and her embrace of improved racket technology—was a reversal of her results against rival Chris Evert (1954–). Navratilova lost twenty-one of her first twenty-five matches with Evert but ended up with a career record of 43-37 against the American. Their rivalry—and contrasting styles of play—dramatically increased the popularity of women's tennis in the 1980s.

Navratilova retired in 1994, only to return to the tour in 2000, mostly to play doubles. She retired for good in 2006, winning the mixed doubles championship in her last career tournament—the US Open.

ADDITIONAL FACTS

1. *Navratilova's twenty Wimbledon titles (singles, doubles, and mixed) ties her for the record with Billie Jean King (1943–).*

2. *Navratilova became a US citizen in 1981.*

3. *Her two most dominant years were 1983 and 1984, when she won three Grand Slam singles titles in both years. In 1983, she posted an 86-1 singles record, and in 1984, she won 74 consecutive matches.*

••●••

Saturday Night Live

The first episode of *Saturday Night Live* aired on October 11, 1975, and the show's format has stayed largely the same ever since: a celebrity host, a regular cast of comedians, and interludes for a musical guest. Now one of the longest-lasting fixtures on network television, the show has weathered many ups and downs in the decades since its inception and has launched the careers of countless comedians.

SNL was originally conceived as a way for NBC to parlay the top spot it enjoyed in weekday late-night television into weekend dominance by adding a late-night weekend show to its roster.

The original *SNL* cast was made up of largely unknown New York City and Toronto comedians. Known as the Not Ready for Prime Time Players, they included Chevy Chase (1943–), Dan Aykroyd (1952–), John Belushi (1949–1982), and Gilda Radner (1946–1989), all of whom would achieve considerable fame. Belushi and Aykroyd reached a wider audience in 1980 when they starred in a successful film based on their "Blues Brothers" routines. Many other films have been based on *SNL* skits, most notably *Wayne's World* in 1992.

Saturday Night Live is notable for the many impersonations its cast has performed, from Chase's bungling, pratfall-prone Gerald Ford (1913–2006) to the Stevie Wonder (1950–) portrayed by Eddie Murphy (1961–).

The show continues to be a breeding ground for new comedic talent. Most recently, *SNL* star Tina Fey (1970–) successfully produced her own sitcom, *30 Rock,* which portrays the behind-the-scenes struggles of a sketch comedy show much like *SNL* itself.

ADDITIONAL FACTS

1. *The host of the first* SNL *episode was the comedian George Carlin (1937–).*

2. *Though none were as successful as* Wayne's World, *the list of feature-length films spawned by* SNL *skits includes* The Coneheads *(1983),* It's Pat! *(1994), and* Stuart Saves His Family *(1995).*

3. *Jim Henson (1936–1990) was an original member of the* SNL *cast, featuring his Muppets in a short-lived series of sketches called "The Land of Gorch."*

••●••

Public Enemy

In the 1980s, the pioneering hip-hop group Public Enemy brought socially conscious and politically motivated lyrics to rap, as well as a harder sound that presaged the gangsta rap era of the 1990s.

Led by front man Chuck D (1960–), the members of Public Enemy tapped into the anger and social unrest among African-Americans in the 1980s and became, in their own estimation, spokesmen for a black community plagued by drugs, violence, and racism—the "black CNN." With songs like "Fight the Power" (1989) and "Don't Believe the Hype" (1988), the group sought to raise the consciousness of black Americans and prompt them to understand their predicaments in wider political and social contexts.

The group—originally consisting of Chuck D, Flavor Flav (1959–), Professor Griff (1961–), and DJ Terminator X (1966–)—formed at Long Island's Adelphi University in 1982. Featuring Chuck D's straightforward and direct rhymes and sidekick Flavor Flav's sometimes nonsensical and wild lyrics, Public Enemy released its first album, *Yo! Bum Rush the Show,* in 1987.

But it was Public Enemy's second album, *It Takes a Nation of Millions to Hold Us Back* (1988), that brought the group to stardom. *It Takes a Nation* went to the top of the R & B charts and is widely considered one of hip-hop's seminal albums and one of the most influential records of the decade.

The following year, Public Enemy reached its cultural zenith with the single "Fight the Power." The theme song to the controversial film *Do the Right Thing* (1989), directed by Spike Lee (1957–), "Fight the Power" was a call to arms for the black community and all young Americans to recognize and take on the oppressiveness of what the group considered a corrupt power structure.

The song helped Public Enemy's third album, *Fear of a Black Planet* (1990), reach number ten on the pop charts, but the band's influence and commercial viability soon waned. Flavor Flav's drug problems and run-ins with the law, as well as Professor Griff's anti-Semitic remarks, damaged the group's credibility, but also, its time had simply passed.

ADDITIONAL FACTS

1. *Flavor Flav is widely credited with inventing the role of the rapping sidekick and is recognizable for his gold teeth, his cartoonish sunglasses, and the oversize clocks he wears around his neck.*

2. *In recent years, Flavor Flav has been ubiquitous on reality television shows, including* The Surreal Life *and* Flavor of Love.

3. *Public Enemy was one of the first hip-hop groups to tour internationally and opened for U2's Zoo TV Tour in 1992.*

··●●··

Postmodernism

Postmodernism in literature took root roughly during the 1940s and remains a thriving genre today. A wide-ranging, vaguely defined movement, postmodernism has encompassed a broad variety of authors of many nationalities writing in many forms. Despite this diversity, postmodernist works often feature many of the same central characteristics: self-referentiality, ironic humor, blurring of different styles and genres, blending of high and low culture, voicing of viewpoints from outside of mainstream society, and reframing of earlier works or figures from new perspectives.

As its name implies, postmodernism developed largely out of modernism, the major Western literary movement that preceded it. Modernist authors, such as James Joyce (1882–1941), Virginia Woolf (1882–1941), William Faulkner (1897–1962), and T. S. Eliot (1888–1965), had seen the rapidly changing twentieth-century world as a shattered landscape, rife with human isolation, alienation, and uncertainty. For postmodernist authors, however, this world was no longer new and unfamiliar; accepting it as a given, they scrutinized it through a more playful, detached, and often humorous lens.

Many postmodernist works employ black comedy and irony to investigate problems of the contemporary world. Novels such as *Catch-22*, by Joseph Heller (1923–1999), and *Slaughterhouse-Five*, by Kurt Vonnegut (1922–2007), use frenetic, cartoonish storytelling to reveal the horrors of modern warfare. The novels of Thomas Pynchon (1937–) and Don DeLillo (1936–) brim with a sense of paranoia, false meaning, and information overload.

In addition, postmodernist works frequently toy with the relationships among the author, the reader, and the work. In *The French Lieutenant's Woman* (1969), John Fowles (1926–2005) inserts himself into the story, includes three alternate endings, and implies that his own characters are beyond his control. *If on a winter's night a traveler* (1979), by Italo Calvino (1923–1985), intersperses chapters of ten wildly different novels of Calvino's invention with passages in which Calvino addresses the reader directly, exploring the experience of reading itself.

ADDITIONAL FACTS

1. *Some of the myriad authors who have been labeled postmodernist include Tom Stoppard (1937–), Jean Rhys (1890–1979), Umberto Eco (1932–), John Gardner (1933–1982), Vladimir Nabokov (1899–1977), Paul Auster (1947–), Truman Capote (1924–1984), Salman Rushdie (1947–), John Barth (1930–), William Gaddis (1922–1998), Jeanette Winterson (1959–), Philip K. Dick (1928–1982), and Toni Morrison (1931–).*

2. *Postmodern literature comprises a number of movements, including postcolonialism and metafiction, that in themselves encompass extensive bodies of work.*

3. *Postmodernism is not confined to literature; in fact, one of its most fruitful arenas has been architecture. Notable examples include the Centre Pompidou in Paris and the AT&T Building in New York City.*

•••••

Stevie Wonder

Stevie Wonder, born in Michigan as Stevland Hardaway Judkins (1950–), signed his first record contract at age twelve and recorded a hit single less than a year later with "Fingertips (Pt. 2)." Over the next eight years, he released a string of pop classics, including "My Cherie Amour" (1969) and "Signed, Sealed, Delivered I'm Yours" (1970).

Despite his success, the young Wonder, who was born blind, became increasingly unhappy with Motown, his record label. At the time, the label and its famous chief, Berry Gordy (1929–), insisted on controlling every aspect of an artist's career. Wonder wanted the freedom to pick his own songs and refused to re-sign with the label in 1971 until he was guaranteed more control over the production of his music.

The next five albums Wonder released were commercial successes and instant classics, allaying the record label's fears. The first was *Music of My Mind* in 1972, quickly followed by *Talking Book* later that year. The latter included the number one hit "Superstition," which represented the full flowering of the unique rhythms and instrumental arrangements that Wonder had experimented with in previous years.

After that, Wonder dominated the pop world for several years. *Innervisions,* his most socially conscious album to date, came out in 1973 and included "Higher Ground" and the epic "Living for the City." He followed this with *Fulfillingness' First Finale* in 1974 and the double album *Songs in the Key of Life* in 1976. He won the Best Album Grammy for all three.

Wonder continues to record new albums and to tour around the world.

ADDITIONAL FACTS

1. *Wonder released an instrumental album in 1968 under the name Eivets Rednow (Stevie Wonder spelled backwards).*

2. *"Happy Birthday," from the 1980 album* Hotter than July, *was part of Wonder's successful campaign to have the birthday of the civil rights leader Martin Luther King Jr. (1929–1968) recognized as a national holiday.*

3. *Some of the biggest hits by other Motown artists, including "Tears of a Clown" (1967) by Smokey Robinson & the Miracles, were written or cowritten by Wonder.*

•••••

Robert Redford

Once the world's top box office star, Robert Redford has emerged in recent years as a leading advocate for independent film. His success as a champion of little-known artists has come to rival his own accomplishments as an actor, director, and producer.

After getting his start on the stage and on television, Redford (1937–) made his screen debut in *War Hunt* (1962) and landed his first starring role opposite Jane Fonda in an adaptation of Neil Simon's hit Broadway play *Barefoot in the Park* (1967). Two years later, he emerged as a Hollywood superstar in George Roy Hill's *Butch Cassidy and the Sundance Kid.* Playing the latter of the two title characters alongside Paul Newman, Redford exuded danger, mystery, and humor—and exhibited the face that made him the desire of women around the world.

Four years later, his collaboration with Hill and Newman peaked with *The Sting,* a story of con men operating in 1930s Chicago. The film earned seven Academy Awards (including one for best picture), and Redford received a best actor nomination for his portrayal of Johnny Hooker.

His other notable acting credits include films focusing on politics (*The Candidate,* 1972; and *All the President's Men,* 1976), sports (*Downhill Racer,* 1969; and *The Natural,* 1984), and espionage (*Three Days of the Condor,* 1975; *Sneakers,* 1992; and *Spy Game,* 2001). He also costarred with Meryl Streep in *Out of Africa* (1985), which won seven Academy Awards.

Redford won an Oscar for Best Director for his directorial debut, *Ordinary People* (1980), though most critics consider *Quiz Show* (1994), an examination of the 1950s scandal at the television game show *Twenty One,* to be his finest work as a director.

In 1981, Redford founded the Sundance Institute outside Park City, Utah, to create an environment in which to nurture and promote independent films produced outside the Hollywood studio system. The most visible outgrowth of the institute is the annual Sundance Film Festival, a forum in which independent films are often launched to mainstream success.

ADDITIONAL FACTS

1. *Redford worked with the director Sydney Pollack on seven films, including* Jeremiah Johnson *(1972),* The Way We Were *(1973),* Three Days of the Condor, *and* Out of Africa.

2. *Redford attended the University of Colorado on a baseball scholarship but was soon kicked off the team for drinking.*

3. *He was given an honorary Academy Award in 2002.*

•●●•

The Imperial Presidency

In 1973, the historian Arthur M. Schlesinger Jr. (1917–2007) published a book entitled *The Imperial Presidency*. In the 500-page volume, Schlesinger—a former advisor to presidents John F. Kennedy (1917–1963) and Lyndon B. Johnson (1908–1973)—accused American presidents of systematically exceeding their constitutional powers in both foreign and domestic affairs.

Schlesinger's book crystallized a growing concern in the 1970s that the office of the presidency had accumulated too much power in the American political system. As a result, Congress passed a series of laws meant to reassert its role as a coequal branch of government.

The "imperial presidency" traced back to Franklin Delano Roosevelt's presidency, when FDR expanded the White House bureaucracy and instituted domestic policies that gave him more direct power over the economy.

After World War II, presidents of both parties sought to expand their power in foreign affairs. Traditionally, Congress was required to pass a declaration of war to commit troops to combat, but President Harry S. Truman (1884–1972) entered the Korean War in 1950 without a declaration of war—a first for a major American conflict.

In the 1960s and 1970s, President Richard M. Nixon (1913–1994) aggressively defended the use of presidential power. In a famous 1977 interview, he explained his belief that the president could do virtually anything he wanted. "When the president does it, that means that it is not illegal," he said.

In part as a reaction against Nixon, Congress passed the War Powers Resolution in 1973. The measure limited the power of presidents to send troops into combat. Congress also expanded its control over federal spending the following year.

More recently, the administration of President George W. Bush (1946–) has resumed Nixon's campaign to expand the president's powers, declaring that the president can order illegal wiretapping and torture in an effort to detect and interrogate potential and accused terrorists. Critics charge that he has revived the imperial presidency, and an indignant Congress has issued a number of press releases denouncing the practices.

ADDITIONAL FACTS

1. *Although American troops have been involved in numerous conflicts since World War II, Congress has not declared war on a foreign country since 1942.*

2. *Congress retains some control over foreign policy with its "power of the purse"; lawmakers were able to bring the Vietnam War to an end by denying funding to American forces there.*

3. *Schlesinger rereleased* The Imperial Presidency *in 2004 to include the Bush administration.*

••••

The Miracle on Ice

The 1980 Olympic Winter Games were held in Lake Placid, New York, at a time when the United States was suffering through high inflation, a gas shortage, and a traumatizing hostage crisis in Iran. The Soviet Union, meanwhile, had just marched its troops into Afghanistan. Morale across the United States was low, and aside from the high expectations for speed skater Eric Heiden (1958–), few believed American fortunes would turn at the Olympics.

Even fewer thought the US hockey team—made up of twenty college kids and coached by Herb Brooks (1937–2003)—would be much of a factor. Three days before the start of the Games, the Soviets—who had won five of the previous six Olympic gold medals—thrashed the Americans 10–3 in an exhibition game.

But once the tournament got under way, US momentum began to build. A late goal earned the Americans a 2–2 tie with medal hopeful Sweden. Next came a stunning 7–3 upset of Czechoslovakia, another medal contender. After three more wins in the early stages of the tournament, the Americans found themselves in the four-team medal round—facing the presumably invincible Soviets on February 22, 1980.

Much to the surprise of everyone—particularly the Soviets—the Americans trailed at only 3–2 entering the third period. Soviet head coach Viktor Tikhonov (1930–) had already replaced his star goaltender, Vladislav Tretiak (1952–), with Vladimir Myshkin (1955–) after the first period—a move that had stunned both teams. Meanwhile, US goaltender Jim Craig (1957–) was playing brilliantly in the American net.

Eight minutes and thirty-nine seconds into the third period, Mark Johnson (1957–) notched his second goal of the game, evening the score at 3–3 and sending the Lake Placid crowd into a frenzy. Just one minute and twenty-one seconds later, captain Mike Eruzione (1954–) fired a wrist shot past Myshkin to give the Americans their first lead of the game.

The seconds ticked off like hours as waves of Soviet skaters attacked for the game's final ten minutes. But Craig and the US defense held firm. When the clock finally ran out, ABC's Al Michaels (1944–) cried out on the air, "Do you believe in miracles? *YES!*" as bedlam broke out in the stands, on the ice, and around the country.

The Americans still had to win one more game to clinch the gold medal. Two days later, the United States beat Finland 4–2 to take the gold.

ADDITIONAL FACTS

1. *The Americans trailed in six of their seven games in Lake Placid. The only game in which they did not fall behind was against Romania.*

2. *In the game against the Soviets, the American goals were scored by Buzz Schneider (1954–), Johnson, who scored twice, and Eruzione. Craig finished with thirty-nine saves.*

3. *One of the famous moments associated with the team's victory occurred when the team captain, Eruzione, called his teammates up onto the medal stand to celebrate their gold medal. Ordinarily, only the captain stood on the podium.*

Who Shot J. R.?

In 1980, the producers of the hit CBS series *Dallas* decided to add a surprise twist to the finale of the show's second season. In the famous episode, one of the drama's main characters—the greedy oil baron John Ross "J. R." Ewing Jr., played by Larry Hagman (1931–)—was shot in his office by an unknown attacker, paralyzing him.

The dramatic plot twist became the talk of the nation in the summer of 1980 as viewers wondered which of the show's characters had fired the shot. Thousands of T-shirts emblazoned with "Who shot J. R.?" were sold. An airplane pilot even threatened not to land a plane unless the *Dallas* actress onboard—Victoria Principal (1950–), who played J. R.'s sister-in-law, Pamela Barnes Ewing—revealed the secret. (The pilot had no choice but to land without learning the secret; Principal, like every other performer on the show, didn't know.)

In preparation for the big revelation, and in order to keep the secret safe, the producers of *Dallas* decided to shoot a scene in which *every* major character shot J.R.

The gambit worked: The ending remained a secret, and the episode revealing the assailant's identity became the highest-ranked show in history at the time, with 41 million viewers, or 53.3 percent of the country's television audience, tuning in on November 21, 1980. Most of the cast and crew of *Dallas* had to wait until the show aired to learn the shooter's identity for themselves, because the producers held off on making the decision until the last possible moment.

Spoiler below!

It was Kristen.

ADDITIONAL FACTS

1. *A one-minute commercial during the episode that revealed who shot J.R. cost half a million dollars, or more than $1.3 million in current dollars.*

2. *"Who Done It?" held the record as the most-watched television episode in history until February 28, 1983, when 125 million viewers watched the final episode of* M*A*S*H.

3. *Hagman threatened to leave the cast of* Dallas *during the summer before it was revealed who'd shot his character unless he was paid $100,000 an episode. The producers relented, and Hagman was given a new contract.*

Stephen Hawking

Stephen Hawking (1942–), who has been called the greatest mind in physics since Albert Einstein (1879–1955), is an internationally celebrated lecturer and cultural figure and has made guest appearances on television shows including *The Simpsons* and *Star Trek: The Next Generation.*

Hawking has managed to achieve all this despite living with amyotrophic lateral sclerosis (commonly known as Lou Gehrig's disease or ALS) for more than forty years. He has been confined to a wheelchair for decades and, for much of that time, has been unable to communicate verbally without the help of a computer-driven voice synthesizer.

Hawking's fields are theoretical physics and quantum theory, with particular focus on black holes, space-time singularities (events in which the laws of physics seem to break down), and the origins of the universe. His childhood interest in mathematics and science earned him a scholarship to Oxford University, from which he graduated in 1962. He later earned his PhD at Cambridge University and eventually became the school's Lucasian Professor of Mathematics, the same post held by the physicist Sir Isaac Newton (1642–1727) three centuries earlier.

Hawking made his early reputation by using Einstein's formulas to develop new ideas and to question the concepts of older, more established physicists. One of his most significant achievements was the discovery of Hawking radiation: subatomic particle emissions from black holes. It had previously been believed that black holes had such powerful gravitational forces that nothing could escape, including radiation or light.

Hawking dramatically raised his public profile with the 1988 publication of *A Brief History of Time: From the Big Bang to Black Holes,* a book that frames ideas on the cosmos in a manner accessible to the average reader. It was a runaway bestseller, spending more than four years on the *London Sunday Times* bestseller list, the longest run for any book in history.

ADDITIONAL FACTS

1. *Hawking was diagnosed with ALS when he was a graduate student in his early twenties. He was given two to four years to live but has survived for more than four decades. In spite of the disease, he fathered three children with his first wife.*

2. *His computer-driven voice synthesizer is triggered by an infrared device that tracks his eye movements.*

3. *In April 2007, Hawking took a zero-gravity flight that allowed him to be weightless outside of his wheelchair for a total of four minutes. He hopes someday to go into space, arguing, "The human race doesn't have a future if it doesn't go into space."*

•••••

Gravity's Rainbow

Gravity's Rainbow (1973), by Thomas Pynchon (1937–), is arguably the foremost work of American postmodernist literature and is regarded as one of the most "difficult" books of the past century. Upon its publication, it elicited strong opinions from critics: Some decried it as self-important and unreadable, while others hailed it as the postmodernist equivalent of James Joyce's modernist masterpiece *Ulysses.*

Gravity's Rainbow takes place during the late stages of World War II, when German forces are raining down their new, technologically advanced V-2 rockets all over London. The plot revolves loosely around a US Army lieutenant named Tyrone Slothrop, whose every sexual encounter, it seems, occurs in the exact spot where a German rocket then lands a few days later. Alerted to Slothrop's apparent predictive abilities, Allied commanders take him in for study. Near the close of the war, he escapes and bounces around Europe, pursued by mysterious individuals who, like him, are trying to discover the nature of a top-secret German rocket and the mysterious payload it contains.

Pynchon's unbelievably dense and convoluted novel shuns a traditional linear plot in favor of a twisting narrative of multiple storylines and hundreds of characters. The story is littered with mathematical equations, songs, and other digressions, and each page is stuffed with allusions and references, from rock music to rocket science to tarot.

Though *Gravity's Rainbow* is nominally about World War II, its thematic concerns are wide-ranging: paranoia, war, sex, death, modern life, and even the nature of meaning itself. The novel wraps actual historical events, surrealist elements, and far-reaching conspiracy theories into a darkly comic hodgepodge not unlike that of Joseph Heller's *Catch-22* or Kurt Vonnegut's *Cat's Cradle*—though far more complex. The result remains one of the more enigmatic, trying, and fascinating books of modern times.

ADDITIONAL FACTS

1. *Pynchon has a physics and engineering background and worked as a technical writer for Boeing during the early 1960s. He wrote the entire massive first draft of* Gravity's Rainbow *by hand on engineer's graph paper.*

2. *In a famous example of the novel's divisive reputation among critics, jurors voted unanimously to award Pynchon a Pulitzer Prize for* Gravity's Rainbow *in 1974, but the award committee vetoed the nomination, calling the book "unreadable."*

3. *Pynchon has avoided the public spotlight throughout his career. Only a handful of photos of him have ever been published, and the only recordings of him in the public sphere are two brief voice cameos on* The Simpsons *in 2004.*

•••••

Brian Eno

The producer Brian Eno (1948–) has been at the forefront of many of the most important pop music trends of the 1970s and 1980s and continues to be one of the best-known producers in contemporary music. Eno was a founding member of the influential rock band Roxy Music and an early pioneer of the "ambient" music style. In addition, he has produced megahits by other artists, including U2's *The Joshua Tree* (1987).

Eno, an art-school graduate from England, joined Roxy Music in 1971 with his university friend Andy MacKay (1946–), and the group released a modestly successful self-titled album in 1972. Its next album was *For Your Pleasure* (1973). It was less successful than the band's debut, but its complex arrangements, liberal use of experimental instruments and sounds, and deliberately flowery lyrics made it a classic of the progressive, or prog, rock style.

After *For Your Pleasure,* Eno left Roxy Music to pursue his own projects. He released four solo albums in the 1970s: *Here Come the Warm Jets* (1973), *Taking Tiger Mountain (By Strategy)* (1974), *Another Green World* (1975), and *Before and After Science* (1977). (The most successful tracks from these albums include "Needles in the Camel's Eye" and "Third Uncle.")

Eno also recorded a series of influential ambient albums—music that was intended to create an atmospheric sound that would transform and interact with an environment, as opposed to a piece that demanded the listener's complete attention. His first album in this style was *Discreet Music,* from 1975. He followed it with his four-part ambient series, most famously *Ambient 1: Music for Airports* (1978).

Since then, Eno has produced records for major rock acts, including David Bowie (1947–), U2, and Coldplay.

ADDITIONAL FACTS

1. *Eno composed the $3\frac{1}{4}$-second-long start-up sound for Microsoft Windows 95.*

2. *Years after Eno left the band, Roxy Music had a hit with its 1981 cover of "Jealous Guy," a song written by John Lennon (1940–1980) for his 1971 album* Imagine.

3. *One of the biggest influences on Eno was "He Loved Him Madly," a song recorded by Miles Davis (1926–1991) in 1974 as a tribute to Duke Ellington (1899–1974).*

••••

Jack Nicholson

When host Billy Crystal introduced the presenter for the Best Picture Oscar at the 1993 Academy Awards, he had only to say one four-letter word and everyone knew whom he was talking about: "Jack."

Since his breakthrough performance as an alcoholic lawyer in Dennis Hopper's *Easy Rider* (1969), Jack Nicholson (1937–) has become an American cultural icon. Known for his intense yet effortless acting style, his pugnaciousness—on-screen and off—his seemingly carefree life of romantic dalliances, and his unyielding devotion to the Los Angeles Lakers, his outsize personality has earned him a rightful place among pop culture's one-named stars.

But before the romances (he has five children by four different women), the drugs, and the public explosions of anger, there were the movies.

From 1969 until 1975, Nicholson appeared in a string of successful films (including Bob Rafelson's *Five Easy Pieces* in 1970 and Roman Polanski's *Chinatown* in 1974), often playing antiestablishment characters with a combination of toughness, cool rage, and laconic irony—modern successors to the Humphrey Bogart characters of *High Sierra* (1941) and *Casablanca* (1942), according to the film historian David Thomson.

Over that seven-year period, Nicholson was nominated for five Academy Awards, winning on the fifth try for his tour de force performance as the rebellious Randle Patrick McMurphy in Milos Forman's *One Flew Over the Cuckoo's Nest* (1975).

Dialogue from several of Nicholson's roles has entered the national lexicon, from Jack Torrance in *The Shining* (1980) ("Heeeeeeeeere's Johnny!"), to the Joker in *Batman* (1989) ("Ever dance with the devil in the pale moonlight?"), to Colonel Nathan R. Jessep in *A Few Good Men* (1992) ("You can't handle the truth!").

Though he has appeared in some films that have been unsuccessful, Nicholson has never had a fallow period in his career. He has been nominated for twelve Academy Awards—more than any other male actor—never waiting more than six years between nominations. In addition to his performance as McMurphy in *One Flew Over the Cuckoo's Nest,* he also won a Best Actor Oscar for *As Good As It Gets* (1997) and a Best Supporting Actor Oscar for *Terms of Endearment* (1983).

ADDITIONAL FACTS

1. *Nicholson got his start in Hollywood working as a mail clerk for MGM, making $30 a day.*

2. *He was raised to believe that his grandmother was his mother and his mother was his sister—he did not find out the truth about his lineage until a* Time *reporter checked up on the actor's background in 1974.*

3. *He is one of two actors to be nominated for acting Oscars in five different decades (the 1960s through the 2000s). Michael Caine is the other.*

•••••

Neoconservatism

Neoconservatism, one of the most controversial intellectual trends in contemporary American politics, emerged in the late 1960s and early 1970s among some liberals as a reaction against the perceived excesses of left-wing policies. Prominent neoconservatives included many ex-liberals and ex-communists who had reconsidered their old beliefs and instead advocated more conservative stances in both domestic and foreign affairs.

Indeed, one of the leaders of the movement, Irving Kristol (1920–), famously defined a neoconservative as a "liberal mugged by reality."

Commentary, edited by Norman Podhoretz (1930–), was one of the key journals of the movement, publishing works by Kristol and other neoconservatives. In the political realm, Senator Henry "Scoop" Jackson (1912–1983), a Democrat from Washington State, was also closely associated with various aspects of neoconservatism.

As a philosophy, neoconservatism initially arose out of a concern that many liberal-backed programs of the 1960s, such as affirmative action and welfare, were ineffective or even harmful. Massive government spending could not wash away social problems such as inequality, they felt, and so they argued against expansion of government social programs.

In foreign affairs, the neoconservatives advocated a robust defense of democracy and human rights abroad. Neoconservatives led the criticism of détente in the 1970s, which they said underestimated the dangers of Soviet military power and turned a blind eye to human-rights abuses.

In the 2000s, President George W. Bush (1946–) appointed neoconservatives to some top positions in his administration and launched an invasion of Iraq in 2003, a long-cherished goal of neoconservative writers.

Critics of neoconservatives have pointed out the seeming contradiction between their reluctance to support social programs in the United States and their readiness to back massive military invasions overseas; the unsuccessful 2004 presidential candidate John Kerry criticized Bush for "opening firehouses in Baghdad and shutting them in the United States of America."

ADDITIONAL FACTS

1. *Advancement based on merit instead of affirmative action has been a favorite cause among neocon-servatives; Podhoretz's son John (1961–) was named to the editorship of* Commentary *in 2007 to continue the magazine's fearless crusade for meritocracy.*

2. *Although the Republican Party embraced many tenets of neoconservatism, many members of the movement remained Democrats; Jeane Kirkpatrick (1926–2006) remained a registered Democrat while serving as a diplomat in the administration of Ronald Reagan (1911–2004).*

3. *The term* neoconservative *was coined by Michael Harrington (1928–1989), a socialist and a critic of the movement.*

••●••

Joe Montana

Known as Joe Cool, Joe Montana (1956–) was renowned for his ability to stay calm in any situation, particularly when the pressure was at its highest. He led the San Francisco 49ers to four Super Bowl titles, was three times named Super Bowl Most Valuable Playere (MVP), and, along with Jerry Rice (1962–) was half of one of the most prolific quarterback-receiver combinations in National Football League (NFL) history.

As quarterback of the San Francisco 49ers (1979–1992) and Kansas City Chiefs (1993–1994), Montana led his teams to thirty-one fourth-quarter comebacks. No comeback was more memorable than the one that clinched Super Bowl XXIII, in 1989. In that game, Montana led a ninety-two-yard touchdown drive to beat the Cincinnati Bengals, throwing the game-winning touchdown pass with thirty-four seconds left. As an illustration of his coolness under pressure, just before the winning drive began, he pointed at a fan and famously asked one of his teammates, "Isn't that John Candy?"

Even though Montana had led Notre Dame to the national championship as a junior in 1977, his NFL greatness was not predictable. He was not particularly big (six foot two, 200 pounds) and did not have an unusually strong arm.

The 49ers made him the eighty-second pick overall in the 1979 NFL Draft, taking him in the third round. (He was the fourth quarterback drafted.) But he would go on to pass for 40,551 yards and 273 touchdowns, earn two league MVP awards (1989 and 1990), and be named to eight Pro Bowls.

Montana, who won all four of his Super Bowls, still owns most of the Super Bowl passing records. After two seasons with the Chiefs, he retired after the 1994 season and was elected to the Pro Football Hall of Fame in 2000.

ADDITIONAL FACTS

1. *Montana was a great all-around athlete—though he played football at Notre Dame, he was also offered a basketball scholarship at Division I powerhouse North Carolina State.*

2. *In 1990, he was named Sportsman of the Year by* Sports Illustrated.

3. *Montana threw the pass in one of the legendary plays in NFL history, known to fans simply as "the Catch"—a touchdown reception by tight end Dwight Clark (1957–) in the 1981 National Football Conference Championship game.*

•••••

Cabbage Patch Kids

Xavier Roberts (1955–) invented Cabbage Patch Kids, a series of quilted dolls, while he was a twenty-one-year-old art student in Georgia. Soon after they were introduced to the public, the dolls' unexpected popularity reached such a fever pitch that television stations broadcast video of mothers pushing and shoving their way through frenzied crowds of other eager parents to "adopt" the toys for their demanding children.

Initially, Roberts called the dolls Little People Originals and marketed them mostly to arts-and-crafts enthusiasts. The dolls caught the eye of Coleco, a toy company, which began mass-producing the toys in 1982.

Each doll arrived with adoption papers, a birthday, and a unique name. Children would fill out the adoption papers and return them to the company; on the doll's first birthday, they'd receive a birthday card from Coleco. Each doll was in some way unique. And in the spirit of the multiculturalism of the 1980s, the dolls came in all colors, races, hair combinations, and freckle statuses (with or without).

However, the toy company couldn't keep up with demand for the must-have toy, and crowds even swarmed delivery trucks as they pulled up to toy stores. Demand was especially strong at Christmas, when stores were forced to hire security guards to keep ill-behaved parents in line. The shortage created a black market full of scalpers, collectors, and Cabbage Patch schemers seeking to cash in on the craze.

Like most crazes, however, the Cabbage Patch fad eventually fizzled out. By 1986, Coleco had overproduced the dolls. Despite efforts to revitalize the line by adding new features, the craze was over, and Coleco declared bankruptcy in 1988.

ADDITIONAL FACTS

1. *Roberts later revealed that he found the names for the dolls in a 1930s book of baby names.*

2. *The Cabbage Patch craze fueled doting mothers to go to extremes for their demanding children. One such story involved a mother in Sioux Falls, South Dakota, who showed up at a local Toys"R"Us store with a spork and a BB gun, demanding that they give her a doll.*

3. *As with the original Little People, Roberts's signature was imprinted on the buttocks of each Cabbage Patch Kid.*

••●••

Donald Trump

According to *Forbes* magazine, in 2007 there were 116 Americans wealthier than the real-estate mogul Donald Trump (1946–), who had a net worth of $3 billion. But no one ahead of him measured up to "the Donald's" flamboyant lifestyle, cocky public persona, and propensity for landing in the tabloids.

Trump learned the New York City real-estate world from his father, Fred (1905–1999), a developer who focused on middle-income housing in Brooklyn and Queens. In the 1970s, Donald turned his attention and his enormous ambitions to Manhattan, where he began borrowing heavily to create huge buildings.

One of his first major projects was the 1982 construction of Trump Tower on Fifth Avenue. He also bought casinos in Atlantic City and turned himself into a billionaire. But the real-estate crash of the early 1990s nearly ruined him, forcing him into personal debt of $900 million.

In a remarkable turnaround, Trump sold many of his assets, paid off his debts, and within a decade had made enough shrewd business deals to return to the billionaire ranks. When *Forbes* listed him as having a net worth of $3 billion in 2007, he disputed the figure. "I'm worth $7 billion," he said.

Part of Trump's national appeal is his outsize personality. He has become a regular in the tabloids for his two high-profile divorces (as well as the extramarital affair that ended the first marriage and led to the second) and for his marriage to his third wife, Melania, who is twenty-four years his junior.

In 2004, he launched the successful reality show *The Apprentice* on NBC, which made him a television star and popularized his catchphrase "You're fired." He also openly feuds with other celebrities, has written several books, and is a ubiquitous presence on late-night comedy shows (as both a guest and a subject of ridicule, particularly for his unique hairstyle).

ADDITIONAL FACTS

1. *Following his near ruin in the early 1990s, Trump signaled his return to celebrity culture when he announced in 1999 that he was considering running for president as a Reform Party candidate. He ultimately opted against running, but in the meantime, he received a lot of media attention.*

2. *He says he's a germaphobe and doesn't like shaking anyone's hand for fear of picking up their germs.*

3. *Trump's nickname, "the Donald," was coined by his Czech-born first wife, Ivana.*

•••••

Postcolonialism

Throughout much of the nineteenth and early twentieth centuries, huge swathes of the globe, from Aruba to Korea to Zimbabwe, were under the control of colonial powers. Although Great Britain and France had the most-widespread colonial empires, a whole host of countries, from Japan to the United States, oversaw lands outside their national borders. When this network of empires and colonies largely disintegrated after World War II, former colonial lands began to demand both political and cultural independence.

The collective body of works by or about people from parts of the world formerly subject to colonial control has since been termed *postcolonial literature*. Confined to neither a specific continent nor a particular language, this genre spans a vast amount of literature produced in Africa, Asia, Australasia, and the Americas. Despite this diversity, though, postcolonial works tend to explore similar themes: cultural and national identity, religious tension, subjugation of one race or ethnic group by another, and other issues related to the mixing and clash of cultures.

Postcolonial literature rose to prominence in about 1978, when the theorist Edward Said (1935–2003) published his landmark work *Orientalism*. This tome highlighted the tendency of Western culture to divide its worldview into the West and the "other," consciously viewing non-Western cultures and peoples as exotic. Other theorists, such as Aimé Césaire (1913–) and Homi K. Bhabha (1949–), expanded on Said's ideas, deepening the pool of postcolonial scholarship.

Major postcolonial authors are countless: Key works include Chinua Achebe's *Things Fall Apart* (1958), Jean Rhys's *Wide Sargasso Sea* (1966), V. S. Naipaul's *A Bend in the River* (1979), and Salman Rushdie's *Midnight's Children* (1981). The genre continues to flourish today, with a new generation of postcolonial authors exploring the experiences of non-Western immigrants living in Britain, the United States, and other Western countries.

ADDITIONAL FACTS

1. *The scores of authors who have been labeled postcolonial include Achebe (1930–), Edwidge Danticat (1969–), Nadine Gordimer (1923–), Jamaica Kincaid (1949–), Hanif Kureishi (1954–), Doris Lessing (1919–), Rohinton Mistry (1952–), Michael Ondaatje (1943–), Zadie Smith (1975–), and Derek Walcott (1930–), among many others.*

2. *Although the bulk of postcolonial literature has been produced in English, a postcolonial tradition also exists in Afrikaans, Arabic, French, Hindi, Spanish, and other languages.*

3. *Occidentalism (2004), by Ian Buruma (1951–) and Avishai Margalit (1939–), applies Edward Said's ideas from* Orientalism *in the opposite direction, exploring non-Westerners' negative assumptions about the Western world.*

••●••

Bob Marley

When a style of Jamaican music known as reggae became internationally popular in the late 1960s, no performer in that genre matched the success of Bob Marley (1945–1981). Marley's talent was recognized early, and his reputation—to say nothing of his legend—has grown steadily in the years since his untimely death.

Robert Nesta Marley was born to a black mother and white father in the Saint Ann Parish of Jamaica and moved to Kingston, the island's largest city, when his father died in 1955. In 1963, Marley formed his first band, eventually called the Wailers, with a group of local musicians. The Wailers released a number of hits in Jamaica the following year, mostly songs in the ska and rock steady genres.

It wasn't until 1966, though, that Marley embraced the two movements with which he will always be identified: reggae and Rastafarianism.

Reggae combines Caribbean rhythms and instruments with American jazz and blues influences. The tempo is usually slow, even languid.

The Jamaican Rastafarian religious movement, which began in the 1930s, regards the Ethiopian emperor Haile Selassie I (1892–1975)—the first monarch of a postcolonial African state—as its God. This aspect of the movement is often overlooked today, as Rastafarianism is more often associated with two other features: the dreadlocks worn by adherents such as Marley and followers' spiritual use of marijuana.

Catch a Fire, the first full-length Wailers album, was released in 1973 and was followed later that year by *Burnin',* which includes the songs "Get Up, Stand Up" and "I Shot the Sheriff." Marley soon achieved international success, beginning with the song "No Woman, No Cry" (1975) and continuing through the *Exodus* and *Kaya* albums in 1977 and 1978, respectively.

Marley was diagnosed with a cancerous toe in 1977 but refused an amputation on religious grounds and continued to record new music. Within a few years, the cancer spread throughout his body, and he died in 1981 at the age of thirty-six. *Legend,* a posthumous compilation of his work, is the best-selling reggae album of all time.

ADDITIONAL FACTS

1. *In 1999,* Time *magazine named Marley's 1977 record* Exodus *the greatest album of the twentieth century.*

2. *In honor of his religion's Messiah and God, Marley used Haile Selassie's 1963 speech to the United Nations as the basis for his song "War."*

3. *Marley's international reputation got its first big boost in 1974, when Eric Clapton (1945–) covered "I Shot the Sheriff," making it a number one hit single.*

••●••

Francis Ford Coppola

Over a remarkable eight-year period, Francis Ford Coppola (1939–) established himself as one of cinema's great directors, completing work on four of the most critically acclaimed films in Hollywood history: *The Godfather* (1972), *The Conversation* (1974), *The Godfather: Part II* (1974), and *Apocalypse Now* (1979). All told, these four movies garnered thirty-three Academy Award nominations (winning eleven Oscars) and turned Coppola into a legendary figure in the film world.

When he was hired to direct the screen version of *The Godfather,* Coppola had no successful directing credits to his name (though he had won an Academy Award in 1971 for cowriting the screenplay to Franklin J. Schaffner's war movie *Patton*).

Despite his relative inexperience—and Paramount's qualms about his hiring—Coppola managed to create a movie that rejuvenated Hollywood during a period of financial insecurity and proved that high artistic ideals could still lead to box office profits. (It grossed more than $133 million domestically, a record at the time.)

The Godfather is an intimate look at one family's place within the New York Mafia underworld during the 1940s and 1950s, connecting classic Hollywood storytelling with a more personal style that would mark many of the most successful films of the 1970s. The cast matched one star—Marlon Brando (1924–2004)—with several then unknowns who would go on to major film careers, among them Al Pacino (1940–), Robert Duvall (1931–), Diane Keaton (1946–), and James Caan (1940–).

Two years after the release of *The Godfather,* Coppola added *The Conversation* and *The Godfather: Part II* to his oeuvre. The former is a claustrophobic study of an audio surveillance expert; the latter, a hit sequel to the original *Godfather* film.

To date, *Apocalypse Now* is Coppola's last masterpiece. Because of typhoons that destroyed sets, star Martin Sheen's heart attack, the outbreak of civil war in the Philippines (where most of the shooting took place), trouble with the mercurial Brando, and Coppola's own financial and emotional problems, the film was almost never completed. But the director persevered, although the film came in about $20 million over its original $11 million budget.

Since *Apocalypse Now,* Coppola has taken on several projects as director and producer, but nothing has matched his brilliant work from the 1970s.

ADDITIONAL FACTS

1. *Three generations of Coppolas have won Academy Awards—Francis; his father, Carmine (Best Original Score,* The Godfather: Part II, *his daughter, Sofia (Best Original Screenplay,* Lost in Translation, *2003), and nephew, Nicolas Cage (Best Actor,* Leaving Las Vegas, *1995).*

2. *Coppola owns Rubicon Estate Winery in Napa Valley, California, which produces wines, pasta, and pasta sauces. He also owns resorts in Guatemala and Belize.*

3. *His sister, Talia Shire, who is also known for playing Adrian in the* Rocky *movies, played Constanzia "Connie" Corleone in the* Godfather *trilogy.*

•●●•

Gay Rights

In 1948, the biologist Alfred Kinsey (1894–1956) published *Sexual Behavior in the Human Male,* a massive, 800-page study that examined the sex lives of thousands of men. One of Kinsey's most controversial findings was that about 37 percent of men reported having had at least one homosexual encounter in their lives—meaning homosexuality was far more common than most Americans realized at the time.

Kinsey's findings helped change attitudes about homosexuality. But it would take decades before age-old prejudices and legal regulations against gay men and women began to fade in the United States.

Homosexuality had been embraced by the ancient Greeks and was not considered controversial in some societies. But most major religions, especially Christianity, condemned the practice. In the United States, most states outlawed sodomy, and many Americans considered gay sex immoral.

In the 1950s and 1960s, a few organized efforts to relax laws against gays were launched. An early gay-rights group, the Mattachine Society, was founded in California in 1950.

But the so-called Stonewall Rebellion of June 28, 1969, escalated these efforts and is often marked as the true beginning of the gay-rights movement in the United States. The incident's name refers to the Stonewall Inn, a gay bar in New York City's Greenwich Village where a group of gay men and lesbians fought back against a police raid, sparking three days of riots.

In the 1970s, most city police forces ended their harassment of gay bars. In the 1980s, some states granted gays legal protection against discrimination. The Supreme Court struck down laws against sodomy in 2003. In 2004, Massachusetts became the first state to extend full-fledged marriage rights to gays.

However, many rules against homosexuality remain, including a ban on gays in the military. In 1996, President Bill Clinton (1946–) signed the Defense of Marriage Act, which allowed states to disregard gay marriages performed in other jurisdictions. In addition, many states have passed referenda explicitly banning gay marriage.

ADDITIONAL FACTS

1. *Though it is still against the law in most of the United States, same-sex marriage has recently become legal in South Africa, Belgium, Spain, the Netherlands, and Canada.*

2. *The American Psychiatric Association listed homosexuality as a disorder in its* Diagnostic and Statistical Manual of Mental Disorders *until 1973.*

3. *Public attitudes about homosexuality have shifted remarkably over the past three decades. As of 2007, 89 percent of Americans believed gays should have equal rights in the workplace, compared with 56 percent in 1977.*

••••

Larry Bird

During the 1980s, few sporting rivalries were as intense and dramatic as the clashes between the Los Angeles Lakers and the Boston Celtics, who met in the National Basketball Association (NBA) finals three times. The teams were led by two of the greatest players in the sport's history: Earvin "Magic" Johnson (1959–) and an unassuming forward from French Lick, Indiana, named Larry Bird (1956–).

In his thirteen-year career with the Celtics, Larry Bird evolved from the self-proclaimed "Hick from French Lick" to "Larry Legend." Bird had the rare combination of outstanding shooting and passing skills, toughness, leadership qualities, and the ability to make his teammates better, all wrapped up in a six-foot-nine, 220-pound package. He also was one of the best clutch performers ever, always there to hit a shot or make a steal at the key point in an important game.

Bird led the Celtics to three league championships and was a three-time Most Valuable Player (MVP), a twelve-time all-star, a two-time NBA finals MVP, and the 1980 Rookie of the Year. He also was cocaptain of the 1992 US Olympic team—dubbed the Dream Team—which won the gold medal in Barcelona.

Before joining the Celtics in 1979–1980, Bird spent two seasons as an all-American at Indiana State University. In his senior year, he led the Sycamores to an undefeated record before they reached the National Collegiate Athletic Association championship game against Michigan State. Led by sophomore Magic Johnson, the Spartans won, and one of basketball's enduring rivalries was born—Bird versus Magic.

Bird and Johnson entered the NBA the next season, and their rivalry helped raise the profile of the NBA. Their teams met for the NBA title three times (1984, 1985, and 1987), with Magic's Lakers winning twice.

Bird was plagued by back and foot injuries in his last four seasons, forcing his retirement after the 1992 Olympics. He was inducted into the Basketball Hall of Fame in 1998. He later coached the Indiana Pacers for three seasons (1997–2000) and has worked as the Pacers' president of basketball operations since 2003.

ADDITIONAL FACTS

1. *Bird finished his NBA career with averages of 24.3 points, 10.0 rebounds, and 6.3 assists per game.*

2. *Bird received a basketball scholarship to play for the legendary Indiana University coach Bobby Knight (1940–), but after a month on campus, Bird was homesick and overwhelmed and returned to his tiny hometown of French Lick. He also briefly attended Northwood Institute, a junior college, before enrolling at Indiana State.*

3. *The Celtics selected Bird as the sixth overall pick in the 1978 draft—after his junior season. Although he returned to Indiana State for another year, the Celtics still retained his draft rights and later signed him to a five-year, $3.25 million contract (at the time, an NBA rookie record).*

• • ● • •

Bill Cosby

The comedian Bill Cosby (1937–) began his career while still in college at Temple University in his hometown of Philadelphia. Tending bar to make ends meet, he was encouraged by patrons to take his humor onstage.

Cosby eventually landed at New York City's Gaslight Cafe in 1962, where he was a hit. He decided to leave college in order to pursue what would become a pioneering career as one of the country's first successful African-American comics.

In 1965, three years after his first appearance at the Gaslight, Cosby landed the role of Alexander Scott, an undercover CIA operative on the television series *I Spy*. The role was a milestone: Cosby was the first black performer with a recurring role in a major series. After ending his stint on *I Spy* in 1968, Cosby went in an unusual direction: With characters based on his childhood friends, he produced a successful cartoon, *Fat Albert and the Cosby Kids*, that first aired in 1972.

Cosby was never able to translate his success onto the big screen, but his television victories continued. In 1984, he began playing the role of Dr. Heathcliff Huxtable, a successful obstetrician living in Brooklyn, on *The Cosby Show*. The series was another milestone for American television: Rather than portraying a poor and dysfunctional minority family, as shows like *Sanford and Son* had in the past, the show depicted a successful middle-class family that featured a dedicated marriage and well-adjusted children. The show was a dominant force on television until it was knocked from its throne in 1992 by another innovative series, *The Simpsons*.

In recent years, Cosby has focused on social advocacy issues and has emerged as a controversial voice in the African-American community. On the fiftieth anniversary of the *Brown v. Board of Education* ruling, which ended racial segregation of schools, Cosby gave a speech criticizing black Americans for supposedly neglecting parenting responsibilities, glamorizing crime, and downplaying the importance of education. Many considered Cosby's speech unfairly harsh, but others commented that he was "carry[ing] forward the work of earlier generations of black leaders."

ADDITIONAL FACTS

1. *The original Bill Cosby Show, debuting in 1969, depicted Cosby as a teacher rather than a doctor. It ran for only two seasons.*

2. The Cosby Show *was originally meant to follow the story of a working-class family.*

3. *Cosby earned a PhD in education from the University of Massachusetts in 1977.*

•••••

Bono

Bono (1960–) is the lead singer of the immensely popular rock group U2 as well as arguably the world's most visible champion of humanitarian causes. He has used his fame and status as the face of U2 to fight poverty and AIDS in the Third World, particularly in Africa.

Bono was born Paul Hewson in Dublin, Ireland, to a Catholic father and Protestant mother. He joined the band that would become U2 in October 1976, even though he could not sing or play the guitar very well. But his new bandmates could already recognize his potent charisma and overwhelming desire for success.

As Bono honed his tenor voice, songwriting skills, and dramatic stage presence, U2 built a following in the early 1980s with its live shows. The band's third album, *War,* released in 1983, turned the group into an international sensation. Four years later, the release of *The Joshua Tree* turned U2 into one of the biggest bands on the planet, and the group filled stadiums around the world.

Subsequent U2 albums, including *Achtung Baby* (1991), *All That You Can't Leave Behind* (2000), and *How to Dismantle an Atomic Bomb* (2004), explored new musical directions and provided further confirmation of the band's international popularity.

As U2 skyrocketed to fame, Bono began developing into a social activist. He and bass player Adam Clayton (1960–) played on the 1984 charity single "Do They Know It's Christmas?" to raise funds for Ethiopian famine relief.

In July 1985, U2 participated in Live Aid, a major international concert for African famine relief at London's Wembley Stadium. U2's stirring performance created thousands of new fans, and after the concert, Bono and his wife, Alison Hewson (1961–), worked for six weeks in Ethiopia on a famine-relief and education project.

More recently, Bono has focused on canceling Third World debts and fighting poverty and global diseases through his work as cofounder of the One Campaign and DATA (Debt, AIDS, Trade in Africa). In 2005, he convinced leaders of the G8 countries to forgive $40 billion worth of debt owed by poorer nations. For his efforts, he has been nominated for the Nobel Peace Prize three times (2003, 2005, and 2006).

ADDITIONAL FACTS

1. *There are many stories about how Bono got his moniker. The most credible version is that the name came from a brand of hearing aid called Bonavox—a close approximation of bono vox, which is Latin for "good voice."*

2. *Perhaps the lyrics that best sum up Bono's brand of activism come from U2's 2004 song "Crumbs from Your Table": "Where you live should not decide / Whether you live or whether you die."*

3. *Among Bono's onstage trademarks are his political speeches (which have made him a lightning rod for criticism), his penchant for pulling women out of the audience to dance with him, and his personas from the 1992–1993 Zoo TV Tour—the Fly, Mirrorball Man, and MacPhisto.*

••●••

Toni Morrison

Born in Ohio in 1931, Toni Morrison is one of the foremost American authors of the past fifty years and a major figure on the international literary stage. After writing several acclaimed novels about the nineteenth- and twentieth-century African-American experience, in 1993 Morrison became the first black woman to win the Nobel Prize in Literature. Her novels are renowned for their poetic language and their exploration of African-American memory, folklore, and ancestry.

Morrison was a voracious reader as a child and grew up amid a family tradition of storytelling. After college and graduate school, she worked for years as a professor before becoming a fiction editor for Random House. During this time she began to write fiction of her own, and in 1970 her first novel, *The Bluest Eye*, was published. A tale of a young black girl who wishes she had blue eyes, the novel introduced what would become Morrison's trademark style: a fragmented, nonchronological narrative tinged with elements of African-American music, culture, and religion.

Morrison's next novel, *Sula* (1973), about a tumultuous friendship between two women, gained greater notice and a National Book Award nomination. But it was her third novel, *Song of Solomon* (1977), that firmly established her reputation. Filled with biblical allusions, the saga follows a young man's attempt to understand the history of his family.

Beloved (1987) is Morrison's best-known work and generally considered her finest. Set around the time of the Civil War, it tells of a runaway slave who, pursued by slave catchers, decides in a desperate moment to try to kill her own young children rather than allow them to face a destiny of slavery. This decision haunts her, literally, throughout the rest of her life. *Beloved* won the Pulitzer Prize in 1988 and a decade later was adapted into an award-winning film.

ADDITIONAL FACTS

1. *In addition to pursuing her career as a novelist, Morrison has been an academic for decades, teaching literature and writing at Texas Southern, Howard, Yale, Princeton, and the State University of New York.*

2. *Morrison does not fit squarely into any one movement or genre. She has been categorized as a modernist, like Virginia Woolf (1882–1941); a black American author, like Ralph Ellison (1914–1994); and a magic realist, like Gabriel García Márquez (1928–).*

3. *Morrison's birth name was Chloe Anthony Wofford, but she dropped her first name (because too many people mispronounced it) and adapted the name Toni from her middle name instead.*

••●●••

Patti Smith

Patti Smith (1946–), who grew up in a poor family in New Jersey, moved to New York City in 1967 to "sort herself out." A bookish, rail-thin young woman, Smith soon joined the city's art scene as a poet and performance artist. Inspired by the emerging punk rock genre of the 1970s, Smith eventually created the Patti Smith Group, a band that combined her poetry with the raw energy of punk. The band became one of the first New York punk acts to score a record contract (just ahead of another seminal punk band, the Ramones).

Uninterested in fame or riches, Smith pens lyrics that reflect her working-class upbringing and her edgy, primitive style. For instance, in the song "Piss Factory" (1974), she sings,

> Sixteen and time to pay off
> I got this job in a piss factory inspecting pipe
> Forty hours thirty-six dollars a week
> But it's a paycheck, Jack.

Smith's lyrics were uncommon for a female musician at the time, and she was dubbed punk rock's poet laureate. But Smith never saw herself as a feminist pioneer—she simply thought of herself as an artist. Her coworkers and compatriots included figures such as the photographer Robert Mapplethorpe (1946–1989) and the poets Jim Carroll (1950–) and William S. Burroughs (1914–1997). Smith's unwillingness to depend on gender as a means of wooing an audience proved inspirational to many other female rockers.

Smith continues to champion the simple do-it-yourself punk aesthetic, urging people to get out and talk, hash out ideas, and make powerful music. She has also been active politically, appearing at events to oppose the American invasion of Iraq in 2003.

ADDITIONAL FACTS

1. *Patti Smith married Fred "Sonic" Smith (1949–1994), guitarist for the rock band MC5. The Smiths dropped out of the music scene temporarily to raise their two children.*

2. *Patti Smith's song "People Have the Power" became a rally song for Ralph Nader's 2000 presidential campaign.*

3. *When the legendary rock club CBGB shut down in 2006, Patti Smith headlined the farewell concert with a 3½-hour-long set. She was the last performer ever to grace the CBGB stage, where many punk bands had made their debuts.*

• • ● • •

The Godfather (1972)

The Godfather is many things. It is Francis Ford Coppola's masterpiece. It is the most celebrated film produced since World War II. It includes arguably the finest screen performance by Marlon Brando (1924–2004). It helped revitalize American cinema. And it proved that artistic ambitions could coexist with commercial viability. Most of all, though, *The Godfather* is great entertainment.

The film, based on a novel by Mario Puzo (1920–1999), focuses on the fictional Corleone family, which Puzo based on one of the five powerful Mafia families that run organized crime in New York City. The period of the film, roughly 1945–1955, encompasses the decline of the aging Don Vito Corleone (Brando), who must make a series of decisions to protect his family's future. The most important decision: which of his three sons will succeed him at the helm of his criminal empire.

Critics hailed *The Godfather* for redefining the gangster genre. Though it is violent and graphically depicts criminal activities, the most significant theme is that of family loyalty. And unlike gangsters of earlier times in Hollywood, the characters in *The Godfather* are treated as sympathetic heroes rather than villains, though the film's visual darkness mirrors their own internal darkness.

That *The Godfather* became one of Hollywood's iconic films was something of a surprise. The studio, Paramount, strongly considered replacing the thirty-two-year-old director on several occasions.

The only star in the cast was Brando. His portrayal of Vito Corleone became one of the renowned performances in film history, and he was rewarded with his second Academy Award for Best Actor. The film also claimed Oscars for Best Picture and Best Adapted Screenplay.

The Godfather broke box office records, grossing more than $133 million on its initial release. (Steven Spielberg's *Jaws* passed that mark three years later.) It also spawned two sequels—*The Godfather: Part II* (1974), which won six Academy Awards, including Best Picture, and *The Godfather: Part III* (1990).

ADDITIONAL FACTS

1. *Paramount was reluctant to cast Brando as Vito Corleone because of his perceived oddities and reputation for being difficult on set. Others considered for the part included Laurence Olivier (1907–1989), Ernest Borgnine (1917–), and Frank Sinatra (1915–1998).*

2. *For the role of Michael, which went to Al Pacino (1940–), Paramount wanted a star with more box office appeal. Warren Beatty (1937–), Jack Nicholson (1937–), and Dustin Hoffman (1937–) were all offered the part, and Robert Redford (1937–) and Ryan O'Neal (1941–) were also considered, but Coppola was adamant that Pacino was his Michael.*

3. *In 2007, the American Film Institute rated* The Godfather *the number two American film ever made, behind only* Citizen Kane *(1941).*

•••••

CNN and the Twenty-Four-Hour News Cycle

Before 1980, most television news consisted of an hour-long broadcast on a network channel—thirty minutes for local news and thirty minutes for national. That year, however, an upstart cable network in Atlanta called Cable News Network (CNN) began broadcasting live, nonstop news—a tactic that would soon revolutionize the media business.

Founded by the entrepreneur Ted Turner (1938–), CNN was an expensive gamble. Critics wondered whether enough viewers would tune in for twenty-four hours of daily news coverage to recoup Turner's investment in overseas bureaus.

The first Gulf War (1990–1991), however, was a major boon for the network. CNN was the only American station that was able to broadcast live reports directly from Iraq, sometimes from the hotel room of its war correspondent, Peter Arnett (1934–). CNN's ratings even surpassed those of the three major networks, a once-unthinkable feat for a cable channel.

For Turner, the station's success led to lucrative rewards: Time Warner purchased Turner Broadcasting for $6.5 billion in 1996.

But CNN also achieved a broader social impact by changing the way many people across the world receive news. Unlike newspapers or traditional television news, CNN allowed viewers to watch the news in real time, as events unfolded. Media observers called it the "twenty-four-hour news cycle" or just "the CNN effect." And because viewers now had access to up-to-the-minute information, political leaders came under increasing pressure to make decisions quickly and respond immediately to events.

Following CNN's success, several other all-news channels went on the air, including MSNBC, CNBC, Fox News, and several offshoots of CNN, such as CNN Headline News.

More recently, the creation of Internet news sources has solidified the dominance of the twenty-four-hour news cycle that CNN pioneered.

ADDITIONAL FACTS

1. *The HBO movie* Live from Baghdad, *a feature about CNN's coverage of the first Gulf War, was produced by Time Warner, the parent company of CNN.*

2. *Among CNN's sister networks, CNN Headline News still broadcasts today, and two channels—the sports channel CNNSI and the financial channel CNNfn—are now defunct.*

3. *Turner is also known for his charitable work. He pledged $1 billion to the United Nations, created the* Captain Planet *television series to educate children about environmental hazards, and owns the largest herd of bison in the world, significantly increasing the population of a species that was once dwindling.*

•••••

Magic Johnson

Earvin "Magic" Johnson has two legacies. One is as a revolutionary, six-foot-nine point guard who helped revitalize the National Basketball Association (NBA) in the 1980s and led the Los Angeles Lakers to five world championships. The other came as a total surprise—on November 7, 1991, Johnson announced to the world that he had tested positive for HIV and would retire from basketball. Since then, he has been an ambassador for HIV/AIDS awareness, writing books, speaking to groups, and raising money for his cause.

On the court, Johnson (1959–) played with unmatched enthusiasm and style, wowing fans around the world with his dazzling passing ability. He was the focal point of the Lakers' vaunted "Showtime" teams, which were renowned for their offensive prowess and their rivalry with Larry Bird's Boston Celtics.

Johnson packed a lot of success into his abbreviated career. As a sophomore, he led Michigan State to the National Collegiate Athletic Association (NCAA) title, beating Bird's undefeated Indiana State team in the championship game. A year later, Magic helped the Lakers to the NBA title, playing one of the signature games of his career in Game 6 of the finals against the Philadelphia 76ers. Filling in for injured center Kareem Abdul-Jabbar (1947–), the twenty-year-old Johnson played the pivot (a position usually filled by the tallest player on the team) and scored 42 points with fifteen rebounds and seven assists. He became the first rookie to be named NBA finals Most Valuable Player (MVP).

Johnson's Lakers added four more championships (1982, 1985, 1987, and 1988), and he was named the league's MVP three times (1987, 1989, and 1990).

After his initial retirement in 1991, he returned to play in the NBA All-Star Game that season and was named the game's MVP. He then led the United States lineup—known as the Dream Team—to the gold medal at the 1992 Barcelona Olympics.

Johnson made another comeback in 1995–1996, playing the final thirty-two games of the season for the Lakers before retiring for good.

Fighting the odds, Johnson has reportedly remained in good health since his 1991 announcement and has become a successful entrepreneur and frequent television commentator.

ADDITIONAL FACTS

1. *Johnson finished his career with averages of 19.5 points, 7.2 rebounds, and 11.2 assists per game. Upon his initial retirement in 1991, he was the league's career assists king, but was later passed by John Stockton (1962–).*

2. *Johnson got the nickname "Magic" in high school from an awestruck sportswriter.*

3. *Within a four-year span, Johnson won a high-school state championship, an NCAA title, and an NBA crown.*

•●●•

Hulk Hogan

Hulk Hogan (1953–) was the best-known face of the World Wrestling Federation (WWF) during the 1980s and 1990s, when pro wrestling exploded in popularity on pay-per-view television. Hogan won the group's "title" six times in televised matches and was wildly popular with fans before a steroid scandal derailed his career.

Hogan, whose real name is Terry Bollea, was born in Atlanta, Georgia, and raised in Tampa, Florida. He began bodybuilding at a young age and made his debut as a pro wrestler in 1978. He was immediately successful and quickly moved on to the WWF and American Wrestling Association (AWA) circuits, both of which staged tightly choreographed fake wrestling matches. Hogan also participated in New Japan Pro Wrestling and became a superstar in Japan.

By the early 1980s, Hogan was an international star; he even appeared in the movie *Rocky III* (1982). He competed in a number of high-profile matches, including the early Wrestlemania matches, which were broadcast in the then-new medium of pay-per-view. Professional wrestling, with its cast of spandex warriors, eventually became so popular that NBC began broadcasting matches in prime time.

Hogan was the perennial champion of Wrestlemania, the most recognizable WWF star, and a household name. His career looked unstoppable, but it was interrupted by a scandal that took over the WWF in the early 1990s. In court testimony, Hogan admitted that he frequently used steroids, and said that steroid use was widespread in the WWF.

Today, Hogan may be best known for a reality show about his personal life: VH1's *Hogan Knows Best*.

ADDITIONAL FACTS

1. *Hogan took the name* Hulk *after appearing on a television show with Lou Ferrigno (1951–), who played the Incredible Hulk on television. The host of the show pointed out that Hogan was significantly larger than Ferrigno, so Hogan decided to use the Hulk moniker himself.*

2. *Hogan's nickname in Japanese wrestling was "Ichiban," Japanese for "number one."*

3. *The WWF was forced to change its name to World Wrestling Entertainment in 2002 after complaints from the World Wildlife Fund (WWF).*

•••••

Bill Clinton

The presidency of Bill Clinton (1946–) spanned eight years of economic prosperity and relative peace abroad—and included one of the most divisive scandals in White House history. His policy achievements, military successes, and record of fiscal responsibility have often been overshadowed by his impeachment for lying about having a sexual relationship with a White House intern, Monica Lewinsky (1973–).

Clinton was educated at Georgetown University, Oxford University (after winning a Rhodes Scholarship), and Yale Law School, where he met his future wife, Hillary Rodham Clinton (1947–).

After graduating from Yale in 1973, he returned to his native Arkansas to begin his political career. By 1978, at age thirty-two, he was governor of the state. He lost his reelection bid two years later before reclaiming the position in 1982.

Clinton considered running for president in 1988 but held off until 1992. That year, he surprisingly won the Democratic nomination, then defeated incumbent president George H. W. Bush (1924–) and billionaire businessman H. Ross Perot (1930–).

The first two years of Clinton's presidency were largely a disaster, thanks to the high-profile failure of his attempt to pass a major health-care initiative his wife had led. A major consequence of the health-care fiasco was the Republican takeover of Congress in 1994, the so-called Republican Revolution. He persevered, though, becoming the first Democratic president since Franklin D. Roosevelt (1882–1945) to win reelection.

Until the Lewinsky scandal, Clinton's presidency featured the successful balancing of the federal budget, the passing of the North American Free Trade Agreement, and military interventions in Haiti and Bosnia.

But scandal slowed his second term, and in 1998, he became the second president ever to be impeached by the US House of Representatives. (Andrew Johnson, 1808–1875, was the first.) The Senate later acquitted Clinton on charges of perjury and obstruction of justice. Although Clinton was found to have lied to the nation—and to his wife—about his relationship with the twenty-two-year-old intern, many Americans felt he had been unfairly targeted by his opponents, and he left the White House with a 65 percent approval rating, the highest of any postwar president.

ADDITIONAL FACTS

1. *The first baby boomer to win the White House, Clinton was a "cool" presidential candidate who donned sunglasses and played the music of Elvis Presley (1935–1977) on his tenor saxophone on* The Arsenio Hall Show.

2. *In his postpresidency years, Clinton has focused on humanitarian causes, particularly raising money for and awareness of HIV/AIDS, poverty, and public health issues.*

3. *Clinton's other major post–White House role has been as a campaigner for Hillary in her successful 2000 run for a US Senate seat in New York and her unsuccessful 2008 race for the presidency.*

•••••

The Color Purple

Alice Walker's *The Color Purple* (1982) tells the harsh but ultimately uplifting life story of a poor, uneducated young black woman living in rural Georgia during the first half of the twentieth century. The prizewinning novel established Walker (1944–) as a major voice in American literature and African-American feminism, alongside figures such as Maya Angelou (1928–) and Toni Morrison (1931–).

The Color Purple is an epistolary novel, meaning that the story is told entirely through a character's letters or diary entries. The protagonist, Celie, writes countless letters—both to God and to her younger sister, Nettie—detailing in a blunt, confessional tone the hardships she encounters. In her teens, Celie is sexually abused and impregnated by her stepfather, who later marries her off to an even more

Alice Walker

abusive husband. Though initially timid and withdrawn, Celie eventually meets and is inspired by several strong female characters who lead her to personal and sexual self-discovery and help her to develop a more assertive, independent voice. Running parallel to Celie's story throughout the novel is the story of Nettie, her intellectually curious sister, who travels to Africa to do missionary work.

Walker's novel caused, and continues to cause, controversy owing to its sexual candor and its unflinching depictions of violence—it still ranks among the most frequently challenged books in American libraries and schools. However, its powerful narrative brought it critical and commercial acclaim and won Walker both the Pulitzer Prize and the National Book Award in 1983. *The Color Purple* has since undergone two popular, successful adaptations—a 1985 film directed by Steven Spielberg (1947–) and starring Whoopi Goldberg (1955–), and a 2005 Broadway musical produced by Oprah Winfrey (1954–).

ADDITIONAL FACTS

1. *Walker was the youngest of eight children born to sharecroppers in rural Georgia.*

2. *During the 1960s, Walker lived in Mississippi and was actively involved in the civil rights movement there.*

3. *She was instrumental in the rediscovery of the early-twentieth-century novelist Zora Neale Hurston (1891–1960). Walker and an academic colleague publicized Hurston's works and even tracked down her unmarked grave in Florida.*

• • • •

The Clash

In 1977, punk rock exploded out of the United Kingdom in a blaze of leather jackets and confrontational lyrics. That year, the Sex Pistols released their hit record *Never Mind the Bollocks, Here's the Sex Pistols*, and the Clash released their self-titled debut album.

Although sometimes lumped together, the two trailblazing punk bands had drastically different outlooks. In contrast to the nihilistic and vitriolic Sex Pistols, the Clash brought a more intellectual and musically reflective approach to their brand of punk.

Indeed, the Clash—guitarist and vocalist Joe Strummer (1952–2002), bassist Paul Simonon (1955–), guitarist Mick Jones (1955–), and drummer Terry Chimes (1955–)—were idealists. The quartet's songs dealt with themes of unemployment, social decay, racism, police brutality, and political malaise. For instance, their debut album featured the song "(White Man) In Hammersmith Palais," which criticized the political apathy of contemporary Britain:

> *White youth, black youth*
> *Better find another solution*
> *Why not phone up Robin Hood*
> *And ask him for some wealth distribution*
> *[. . .]*
> *The new groups are not concerned*
> *With what there is to be learned*

The Clash truly believed that rock and roll meant something and could change society for the better. Punk rock proved to be the ideal complement to their left-leaning political outlook and their love of reggae, dub, dance, and jazz music. The fusion of white and black musical heritages was the perfect snapshot of a British culture in flux after the 1960s.

The Clash released several critically acclaimed albums but broke up in 1986 amid internal disagreements.

ADDITIONAL FACTS

1. *Lead singer Joe Strummer was the son of a diplomat.*

2. *In 2006,* Time *magazine chose* London Calling *(1979) as one of the 100 best albums of all time.*

3. *Strummer scored the sound track to the 1997 movie* Grosse Pointe Blank.

Martin Scorsese

Along with Woody Allen (1935–) and Spike Lee (1957–), Martin Scorsese (1942–) is among the quintessential contemporary New York City filmmakers. Much of Scorsese's work is heavily influenced by his upbringing in the Little Italy section of Manhattan.

His exposure to street violence, local mafiosi, and the claustrophobia of city life, coupled with his interest in the Catholic Church, informs the duality of many of his protagonists—whose lives of sin collide with their (often fruitless) desires for redemption.

Scorsese's work is marked by an energetic visual style, frequently featuring abrupt cuts from one scene to the next, rock-and-roll sound tracks, and extreme violence. His best and most successful films are explorations of alienation, paranoia, and bloodshed, often with New York City as not only a backdrop but also a character unto itself.

Scorsese's breakthrough film was *Mean Streets* (1973), a study of a young man's attempt to reconcile his life as a petty gangster with his desire for godliness. The first words of the film—spoken in a voice-over by Scorsese himself—sum up much of the director's future work: "You don't make up for your sins in church. You do it in the streets. You do it at home. All the rest is bullshit and you know it."

That sentiment has carried on through Scorsese's most acclaimed work, from his masterpiece on obsession, loneliness, and urban decay, *Taxi Driver* (1976), to the first-person tale of New York gangster life in *Goodfellas* (1990), to *The Departed* (2006), which won the Best Picture Oscar and earned Scorsese his first Academy Award for Best Director.

Scorsese's career is also marked by his collaboration with three particular actors—Harvey Keitel (1939–, five features), Robert De Niro (1943–, eight films, including *Raging Bull*, for which De Niro won an Academy Award for Best Actor), and Leonardo DiCaprio (1974–, three films).

ADDITIONAL FACTS

1. *Scorsese has said that his love of cinema diverted him from a life in the priesthood.*

2. *Although he was nominated for the Best Director Oscar five times, Scorsese did not win the award until 2007, when he won for* The Departed. *The film was also the first Scorsese directed to win the Academy Award for Best Picture.*

3. *Scorsese is a member of the so-called movie brats: American directors (most of them film-school educated) who reinvigorated the Hollywood system in the 1970s—similar to the French New Wave auteurs who had an encyclopedic knowledge of Hollywood movies and directors. Other principal members of the group include Steven Spielberg, Francis Ford Coppola, and George Lucas.*

•••••

Yuppies

In 1984, a cover story in *Newsweek* magazine warned of the arrival of a new breed of American: the yuppie. Short for "young urban professional," the magazine coined the term to capture the rapidly changing face of the baby boom generation, which had grown up from being the idealists of the 1960s to become the careerists of the 1980s, trading in their bell-bottoms for BMWs.

Indeed, critics portrayed the 1980s as an era of unmitigated and unprecedented greed. Fiction about yuppies, including *The Bonfire of the Vanities* (1987), by Tom Wolfe (1931–), depicted young white-collar traders in New York City as shallow and avaricious. The Bret Easton Ellis (1964–) novel *American Psycho* (1991) tells the story of a wealthy young investment banker whose empty life is punctuated only by decisions about the color of his tie and the font for his business cards.

As a demographic group, young Americans in the 1980s waited longer than previous generations to have children, and thus had much more disposable income to spend on high-end bric-a-brac, plastic surgery, Perrier, and the other trappings of yuppiehood. Many members of the generation complained that the pejorative term stereotyped them unfairly, but it captured a widespread sense that the baby boomers had turned inward from the idealism of the 1960s.

But the yuppies themselves receded, and in 1991 *Time* published an "obituary" for the yuppie, citing a downturn in the economy. The term is still used, albeit often as a form of mockery, to refer to wealthy, young professionals.

ADDITIONAL FACTS

1. *The term* yuppie *has spawned several offshoots, including* buppie *(black urban professional) and* scuppie *(socially conscious upwardly mobile person).*

2. *After the publication of* American Psycho, *Bret Easton Ellis received numerous death threats and large amounts of hate mail for his pitiless depiction of yuppie greed and selfishness.*

3. *During the 1980s, the illness now known as chronic fatigue syndrome was often referred to as "yuppie flu" because it most often occurred in people characterized as yuppies.*

Wayne Gretzky

There's a reason why Wayne Gretzky (1961–) is called the Great One: He was the most dominant player in hockey history. No North American athlete in a team sport, with the possible exception of Babe Ruth (1895–1948), rewrote his sport's record books like Gretzky. And unlike the Babe, Gretzky was not a physically dominating player—as he once put it, "My eyes and mind have to do most of the work."

The slightly built center from Brantford, Ontario, played under the strain of immense national expectations in Canada from age nine, when reporters were already comparing him to hockey's foremost legend, Gordie Howe (1928–).

Remarkably, Gretzky exceeded the expectations. He led the Edmonton Oilers to four Stanley Cups, was the National Hockey League's (NHL) Most Valuable Player (MVP) nine times and its scoring leader ten times, and was twice named the MVP of the play-offs. When he retired in 1999, he owned sixty-one NHL records, including the marks for career goals (894), assists (1,963), and points (2,857).

In a measure of his staggering dominance, no other hockey player has more career *points* than Gretzky has *assists*.

Gretzky made his professional debut for the Indianapolis Racers of the World Hockey Association (WHA) in 1978 and was sold later that year to the Edmonton Oilers. He was the WHA's Rookie of the Year.

The WHA folded after that season, and the Oilers joined the NHL for the 1979–1980 season. Gretzky immediately dominated, winning the first of eight consecutive MVPs.

Among his most remarkable feats: scoring fifty goals in the first thirty-nine games of the 1981–1982 season, then finishing the year with a record ninety-two goals; starting the 1983–1984 season with points in fifty-one consecutive games; racking up forty-seven play-off points in 1984–1985; and setting a record with 215 points in 1985–1986.

Gretzky also helped popularize hockey in warm-weather areas of the United States when he was traded from Edmonton to the Los Angeles Kings in 1988. He led the Kings to the Stanley Cup Finals in 1993 and later finished his career with the St. Louis Blues and New York Rangers.

ADDITIONAL FACTS

1. *Gretzky played for Canada in the 1998 Nagano Olympics, then returned to the Games as Canada's executive director at the 2002 Salt Lake City Olympics, putting together his country's first gold-medal-winning team in fifty years. He served in the same capacity at the 2006 Turin Games.*

2. *Gretzky topped the 200-point mark for a season four times during his NHL career; no other player has done it even once.*

3. *At the 2000 NHL All-Star Game, his number, 99, was retired by the entire league.*

•• • ••

New Kids on the Block

Formed in Boston in 1984, New Kids on the Block was a peppy, all-male pop group that for a brief, terrifying moment appeared to represent the future of American popular music.

The group was assembled by the producer Maurice Starr (1953–) and consisted of Joey McIntyre (1972–), Donnie Wahlberg (1969–), Danny Wood (1969–), Jordan Knight (1970–), and Jordan's brother Jonathan (1968–). At the time the group was formed, none of its members was over the age of sixteen.

The band's self-titled debut album was roundly considered a flop when it came out in 1986. In danger of being dropped by Columbia Records, the band released its second album, *Hangin' Tough*, a year and a half later.

While the group was on tour in 1988 with the pop act Tiffany, its second single from *Hangin' Tough*, "You Got It (The Right Stuff)," started getting regular exposure on MTV. The single was followed up with "I'll Be Loving You (Forever)," which reached number one on the Billboard music charts. The success of this single and the band's next album, *Step by Step*, resulted in the group's embarking on a world tour sponsored by Coca-Cola.

However, the band's meteoric rise halted in 1992 when a former sound engineer alleged that the group had lip-synched a number of songs on *Hangin' Tough*. This accusation, combined with the waning popularity of teenybopper acts and so-called boy bands, was the beginning of the end for the teen group.

Their last album, *Face the Music*, was released in 1994 and received mediocre reviews. The group announced that it was disbanding in June 1994, at its final concert date in promotion of the album.

ADDITIONAL FACTS

1. *In March 1991, band member Donnie Wahlberg was charged with first-degree arson in connection with a fire at the Seelbach Hotel in Louisville, Kentucky.*

2. *Starr was also responsible for putting together the band New Edition.*

3. *Although not a New Kid, perhaps the most famous descendant of the group is Donnie's younger brother, Mark Wahlberg (1971–). Mark Wahlberg emerged as a recording artist with the group Marky Mark and the Funky Bunch. He survived pop stardom seemingly unscathed and now earns top box office billing under his given name.*

4. *Mark Wahlberg is the executive producer of the HBO TV series* Entourage. *It is widely believed that the fictional character of Johnny Drama (a washed-up actor who's the elder brother of Vincent Chase) is based on Mark's real-life older brother, Donnie.*

• • • • •

Rush Limbaugh

Loved and hated for his combination of irreverent humor and staunchly conservative political views, Rush Limbaugh (1951–) has developed the highest-rated national radio talk show in America. Listened to by about 20 million people each week on nearly 600 stations, he has become a hero to the Right and an enemy of the Left.

Limbaugh is, at his core, an entertainer. But it is his political commentary that stirs the blood of Republicans and Democrats alike. Proponents credit him with playing a significant role in helping the Republicans take control of Congress in 1994; opponents say he is disingenuous at best, an outright liar at worst. Either way, he is a giant in broadcasting.

Limbaugh comes from a family of lawyers, and his grandfather (also named Rush) was the US ambassador to India under President Dwight D. Eisenhower (1890–1969). Limbaugh got his start in radio in 1967 as a disc jockey on his hometown station in Cape Girardeau, Missouri, while still in high school. After failing to make a career in radio with several unsuccessful jobs, he left the business in 1979 to work in sales for the Kansas City Royals baseball team.

He returned to radio in 1983, becoming a political commentator at KMBZ in Kansas City. A year later, he was hired at KFBK in Sacramento, where he became a dramatic success, nearly tripling his ratings over the next four years.

In 1988, he signed a syndication deal and moved to New York City, from where he has been the scourge of liberals across the country for the past two decades. Limbaugh's success has also inspired dozens of conservative talk-radio imitators, including Sean Hannity (1961–) and Michael Savage (1942–), and a smaller number of liberal commentators, such as Al Franken (1951–).

ADDITIONAL FACTS

1. *Limbaugh began his career using the on-air pseudonym Rusty Sharpe for his first radio show in high school. He later used the name Jeff Christie while working in Pittsburgh.*

2. *He was inducted into the Radio Hall of Fame in 1993 and the National Association of Broadcasters Hall of Fame in 1998. He also won the Marconi Award for Syndicated Personality of the Year in 1992, 1995, 2000, and 2005.*

3. *In 2003, ESPN hired Limbaugh as a commentator for its Sunday NFL Countdown show. But less than a month into his tenure, he resigned after making a controversial comment about the role race played in the media's treatment of the Philadelphia Eagles quarterback Donovan McNabb (1976–).*

••●••

The Unbearable Lightness of Being

The Unbearable Lightness of Being (1984), by the Czech novelist Milan Kundera (1929–), is probably the most prominent work of eastern European fiction of the modern era. An intriguing combination of genres, it mixes fiction, politics, philosophy, and history, all set against the backdrop of intellectual and artistic repression under the communist regime of the former Czechoslovakia.

The novel's unusual title refers to its main theme: the idea that life can be lived with either "lightness" or "weight." At the novel's outset, Kundera contemplates the philosopher Friedrich Nietzsche (1844–1900), who famously asked what it might be like if we as humans were forced to relive our lives over and over eternally. Nietzsche believed that the prospect of such "eternal recurrence" was horrible—even the mere thought of it was a weighty burden. To Kundera, though, it is even more distressing to know that we have only one shot at life. Because we have no way to compare the different potential outcomes of each important decision we make, life has an essential arbitrariness or meaninglessness—an "unbearable lightness."

This discussion sets the stage for Kundera's story, set in 1960s Prague, about a surgeon named Tomas who lives life quite lightly. An avid womanizer, he enjoys pleasures that come and go in a moment. His photographer wife, Tereza, however, sees life as a weighty thing, in which every action is laden with significance. Though Tomas and Tereza love each other, these differing worldviews complicate their marriage considerably.

When Tomas loses his job after criticizing the Czech Communist Party, he is forced to flee abroad and must finally choose between Tereza and his mistress, Sabina, a free-spirited artist and fellow devotee of lightness. Throughout, all three characters navigate the complex intersection between art and politics—as Kundera himself did, writing amid the restrictions of a communist regime.

ADDITIONAL FACTS

1. *Although Kundera wrote his early novels in his native language, Czech, he moved to France in 1975 and has written his most recent novels in French.*

2. *In 1988,* The Unbearable Lightness of Being *was made into a film starring Daniel Day-Lewis (1957–) as Tomas, Juliette Binoche (1964–) as Tereza, and Lena Olin (1955–) as Sabina.*

3. *Many of the events that befall Tomas in* The Unbearable Lightness of Being *stem from Kundera's own experience during the Prague Spring of 1968—a brief period of increased political freedom in Czechoslovakia that the Soviet military quickly brought to a brutal halt.*

••••

Philip Glass

Though he is uncomfortable with the description of his work as minimalist, Philip Glass (1937–) is regarded as one of the world's leading composers of minimalist music. Minimalism has no clear definition. Rather, it refers to a series of traits that works by Glass and like-minded composers have in common. Among these are the repetition of very short musical phrases and an extremely steady, almost mathematical beat.

Born in Baltimore, Glass studied music at Juilliard and in Paris. He returned to New York City in the 1960s, joining a community of other young, struggling avant-garde composers, including Steve Reich (1936–).

The musicians in the group were notable for drawing their artistic inspirations from non-Western sources. (Reich, for instance, took a five-week trip to Ghana to study with African drummers.) For Glass, the most significant influences came from India. In fact, after studying Indian rhythms and working with the sitar player Ravi Shankar (1920–), Glass renounced all his earlier works and set out on the direction for which he is famous today. The most ambitious piece from this period is his four-hour-long *Music in Twelve Parts* (1971–1974).

Glass never embraced the term *minimalist,* and instead offered an alternative: *theater composer.* Indeed, Glass's most ambitious works have been his two opera trilogies. The first was his *Portrait Trilogy,* which contains one of his most famous works, *Einstein on the Beach* (1976). (The title refers to the great scientist's remark that he did his best thinking while strolling on the beach.) The second was the *Satyagraha* (1980), based on the early life of Mohandas Gandhi (1869–1948), who began his career as a lawyer in South Africa. The last was *Akhnaten* (1983), a work based on the story of an Egyptian pharaoh. He released another acclaimed trilogy in the 1990s.

Glass's most recent operatic work is *Waiting for the Barbarians* (2005), based on the novel of that name by the Nobel Prize–winning South African writer J. M. Coetzee (1940–). A Glass opera about the American Civil War titled *Appomattox* premiered in 2007.

ADDITIONAL FACTS

1. *Glass is an advocate of the Tibetan cause and first met the Dalai Lama (1935–) in 1972.*

2. *An earlier version of Glass's Academy Award–nominated score for* The Hours *(2002) was used in the 1988 documentary* The Thin Blue Line.

3. *To earn money when he was starting out, Glass drove a taxicab in New York City and started a moving company with Reich.*

• • ● • •

Robert De Niro

Robert De Niro (1943–) is one of the most acclaimed male actors of his generation. Born in New York City, he made his feature debut in Brian De Palma's 1968 comedy *Greetings*. Five years later, De Niro's breakthrough came in two films—*Bang the Drum Slowly*, in which he played a terminally ill baseball player, and *Mean Streets*.

The latter of those two films set him on a course to stardom. *Mean Streets* represented the first of eight collaborations with the director Martin Scorsese. In it, De Niro's emergence on the screen is literally explosive—the first time he appears as the self-destructive Johnny Boy, he blows up a mailbox and runs away, giggling.

His performance as Johnny Boy set the standard for what would become De Niro's trademark acting style. An adherent of the Method acting school, he is known for his immersion in roles, and many of his later characters are combustible, aggressive, and sometimes truly crazy.

A year after his eye-opening performance in *Mean Streets*, De Niro starred as the young Vito Corleone in Francis Ford Coppola's *The Godfather: Part II*, earning an Academy Award for Best Supporting Actor.

In 1976, he returned to work with Scorsese on *Taxi Driver*, in which De Niro inhabited one of Hollywood's most enduring and troubled characters, Travis Bickle. His line "Are you talkin' to me? Well I'm the only one here" represents the character's intense loneliness and alienation and has gone down in Hollywood history as one of the most memorable pieces of dialogue ever spoken.

De Niro helped Michael Cimino's *The Deer Hunter* (1978) win an Academy Award for Best Picture, then created another of his signature characters in Scorsese's *Raging Bull* (1980). As the middleweight champion Jake La Motta, De Niro earned an Oscar for Best Actor, putting on more than fifty pounds to play the boxer in his later years.

In recent years, De Niro's body of work has been marked by quantity but in most cases not by quality. But he has costarred in two hugely successful comedy franchises, *Analyze This* (1999)/*Analyze That* (2002) and *Meet the Parents* (2000)/*Meet the Fockers* (2004).

ADDITIONAL FACTS

1. *De Niro has directed two films:* A Bronx Tale *(1993) and* The Good Shepherd *(2006).*

2. *Marlon Brando and De Niro are the only actors to win Academy Awards for playing the same role—Vito Corleone. Brando won Best Actor for* The Godfather *(1972), and De Niro won Best Supporting Actor for* The Godfather: Part II *(1974).*

3. *De Niro cofounded the TriBeCa Film Festival, following the September 11, 2001, attacks on New York City. One of the missions of the festival is to bring vitality back to Lower Manhattan, which was devastated by September 11.*

·•●●·•

Glasnost

Glasnost, a Russian word meaning "openness," refers to a set of reforms introduced by the Soviet leader Mikhail Gorbachev (1931–) in the USSR during the 1980s to allow more free speech in the communist nation. Gorbachev hoped that permitting more civil liberties would revitalize the Soviet system, but instead his reforms unleashed withering criticism of the communist government and hastened the demise of communism around the world.

Gorbachev introduced the first reforms shortly after he took power in 1985. On his orders, previously banned books and films were made legal, political dissidents were freed, and restrictions on mass media were abolished.

A key test of glasnost occurred in 1986, when an explosion and meltdown at a nuclear power plant in the Ukraine killed dozens. After a thirteen-day cover-up, Gorbachev allowed the press to report on the Chernobyl disaster, an unprecedented decision that spurred investigations into other Soviet blunders.

The information unleashed under glasnost shocked the Russian people. In a nation that called itself "the world's most advanced society," it turned out that millions waited daily in long lines for basic necessities such as soap and milk.

Glasnost also allowed discussion of the country's painful past, including the deaths of millions in purges and famines under former Soviet leader Joseph Stalin (1879–1953). Even the Soviet victory in World War II was tarnished when it was revealed that government incompetence had caused millions of unnecessary deaths.

Confidence in the Communist Party quickly eroded, both in the Soviet Union and throughout the Warsaw Pact nations. By 1989, 60,000 independent groups and clubs were active in the Soviet Union, and reformist candidates won seats in fifty Russian cities in 1990 elections. Mass demonstrations in major cities and a national mining strike in 1991 solidified what national polls had already shown: that a majority of Russians felt that their political system needed radical transformation.

Gorbachev borrowed the term *glasnost* from Vladimir Lenin (1870–1924), who saw it as a tool of propaganda. Implementing the policy in part to protect his position of power, General Secretary Gorbachev never could have imagined that glasnost would bring down the Soviet Union and change the world.

ADDITIONAL FACTS

1. *Glasnost was accompanied by perestroika, a set of economic reforms that Gorbachev hoped would revive the moribund Soviet economy.*

2. *Glasnost-themed advertisements for companies such as PepsiCo and McDonald's dominated American media beginning in 1988. These commercials abandoned the mocking stereotypes of Russian life popular before glasnost and showed Russia in a favorable light.*

3. *In 1990 the works of twenty-six Russian artists were featured in* Interview *magazine under the title* Absolut Glasnost. *Gorbachev was presented with the first issue.*

··●●··

Carl Lewis

In track and field, Carl Lewis's achievements are unparalleled. His nine career gold medals place him in a tie for the most in Olympic history. He is one of just three athletes to have won the same Summer Olympic event (the long jump) four times. In 1984, he repeated Jesse Owens's historic feat of winning the 100 meters, 200 meters, 4x100-meter relay, and long jump at a single Games. And over a ten-year span, Lewis won a record sixty-five consecutive long-jump events.

His accomplishments earned him an array of accolades, including being named Sportsman of the Century by the International Olympic Committee and Olympian of the Century by *Sports Illustrated*.

But for all his success, Lewis (1961–) was never embraced in the United States as warmly as he was in Europe and Asia. Some blamed his supposed lack of humility and attempts to "cash in" on his success at the 1984 Olympics in Los Angeles with lucrative endorsement deals and a career in entertainment and fashion.

Yet, considering Lewis's stature in the sporting world, he certainly had reason for arrogance. After winning four golds at the 1984 Games, he added two more victories in 1988, becoming the first athlete to successfully defend the Olympic 100-meter and long-jump titles. He won another pair of golds in 1992, in the long jump and 4x100-meter relay.

And his most improbable—and dramatic—Olympic victory came at the 1996 Games in Atlanta. He had barely qualified for the US team in the long jump, but he stunned everyone by upsetting the field to win the final gold medal of his illustrious career.

ADDITIONAL FACTS

1. *Although Lewis won gold in the 100 meters at the 1988 Seoul Olympics, he did not finish first in the actual race—the Canadian sprinter Ben Johnson (1961–) did. But Johnson tested positive for the banned steroid stanozolol, and Lewis was awarded the gold medal.*

2. *Lewis also won ten medals (eight golds, one silver, and one bronze) in World Championship competition. His most memorable contest was the 1991 World Championships in Tokyo, where he broke the 100-meter world record (9.86 seconds) but saw his ten-year unbeaten streak end in the long jump. He was bested by fellow American Mike Powell (1963–), who topped a world record set by Bob Beamon (1946–).*

3. *Even though Lewis did not play basketball or football, he was drafted in 1984 by the NBA's Chicago Bulls (tenth round) and the NFL's Dallas Cowboys (twelfth round).*

•••••

Graphic Novels

In 1986, the cartoonist Art Spiegelman (1948–) released the first volume of *Maus: A Survivor's Tale*. A book-length cartoon about the experiences of Spiegelman's father during World War II, *Maus* tackled the most sensitive of topics: the Holocaust. Spiegelman's book elevated cartoons to a serious literary form and helped define an emerging new genre—the graphic novel.

Until the 1970s, most mainstream comics were daily strips published in newspapers or one-dimensional superhero comics like *Superman* and *Batman*. But graphic novels such as *Maus* were highly realistic and dramatic. Spiegelman's book told the story of the Nazi invasion of Poland and the subsequent roundup of the country's Jewish population. In 1992, the second volume of Spiegelman's work, *Maus II,* which explored the psychological toll of the Holocaust on survivors, won a special Pulitzer Prize.

Graphic novels continued to grow in popularity during the 1990s and 2000s. *Jimmy Corrigan, the Smartest Kid on Earth* (2000), by Chris Ware (1967–), a critically acclaimed story of a child growing up without a father, was published in 2000. Other major works have included *Black Hole* (2005), by Charles Burns (1955–), which follows the story of Seattle teenagers who develop mutations as a result of a sexually transmitted disease, and *Persepolis* (2003), by Marjane Satrapi (1969–), a memoir of the Islamic revolution in Iran.

In the wake of the success of books like *Persepolis,* many major publishing houses have begun releasing graphic novels, and the books have started to attract increasingly positive critical attention as bona fide works of literature. (*The New Yorker* called *Jimmy Corrigan* a "masterpiece.") The graphic novelists broke the association between comics and children, creating mature literary works in what had been considered a medium for kids.

ADDITIONAL FACTS

1. *The graphic novel* V for Vendetta *(1988), which imagines a totalitarian government taking power in the United Kingdom, was made into a 2006 movie and was cited as one of the inspirations for the grassroots support of Ron Paul (1935–) in his unsuccessful bid for the Republican candidacy in the 2008 presidential primary.*

2. *Spiegelman was a cocreator of the* Garbage Pail Kids, *a series of wacky trading cards issued by Topps in 1985.*

3. *In 2007, Satrapi's* Persepolis *was adapted into an animated feature film.*

•••••

Diana, Princess of Wales

She was known as the People's Princess, a global celebrity and humanitarian whose tragic death stunned the world. As a shy girl of twenty, Diana Spencer (1961–1997) married Great Britain's Prince Charles (1948–) in 1981, in what many believed was a fairy-tale romance. Hundreds of millions of people tuned in to watch the wedding on television; sixteen years later, an estimated 2.5 billion watched her funeral.

Diana united the grandeur of the British royal family with movie-star charisma to create a persona that people around the world found irresistible. She was a fixture in the fashion and celebrity worlds and was also one of the planet's most socially powerful women, working tirelessly on behalf of victims of AIDS, leprosy, and cancer, among other causes.

Along with her power, though, came vulnerability, which emerged when her personal life unraveled in public view. Her marriage to Prince Charles was an unhappy one. As time passed, the two rarely appeared in public together and seemed unhappy when they did. Soon, the truth came out: Diana suffered from depression, developed an eating disorder, and attempted suicide, while Charles rekindled an old romance with Camilla Parker Bowles (1947–). Diana responded to her husband's infidelity with affairs of her own until they officially separated in 1992.

As this personal drama unfolded, Diana attempted to raise her two sons, Prince William (1982–) and Prince Harry (1984–), while the paparazzi followed her relentlessly.

Diana and Charles divorced in 1996, leaving the princess to create an independent life for herself. The public remained fascinated with her, and photographers continued to trail her. When she and her boyfriend, Dodi Fayed (1955–1997), died in a high-speed car accident in Paris, many said they were fleeing the prying eyes of the paparazzi.

Investigations determined that the crash was a tragic accident and that their driver, Henri Paul (1956–1997), was drunk. Still, many conspiracy theories abound, including one put forth by Fayed's father, Mohamed Al-Fayed (1933–).

More than a million people lined the route from Kensington Palace to Westminster Abbey for Diana's funeral. She died at age thirty-six.

ADDITIONAL FACTS

1. *Diana was from an aristocratic family herself. She was the daughter of the eighth Earl Spencer and was a descendant of King James II.*

2. *She was a kindergarten teacher before marrying Prince Charles.*

3. *Elton John (1947–) rewrote the lyrics of his hit song "Candle in the Wind" in Diana's memory. (The original version was a 1973 tribute to Marilyn Monroe.) He performed the new version at Diana's funeral.*

••●••

The Satanic Verses

The international furor that erupted over *The Satanic Verses,* a novel by Salman Rushdie (1947–), is unparalleled in modern literature. When the book was published in 1988, allegations that it blasphemed Islam set off a firestorm of worldwide protest, leading to book burnings, riots, bombings, a bounty on Rushdie's head, and dozens of deaths.

Although *The Satanic Verses'* main subject is Anglo-Indian cultural identity and migration, it contains passages that touch on sensitive aspects of Islam. The novel's title refers to several verses that, according to some scholars, were originally part of the Qur'an but were quickly removed by the Prophet Muhammad, who claimed that he included them in the first place only because Satan had tempted him into doing so. These "satanic verses" allegedly acknowledged the divinity of three minor goddesses that certain Arab tribes worshipped—a direct contravention of Islam's belief in one single God.

The very existence of these verses, let alone any story behind them, is a long-standing source of contention in Islamic scholarship, and Rushdie's novel touched a nerve. Moreover, one particular section of the novel—a dream sequence in which the prostitutes at a brothel try to attract business by assuming the names of Muhammad's wives—was seen as a grievous insult to both Muhammad and Islam.

In 1989, the Ayatollah Ruhollah Khomeini (c. 1900–1989) of Iran, the country's religious leader, issued a fatwa, or judicial edict, calling for the execution of Rushdie and anyone else associated with the publication of *The Satanic Verses.* A reward was placed on Rushdie's head, prompting him to cancel his book tour and go into hiding. Dozens of protesters in several countries were killed in anti-Rushdie riots, and three assassination attempts—one successful—were carried out against foreign-language translators of the novel. Ironically, Western critics generally found *The Satanic Verses* outstanding, citing it as a complex, deftly told tale of modern multiculturalism.

ADDITIONAL FACTS

1. The Satanic Verses *was banned in more than twenty countries, including Singapore, South Africa, Pakistan, Egypt, Saudi Arabia, and even Rushdie's native India.*

2. *Rushdie formally apologized in 1990 for writing* The Satanic Verses *but later rescinded the apology, describing it as the "biggest mistake of my life."*

3. *Although Iran's leaders stated in 1998 that they would not attempt to carry out Rushdie's execution, they reconfirmed in both 2005 and 2006 that the death sentence was permanent.*

••••

DJ Kool Herc

Clive Campbell, better known by the stage name DJ Kool Herc, is considered one of the founders of hip-hop. Along with a handful of other New York City artists, such as Grandmaster Flash (1958–), Herc invented many of the techniques that turned rap into a global musical phenomenon in the 1980s and 1990s.

Born in Kingston, Jamaica, in 1955, Herc immigrated to the United States at age twelve. He settled in the Bronx and began deejaying at block parties in poor neighborhoods while still a teenager. At the time, the Bronx suffered from massive unemployment, violence, and social malaise, conditions that were reflected in many of the first rap lyrics.

Campbell's greatest innovation as a DJ was to pick out the most danceable section of a song—the "break"—and repeat it continuously on his turntables, providing a pulsating backdrop for the rappers whose lyrics accompanied his beats. As he put it in an interview in 2005, "I played records to get you up; I get a record to sit you down; I played records you could talk over; and, I get you back on the dance floor. That's my format." Herc scavenged old funk records for good breaks, which he then incorporated into his shows; continuously looped breaks of funk songs later became a staple of hip-hop.

In its earliest days, rap music was performed almost exclusively by African-American artists and was confined geographically to an impoverished corner of New York City. That changed in 1979, when a group called the Sugar Hill Gang recorded the single "Rapper's Delight," which sold more than 8 million copies. Throughout the 1980s, rap moved into the mainstream thanks to groups like Public Enemy and was eventually embraced by some white artists as well.

DJ Kool Herc, however, never left the Bronx. He was stabbed after a party in the late 1970s, slipped into obscurity, and was largely bypassed when rap became big business. However, today he is recognized as one of the godfathers of rap. He continues to deejay occasionally.

ADDITIONAL FACTS

1. *In 2006, Herc and other rap legends headlined the opening of the Smithsonian Institution's "Hip-Hop Won't Stop," a collection of early New York City rap memorabilia at the National Museum of American History in Washington, DC.*

2. *Although best known for using breaks from African-American funk artists such as James Brown (1933–2006), Herc and Grandmaster Flash also sampled from white heavy-metal groups, such as the Australian band AC/DC.*

3. *In the 1970s, Herc was renowned as the DJ with the loudest sound system in New York City; he sometimes powered his system by tapping illegally into the city's electrical grid.*

••●••

Steven Spielberg

Steven Spielberg (1947–) is his generation's most successful film director. He has achieved unparalleled commercial triumphs with such blockbusters as *Jaws* (1975), *Raiders of the Lost Ark* (1981), *E.T.: The Extra-Terrestrial* (1982), and *Jurassic Park* (1993), as well as artistic achievements with *Close Encounters of the Third Kind* (1977), *Schindler's List* (1993), and *Saving Private Ryan* (1998).

Spielberg came to Hollywood as a film-school reject but a successful television director. His made-for-TV film *Duel* (1971) earned him some early notice, and he made his feature debut with *The Sugarland Express* (1974).

Spielberg truly arrived with *Jaws,* a revolutionary film that turned summer into blockbuster movie season in Hollywood. The picture cost $12 million and went on to become the highest-grossing film up until that time, with domestic receipts of $260 million. Tapping into the fear of the unseen and unknown, Spielberg allowed the near-mythic great white shark to be seen only rarely throughout the film.

Spielberg followed *Jaws* with *Close Encounters,* a special effects marvel that helped usher in the era of blockbuster science-fiction movies (along with *Star Wars,* 1977).

His Indiana Jones series, beginning with *Raiders of the Lost Ark* (1981) and starring Harrison Ford in the role of the swashbuckling archeologist, was hugely success-ful—each film grossed more than $179 million domestically. (A fourth Indiana Jones movie was released in 2008.)

E.T. was another science-fiction phenomenon, passing *Star Wars* as the top-grossing film up to that time ($359 million in the United States). The film centers on the relationship between a fatherless suburban boy and a lost visitor from another planet, and Spielberg gave the story particular poignancy by shooting from a lower camera angle in order to present a child's perspective on reality.

The year 1993 proved Spielberg's ability to make both commercially and artistically viable films. *Jurassic Park,* which features the most realistic re-creation of dinosaurs ever captured on film, was an enormous hit, and his Holocaust film, *Schindler's List,* won seven Academy Awards (including Best Picture and Best Director).

He picked up another Oscar for Best Director for *Saving Private Ryan* (1998), which redefined the war genre with its realistic portrayal of combat violence.

ADDITIONAL FACTS

1. *In addition to his success as a director, Spielberg has produced hits such as* Poltergeist *(1982),* Back to the Future *(1985),* Who Framed Roger Rabbit *(1988),* Men in Black *(1997),* Flags of Our Fathers *(2006), and* Letters from Iwo Jima *(2006).*

2. *Though his films are often lauded for their optimism and naïveté, Spielberg has also tackled serious subjects, including the Holocaust (*Schindler's List*), slavery (*Amistad, 1997*), racism (*The Color Purple, 1985*), and terrorism (*Munich, 2005*).*

3. *Spielberg has been nominated for twelve Academy Awards, winning three (two for best director and one as coproducer of a best picture).*

•••••

Political Correctness

In the 1980s and 1990s, the campuses of many American colleges and universities erupted into rancorous, emotional debates over "political correctness." The controversies pitted the right to free expression against the desire on the part of many university officials to make campuses more welcoming to people of all races and beliefs by imposing some limits on potentially offensive speech.

For instance, in 1989 the University of Connecticut adopted a rule that barred students from telling "inconsiderate jokes" or engaging in "inappropriately directed laughter" that could be construed as offensive. In 1993, a student at the University of Pennsylvania was investigated and faced disciplinary action for yelling the term "water buffalo" at a group of students.

Rules adopted at other schools outlawed racial epithets, Holocaust denial, sexist terms, or jokes deemed damaging to another student's self-esteem.

To critics of political correctness, the "speech codes" were at best a clumsy attempt to legislate good manners, but at worst a system of censorship that violated the spirit of free speech.

Furthermore, critics said, political correctness could squelch discussion of serious but sensitive political topics such as affirmative action solely because opinions might offend some.

In the world outside of college campuses, political correctness also referred to a transformation in the language used to describe many ethnic and social groups. During this time, for instance, *retarded* became *developmentally disabled, Negro* became *African-American,* and *Indian* became *Native American,* in a shift toward terms that were regarded as more culturally sensitive.

Speech codes faded as a source of contention after the 1990s, although the proper balance between speech and civility in a diverse society has been—and seems likely to remain—a source of endless debate.

ADDITIONAL FACTS

1. *The comedian and political commentator Bill Maher (1956–) hosted a popular television show called* Politically Incorrect. *Ironically, the show was canceled after Maher made some rather un-PC comments about America's policies in the war on terror.*

2. *The University of Pennsylvania eventually dropped its case against the student accused of using the term "water buffalo."*

3. *The term* politically correct *derives from Marxism, whose adherents were expected to subscribe to the "party line" on political questions.*

••••

Jackie Joyner-Kersee

When Jacqueline Joyner was born in East St. Louis, Illinois, in 1962, she was named after the First Lady of the United States, Jacqueline Kennedy (1929–1994). Joyner-Kersee's grandmother announced, "Someday this girl will be the First Lady of something"—and she was right. Jackie Joyner-Kersee would become the First Lady of Track and Field and arguably the greatest female athlete of the twentieth century.

Joyner-Kersee's signature event was the heptathlon, a grueling test consisting of seven components—the 100-meter hurdles, high jump, shot put, 200-meter run, long jump, javelin, and 800-meter run. She won two Olympic gold medals (1988 and 1992) and one silver (1984) in the event and set the world record in 1988.

She also claimed three Olympic long-jump medals (gold in 1988 and bronze in 1992 and 1996). Perhaps her most memorable Olympic performance came at the 1996 Atlanta Games. She had pulled out of the heptathlon due to an injury to her right hamstring, but she decided to compete in the long jump six days later. Entering her final jump of the competition, she overcame obvious pain to leap into third place and win the bronze.

Joyner-Kersee played an important role in the growth of women's sports in America. She was inspired by Babe Didrikson (1911–1956), the other female athlete considered to be the best of the twentieth century. And along with the high-scoring soccer player Mia Hamm (1972–), Joyner-Kersee, one of the first major stars of the Title IX era, in turn inspired the next generation of American girls.

Hobbled by injuries and health problems, Joyner-Kersee retired from track and field in 1998.

ADDITIONAL FACTS

1. *Joyner-Kersee's brother, Al Joyner (1960–), won gold in the triple jump at the 1984 Los Angeles Olympics. He later married 1988 triple Olympic gold medalist Florence Griffith Joyner (1959–1998).*

2. *Joyner-Kersee married her coach, Bob Kersee (1954–), in 1986. They first met at UCLA, where he was a coach and she was a star on the basketball and track teams. She was a four-year starter and all-American on the Bruins basketball team.*

3. *Her world record of 7,291 points in the 1988 Olympic heptathlon still stands.*

•••••

Jerry Seinfeld

Famously described as "a show about nothing," *Seinfeld* was one of the biggest hit television series of the 1990s and made a household name of its star, comedian Jerry Seinfeld (1954–). The show's final episode was one of the most watched in television history, and the series is still frequently broadcast in syndication.

Born in New York City, Seinfeld got his start on the stand-up circuit and eventually appeared on the *Tonight Show* with Johnny Carson (1925–2005) and *The Late Show with David Letterman* (1947–).

In 1980, Seinfeld had his first shot at a part in a sitcom, playing Frankie in the television series *Benson*. He was fired after a handful of episodes and decided that he wouldn't return to sitcoms unless he had a significant degree of control.

Seinfeld got that opportunity in 1989, when NBC agreed to pick up the show that bore his name. *Seinfeld* was the story of the title character and a group of his closest friends: George Costanza, played by Jason Alexander (1959–); Cosmo Kramer, played by Michael Richards (1949–); and Elaine Benes, played by Julia Louis-Dreyfus (1961–).

The series was not a popular success at first, but it was an immediate critical success. Eventually, *Seinfeld* became one of the most successful television programs of all time. It ranked in the top two in the Nielsen ratings every year from 1994 to 1998, and in 2002, *TV Guide* named it the greatest television show in history.

After deciding to leave the show in 1998, following its ninth season, Seinfeld returned to stand-up. In August 1998, he performed three routines using his old material in New York City, vowing never to use the material again. (One of the routines was broadcast by HBO as *I'm Telling You for the Last Time*.)

Seinfeld then returned to the stage with new material, and his work is chronicled in the 2002 documentary *Comedian*, which also followed a young comic named Orny Adams (1971–). In 2007, Seinfeld released his first feature-length film, the animated feature *Bee Movie*, in which he performed the voice of a talking bee named Barry B. Benson.

ADDITIONAL FACTS

1. Seinfeld *cocreator Larry David (1947–) followed his success on network television with the highly acclaimed HBO series* Curb Your Enthusiasm, *in which he stars.*

2. *In 2006, Richards was widely criticized after being caught on a cell-phone camera using a racial epithet at a comedy club. He later apologized for the outburst in a televised appearance.*

3. *Seinfeld owns an estate in the Hamptons, in Long Island, New York, that he purchased from the singer Billy Joel (1949–).*

•• • ••

Timothy McVeigh

Before the tragic events of September 11, 2001, the worst terrorist attack in US history was perpetrated not by a radical Islamic extremist but by an American who had served his country with distinction in the Gulf War.

On the morning of April 19, 1995, Timothy McVeigh (1968–2001) parked a yellow rental truck loaded with a 7,000-pound homemade bomb a few steps away from the Alfred P. Murrah Federal Building in Oklahoma City, Oklahoma. He then got out of the truck's cab and walked away. Moments later, at 9:02 a.m., the bomb exploded, killing 168 people.

About an hour later, McVeigh was arrested in Perry, Oklahoma, for an unrelated traffic violation and weapons charge. Two days later, authorities announced that the man sitting in the Perry prison was responsible for the bombing.

McVeigh later said he had committed the act as retribution against the federal government, which he believed to be trampling on the individual rights of its citizens. He was specifically angered by the federal raids at Ruby Ridge, Idaho, where agents killed the wife and son of separatist Randy Weaver (1947–), and at a compound near Waco, Texas, where agents killed seventy-six members of the Branch Davidian religious cult.

That the Oklahoma City bomber was an American and not a foreign attacker stunned the nation and alerted the public to the danger of homegrown terrorism. McVeigh was born and raised in upstate New York, and after high school, he enlisted in the US Army, earning a Bronze Star during the Gulf War.

Following his honorable discharge in 1991, he lived a largely transient life, driving around the country to attend gun shows. He was involved with right-wing separatist groups in Michigan and was inspired by racist and antigovernment literature.

After the attack, he said his only regret was that the bomb did not level the entire building.

On June 2, 1997, McVeigh was convicted of eleven counts of murder and conspiracy in the deaths of eight federal agents in the building. Eleven days later, he was sentenced to death. He was put to death by lethal injection on June 11, 2001, becoming the first federal prisoner to be executed since 1963.

ADDITIONAL FACTS

1. *Five minutes before McVeigh was to due to go before the Noble County, Oklahoma, court—where he might have walked away on $500 bail for his traffic and weapons charges—the FBI called to tell the district attorney to hang on to the prisoner.*

2. *Terry Nichols (1955–), a coconspirator of McVeigh's, was later convicted on murder and manslaughter charges and was sentenced to life in prison.*

3. *At his execution, McVeigh offered no last words. But he had previously given the warden of the prison in Terre Haute, Indiana, a copy of the 1875 poem "Invictus," by the British poet William Ernest Henley (1849–1903), to distribute as his final words.*

•••••

Amy Tan

Oakland, California–born novelist Amy Tan (1952–) has been a leading figure on the world literary scene since the 1980s. Although her works tend to focus on relationships between Chinese-American mothers and daughters, their insights into generational conflict, family dynamics, immigration, and cross-cultural living have appealed to far wider audiences.

The bulk of Tan's work is based on her own experience growing up as an American in an ethnically Chinese family. After receiving a master's degree in linguistics and embarking on a lucrative career in freelance business writing, Tan decided in 1987 that she wanted to return to China with her mother to meet her two half sisters for the first time. This trip and its emotional family reunion formed the inspiration for Tan's first major work, *The Joy Luck Club* (1989), which remains her best-known and most widely read book.

Though *The Joy Luck Club* is often termed a novel, it actually consists of sixteen interlocking short stories told by four sets of Chinese-American mothers and daughters living in the San Francisco Bay Area. Because of miscommunication and cultural differences, the thoroughly Americanized daughters and their traditionally Chinese mothers frequently misunderstand one another: The daughters view their mothers as meddlesome, disapproving, and out of touch with the demands of modern American life, whereas the mothers see their daughters as impudent, misguided, and contemptuous of their Chinese heritage. By using multiple narrators from both generations, Tan reveals gradually that neither generation's picture of the other is accurate, and that good intentions and rich personal histories often fail to translate across linguistic and cultural barriers.

After the runaway success of this first book, Tan's subsequent works have included *The Kitchen God's Wife* (1991) and *The Bonesetter's Daughter* (2001). Both continue in the same vein, portraying Asian-American families and, in particular, the relationships among mothers, daughters, and sisters.

ADDITIONAL FACTS

1. *Tan also wrote the screenplay for the successful 1993 film adaptation of* The Joy Luck Club, *directed by Wayne Wang (1949–) and produced by Oliver Stone (1946–).*

2. *Tan is often compared to fellow Bay Area native Maxine Hong Kingston (1940–), whose acclaimed memoir* The Woman Warrior *(1976) paved the way for much of the Asian-American literature that has followed.*

3. *Along with fellow writers Stephen King (1947–), Dave Barry (1947–), Mitch Albom (1958–), and others, Tan plays in a charity rock band called the Rock Bottom Remainders. Her signature number is a cover of Nancy Sinatra's "These Boots Are Made for Walkin'."*

••●••

Thriller

By the time Michael Jackson (1958–) released the blockbuster album *Thriller* in 1982, he was already one of pop music's most successful artists. The album's phenomenal success, however, elevated him to the role of global icon.

Jackson started his musical career in 1963, at the age of five, when he formed the Jackson 5 with his siblings. Michael was soon leading some of the group's biggest singles, including "ABC" (1970) and "I'll Be There" (1970). He released the solo album *Off the Wall* in 1979, his first record to be arranged by the composer and producer Quincy Jones (1933–); it contained two number one singles: "Don't Stop 'Til You Get Enough" and "Rock with You."

As successful as his debut album was, however, it was completely eclipsed by *Thriller*. To date, *Thriller* has sold well over 100 million copies, making it the best-selling album of all time. Seven of its ten tracks went to the top ten on the Billboard charts. The first single to climb the charts was "The Girl Is Mine," a duet with the former Beatle Paul McCartney (1942–). Others included "Wanna Be Startin' Something," "Beat It," "Billie Jean," and the title track, "Thriller."

Thriller also spawned some of the most unique and revolutionary music videos ever. The most famous videos are those for "Billie Jean," "Beat It," and "Thriller." The video for "Billie Jean," a controversial song dealing with illegitimacy, was one of the first by a black artist to air on the music video channel MTV. While most music videos in the early 1980s were cheaply and quickly produced, the videos for "Billie Jean," "Beat It," and "Thriller" were treated and produced like short films, setting a new standard for the music video.

Still, not all of Jackson's milestones required such elaborate productions. In 1983, Jackson performed "Billie Jean" at a twenty-fifth-anniversary concert for Motown Records. During the show, he unveiled his "moonwalk," a dance move, for the first time. It was one of the most famous moments of his career—and no special effects were required.

ADDITIONAL FACTS

1. *Though Jackson and Paul McCartney were friends for many years, their friendship came to an end when Jackson bought the publishing rights to the Beatles' catalogue in 1985, beating out a bid by McCartney himself.*

2. *The spoken section of "Thriller" is performed by the film legend Vincent Price (1911–1993), who played the villain in many famous horror movies.*

3. *Only two other artists have tied* Thriller's *record for most hit singles on an album: Bruce Springsteen (1949–), with* Born in the U.S.A. *(1984), and Michael's sister Janet Jackson (1966–), with* Rhythm Nation 1814 *(1989).*

• • ● • •

Star Wars (1977)

"May the Force be with you."
—Alec Guinness (1944–) as Obi-Wan Kenobi

George Lucas's (1944–) space epic *Star Wars* not only revitalized the science-fiction genre, it also revolutionized the business of Hollywood and added such terms as *Jedi, the Force,* and *lightsaber* to the world's vocabulary.

The film is a classic good-versus-evil story in which a naïve youth, Luke Skywalker (played by Mark Hamill, 1951–), rallies a band of underdog rebels to fight the evil Galactic Empire, led by part-man, part-machine Darth Vader (played by David Prowse, 1935–, and voiced by James Earl Jones, 1931–). The film combined some of man's most traditional archetypes, myths, and legends with cutting-edge special effects to create one of the most popular films of all time.

Star Wars also contributed to an era in Hollywood—which largely persists today—in which studios pursue major blockbuster films in the hope of producing sequels and lucrative merchandise, rather than the more personal, often cynical films that had taken hold during the mid-1970s.

The picture also broke with recent Hollywood tradition in that previous Hollywood hits had been adapted from best-selling novels, Broadway musicals, or other popular sources. *Star Wars* had an original script (written by Lucas) and no stars in leading roles. The primary actors would all become stars after the film's release, especially Harrison Ford (1942–) who played the mercenary pilot Han Solo.

That *Star Wars* was a box office smash only begins to describe its impact on the film industry. It is the first film to legitimately claim to have launched a "franchise" that included five subsequent films (two sequels and three prequels) and an array of merchandising offshoots, including toys, video games, home videos, DVDs, and various published materials. All told, in 2005, *Forbes* estimated that the *Star Wars* franchise had generated more than $20 billion.

Including rereleases, the six films grossed more than $4.3 billion at worldwide box offices. The original movie became the most commercially successful film in history, surpassing *Jaws* (1975) and coming in second in domestic gross to *Titanic* (1997). Adjusted for inflation, its $460 million US gross (including rereleases in 1982 and 1997) translates to $1.1 billion, second of all-time only to *Gone with the Wind* (1939). The budget of *Star Wars* is estimated at a mere $13 million.

ADDITIONAL FACTS

1. *The film's full name is* Star Wars, Episode IV: A New Hope. *Lucas originally envisioned a nine-film series, of which the first six have been made. There are no current plans for the final three films.*

2. *Lucas founded the firm Industrial Light and Magic to provide the special effects for* Star Wars; *the company has gone on to become an industry leader in Hollywood special effects production.*

3. *Lucas took only $175,000 for writing and directing the original film in exchange for 40 percent of the merchandising rights. That turned out to be a smart move—*Star Wars *merchandising has dwarfed the film's box office gross.*

•••••

The Internet

Reflecting on the growth of the Internet in its early years, the Romanian author and poet Andrei Codrescu (1946–) wrote, "The speed with which the industrial world became networked in cyberspace was miraculous, like watching something in a Petri dish grow to the size of a flying rhino in three days."

The Internet didn't just grow from something small to something large; it grew from something extremely small and specialized—a military communications network called ARPAnet—into something vast and unlike anything ever before seen. The Internet made communication across vast distances easy and virtually free, changing the way people shop, socialize, and learn.

ARPAnet, an experimental Pentagon research project, went online in 1969. At first, it was used by only a handful of military researchers and university specialists. Even by the mid-1980s, the number of users was estimated at no more than a few thousand.

By the late 1980s, civilians outnumbered military users on the network. But to the general public, the Internet was still a confusing and esoteric computer group.

The concept of *hypertext* finally made the network accessible to nonspecialists, triggering the revolution described by Codrescu. Hypertext "linked" documents on the Internet to one another in a visible fashion, making it easier to navigate the system.

In the mid-1990s, a small firm called the Mosaic Communications Corporation developed a tool for hypertext "browsing" through the Internet by using a graphical interface rather than complex typed commands. The tool was soon renamed the Netscape browser, which allowed home computer users to take advantage of what was once a forbidding Pentagon network. Today, those users number more than one billion people worldwide.

ADDITIONAL FACTS

1. *The first signal sent over the military ARPAnet was supposed to be the term* log-in. *However, the system crashed after the* l *and* o *were transmitted, so the first signal was in fact* lo.

2. *ARPA stood for* Advanced Research Projects Agency, *the agency at the Defense Department that funded early Internet research in the 1960s.*

3. *Today, the Netscape browser is used by less than 1 percent of Internet users.*

•• • ••

Michael Jordan

In the 1980s and 1990s, there was no more iconic figure in sports around the world than Michael Jordan (1963–). The six-foot-six guard for the Chicago Bulls was at once an otherworldly basketball player, an international marketing titan, and a cultural trendsetter.

On the court, he put together a compelling case for the title *greatest basketball player ever*. He developed from a tongue-wagging, high-flying scoring machine into a six-time National Basketball Association (NBA) champion with the Bulls. He won a record ten scoring titles and five Most Valuable Player (MVP) awards, and was named MVP of the NBA finals six times.

Most observers would agree, though, that what separated Jordan from other immensely talented players was his unparalleled desire to win, along with his ability to make a dramatic shot with the game on the line.

Off the court, no athlete was more successfully marketed than Jordan. He was a pitchman for an array of high-profile corporations, and his Air Jordan sneakers set the marketing standard for all athletic footwear to follow. Everyone wanted to be "like Mike," as a song in a Gatorade commercial famously said. When he shaved his head or wore an earring in his left ear, legions of basketball players and fans did the same.

In his first few years with the Chicago Bulls, Jordan was considered a great scorer and dunker, but critics questioned whether he could take a team to a championship. He put those questions to rest in 1991, when the Bulls beat the Los Angeles Lakers for the NBA title. His teams would add five more crowns, in 1992, 1993, 1996, 1997, and 1998.

Jordan retired three times. He first left basketball before the 1993–1994 NBA season, following the murder of his father and while he was beset by allegations of gambling troubles. He spent that year playing minor-league baseball for the Class AA Birmingham Barons, with little success. He returned to the Bulls in 1995.

He retired again after winning the 1998 NBA title, only to return three years later to play two seasons with the Washington Wizards. Jordan had been a minority owner of the Wizards but sold his shares to return to the court. He failed to help Washington to the playoffs and was criticized for damaging his legacy.

ADDITIONAL FACTS

1. *Jordan's legend was born in his freshman year at the University of North Carolina, when he made the title-winning shot in the 1982 National Collegiate Athletic Association (NCAA) Championship game. Two years later, he left school for the NBA as the best college player in the nation. Amazingly, he was selected after two other players in the 1984 draft, Hakeem Olajuwon (1963–) of the Houston Rockets and Sam Bowie (1961–) of the Portland Trail Blazers.*

2. *Jordan won two Olympic gold medals—in 1984 as an amateur and in 1992 as a leading member of the Dream Team.*

3. *In 1999, Jordan was named the greatest North American athlete of the twentieth century by ESPN. He has also been on the cover of* Sports Illustrated *more times than any other person (forty-nine).*

•• • ••

O. J. Simpson

Football superstar, comedic actor, Hertz spokesman, and world-famous murder suspect, O. J. Simpson (1947–) went from Hollywood celebrity to national pariah after his acquittal on charges of killing his ex-wife in 1995.

Orenthal James Simpson was born in San Francisco and earned a scholarship to play running back for the University of Southern California. He won the Heisman Trophy, awarded annually to the most outstanding collegiate football player in the United States, in 1968.

Simpson's professional career in the National Football League (NFL) was equally remarkable. He was the league's Most Valuable Player in 1973, when he became the first player to rush more than 2,000 yards in one season for the Buffalo Bills.

While he was still in the NFL, Simpson began his acting career. He played small parts in projects ranging from the television miniseries *Roots* to the *Naked Gun* comedy film series. He also became the face of Hertz Rent-a-Car in its TV ads.

On June 12, 1994, Simpson's ex-wife Nicole Brown Simpson (1959–1994) was found dead alongside her friend Ronald Goldman (1968–1994) outside of her home. Suspicion quickly centered on Simpson, who famously attempted to flee in a white Ford Bronco. The trial that followed was one of the most controversial events of the decade.

The 134-day trial pitted lead prosecutor Marcia Clark (1953–) against Simpson's "Dream Team" of defense attorneys, which included F. Lee Bailey (1933–), Barry Scheck (1949–), Robert Shapiro (1942–), Robert Kardashian (1944–2003), Alan Dershowitz (1938–), and Johnnie Cochran (1937–2005).

Two critical events in the trial were the revelation that a police investigator on the case, Mark Fuhrman (1952–), had used racial epithets to refer to African-Americans, and the moment when Simpson tried on the gloves found at the crime scene, and they didn't fit.

In an extremely controversial—and racially charged—decision, the jury found Simpson not guilty of the murders, on October 3, 1995. However, Goldman's family was later awarded $33.5 million in a wrongful-death civil suit against Simpson, further adding to the controversy over the verdict.

ADDITIONAL FACTS

1. *Simpson still holds the record for the largest margin of victory for the Heisman trophy, defeating the runner-up, Leroy Keyes (1947–) of Purdue, by 1,750 points.*

2. *Before Arnold Schwarzenegger (1947–) was cast for the role, Simpson was considered for the lead in the 1984 film* The Terminator. *The producers passed because they didn't think he would be convincing in the role of a villain.*

3. *In 2007, Simpson worked with a ghostwriter to produce* If I Did It, *a book about the 1994 murder. It was blocked from publication until the rights were assigned to the Goldman family as part of the judgment in an unpaid settlement in the civil suit the family won against Simpson.*

•••••

Garry Kasparov

World chess champion Garry Kasparov (1963–) ruled his sport for decades but lost one of the most publicized games in history, against an IBM computer in a dramatic matchup of man against machine. After retiring from competitive chess in 2005, Kasparov reemerged as a prodemocracy activist and a leading opponent of Russian leader Vladimir Putin (1952–).

Kasparov was born in the Soviet province of Azerbaijan and was recognized as a chess prodigy at an early age. He attended special chess schools as a child and won the world crown in 1985. At twenty-two, he was the youngest chess champion ever.

Over the next fifteen years, Kasparov defended his title against some of the biggest stars of chess, including fellow Soviet grand master Anatoly Karpov (1951–). Kasparov's most famous matchup, however, came in 1997, when he agreed to play a six-game match in New York City against Deep Blue, a chess supercomputer built by a team of engineers at IBM.

Deep Blue had been designed specifically to defeat Kasparov and could analyze 200 million chess moves every second. Still, after the first five games of the match, Kasparov and Deep Blue were tied with one win each and three draws.

In the sixth and deciding match, however, the computer demolished Kasparov, defeating the champion in only nineteen moves. Kasparov had never lost a game so quickly.

The match was followed closely on front pages across the world and was televised in some countries. Kasparov's defeat in a traditional test of human intelligence was widely seen as a symbol of the increasing power and sophistication of computer technology in the late twentieth century.

Against a human opponent, Kasparov lost his world championship in 2000. He retired from chess five years later, claiming he had nothing left to prove.

After his retirement, Kasparov started a second career as a political dissident. He was briefly imprisoned and, in one infamous incident, beaten with a chessboard by a pro-Putin thug for his opposition to the Russian president. Kasparov was an unsuccessful candidate for president of Russia in the 2008 election.

ADDITIONAL FACTS

1. *Deep Blue weighed 1.4 tons.*

2. *The day after its computer defeated Kasparov, IBM's stock rose by 3.6 percent, or $6 a share.*

3. *After he was pummeled with a chessboard in 2005 by a political opponent, Kasparov quipped, "I am lucky that the popular sport in the Soviet Union was chess and not baseball."*

•••••

Metafiction

The Greek prefix *meta*, meaning "after" or "beyond," has worked its way into many academic terms, from *metaphysics* to *meta-analysis*. The word *meta* has even come to stand on its own, denoting ideas or situations that are self-referential or self-reflexive. In the literary world, metafiction—fiction about fiction—has emerged as an important, interesting genre in recent years.

Metafiction encompasses a variety of devices and approaches that help investigate the relationship between the author and a literary work, between the reader and a literary work, or between one literary work and another. By its very nature, a work of metafiction is acutely self-aware, drawing attention to its status as an artificial, created object.

One common metafictional device is for the author to insert himself into his work as a character. John Fowles's *The French Lieutenant's Woman* (1969) and Kurt Vonnegut's *Breakfast of Champions* (1973), for instance, take this approach. Other metafictional works engage the reader directly: Italo Calvino's *If on a winter's night a traveler* (1979) makes the reader a character in the novel, while Dave Eggers's *A Heartbreaking Work of Staggering Genius* (2000) includes a reader's guide to itself and a discussion of its own use of symbolism.

Another popular metafictional technique is to reexamine a previous literary work, often from the perspective of a character different from the original protagonist. For example, John Gardner's *Grendel* (1971) revisits the ancient epic poem *Beowulf* from the perspective of the monster, while Gregory Maguire's *Wicked* (1995) recasts *The Wonderful Wizard of Oz* through the eyes of the Wicked Witch of the West.

Although metafiction may seem like a recent gimmick, arguably it is as old as Miguel de Cervantes's *Don Quixote,* which was published in two volumes in 1605 and 1615 and is considered one of the foundations of Western literature. In the second volume of this classic, Don Quixote and his sidekick, Sancho Panza, learn that a Cervantes impostor has published a fake sequel about their alleged exploits, a development based on the actual imitators who published stories using Cervantes's characters after the huge success of the first volume of *Don Quixote*. The two characters mock the idea heartily.

ADDITIONAL FACTS

1. *Stephen King (1947–) has brought elements of metafiction to popular literature: Misery (1987) concerns a romance novelist held captive by a crazed fan who dictates what he writes; The Dark Half (1989) depicts a writer whose pseudonym comes violently to life.*

2. *When the screenwriter Charlie Kaufman (1958–) had difficulty adapting the Susan Orlean (1955–) novel The Orchid Thief (1998) into a film, he wrote himself into the screenplay. The result was the film Adaptation (2002), a quintessential work of metafiction.*

3. *Other notable authors who have dabbled in metafiction include Paul Auster (1947–), Julian Barnes (1946–), Milan Kundera (1929–), Yann Martel (1963–), Vladimir Nabokov (1899–1977), Zadie Smith (1975–), and John Updike (1932–).*

•••••

Madonna

Madonna (born Madonna Louise Ciccone in 1958) is the most successful female recording artist of all time and an international pop icon. In her career, she has sold more than 200 million albums worldwide. Her Confessions Tour in support of the 2005 album *Confessions on a Dance Floor* was the highest-grossing concert tour by a female artist; her 1991 documentary *Truth or Dare* was the highest-grossing documentary ever at the time of its release; and her risqué 1992 book *Sex* remains the best-selling coffee-table book of all time.

Born in Michigan and originally trained in ballet, Madonna released her self-titled debut album to modest success in 1983. Her second album, *Like a Virgin* (1984), rose to number one on the strength of its title track as well as the hit single "Material Girl," whose title became a nickname still associated with the singer. Around this time, Madonna was also famous for her unique fashion sense, mostly drawn from New York City's hipster scene in the East Village neighborhood.

In the years following, she drew on a number of influences, particularly in her video work. Images in the video for "Express Yourself" (from her 1989 album *Like a Prayer*) were inspired by Fritz Lang's 1927 silent film *Metropolis;* the controversial video for "Justify My Love" (1990) drew from the underground subculture of sadomasochism; and the video for "Vogue" (1990), perhaps her most famous, was a direct nod to the glamorous photos taken of some of Madonna's film heroines, including Marlene Dietrich (1901–1992) and Rita Hayworth (1918–1987). (Madonna has also drawn inspiration from more obscure sources: Some critics, for instance, have noted similarities between her videos and the 1965 film *Vinyl,* Andy Warhol's unreleased adaptation of the novel *A Clockwork Orange.*)

Madonna took a completely different turn in the late 1990s with *Ray of Light,* an electronic album largely inspired by her then-new interest in kabbalah, or Jewish mysticism. She later moved to the United Kingdom, where she continues to produce new music.

ADDITIONAL FACTS

1. *Not everything Madonna touches turns to gold: Her 1987 film* Who's That Girl *was a flop.*

2. *Madonna has often courted controversy with her live performances, which have included acts ranging from the erotic use of religious iconography to rubbing the Puerto Rican flag between her legs onstage.*

3. *Madonna's first band was called the Breakfast Club. She played drums for the group before becoming the lead singer.*

•• ●●••

Meryl Streep

Meryl Streep (1949–) has been Hollywood's dominant lead actress for the past twenty-five years. She is the most respected and honored actress of the era, earning fourteen Academy Award nominations (the most of any actor or actress) and winning six Golden Globes (the most of any actress) as well as two Emmy Awards.

After her film debut in *Julia* (1977), the Yale Drama School graduate appeared in a series of critically acclaimed films, including *The Deer Hunter* (1978), for which she received her first Academy Award nomination; *Manhattan* (1979); and *Kramer vs. Kramer* (1979), for which she earned an Oscar for Best Supporting Actress.

She turned in acclaimed performances throughout the 1980s, particularly in *The French Lieutenant's Woman* (1981) and as a Polish concentration-camp survivor in *Sophie's Choice* (1982), which earned her an Oscar for Best Actress.

Streep's critics, while recognizing her talents, have said that she is too clinical an actress. And most of her performances over the past two decades, since costarring with Robert Redford (1937–) in Sydney Pollack's *Out of Africa* (1985), have been in movies few would consider great films.

In the 1990s, Streep branched out into dark comedies (*Death Becomes Her*, 1992) and adventure films (*The River Wild*, 1994), as well as an admired turn in Clint Eastwood's 1995 adaptation of the romantic novel *The Bridges of Madison County* (in which Eastwood also costarred).

After six years without an Academy Award nomination for Best Actress, she received her eleventh such nomination (and fourteenth acting nomination overall) for *The Devil Wears Prada* (2006). She earned a Golden Globe for the performance.

ADDITIONAL FACTS

1. *Streep received the American Film Institute's Life Achievement Award in 2004.*

2. *Streep passed Katharine Hepburn (1907–2003) as the recipient of the most Academy Award nominations for acting with her thirteenth nod, for* Adaptation *(2002).*

3. *Her given name is Mary Louise Streep.*

••●••

Cloning

In 1952 two Philadelphia researchers, Robert Briggs (1911–1983) and Thomas King (1921–2000), cloned the first animal—a tadpole—followed by a carp, cloned by the Chinese researcher Tong Dizhou (1902–1979) in 1963. Decades later, after years of research in the controversial field, scientists produced a far more impressive result: On July 5, 1996, a cloned female sheep named Dolly was born in Scotland.

To its supporters, cloning—producing an exact replica of a living animal—is one of the great scientific achievements of the late twentieth century, a technology that could help scientists cure diseases and develop a greater understanding of nature. Some scientists predict that cloning of human cells could help them find cures to diabetes, Parkinson's disease, Alzheimer's disease, and other serious illnesses.

But to critics, concocting clones in a laboratory represents the height of scientific hubris—a dangerous way for researchers to play God. Cloning has figured, usually in a sinister light, in countless science-fiction novels and movies, and several countries have imposed legal limits on cloning.

In the years after Dolly's birth, researchers were able to clone mice, rats, rabbits, cats, dogs, pigs, goats, cows, horses, and mules. Dolly, however, died in 2003.

Still, scientists have not succeeded in cloning monkeys, and this puts the researchers many steps away from cloning the most advanced primate of all: human beings. In the meantime, however, guidelines in several countries have been established to forbid human cloning, and polls show strong public opposition to cloning humans.

ADDITIONAL FACTS

1. The word clone *comes from the ancient Greek word* klon, *meaning "twig." It refers to the process of duplicating a plant by planting or grafting a cutting from it.*

2. The public radio show This American Life *dedicated an episode to the story of Second Chance, the clone of a Brahman bull named Chance, that was produced at Texas A&M University at the instigation of the original bull's owner.*

3. The first science-fiction novel to use the word clone *in the title was P. T. Olemy's 1968 book* The Clones.

4. A Gallup poll in 2005 found that 87 percent of Americans would consider human cloning morally wrong; 9 percent said it would be acceptable.

•●●••

Lance Armstrong

By the time Lance Armstrong (1971–) turned twenty-five, he was known as an arrogant, brash Texan with immense raw cycling talent and an ego to match. During the next decade, he would become one of the most celebrated and beloved sports figures in history, a seven-time Tour de France champion, a cancer survivor, and an inspiration to millions around the world.

In 1996, Armstrong ascended to the world number one ranking and was considered one of the most promising young cyclists in the world. Then, disaster struck: In October, he was diagnosed with testicular cancer, which had spread to his lungs and brain. Doctors gave him less than a 50 percent chance of survival before putting Armstrong on an aggressive chemotherapy regimen.

Miraculously, Armstrong beat the cancer and returned to competition in 1998, cycling for the US Postal Service team. But his postcancer transition was not smooth—after quitting during the Paris-Nice race, he nearly gave up the sport. Instead, he went to North Carolina to train with coach Chris Carmichael (1961–) and rediscovered the joy of cycling. Later that year, he posted top-five finishes in the Tour of Spain and at the World Championships.

At the 1999 Tour de France, Armstrong won the prologue and never looked back, becoming the first American since Greg LeMond (1961–) to win cycling's most prestigious race. He would never lose another Tour de France, winning each of the next six years before retiring in 2005. No other rider has ever won the race more than six times.

His work through the Lance Armstrong Foundation—including the introduction of the popular Livestrong bracelets in 2004—has helped raise money and awareness to fight cancer. And Armstrong says that getting cancer was "the best thing that ever happened to me."

Armstrong has faced allegations that he used performance-enhancing drugs during his career. He has adamantly proclaimed his innocence, noting that he has never tested positive for drugs.

ADDITIONAL FACTS

1. *Armstrong is a four-time selection by the Associated Press as the Male Athlete of the Year (2002–2005). He was also selected as the* Sports Illustrated *Sportsman of the Year in 2002.*

2. *Armstrong is a three-time Olympian (1992, 1996, and 2000) and won a bronze medal in 2000 in the time trial.*

3. *In 1993, he was the world road-race champion and, at twenty-one, became the youngest rider to win one of the sections of the Tour de France.*

•••••

Friends

For ten years, American audiences tuned in to NBC's hit sitcom *Friends* for a weekly dose of good-natured frivolity. The show transformed its six costars— and their television alter egos—into national celebrities.

Created by Marta Kauffman (1956–) and David Crane (1957–) as a follow-up to their HBO series *Dream On, Friends* followed the lives of six young, single (at least initially; several characters ultimately married) New Yorkers who lived in the same neighborhood and frequented the local café, Central Perk.

Conceptually, the show didn't exactly break ground. However, the stories resonated with the Starbucks sensibility of the 1990s. Through the misadventures of Ross (David Schwimmer, 1966–) and Rachel (Jennifer Aniston, 1969–), Monica (Courteney Cox, 1964–) and Chandler (Matthew Perry, 1969–), and Phoebe (Lisa Kudrow, 1963–) and Joey (Matt LeBlanc, 1967–), young adults saw their serial dating and extended independence portrayed in a benign, admiring light.

Despite average writing and acting, *Friends*'s cultural impact was considerable. The show's female stars—especially Jennifer Aniston—were major trendsetters, and hair salons around the world still get requests for the Aniston—a layered, midlength cut.

The show's language also seeped into the pop lexicon, especially the use of the word *so* in the sense of "surely" or "decidedly" (e.g., "You are *so* moving to a new apartment"). Referring to an on-again, off-again, "will they or won't they?" couple as a "Ross and Rachel" may be the show's most enduring legacy; an episode of the NBC hit *Scrubs* even used this phrase to describe the tumultuous relationship of J.D. (Zach Braff, 1975–) and Eliot (Sarah Chalke, 1976–).

With a slew of Emmy and Golden Globe wins, *Friends* finally called it quits on May 6, 2004.

ADDITIONAL FACTS

1. *The program's initial working titles included* Across the Hall, Friends like Us, Six of One, *and* Insomnia Café.

2. *The character of Ross was written with David Schwimmer in mind.*

3. Friends *has been broadcast in more than 100 countries; the final episode drew an estimated 51 million viewers worldwide.*

••●••

Oprah Winfrey

She is one of those rare icons of pop culture known throughout the world simply by her first name: Oprah. But Oprah Winfrey's impact on modern culture has not been singular in scope. She is at once a broadcasting giant, a publishing mogul, a philanthropist, and, to the millions who watch her nationally syndicated television show, a friend.

According to *Forbes,* Winfrey's vast media empire has made her one of the wealthiest people in the world, with an estimated net worth of $2.5 billion, and *Time* magazine rated her in 1998 as one of the most influential people of the twentieth century.

Winfrey (1954–) was raised by her grandmother on a Mississippi farm with no indoor plumbing. Her unlikely rise to fame began when she started working at a Nashville radio station while in high school. By age nineteen, she had become the youngest person and first African-American woman to anchor the news, at Nashville's WTVF-TV.

After a stop in Baltimore, she arrived in Chicago in 1984, hosting a morning talk show that was soon renamed *The Oprah Winfrey Show.* Within two years, her show had gone into national syndication and had become the highest-rated talk program in television history.

Her popularity largely stems from her combination of intelligence, media savvy, and honesty in dealing with her audience. In sharing her own story—talking about being a victim of sexual abuse, using drugs, gaining and losing weight, and having romantic crises—she has created a unique bond with her viewers.

In recent years, Winfrey has expanded her empire to include a television, film, radio, and music production company (Harpo Entertainment Group) and a magazine (*O, The Oprah Magazine*), and her book club has launched dozens of books to bestseller status.

Winfrey is also one of the country's most visible philanthropists. Her various foundations have awarded grants to organizations that support the education and empowerment of women, children, and families around the world. She also contributed $40 million toward the creation of the Oprah Winfrey Leadership Academy for Girls in South Africa, which opened in January 2007.

ADDITIONAL FACTS

1. *The Oprah Winfrey Show is seen by an estimated 49 million viewers each week and is broadcast in 134 countries.*

2. *Winfrey also has compiled an impressive acting résumé. She made her acting debut in Steven Spielberg's The Color Purple (1985), for which she received Academy Award and Golden Globe nominations.*

3. *Part of Winfrey's power lies in her ability to inspire her viewers to act. In 1998, she founded Oprah's Angel Network, a charity organization that is largely funded by audience contributions. It has raised more than $70 million.*

••●••

Don DeLillo

New York City native Don DeLillo has for decades been one of the leading figures in postmodern literature. In more than a dozen novels, he has used dark humor and wit to satirize the consumerism, materialism, media saturation, and information overload that characterize modern American culture.

Born in the Bronx in 1936, DeLillo grew up in a working-class Italian-American neighborhood and attended college at Fordham University. After graduating, he got his professional start as an advertising copywriter before growing bored with the job and moving on to writing fiction. Beginning with his first major work, *Americana* (1971), DeLillo released a series of novels that were largely praised by critics but did not sell well among the general public.

DeLillo finally found major success with *White Noise* (1985), still considered one of his best and most important works. The novel is an absurd, darkly comic story of a man named Jack who is the chair of the Hitler studies department at a small-town college. His wife, Babette, secretly medicates herself to combat her fear of death; when a massive chemical spill causes an "airborne toxic event" near their home, Jack becomes obsessed with death as well.

White Noise is a quintessential postmodern novel. Plot is only a secondary concern; instead, the story is a zigzagging mishmash of brand names, esoteric academic debates, pop culture references, and comic flourishes such as a hospital run by atheist nuns. DeLillo depicts a society obsessed with technology, mass culture, health risks, and material excess—and surrounded by a constant "white noise" of media and information that is continually beamed across the airwaves. Paradoxically, in this world in which everyone seems connected and informed, individuals actually feel more confused and isolated than ever before.

ADDITIONAL FACTS

1. *DeLillo's post–*White Noise *novels include* Libra *(1988), about Lee Harvey Oswald (1939–1963);* Mao II *(1991), an exploration of terrorism; and* Underworld *(1997), a sprawling history of twentieth-century America featuring both fictional and real-life characters.*

2. *DeLillo cites jazz music, abstract expressionist painting, and foreign films as his three greatest artistic influences.*

3. *He has claimed that one of the primary ways he became a writer was by "avoiding serious commitment to anything else."*

•••••

Nirvana

Nirvana, one of the most influential rock bands of the early 1990s, formed in Aberdeen, Washington, in 1987 and featured front man Kurt Cobain (1967–1994), bassist Krist Novoselic (1965–), and drummer Dave Grohl (1969–) who joined the group in 1989. After the group struggled in obscurity for several years, Nirvana's first major label release in 1991, *Nevermind,* thrust the band and the Seattle music scene known as grunge into the mainstream. Almost overnight, Nirvana became the inadvertent torchbearers of what was then dubbed alternative rock and came to epitomize the so-called Generation X.

Nevermind sold nearly 20 million copies worldwide and produced the band's biggest hit, their debut single "Smells Like Teen Spirit." Set at a high-school pep rally–turned–mosh pit, the video for the single featured the band playing to flannel-clad teenagers and despondent cheerleaders. MTV placed the video in heavy rotation, and the media descended on the words *alternative* and *grunge.* Nirvana quickly became associated with all things Gen X—alienation, angst, and ennui. This aimless frustration is captured in the lyrics of "Smells Like Teen Spirit":

> *I feel stupid and contagious*
> *Here we are now*
> *Entertain us*

Kurt Cobain

The band's sound was raw, lyrical, and loud. Although an obvious challenge to mainstream pop, alternative music quickly became a definitive category of popular music. Impressed by Nirvana's success, record labels rushed to develop their alternative rosters with bands like Alice in Chains and Soundgarden. *Alternative* became a general term for many niche genres that formerly didn't fare well on major record labels. (To many, the term seemed more a marketing word than an actual musical movement.)

At the peak of its popularity, however, Nirvana began to unravel. Cobain's personal life had always been difficult, and after struggling with a painful stomach ailment and heroin addiction, he committed suicide in 1994.

ADDITIONAL FACTS

1. *In 1992, Cobain married Courtney Love (1964–), the lead singer of the band Hole.*

2. *After Cobain's death, Grohl went on to become one of the founders of the Foo Fighters.*

3. *The title "Smells Like Teen Spirit" refers to Teen Spirit, a brand of women's deodorant that was reportedly used by one of Cobain's girlfriends.*

··●●··

Spike Lee

Spike Lee (1957–) is the most accomplished African-American director in movie history and also one of the most controversial. Most of his work has been devoted to exploring racial themes, particularly *School Daze* (1988), *Jungle Fever* (1991), and *Do the Right Thing* (1989), his most critically acclaimed film. Race also played a large role in *Malcolm X* (1992), his epic biopic of the black leader.

Lee parlayed his award-winning short student film, *Joe's Bed-Stuy Barbershop: We Cut Heads* (1983), into a chance to direct his first feature. On a budget of $175,000, collected largely from foundation grants, he wrote, directed, edited, and appeared in *She's Gotta Have It* (1986). Shot in two weeks, partly in color, partly in black and white, the film went on to gross more than $7 million at the US box office.

Lee dramatically increased his public visibility when he appeared in a series of Nike commercials alongside Michael Jordan as his *She's Gotta Have It* character, Mars Blackmon.

Do the Right Thing made Lee an international sensation. The film explores a sweltering day in a black Brooklyn neighborhood that explodes into racially charged violence. *Do the Right Thing* was instantly controversial: Some critics argued that the film did not work toward racial harmony and that it would only incite more racial violence and intolerance.

Regardless, the film garnered two Academy Award nominations, including a screenplay nod for Lee; received four Golden Globe nominations (screenplay and directing nods for Lee); and was considered for the Palme d'Or at the Cannes Film Festival.

Malcolm X had a significant cultural impact, particularly in the black community. The film exposed many young African-Americans to the teachings of Malcolm X for the first time, and many fans proudly wore an array of clothing emblazoned with the letter *X*.

In recent years, Lee has satirized the television industry and American pop culture in *Bamboozled* (2000), explored the remaining hours of a convicted drug dealer in post-9/11 New York in *25th Hour* (2002), and chronicled the aftermath of Hurricane Katrina in a made-for-television documentary series, *When the Levees Broke: A Requiem in Four Acts* (2006).

ADDITIONAL FACTS

1. *Lee has collaborated on multiple films with several actors, most notably with Denzel Washington (1954–). Lee has directed Washington four times—in* Mo' Better Blues *(1990),* Malcolm X, He Got Game *(1998), and* Inside Man *(2006).*

2. *In addition to his Oscar nomination for the screenplay for* Do the Right Thing, *Lee was also nominated for best documentary feature for* 4 Little Girls *(1997).*

3. *Lee's father, the jazz bassist Bill Lee, has composed music for four of Lee's features—*She's Gotta Have It, School Daze, Do the Right Thing, *and* Mo' Better Blues.

•••••

Antiglobalization

In 1993, the United States Senate approved the North American Free Trade Agreement (NAFTA), a treaty with Mexico and Canada that abolished most restrictions on trade between the three countries. For the rest of the 1990s, the United States and many other nations signed a series of similar accords that lowered tariffs and other trade barriers, a process dubbed *globalization*.

To proponents, globalization promised to raise living standards in poor countries across the world by allowing them to sell goods to richer countries in Europe and North America.

But by the end of Clinton's second term, powerful opposition had emerged against globalization. Trade agreements like NAFTA, opponents argued, destroyed thousands of jobs in the United States by forcing American manufacturers to compete with factories in low-wage countries such as China and Vietnam. In many cases, American companies simply laid off their workers and relocated to foreign countries, a process known as *offshoring*.

The first high-profile event of the antiglobalization movement was a series of protests during a World Trade Organization meeting in Seattle in 1999. Over the course of several days, about 40,000 demonstrators marched to protest global trade policies.

Similar protests followed in Montreal in 2000 and Genoa, Italy, in 2001.

Opponents of globalization also argued that trade agreements often had pernicious effects in the developing world, where many workers ended up in low-wage sweatshops putting together garments, cars, and electronics for sale to the West.

Globalization remains one of the most divisive ideas in American politics, with labor unions generally opposed to free trade agreements and Wall Street in favor.

ADDITIONAL FACTS

1. *In 2004, a poll found that 38 percent of Americans thought NAFTA had been good for the United States, while 46 percent thought its impact was negative.*

2. *While the term* sweatshop *is often used today to describe working conditions in the Third World, critiques of sweatshop conditions form a long tradition that includes Upton Sinclair's classic 1906 exposé of the American meatpacking industry,* The Jungle.

3. *The word* globalization *was first used by academic economists in the early 1980s.*

•• • ••

Mia Hamm

No player—male or female—has scored more goals in international soccer history than Mia Hamm (1972–). During her seventeen-year career with the United States national team, she scored 158 goals, leading the Americans to two World Cup titles (1991 and 1999) and two Olympic gold medals (1996 and 2004). She retired after the 2004 Athens Olympics as one of the highest-profile female athletes in the world.

Spearheaded by Hamm's dynamic play, the national team turned women's soccer from a completely insignificant sport on the national stage to one that, in 1999, drew more than 650,000 fans and 40 million television viewers in the United States alone for the women's World Cup. For the 1999 championship game, 90,185 spectators packed the Rose Bowl to watch the Americans defeat China on penalty kicks—a feat capped by Brandi Chastain (1968–) scoring the winning goal and famously ripping off her shirt.

With Hamm, though, there were no such histrionics. Her demeanor on the field was always fiery, but she never called attention to herself. In fact, as often as possible, she would deflect attention to her teammates. But despite her unease in the spotlight, she became the face of women's sports in America.

The success of the Women's World Cup led to the formation of Women's United Soccer Association (WUSA), a women's professional soccer league, in 2001. (Hamm was a founding member, but the league lasted only three seasons.)

Among Hamm's national endorsement deals is her contract with Nike, which named the largest building on its Oregon campus for her. In 1997, she was also named to *People* magazine's 50 Most Beautiful People list.

In November 2003, Hamm married Los Angeles Dodgers shortstop Nomar Garciaparra (1973–), and she gave birth to twins in March 2007.

ADDITIONAL FACTS

1. *In 1987, Hamm became the youngest member of the women's national team, at age fifteen.*

2. *Hamm led the University of North Carolina to four college soccer titles and finished her college career as the all-time leading scorer in Atlantic Coast Conference history (103 goals, 72 assists, 278 points).*

3. *She was US Soccer's Female Athlete of the Year from 1994 to 1998 and was the Fédération Internationale de Football Association Women's Player of the Year in 2001 and 2002 (the first two years of the award).*

••●••

Martha Stewart

Martha Stewart's name has become synonymous with a certain style of high-class living: rustic but elegant, handmade but professional, convicted but paroled. While this style seems to come naturally to Stewart, she didn't grow up among flowing rivers and rolling hills. She was born Martha Kostyra (1941–) in Jersey City, New Jersey, a New York City suburb.

Despite the urban surroundings, in her childhood Stewart did get an important start on her later career. Her father taught her to garden, and her mother taught her to cook and sew.

Beginning in 1967, Stewart worked as a stockbroker on Wall Street. She left the job a few years later, and in 1976 she opened a catering business. It began modestly but brought in more than $1 million in revenues by 1986.

While running her business, Stewart also wrote about elegant living for newspapers and magazines. In 1982, she published her first book, *Entertaining*, which brought her national recognition. She became even better known when she made the move to television, appearing often on the *Today Show* and *The Oprah Winfrey Show* in the 1980s and hosting her own weekly television program beginning in 1993. The show was canceled, but the magazine to which it was launched as a companion— *Martha Stewart Living*—is still being published.

In 2004, Stewart was convicted of insider trading and received a five-month prison sentence. Since her release, Stewart has continued to expand her business, adding numerous product lines, a daily talk show, and a twenty-four-hour channel on the Sirius Satellite Radio network. Every one of these ventures has been a success. Today, her net worth is estimated at more than $600 million.

ADDITIONAL FACTS

1. *Stewart divorced her husband in 1990 but has kept her well-known married name rather than readopting her maiden name.*

2. *While a student at Barnard College in New York, Stewart modeled to earn extra money.*

3. *Stewart has licensed her name for a variety of products, including housewares at Kmart and Macy's and paints at Lowe's.*

• • ● ● •

Rupert Murdoch

Rupert Murdoch (1931–) is a modern incarnation of the old-fashioned titans of journalism—and probably the last of the breed. Following in the path of the media barons William Randolph Hearst (1863–1951), Henry Luce (1898–1967), and others, Murdoch personally oversees a global empire that encompasses newspapers, magazines, film studios, television and cable networks, satellite services, and Internet outlets.

Murdoch did not begin his career as a mogul. In 1953, at age twenty-three, he inherited a money-losing Australian newspaper, the *Adelaide News,* from his father. He managed to turn it into a profitable enterprise, the first of many such successful reclamation projects.

More than fifty years later, his News Corporation is the world's third-largest media conglomerate, worth an estimated $62 billion and extending from North America to Asia. It is one of the few huge corporations still controlled by a single owner.

Murdoch himself is frequently in the news that his outlets cover, not only for his flashy business maneuvers but also for his sometimes tumultuous personal life, which has included three marriages, two divorces, and six children.

Born in Australia and educated in England, Murdoch first conquered those two countries with shrewd business decisions and, by some estimates, by catering to the lowest common denominator in terms of journalistic content. After Murdoch purchased London's *Sun,* the paper quickly established itself with its splashy, tabloid-style headlines and photos of topless women.

Murdoch turned his attention to the United States in the 1970s, first purchasing the *San Antonio News* in 1973 before adding the *New York Post* and *New York* magazine. Under Murdoch's leadership, the *Post* adopted the tabloid style of the *Sun* (one memorable headline: "Headless Body in Topless Bar") and a conservative political slant.

News Corporation has since acquired 20th Century Fox, one of the six major American film studios, as well as the Fox Broadcasting Company, DirecTV, and MySpace.com. In 2007, Murdoch pulled off a controversial $5 billion purchase of the *Wall Street Journal,* the second-largest newspaper in America.

ADDITIONAL FACTS

1. *In 2007,* Forbes *listed Murdoch as the thirty-third-richest person in America, with an estimated fortune of $8.8 billion.*

2. *Among the most famous headlines in the* Sun *was "GOTCHA," to commemorate Britain's sinking of an Argentinean cruiser during the Falklands War in 1982.*

3. *In 1964, Murdoch founded the* Australian, *the country's first national newspaper.*

•••••

Kazuo Ishiguro

Among the outsize personalities of the contemporary fiction scene, the novelist Kazuo Ishiguro (1954–) is a decidedly low-key figure. Critics esteem him, though, as one of the most accomplished literary craftsmen of the present day. In particular, he is renowned for creating meticulous first-person narratives that explore the human reluctance to confront past sorrows and missed opportunities.

Born in Japan in 1954, Ishiguro moved to England as a child and was raised near London. He has remarked that he feels like an outsider in both cultures, and indeed it is difficult to label him as either a British or a Japanese writer. Fittingly, his first major novel, *A Pale View of Hills* (1982), concerns a Japanese immigrant in England, while his second, *An Artist of the Floating World* (1986), tells of an elderly Japanese man who struggles to acknowledge the unsavory political loyalties of his past.

Ishiguro received nearly unanimous acclaim for *The Remains of the Day* (1989), his Booker Prize–winning tale narrated by an aging butler named Stevens, who manages an English manor. Serious and stoic, Stevens immerses himself—and the reader—in his consummate belief in duty, professionalism, and dedication to his former employer, an English nobleman. Gradually, though, cracks appear in Stevens's stiff narration: It becomes heartbreakingly clear that he has wasted his life serving an unworthy master, and in the process closed himself off from a potentially life-changing love.

Stevens exemplifies the so-called unreliable narrator: Unwilling to confront the uncomfortable truth that he has misplaced his loyalties and priorities, he attempts to delude both himself and the reader that he has made the right decisions in life. In this sense, Stevens also exemplifies Ishiguro's protagonists as a whole: Although they reveal much in what they say, they reveal even more in what they do not say.

ADDITIONAL FACTS

1. *The acclaimed 1993 film adaptation of* The Remains of the Day, *starring Anthony Hopkins (1937–), Emma Thompson (1959–), and Christopher Reeve (1952–2004), was nominated for eight Oscars.*

2. *In a 1990 interview, Ishiguro stated that his novels investigate "the way people can't face certain things . . . when people resort to self-deception and tell themselves stories that aren't quite complete about what happened in their past."*

3. *Ishiguro's most recent efforts include* When We Were Orphans *(2000) and* Never Let Me Go *(2005), both of which were finalists for the Booker Prize, a prestigious award given annually to the best English-language novel written by a citizen of the United Kingdom or one of its former colonies (except the United States).*

•••••

2Pac and Biggie

In the early 1990s, as hip-hop music became enormously popular around the world, leading American rap artists were divided by an intense rivalry between East Coast and West Coast styles. For a time, that rivalry pushed artists such as Dr. Dre (1965–) and the twosome Mobb Deep to create ever-more-innovative works.

Eventually, however, what started as an artistic rivalry took a tragic turn, erupting into real-life violence. No story better exemplifies both of these aspects than that of the rivalry between the West Coast rapper Tupac Shakur (1971–1996) and an East Coast competitor, Biggie Smalls (1972–1997), later known as the Notorious B.I.G.

Shakur released his first solo album—*2Pacalypse Now*—in 1991. The album was modestly successful and, because of its graphic lyrics about violence and inner-city life, extremely controversial. He gained even more fame after his performance in the 1992 film *Juice,* and more still after sexual assault charges landed him in prison in 1995. Shakur was released early after an appeal that was paid for by Marion "Suge" Knight (1965–). In return for the help, Shakur agreed to a three-record deal with Knight's Death Row Records label and fulfilled his obligations for the first two records with the 1996 double disc *All Eyez on Me.*

One of Shakur's fiercest competitors was Smalls, a New York City rapper who was credited with revitalizing East Coast hip-hop. Smalls's 1994 album *Ready to Die* was a major hit. However, many West Coast rappers disdained Smalls, and Shakur taunted him by releasing "Hit 'Em Up" (1996), in which he claimed to have had sex with Smalls's wife.

Soon afterward, the artistic rivalry between rappers on the two coasts took a far more serious turn when Shakur was killed in a 1996 drive-by shooting. Many hoped that this tragic incident would bring an end to the increasingly violent rivalry, and leading hip-hop figures called an "antiviolence summit" to discuss the issue after Shakur's death. Smalls did not attend, and, the following year, he himself was murdered while promoting his album *Life After Death* in California.

Neither murder case has been solved.

ADDITIONAL FACTS

1. *Shakur was serving time on sexual assault charges when his third album,* Me Against the World, *rose to number one, making him the first artist to have a number one album while in prison.*

2. *Smalls was a mentor to (and, allegedly, lover of) the rapper Lil' Kim (1974–), whose 1996 debut album* Hard Core *was the most successful album by a female rapper up to that point.*

3. *After a Texas youth claimed that his shooting of a state trooper was influenced by* 2Pacalypse Now, *Vice President Dan Quayle (1947–) said, "There's no reason for a record like this to be released. It has no place in our society."*

•••••

Titanic (1997)

"I'm the king of the world!"
—Leonardo DiCaprio as Jack Dawson

No film has ever won more Academy Awards (eleven), been nominated for more Academy Awards (fourteen), or grossed more money at the US box office ($600 million) or worldwide ($1.8 billion) than *Titanic* (1997). All at once, it is a historical epic, a romance, an adventure, and a disaster film—and one of the most popular movies of all time. Its only true cinematic antecedent is *Gone with the Wind* (1939).

James Cameron (1954–) directed *Titanic* with (at the time) the most expensive budget in Hollywood history, approximately $200 million. When the film's release was delayed from the summer of 1997 to December of that year, many critics speculated that it would be a box office bust, unable to recoup its huge costs. Those critics were wrong.

The film tells the story of the 1912 sinking of the *RMS Titanic*—a state-of-the-art ocean liner that was thought to be unsinkable—through flashbacks from the present day. The plot centers on the romance between upper-class teenager Rose DeWitt Bukater (played by Kate Winslet, 1975–) and Jack Dawson (played by Leonardo DiCaprio, 1974–), a brash kid from the third-class, or steerage, section of the ship. Looming over their love affair, of course, is the doomed maiden voyage of the *Titanic*.

Cameron re-creates the sinking of the massive ship with remarkable special effects, including the use of several scale models of the vessel—some small, some large. One such model was about 90 percent of the size of the original 882-foot ship.

The film was generally well received, though some critics pointed to a weak script and found the romance between Winslet and DiCaprio's characters too clichéd. But audiences around the world did not agree. At the Academy Awards, Cameron quoted Jack Dawson, announcing, "I'm king of the world!"

ADDITIONAL FACTS

1. Titanic's *fourteen Oscar nominations equaled the record set by* All About Eve *(1950).* Titanic's *eleven Oscar wins tied it for the most with* Ben-Hur *(1959), a mark that was later matched by* The Lord of the Rings: The Return of the King *(2003).*

2. *Gloria Stuart, who played Rose in the present day, became the oldest person to be nominated for an Oscar (for Best Supporting Actress), at age eighty-seven.*

3. Titanic *was the first film to top $1 billion in unadjusted worldwide gross.*

••●••

European Union

The European Union (EU), an international organization of twenty-seven demo-cratic European countries that has brought many ex-enemies together under a single flag, traces its origin to the bleak aftermath of World War II. The utter dev-astation of war inspired the leaders of Europe to seek tighter political and economic links with one another, hoping to avoid future conflicts and speed the postwar recovery.

The Treaty of Rome, approved in 1957 by Italy, West Germany, France, Belgium, the Netherlands, and Luxembourg, created a common market that allowed people and goods to move quickly between the six countries. Ireland, Denmark, and the United Kingdom joined the common market in 1973, and Greece, Portugal, and Spain joined after the restoration of democracy in those nations.

Forging the European Economic Community, as the organization was initially called, required protracted diplomacy to quell the lingering antagonism between France and Germany, foes in both world wars. Some citizens also feared that their countries would lose national sovereignty by joining the organization, a concern that many Europeans continue to express today. (Voters in Norway, for instance, rejected EU membership altogether to preserve their national sovereignty.)

After the end of the Cold War and the reunification of Germany, however, the pace of European integration accelerated. The Treaty of Maastricht (1992) renamed the group the European Union and gave the union many of the trappings of statehood: a flag, an anthem, and, most important, a currency, the euro. Most member coun-tries abandoned their national currency in favor of the euro, a conversion process that was completed in 2002.

The European Union is considered one of the greatest diplomatic accomplishments of the twentieth century and a new model of international globalization, yet its future is unsettled. After 2004, when the group admitted twelve new members, mostly former communist countries from Eastern Europe, some critics said the EU had grown too large. Turkey is currently seeking membership, but many Europeans are opposed to letting the predominantly Muslim country join their club. In addi-tion, after voters in France and the Netherlands in 2005 defeated a proposed Euro-pean constitution that would have expanded the union's powers in foreign affairs, the group's future seems uncertain.

ADDITIONAL FACTS

1. *Traditionally neutral Switzerland is not an EU member; other nonmembers include Iceland, Ukraine, and Russia.*

2. *In 2004, many of the former Eastern bloc countries joined the EU. The ten countries that acceded to EU membership in 2004 were Cyprus, the Czech Republic, Estonia, Hungary, Latvia, Lithuania, Malta, Poland, the Slovak Republic, and Slovenia.*

3. *Denmark and the United Kingdom are EU members but have opted to keep their currencies, the krone and the pound, respectively.*

•• ● ● ••

Tiger Woods

The golfer Tiger Woods (1975–) is arguably the most dominant athlete of his generation—in any sport. By age thirty-one, he had won more major golf championships—twelve—than anyone in history other than Jack Nicklaus (1940–). Woods was the first player to hold all four major titles simultaneously (known as the Tiger Slam) and was the youngest to complete the career Grand Slam (which he has now done twice).

Woods has won more money than any player in PGA Tour history (more than $70 million), and he commands an estimated $75 million more through his endorsement deals. According to some estimates, by 2010, he could become the first athlete to earn $1 billion.

In addition to his dominance on the course and on Madison Avenue, Woods has also been a force for progress in golf because of his race. As a self-styled "Cablinasian"—with African-American, Chinese, Native American, Caucasian, and Thai ancestry— he has inspired a generation of minority players to take up the game.

Woods was the ultimate child prodigy. At nine months, he grabbed a club and emulated the swing of his father, Earl. At age two, Tiger appeared on *The Mike Douglas Show* and putted against the entertainer Bob Hope (1903–2003). At age three, Woods shot forty-eight for nine holes, and by age five, he was featured in *Golf Digest*.

After one of the most successful amateur careers in history, he turned professional at age twenty in August 1996. He immediately signed endorsement deals worth $60 million and went on to win two tournaments as a rookie. Within a year, he had claimed his first major championship by dominating the 1997 Masters.

His most overpowering season was in 2000, when he won three majors, joining Ben Hogan (1912–1997) as one of the only two men to do so. (Hogan notched his trio of majors in 1953.) Woods punctuated that year by winning the US Open by fifteen strokes, the largest spread in major championship history.

ADDITIONAL FACTS

1. *Woods's given name is Eldrick. He shares the nickname "Tiger" with Vuong Dang Phong, a Vietnamese soldier whom Earl Woods befriended during the Vietnam War. Earl Woods said that Phong had saved his life.*

2. *Among Woods's trademarks is that he wears a red shirt on Sundays.*

3. *Woods is the only person to be named* Sports Illustrated's *Sportsman of the Year twice (1996 and 2000). He has also been named Male Athlete of the Year by the Associated Press three times (1997, 1999, and 2000).*

•••••

The Sopranos

The Sopranos was a landmark television program that achieved unprecedented critical and popular success for its unsparing portrayal of the lives of a New Jersey Mafia family. Created by David Chase (1945–), the program ran on the cable network HBO from January 10, 1999, until June 10, 2007.

The series focused on the life of Anthony "Tony" Soprano, the boss of the fictional Di Meo crime family. The show followed Soprano, played by James Gandolfini (1961–), as he tried to balance his family life with his life of crime. Both lives were dissected on the couch of Soprano's psychiatrist, Dr. Jennifer Melfi, played by Lorraine Bracco (1954–).

The Sopranos not only captivated audiences with its uncensored format and its depiction of the dark underbelly of organized crime, it also drew people in with unexpected plot lines that kept audiences guessing from one episode to the next. In a 2001 article in the *Nation,* the critic Ellen Willis wrote that the show had "the feel of an as yet unfinished nineteenth-century novel . . . the sheer entertainment and suspense of the plot twists are reminiscent of Dickens and his early serials."

Not long after the series debuted in 1999, the *New York Times* declared that the show "just may be the greatest work of American popular culture of the last quarter century."

The Sopranos not only garnered critical respect, but also set the bar for ratings for a program on a premium cable network. The premiere of the show's fourth season attracted 13.4 million viewers, the largest audience ever for an HBO program.

ADDITIONAL FACTS

1. *In early 2005, the A&E network paid $195 million for the exclusive rights to run edited versions of every* Sopranos *episode.*

2. *In 2002,* TV Guide *rated* The Sopranos *5th on its list of the Top 50 Greatest Shows of All Time, behind* Seinfeld, I Love Lucy, The Honeymooners, *and* All in the Family.

3. *Tony Soprano's wife, Carmela, is named after Vito Corleone's wife in the novel* The Godfather, *by Mario Puzo (1920–1999).*

• • ● • •

J. K. Rowling

No other series of novels in publishing history has had the cultural and financial impact of the *Harry Potter* books by the British author J. K. Rowling (1965–). With more than 300 million copies in print worldwide, along with a series of hugely successful feature films, video games, and even a musical, Rowling has turned her boy-wizard protagonist into a giant industry and made herself a billionaire in the process.

Rowling first conceived of the character (a young boy who is not yet aware that he is a wizard) in 1990, when she was on a train from Manchester to London. The train was delayed for four hours and, during the holdup, she began constructing Harry Potter's world.

Four years later, she was residing in Scotland, a divorced mother of one, living on welfare and in government housing.

She finally completed the book in 1995, but it would be another two years before its publication in Britain. In 1997, Bloomsbury published *Harry Potter and the Philosopher's Stone* with an initial run of 1,000 copies. And so began Rowling's unlikely rise to literary and cultural stardom.

Scholastic paid $105,000 (a hefty sum for a work by an unknown author) for the US rights, then published the first book as *Harry Potter and the Sorcerer's Stone*.

As Rowling released subsequent books, each broke the records of the previous ones. The seventh and final novel in the series, *Harry Potter and the Deathly Hallows*, had a record-setting print run of 12 million copies in the United States alone and sold 8.3 million copies in the first twenty-four hours of its American release in 2007.

Beyond the incredible sales records and the films' enormous receipts (the first five films grossed $4.4 billion worldwide), some studies have shown that the *Harry Potter* books have also had a significant impact on children's reading habits. In 2005, Gordon Brown (1951–), then British chancellor of the exchequer (who became prime minister in 2007), said, "I think J. K. Rowling has done more for literacy around the world than any single human being."

ADDITIONAL FACTS

1. *Rowling used her first initial (J, for Joanne) and the first initial of one of her grandmothers (K, for Kathleen) as her pseudonym rather than her first name, Joanne, to attract more young male readers.*

2. *Rowling says she has been writing almost continuously since age six. She developed her storytelling skills to entertain her younger sister, Di.*

3. *On the train ride during which she first conceived of Harry Potter and his world, she did not have a pen and was too shy to ask a stranger for one. So once she got home, she wrote furiously to document all her ideas.*

•••••

Index

•••••

•••••

••●••

• • • • •

••●••

••••

Image Credits

Miriam and Ira D. Wallach Division of Art, Prints and Photographs, The New York Public Library, Astor, Lenox and Tilden Foundations: 1

Humanities and Social Sciences Library, Manuscript and Archives Division, The New York Public Library, Astor, Lenox and Tilden Foundations: 3

Time Life Pictures/Getty Images: 4, 86

Hulton Archive/Getty Images: 6, 10, 26, 58, 61, 67, 102, 104, 110, 119, 126, 136, 138, 198, 276

Mid-Manhattan Picture Collection, The New York Public Library, Astor, Lenox and Tilden Foundations: 7

Alex Wong/Getty Images: 14

Imagno/Getty Images: 17

AFP/Getty Images: 22, 170, 188

Edward Gooch/Getty Images: 23

Jon Brenneis/Getty Images: 28

Michael Ochs Archives/Getty Images: 31, 59, 63, 66, 129, 141, 150, 178, 255, 269, 283, 290, 297, 308

Bernard Hoffman/Getty Images: 37

Frank Driggs Collection/Getty Images: 38

National Baseball Hall of Fame/Getty Images: 41

Eric Schaal/Getty Images: 52

CORR/Getty Images: 55

Hy Peskin/Getty Images: 69

Olen Collection/Getty Images: 76

Genevieve Naylor/Corbis: 82

Transendental Graphics/Getty Images: 83, 167

Eliot Elisofon/Getty Images: 90

Ann Rosener/Getty Images: 96

Popperfoto/Getty Images: 98, 346

Keystone/Getty Images: 101, 156, 164, 184, 226

Fox Photos/Getty Images: 105

Greg Forwerck/Getty Images: 111

NBC Television/Getty Images: 112

Ruth Berlau/Getty Images: 121

Ralph Morse/Getty Images: 125

Kidwiler Collection/Getty Images: 132

Hank Walker/Getty Images: 134

Billy Rose Theater Collection, New York Public Library, Astor, Lenox and Tilden Foundations. Photo by Henri Cartier-Bresson/Magnum Photos: 135

Robert Laberge/Getty Images: 139

Columbia Pictures/Getty Images: 140

Leonard McCombe/Getty Images: 142

Ray Fisher/Getty Images: 143

Rogers Photo Archive/Getty Images: 146

Bill Bridges/Getty Images: 147

Lee Lockwood/Getty Images: 148

Focus on Sport/Getty Images: 153, 300

Hector Mata/Getty Images: 154

J. Wilds/Getty Images: 157

Nathaniel S. Butler/Getty Images: 160

Baron/Getty Images: 161

Evening Standard/Getty Images: 163, 247

Reg Speller/Getty Images: 166

Carsten/Getty Images: 168

Allan Tannenbaum/Getty Images: 169

Frank Scherschel/Getty Images: 173

Henry Barr Collection/Getty Images: 174

ABC Television/Getty Images: 175

Ron Galella/Getty Images: 177

Roy Jones/Getty Images: 189, 210

Tom Copi/Getty Images: 192

Horst Tappe/Getty Images: 196

Haywood Magee/Getty Images: 212

Arnold Newman/Getty Images: 219, 352

Homer Sykes/Getty Images: 229

Betmann/Corbis: 233, 287

Arthur Jones/Getty Images: 237

Nancy R. Schiff/Getty Images: 238

Derrick Ceyrac/Getty Images: 239

Sony BMG Music/Getty Images: 241

CBS Photo Archive/Getty Images: 245

Joel Axelrad/Getty Images: 248

Katy Winn/Corbis: 252

Isreal Shenker/Getty Images: 254

Jerry Cooke/Corbis: 258

Ulf Andersen/Getty Images: 261

Getty Images: 268

Rolls Press/Popperfoto/Getty Images: 272

Paul Natkin/Getty Images: 280

Agence France Presse/Getty Images: 282

Gary M. Prior/Getty Images: 286